KT-474-520

BORN AGAIN

BORN AGAIN

Charles W. Colson

HODDER AND STOUGHTON
LONDON SYDNEY AUCKLAND TORONTO

Scripture quotations identified KJV are from the King James Version of the Bible.

Scripture quotations identified RSV are from the Revised Standard Version of the Bible, copyrighted 1946, 1952, © 1971 and 1973.

Scripture quotations identified LB are from the Living Bible, Copyright © 1971 by Tyndale House Publishers, Wheaton, Illinois 60187. All rights reserved.

Scripture quotations identified PHILLIPS are from THE NEW TESTAMENT IN MODERN ENGLISH (Revised Edition), translated by J. B. Phillips. © J. B. Phillips 1958, 1960, 1972. Used by permission of William Collins and Sons Ltd.

Excerpt from the column "Getting Right with Granny" is used by permission of Art Buchwald.

Excerpts from MERE CHRISTIANITY by C. S. Lewis, Copyright 1943, 1945, 1952 by William Collins and Sons Ltd are used by permission.

To my Dad – whose ideals for my life I have tried, not always successfully, to fulfil – and whose strength and support is with me today.

To Patty – the gentle spirit who comforts me when I fail, keeps me humble in success, giving of herself always – in love.

The butterfly is nature's most visible illustration of rebirth. Once drab and earthbound as a caterpillar, the butterfly emerges from its cocoon in beautifully radiant colours, soaring upward into the sky. Free – BORN AGAIN – just as each of us can be when we are, through Christ, born again in the Spirit.

Contents

Before We Begin . . .

The origins of this book go back to a sultry late-summer day in 1974. President Nixon had only recently resigned; the government was in disarray and the country, exhausted by the convulsions of Watergate, was in numbed shock. I was languishing in an Alabama prison, a casualty of the greatest political upheaval in American history.

My own spirit was crying out in agony. How could all this have happened? My mind wandered back over two decades from the days when I was a crew-cut Marine lieutenant to the years when I sat in the Oval Office at the side of the President of the United States. I had served all the time with a burning idealism about my country.

How could we who had the trust of the nation have strayed so far afield? There must be lessons for my life – for others – for an anguished nation. What was the redemptive answer?

Around me in the dreary confines of that prison were hundreds of men trapped as much by the circumstances of their own lives as by their captor's chains. On their sorrowful, forlorn faces were written countless tales of human tragedy. I reflected back on the men with whom I served – Haldeman, Ehrlichman, Mitchell, Nixon. They had been trapped as well – by their own pretensions of power, victims of their own human frailties.

As I kept probing for the deeper meaning of what had

happened to me and to so many others, I began writing – pages of copy evaluating the men and events, forming conclusions, groping for corrective ideas. My focus was on institutions and the words as I reread them day after day seemed heavy, ponderous, and wide of the mark.

Prayer was still new to me. In my own inadequacy I sought God's help. First of all, was I supposed to write a book? There were offers – one very attractive – to write about the Nixon years. But the more I prayed and searched, the more my thoughts centred about my own experiences. What had I discovered in my own life?

Then answers were supplied in unexpected ways. As I wrote letters to my new Christian friends in Washington, I tried to tell them how real God was to some of us in prison. Somehow the Lord helped me make the words in my letters come alive. Convictions deepened. Yes, I was to write a book – but only if I sought His guidance as I wrote.

What form was it to take? Again I prayed for help. Again the answer came through events. As I recorded more of my prison experiences in letters to my friends, I felt God's hand on my shoulder. "Put aside all their theories for now," I seemed to hear. "Tell the story of one life – yours."

But who was I to moralise, to preach to others? I'd botched it, was one of those who helped bring on Watergate and was in prison to prove it. Yet maybe that very fact, plus some unusual things which had happened to me, could give me some insights that would help others. Could there be a purpose to all that had happened to me?

And then I began to see it. The nation was in darkness; there was anger, bitterness, and disillusionment across the land. While my inclination was to think in terms of grandiose reforms, God seemed to be saying that the renewal of our national spirit can begin with each person – with the renewal of individual spirit. *If you want to do something, submit yourself to Me and I will guide you* were the words implanted on my mind.

Submit yourself. Our founding fathers had built a nation on this principle, that fallible men are nothing unless they learn to depend upon God. It was to establish a true community of believers that the Puritans came to this continent. Somewhere at sea, aboard the *Arbella*, John Winthrop articulated the vision: "The God of Israel is among us ... we shall be as a city upon a hill." They saw their destiny, not as political conquerors but as disciples of Jesus Christ.

"With a firm reliance on the protection of Divine Providence ..." are the solemn words of the Declaration of Independence. And our greatest President – Abraham Lincoln – humbly acknowledged that without God, "I must fail."

How magnificently has God honoured the covenant of our forefathers. How richly has He blessed our nation. So deep are our religious roots, but so far have we strayed.

As I wrote, it became clear to me that Watergate could work a healthy cleansing in the nation if it is understood for what it truly is. Were Mr. Nixon and his men more evil than any of their predecessors? That they brought the nation Watergate is a *truth*. But is it not only part of a larger *truth* – that all men have the capacity for both good and evil, and the darker side of man's nature can always prevail in any human being? If people believe that just because one bunch of rascals are run out of office all the ills which have beset a nation are over, then the real lesson of this ugly time will have been missed – and that delusion could be the greatest tragedy of all.

Watergate has raised so many questions. Can humanism ever be the answer for our society? There is an almost sanctified notion that man can do anything if he puts his will to it. This was once my credo. Having seen through Watergate how vulnerable man can be, I no longer believe I am master of my destiny. I need God; I need friends with whom I can honestly share my failures and feelings of inadequacy.

It was in this framework that I wrote this book: an inexperienced writer and a baby Christian, but in submission to the Almighty, praying that others might find hope and encouragement from my experiences. Out of prayer has come the help needed from experienced editors and publishing specialists.

From prayers answered by events came the title, which may amuse those who believe that *Born Again* is an overworked Protestant cliché. While accompanying my wife at her Roman Catholic church one Sunday, Patty flipped open the hymnal, smiled and nudged me. We both knew at that moment that after long weeks of searching and rejecting hundreds of ideas, the title was on that page; the hymn was "Born Again."

For me it is anything but a cliché suggesting that someone has arrived at some state of spiritual superiority; it means only a fresh start at putting my life in order – but it had come with the renewing of my spirit.

I have prayed especially for honesty in my writing, knowing only too well that my basic nature would want to present myself in the most favourable light. As I have fallen down, picked myself up, and fallen down again during the past few years, I am learning how God can break us in order to remake us. And through my dependence on Him has come a surprising sense of freedom – and an exhilaration in my spirit.

I have been given a tremendous eagerness to share all this with others. As you travel with me through these pages, my hope is that you will ask for God's hand on your life. And my most sincere and humble prayer now in this time of judgment is for a revival of the flagging national spirit. It can come in only one way – as each of us bows in submission to Him and as the Almighty leads us from darkness into light – so that once again we might stand together, truly one nation under God.

CHARLES W. COLSON
October 31, 1975

1

Something Wrong

I stood there with my wife, Patty, and son Wendell, puzzled. This night – election night, 1972 – should have been the proudest of my life. Certainly a Victory Party was called for – the landslide re-election of Richard Nixon to the Presidency of the United States.

Nothing was amiss about the setting. The high-ceilinged ornate ballroom of Washington's Shoreham Hotel was packed with distinguished grey-suited men, elegant ladies in rich furs. Yet the picture was out of focus. Something wrong.

I stood there thinking that, unlike any celebration I had attended in twenty years in politics, there was no air of triumph here. The faces before us were unsmiling, looking, in fact, disappointed and even imposed upon. Around the big boards where the continuing returns were posting record-breaking margins for Nixon, there was scarcely a ripple of excitement.

My mind went back to the comparable scene four years before at the Waldorf in New York. What a contrast! That 1968 Victory Party had been alive, high drama indeed. I recalled the scene so vividly – the Waldorf ballroom jammed with eager young people who had worked so hard for months to oust the Democrats. All that long night as the brass ring neared their grasp, the excitement mounted until the sweet smell of victory filled the air. As the vote count on the big boards edged up, precinct by precinct, how they *oohed* and sighed and laughed and slapped one another on the back and roared their approval.

But tonight?

Patty turned to me. "What's wrong, Chuck? You're so quiet."

"I don't *know* what's wrong. Just exhausted, I guess." With a nod and a gesture I indicated the throng pushing and shoving four deep around the bar. "The only thing these people seem to care about is the free booze."

"Let's walk around," Wendell suggested. "See what people are saying." In only two weeks as a campaign volunteer, Wendell had learned a lot. Now he sought further insights to take back to his political-science course at Princeton.

And I wanted insights, too.

In the VIP area the comments were gripping ones.... Where was Nixon? Shouldn't their $25,000 contributions entitle them to at least a handshake on election night? Then we were cornered by Senator Bob Dole, the Republican national chairman. Angrily he jabbed his finger at me: "The President didn't even mention the Committee in his speech."

After that a group of dour-faced party hangers-on surrounded us. "I want to see you about my job," one old stalwart said unsmilingly as he clutched my arm. None of the other senior White House staffers were there, and in minutes I was being swamped with requests.

No, I wasn't imagining the sour mood. But something was also wrong in me. My insides were as deadened as the air in the room and the slow beat of the music. My lack of exhilaration made no sense. Being part of electing a President was the fondest ambition of my life. For three long years I had committed everything I had, every ounce of energy to Richard Nixon's cause. Nothing else had mattered. We had had no time together as a family, no social life, no vacations. So why could my tongue not taste the flavour of this hour of conquest?

Just then my little beeper, the radio receiver which I snapped to my belt whenever I was out of telephone reach, went off. There was a shrill whistle. Then as I lifted the gadget to my ear, came the command, "Colson, Colson, report to the White House operator."

It was the President. He wanted me at once in his office, the operator said when I called in. A limousine sped Patty, Wendell, and me through the darkness, past nearly deserted Rock Creek Park, to downtown Washington, and at last through the iron gates to the White House grounds.

A blue-suited officer, his braid glittering in the glow of floodlights, snapped a salute and told me that Mr. Nixon was in his "working" office in the Executive Office Building, called the E.O.B. Nixon used the traditional Oval Office in the west wing of the White House chiefly for formal meetings, preferring to work in the quiet intimacy of the denlike office in the E.O.B. across the alleyway. This mammoth grey Victorian structure bristling with gingerbread, arches, and turrets had once held the entire State and War Departments, but now housed only the White House staff.

When we got there we found one lone Secret Service agent in the marble-floored hallway. He waved us in and watched while I deposited Patty and Wendell in my office next to the President's. "I'll only be a few minutes," I told them. "Then we'll go home to bed."

Back in the darkened hall, the Secret Service agent spoke softly: "He's waiting for you, Mr. Colson." I swung open the ten-foot-high door to find Richard Nixon reclining in his favourite easy chair, smiling and puffing contentedly on his pipe. The President was wearing the light-blue checked sport jacket he always slipped on when in the privacy of his office and I blinked a little at the eye-blurring combination of blue checks with the dark blue pinstripe of his trousers.

A few feet away Bob Haldeman, Nixon's chief of staff, was sitting at a small antique table poring over election returns. His back was to the door and he never looked up as I walked in.

The President greeted me with a big grin and, "Good job, boy, good job." Haldeman still did not look up.

"Sit down, Chuck, and have a drink with me," he said. The President rang for Manola, his Cuban valet, who scurried in with two Scotch and sodas.

Haldeman never drank, and I imagined Nixon had been anxiously awaiting my arrival. "Here's to you, Chuck. Those are your votes that are pouring in, the Catholics, the union members, the blue-collars, *your* votes, boy. It was your strategy and it's a landslide!" Nixon lifted his glass to me and then gulped almost half its contents in one swallow.

"The way the votes are piling up, you are going to top sixty-one per cent, Mr. President. That's a record," I said and then reminded him of a modest bet we'd made the day before.

Haldeman was still busy totalling up numbers, once snatching the phone beside him to berate his young assistant, Larry Higby, for not providing the latest figures. Watching Bob's scowling face, I saw a replay of the faces at the Shoreham. From Bob's attitude, I could have thought we were losing the election.

"Bob and I were just talking before you came in, Chuck," the President rambled on. "It was ten years almost to the day that they wrote us off. We were 'dead' in California, finished, all through. Look at us now – on top – biggest vote ever," he chortled. "I guess we showed 'em! Right?" He smacked a fist into his outstretched palm.

Nixon drank again, emptying his glass, then went into the large lavatory off the far side of the room. I turned to the grim-lipped Haldeman. "What's eating you?"

Bob's eyes, blue and steely cold, darted up from his papers, meeting mine for the first time, a deep frown on his forehead. His short crew cut seemed to bristle, too. "I'm trying to add the actual figures – don't be giving him your guesses," he snapped.

Haldeman, I assumed, was tired. Perhaps he was also resenting the fact that I was sharing this moment of victory with the President. Of course there were always petty jealousies in the White House.

"What's wrong, Chuck? Why aren't you celebrating?" Nixon asked, returning to his chair.

"I guess I'm a bit numb, sir."

"This is a night to remember. Have another drink. Let's enjoy this." I had always followed Nixon's orders, but you can't order somebody to be happy.

The President then began composing one draft after another of a telegram to send to his vanquished opponent, Senator George McGovern. It was now close to two in the morning. McGovern had conceded hours earlier. By the rules of the game Nixon's response was long overdue. Yet as fast as the words rolled off his tongue, he would reject them. "How can I say something nice after he kept comparing me to Hitler?"

Haldeman handed him a draft written by another aide. Nixon scanned it. "No, I won't say that." He flung the sheet of paper across the little table between Haldeman and myself.

That he could show no charity in this hour of his greatest triumph dramatised the paradox of Richard Nixon. In 1960 evidence suggested that the cliff-hanger had been stolen from him. "Demand a recount," his aides urged. But Nixon had refused: it would create uncertainty, be bad for the country, and it was his job to help unite the electorate behind the man who defeated him. Noble in defeat, he was now without grace in victory.

Time and again I had seen the President show rare courage when others around him shrank in fear. For this he had won my deepest admiration. Since I had come to respect the President for what he was in his best moments, I learned to accept him for what he was in his worst. I suppose loyalty, like love, creates its own image of what we see.

If someone had peered in on us that night from some imaginary peephole in the ceiling of the President's office, what a curious sight it would have been: a victorious President, grumbling over words he would grudgingly say to his fallen foe; his chief of staff angry, surly, and snarling; and the architect of his political strategy sitting in a numbed stupor. Yes, the picture was out of focus. If this was victory, what might these three men have looked like in defeat?

Nixon told Manola to find us something to eat. That meant waking up a couple of the White House stewards. Shortly before 3:00 a.m. they appeared, sleepy-eyed, carrying three plates of fried eggs and ham. I wished that they had brought some food for Patty and Wendell next door, but decided not to trouble the tired stewards further. The President was chattering on about one Senate race after another, on such a reminiscing kick that we could easily be there until dawn. How could I rescue Patty and Wendell?

The answer came in a report from Haldeman's assistant; both the Associated Press and United Press wire services had shut down for the night; there would be no more vote totals until morning. That welcome news plus my drooping eyelids must have convinced the President to call it a night.

As we were leaving, Mr. Nixon paused at the top of the long flight of grey cement steps leading to the driveway. Directly in front of us the chalk-white mansion rose up majestically in the darkness. "Chuck," he said, "I just want you to know – I'll always be . . ."

Knowing how hard it always was for him to show emotions, I interrupted. "Thank you, Mr. President. Tomorrow will be a good day."

With that he turned and started down the steps, with the Secret Service agent in front of him, glancing mechanically from side to side. I stood for a moment, watching the Thirty-seventh President of the United States, now with the greatest mandate in history by which to govern, slowly descending before me. Lights still burning in a few windows cast an orange glow over the green shrubs and velvety lawns. The night air was clear. In the background rose the Washington Monument, tall and proud, a sight which had never ceased to thrill me. But tonight not even this could penetrate the deadness inside me. . . .

The shrill sound kept hammering at my eardrums. I pulled the blanket from over my head, rubbed my eyes and stared at the clock – 8 : 00 a.m. The ringing came from the White House phone beside my bed. I nearly knocked the phone off the nightstand fumbling for the receiver.

"Chuck, sorry, but *he* wants you in his office right away." It was Steve Bull, the President's scheduler and office aide-de-camp.

"Come off it, Steve; I've only had four hours of sleep. The election is over, and the top of my head is coming off."

"Sorry, but the President wants you."

A few shaving nicks and two cups of coffee later, I was on my way, blurry-eyed, with a throbbing head. When I arrived at the White House, the senior staff was already assembling in the Roosevelt Room for a meeting with the President. *If the President wanted to thank us,* I thought to myself, *why doesn't he do it by letting us sleep late?* He ought to be walking on air; the morning vote totals were confirming our most optimistic projections – a record-breaking 49 states for Nixon, 61 per cent of the total vote.

The assembled staff, most red-eyed like myself, rose to their feet when the President entered, applauding enthusiastically. Nixon smiled and waved for us to be seated. The clapping continued and the chief dropped his eyes for a moment, gripping the back of his chair at the end of the long conference table. Richard Nixon looked fresh, surprisingly rested, in fact. He was precise, crisp, and to the point.

"I believe men exhaust themselves in government without realising it," he began. Turning to a favourite period in history, the mid-nineteenth century in England, Nixon recalled that Disraeli defeated Gladstone immediately after Gladstone's great work in reforming the British government. Gladstone was "an exhausted volcano," Disraeli had charged. The parallel as Nixon meant it was clear : We had done well, but were we exhausted volcanoes with no fire left for the battles ahead?

The President turned to Bob Haldeman, who was glaring sternly at the rest of the staff. "Bob will explain the procedures we've worked out. We need new blood, fresh ideas. Change is important."

Why is he doing this? I wondered, as my eyes quickly scanned the still figures around the table.

"You are my first team," he continued, "but today we start fresh for the next four years. There are great goals to be achieved for the country and we must not lose a day. Bob, you take over." With that, he smiled and headed for the door leading to the hall. It took a long painful moment for us to realise the President was through – it had taken exactly twelve minutes – and the applause, more restrained now, had scarcely begun when he was gone.

Haldeman was blunt. "I will expect resignations from every member of the staff to be delivered to the staff secretary by noon on Friday, from each of you and each person who works for you. Also submit memos stating your preferences for new assignments." He cleared his throat, paused, and added, "That is, of course, the courtesy customarily extended a President at the start of each new Administration." He then passed out envelopes filled with detailed instructions and forms.

His last point did not altogether take the sting out of the chilling announcement. *Okay, Bob,* I thought, *everyone appointed by a President serves at his pleasure. But why this, so soon and so crudely?* I had forbidden my staff any vacations during the election year, promising them instead a rousing celebration, good vacations, and help in finding better positions if we won. Now, according to Haldeman, I was to convene all thirty men and women in my office and inform them they were to look for new jobs.

I told myself that I didn't care. I had already told the President in July that I was leaving his staff after the election to return to my law practice. Even so, I felt surprisingly let down. Perhaps I had thought that the out-of-focus picture of the night before would disappear with the bright morning light. It was a shock to encounter the same sourness in this room.

Men stared at one another in disbelief, dazed by the suddenness of it all. Then the grumbling began, first only murmurs of surprise, soon everyone seemed to be talking at once as anger replaced incredulity. Herb Klein, the long-time loyal press aide who had been with Nixon for twenty-five years, quietly left, his head bowed and the bounce gone from his short quick steps.

Just as the din in the room was reaching a crescendo, Steve Bull summoned me to the President's formal Oval Office. Ill at ease. Mr. Nixon explained that I was not in the same category with the others. Before he left that day for Key Biscayne, he said, he wanted to ask me again to reconsider my resignation.

I convened my staff and assured them that notwithstanding the formality of submitting letters of resignation I would assist each of them in locating the right positions in the new Administration, and told them to take vacations.

But the mood was subdued. The victory that had come as the result of such long months of gruelling work now seemed tasteless.

I saw Nixon off that afternoon, watching as *Marine One*, the Presidential helicopter, lifted gracefully from the South Lawn. Then I headed back to my office, walking slowly through the west wing. It was always calm when the President was travelling because half the staff went with him. Normally there would be a few secretaries typing, workmen in the halls repairing lights, a few staffers standing around chatting. But this afternoon, there was only one lonely uniformed policeman, standing at the open door of the Oval Office. The emptiness was unreal, the stillness haunting – as if some deadly plague had swept through ... I could almost hear the muffled drumroll of distant artillery.

The President had spoken of great goals, and at long last they seemed within reach. For the first time in years, there was stability in the country. The war in Vietnam was nearly over and we had won an overwhelming vote of public confidence. What was it that was now unsettling us, invading our midst, right here at the heart of governmental power?

Bringing the question closer to home, what was spoiling inside of me? Just tired? Or was there something very wrong?

2

"Good Enough"

The afternoon papers headlined the huge Nixon victory and already contained speculation about personnel changes. Briefly I thought about my own decision. Always in the past it was the drive to climb new heights which gave life meaning. But what happened when there were no more mountains to scale? I was only forty-one. Surely there must be other stiff challenges. But what? What could I do next that would ever be as fulfilling as helping elect a President, being one of the small handful of men who each day made decisions that shaped the future of a nation?

Yet I knew I must move on. I was one of those "exhausted volcanoes" the President spoke about in his strange speech. Back to my law practice? It was the obvious thing to do and right for my family. This way I could replenish the bank account we had drained while living on a government salary. But money – is that any real goal in life?

No, the more I thought about it, the more one word seemed to sum up what was important to me. *Pride*. Richard Nixon's deep sense of pride in his office was the quality which I most admired. In fact, pride was at the heart of the Nixon Presidency in its reach for historical importance and greatness. And pride had been at the heart of my own life, too, as far back as I could remember. . . .

It was a sunny day in early June 1949 for graduation ceremonies at Browne and Nichols, a small private school in Cambridge. Rows of wooden chairs were stretched across the football field on the banks of the gently flowing

Charles River. A half-mile away were the ivy-covered, Colonial brick buildings of Harvard Yard. Editor of the school newspaper, voted most likely to succeed by my classmates, and an honour student, I was elected to give the valedictory for the graduating class. Seated behind me on a raised wooden platform were my forty classmates, over half of them ready to take their places in the fall as Harvard freshmen.

Pride was the keynote of my speech. "We are proud, very proud, of the lessons we have learned in democracy – of the school – of our class." As I looked out over the rows of distinguished Bostonians, there were no faces in the crowd more filled with pride than those of my mother and dad, who had sacrificed to send me to school beyond our means or status.

My parents' example moulded my early life. Dad had to drop out of high school before earning a diploma, in order to support his mother and sister after his father died in the influenza epidemic which followed World War 1. He married my mother, then spent twelve years in night school, first accounting, then law, all the while holding down a thirty-two-dollar-a-week job as a bookkeeper in a meat-packing plant. How impressed I'd been at age eight, sitting in the crowded auditorium watching my father in black cap and gown, graduating from Northeastern Law School.

When Dad wasn't studying, maybe late on a Sunday afternoon, we would talk. "Work hard, study hard; nothing comes easy in this life," he used to say. "There are no short-cuts. No matter how menial the job you have, the important thing is to do it well." It was the Puritan-inspired work ethic. And then he would always add: "Tell the truth – always – lies destroy you." I'd tried to follow that and always did with him.

Our home was a walk-up rented apartment in an old Victorian house in Winthrop, a small middle-class town on a jetty of land north across the harbour from Boston. By depression standards, we lived fairly well; my mother saw to that, always spending slightly more than my dad earned. Moderately comfortable, we were also moderately in debt. When bills mounted too high, Mother would hold

sales of our furniture and other possessions. I remember
the shock of coming home from school one day, seeing perfect strangers carrying chairs out of our living room. Being
in debt, being unsure where next month's rent would come
from, created an insecurity which, combined with my
father's exhortations, doubtless fuelled my later drive to
achieve.

With his law degree my dad shot ahead in business, but
his success was soon curtailed by poor health. He was
forced to quit his job with General Foods, the company
which had acquired the meat-packing plant he once worked
in. By the time of my graduation, Dad was struggling to
make it as a lawyer practising on his own in a city whose
legal fraternity, like most of its institutions, was tightly
controlled by Harvard men. Only by a stroke of good fortune was my father able to land a small case in the spring
of 1949 that enabled him to pay my last tuition instalment
at Browne and Nichols. Without it I would not have
graduated.

Though so bursting with pride on that day in June that
I was straining the seams of my new blue double-breasted
suit, I was also filled with uncertainty over how I would
possibly meet the tuition payments in college. Every summer since I was eleven I had worked to help with school
expenses. But college would be exactly double prep-school
costs. I took the highest-paying job I could find that
summer as a messenger for a Boston brokerage firm and
anxiously awaited the results of scholarship application
I had filed at Harvard and Brown.

Brown was the first heard from – a notification that I
had been accepted for a full Navy ROTC scholarship, plus
fifty dollars a month for living expenses. Then in early
June I was invited for an interview with the dean of ad-
missions at Harvard.

Promptly at the appointed hour I was ushered into a
handsome corner office in the two-hundred-year-old administration building looking out over the quiet Harvard
Yard on one side and bustling Harvard Square on the
other. The office had a slightly musty smell, the patina of
fine antique brass, glowing random-width floorboards. An

elegant old Colonial desk sat between sagging bookshelves filled with memorabilia of Harvard. The dean, perfectly cast for his role, wore a baggy tweed coat, with wiry grey hair close cropped and the unmistakable air of fine breeding essential for Harvard men of those years.

"I am very happy to inform you, Mr. Colson – you are a fortunate young man – that the Board of Overseers has granted you a full scholarship to Harvard University." He paused a moment for me to express my elation.

I felt it, all right, but I was aware of a second reaction deep inside me: resentment built up over the years to the superior attitude of the whole Harvard academic establishment, the condescension of aristocratic men to those who came out of less fortunate backgrounds. I thanked him politely and waited.

There was a pause as he lighted his pipe and took a long puff. "Well, I assume you have a lot of questions, the house you will live in, and of course your academic schedule," he said.

"But I haven't really decided, Dean, whether I will be coming to Harvard," I said.

He stared at me for a moment, openly nettled. "I can't imagine anyone turning down a scholarship to Harvard," he said.

Pride. As a boy I used to stand on the pebbly beach looking across the grey-green waters of the harbour at the city then run by the Brahmins, the Beacon Hill establishment which traced its ancestry through generations of Harvard classes back to the *Mayflower*. We were neither the new ethnics – Italians, Irish Catholics just seizing political power in the wards of Boston – nor old stock. "Swamp Yankees," we were called. Acceptance was what we were denied – and what we most fervently sought. Now in this one moment, I had it – admission to the elite. And in my pride I believed I had something better still – the chance to turn them down. It was warped pride, no doubt, but the resentment against Eastern intellectualism stayed with me and shaped some of the tumultuous events of my later life.

And so that September, with twenty dollars in the pocket of my blue graduation suit. I headed for Brown University in Providence, Rhode Island, which Harvard men looked upon as a poor Ivy League cousin.

Pride – mixed with a deep-seated patriotism I'd felt since a small boy – was also the reason for my joining the Marines. With the Korean War at its height during my sophomore year at Brown, and the Marines needing volunteers, a strong recruiting pitch was made on our campus. A senior in my fraternity whom I greatly admired, also in the NROTC, Bill Maloney, had decided to take his commission in the Marine Corps. Bill talked about the Marine Corps with such pride and feeling that a week later I found myself standing before the desk of a Marine recruiting officer, a tall arched-backed first lieutenant named Cosgrove.

"Midshipman Colson, sir," I said. "I'd like to inquire about the Marine Corps."

Cosgrove, a Naval Academy graduate, frowned, looked me up and down, and snapped, "You are a bit premature, Colson. First, we will have to see whether you are *good enough* for the Marine Corps."

I stood before his desk speechless for a long moment. What did he mean – "good enough"? I ranked high in my class in all military attributes. For the next two months I smarted over Cosgrove's putdown. One day a week NROTC students wore uniforms to class and afternoon drill sessions. From then on, the night before I spit-shined my shoes, polished my uniform brass, studied every detail of the next day's drill. I began to try to walk like Cosgrove, back straight, chin in. At every drill session I noticed Cosgrove watching me.

Finally, one day in the spring, I found a typed notice on the bulletin board: "Midshipman Colson, report to Lt. Cosgrove." My heart fluttered for a moment; I never had really decided I wanted the Marine Corps; I just wanted to be "good enough."

When I stood stiffly at attention in front of Cosgrove's desk, he leaned back in an old wooden swivel chair, twirling his pencil in front of him. Finally he sat upright and scowling fiercely said, "Colson, we think you're good enough."

Before he could continue, I interrupted with – "Where do

I sign up, sir?" I later discovered that the Marine Corps was under its allowed quota and needed recruits badly.

How different the world around me looked from inside the suit of Marine green, with the globe and anchor on my cap. As a young platoon commander, I was assigned to the division led by General "Chesty" Puller, the salty old warrior whose heroic exploits made him the only man in history to earn five Navy Crosses. The gruff-talking Puller was a Marine's Marine; though he led men to die, they loved him. Like thousands of my comrades I would have walked off a cliff if he so ordered me and, in fact, one day almost did.

On one training exercise in the Caribbean (the Korean War having ended) my platoon was landed on a small stretch of beach on the mountainous island of Vieques. There were two routes to our assigned objective: one around a long circuitous path over relatively flat terrain, the other straight up a craggy cliff rising sixty feet in the air. The order came: "Up the cliff."

For a few moments I couldn't believe it. It was only a training exercise and as I stared at the menacing volcanic ash, I thought it was not only foolhardy but impossible. *Someone, maybe me, would get killed. But Marines can do anything,* I reminded myself, and then led my forty-five men up and over the cliff, clawing every inch of our way with picks, ropes, and bare hands. When we got to the top I looked back at the beach below, the sea beyond, and in that instant realised that Puller was right; when a man throws everything into it, he can do the impossible.

It was that same summer of 1954 when orders came to me at Camp Lejeune: "Report at once with seabag, an emergency." Within hours my battalion was loaded aboard an old World War II "rust bucket," the U.S.S. *Mellette.* With several tons of ammunition in the hold beneath us, we headed for Guatemala, then in the midst of a Communist uprising. Our overt mission was to protect American lives. Off the rocky coast of the tiny Latin American republic, live ammunition was handed out to the troops while I and other platoon leaders were briefed on landing plans. Final orders were to come from Washington.

The sea that night was like glass, the air heavy and hot. As I stood on deck everything was blackness except for the red and green running lights of other ships in our task force and the thousands of stars flickering in the sky. I'd never seen so many stars, a shower spray of tiny pinpoints of light, like a Fourth of July sparkler.

It was almost midnight and I was fearful about what might lie ahead, how I would handle myself, realizing that I was responsible for the lives of forty-five men. I felt suddenly insignificant staring out into the universe, knowing that I was but a tiny dot standing on a slightly larger dot, floating on a sea that was huge and endless to me, but was only another dot compared to the vastness around me. *Where does it all end?* I wondered.

My parents had taken me to an Episcopal Sunday school and church as a boy, but it had never made much impression on me. That night I suddenly became as certain as I had ever been about anything in my life that out there in that great starlit beyond was God. I was convinced that He ruled over the universe, that to Him there were no mysteries, that – He somehow kept it all miraculously in order. In my own fumbling way I prayed, knowing that He was there, questioning only whether He had time to hear me.

Later that night the emergency was cancelled: the pro-U.S. regime in Guatemala beat back the Communists without our help, though we stayed for six weeks just to be sure. And my awareness of God faded as personal interests crowded my life.

Feeling I had proved myself in the Marines, eager for new challenges, I resigned and switched my commission to the Reserves. Law school beckoned. Also politics. A job in a much-heralded management intern programme in the Navy Department in Washington enabled me to work days and go to law school at night at George Washington University.

The first year in Washington I met the senior senator from Massachusetts, a grand old patrician gentleman, Leverett Saltonstall, who offered me a job in his office and two years later, despite my youth and inexperience, named me his chief assistant.

Saltonstall was a towering and respected figure in the Senate but he'd neglected his political fences back home in a state whose politics were changing fast as the Italians and Irish displaced the Old Guard. John F. Kennedy, the junior senator, was the rising star and leading candidate for the Democratic Presidential nomination.

Since 1948, when I became a volunteer worker in the losing effort of Massachusetts Governor Bradford, I had been getting an education in practical politics, Boston-style. I learned all the tricks, some of which went up to and even slightly over the legal boundaries. Phoney mailings, tearing down opposition signs, planting misleading stories in the press, voting tombstones, and spying out the opposition in every possible way were all standard fare.

As the 1960 elections approached, Saltonstall asked me to manage his campaign. The polls showed him trailing the popular Democratic governor, Foster Furcolo, the first Italian-American to occupy the executive mansion in the Bay State. It looked like a hopeless uphill struggle, particularly with Kennedy leading the ticket on the other side. So the challenge was appealing.

We encouraged Tom O'Connor, the young, obscure mayor of Springfield, to run as a Democratic primary candidate against Furcolo. He did so well that he upset the governor and to our shock then appeared even more formidable in the polls than Furcolo had been.

We went all out. When your candidate is of the integrity and standing of a Saltonstall, the shrewd campaign manager sees that his man travels the high road and doesn't know what his manager is doing down on the plains of battle. After several bogus mailings, plus inciting a taxpayers' revolt in O'Connor's hometown, we pulled neck and neck.

A late September poll showed that we were gaining among the Irish bloc whose votes held the key to the election. That information dictated a special tactic. I secretly rented a few rooms in a third-rate Boston hotel, installed new locks on the doors, and packed it with young campaign volunteers who began addressing plain envelopes to every Irish-sounding name in the phone book, some three hundred

thousand families. Then we inveigled six prominent Irish
Democrats to sign a letter endorsing Kennedy (running
against Nixon) for President and Saltonstall for the Senate.
The two senators, though in opposing parties, had worked
together for so many home-state projects that the Salton-
stall-Kennedy hyphenation was synonymous with every
federal goodie that had come to Massachusetts. The letter
was a blatantly provincial appeal to help Saltonstall ride
in on the Kennedy vote. Saltonstall knew nothing of the
ploy. In his speeches, of course, he continued to back Nixon.

The Friday night before the election I visited the hideaway hotel rooms. Twenty nearly exhausted volunteers
were hand stuffing the mountain of envelopes. At midnight
we'd scheduled two station wagons to arrive at the back-
alley entrance; the kids would load box after box into the
wagons and then drive them to an out-of-the-way post
office where a friendly postmaster would process them for us.

There was only one hitch. A Harvard freshman named
Tom, in charge of the secret project, asked to see me alone.
We stepped out of the room and walked together down the
dimly lit corridor. "Chuck," he said, "I'm worried about
one of our girls. Her father is an avid party man and she
thinks we're being disloyal to Nixon. I overheard her talking about going to Republican headquarters to tell the
chairman what's going on here."

"Oh, no," I moaned. "That'll blow us right out of the
water. Any publicity and this will boomerang. Nixon
hasn't a chance in this state and I've told his people what
we're doing. We're trying to save a Republican senator,
that's all."

I stood with my head down staring at the grease-stained
carpet, a sick feeling in my stomach. We couldn't let anyone know that Saltonstall's committee was behind the mailing. It had to look independent, a genuine letter from
Kennedy supporters. The election could be riding on this
one last-minute appeal which our opponent would never
have time to rebut.

"Tell you what, Tom," I looked up into his tired eyes.
"Take this." I handed him ten crisp ten-dollar bills, all I
had in my wallet. "Take the girl out tonight and get her

loaded. Keep her diverted, whatever you have to do until Election Day."

Tom, a ladies' man, happily followed orders. The letters arrived in three hundred thousand Irish homes across the state the next Monday morning. Saltonstall, securely attached to Kennedy's coat tail, was re-elected handily by that many votes.

Heady over my success in managing the Saltonstall campaign, I spurned the senator's urgings to remain his administrative assistant, a secure, well-paying job for the next six years. I turned down bids to join a number of Boston law firms. Instead, with five thousand dollars representing my accumulated savings, I joined forces with Charles Morin, a brilliant young lawyer I'd met in my political travels and who was soon to become my closest personal friend. Charlie, though Harvard educated, was a Catholic of Canadian and Irish descent, like myself an outsider to the establishment, striving to make it. We opened a Boston-Washington law practice. I manned a two-room Washington office; Morin, a three-room Boston suite.

Fortunately, the clients began to come before the last of the five thousand dollars was gone; by midyear we had even hired our first lawyer, a bright young man named Joe Mitchell, recommended to us by our close friend, Elliot Richardson, who was then the U.S. Attorney. Joe was exceptionally well qualified and would have been snapped up by any firm but for one small drawback: he was black. Two months after Morin and I hired him and it was obvious he hadn't "hurt" our business, several law firms in Boston were bidding for him. We not only had gotten a gifted lawyer but had broken the colour line among the Boston Bar as well.

The firm grew fast, but not without anxious moments. Shortly before Christmas of 1962, Charlie and I spent a long evening in our Boston office, shirt sleeves rolled up and the ledger books of our young firm spread out on a rented conference table. Sometime after midnight Morin, anxious furrows across his brow, summed it all up: "We still owe ten thousand dollars for the furniture, the payroll is up to twenty thousand dollars a month, we are hiring too many people, the big firms are putting the blocks to us, and I don't see enough business to get us through the spring."

I couldn't argue with a thing Charlie said. We had moved fast, maybe too fast. The next day, flying back to Washington, I found myself staring out of the window of the DC-6 at the snow-covered countryside below. But I wasn't seeing sleepy New England towns, rather blue Caribbean water, an expanse of white beach, and the craggy cliff I had scaled eight years before. The adrenaline started flowing. I began a long handwritten memo to Charlie.

"Next week I will see my friend at Grumman Aircraft. I feel sure he will retain us. With one trip to California, there are two companies...." I went on for several pages, listing the new business I knew we could get – if we threw everything into it. Charlie kept the memo for years; we landed every one of those accounts.

Although I refused to admit it, my personal life was suffering from my preoccupation with politics and business. Nancy Billings, a lovely Boston-bred girl, whom I married the day I graduated from college, shunned the excitement I found so fulfilling in the political arena, spending all of her time tending our three young children – Wendell, born in 1954, Christian, born in 1956, and Emily, born in 1958. As the years passed we found less and less in common. Her parents' fine home and social standing, the correct wedding, had been, however subconsciously, important to me in my eager drive for acceptance; but the insecurity of my college days had long since given way to assurance, the certainty that I was totally self-sufficient. After a few years' separation, divorce came in January 1964.

Later that year I married Patty Hughes, a wholesome and warm-hearted girl from Springfield, Vermont, whose radiant smile and winsome ways made her one of the best-liked secretaries on Capitol Hill. Her zest for life and love of politics were like mine. Descended from Irish Catholic immigrants, her religion created our one problem. Patty, a onetime Cherry Blossom Princess with scores of friends, had to forego a formal wedding; we were married in a simple civil service at an Army chapel adjacent to Arlington Cemetery. For a while I studied Catholicism, but my divorce appeared an insurmountable barrier to the blessing of her church and in time I dropped it.

Several years later Patty and I, with no children of our own, filed an application with a Washington adoption agency. The matronly interviewer suspiciously probed every facet of our lives. "You seem to have a very successful record, Mr. Colson. Why do you feel you need more children?"

After some sparring back and forth I realized she was implying that I was too busy for children and that I probably hadn't done a very good job with the first three. I explained how much I loved Wendell, Christian, and Emily, how we spent every minute possible together, but that Patty and I wanted children of our own as well.

"You're very clear about what you want, aren't you? I suppose you don't think you have ever failed in anything in your life," she said.

"That's right, I haven't," I replied loftily.

"Don't you think your divorce was a failure?" she pressed on.

The question stung. Deep down I knew I had failed but I couldn't admit it to myself or anyone else. The turndown by the agency could have been a valuable checkpoint for me: a chance to take a hard look at the person I was becoming. But it wasn't. I blamed it on the baby shortage, the pill, and liberalised abortion. The tough exterior coating that I had layered over myself during all the years of driving and succeeding was impenetrable.

I first met Richard Nixon when he was Vice-President during the Eisenhower Administration. My brushes with him over the years impressed me; here was a man of uncommon intellect and capacity, with visions for his country and party which I enthusiastically shared. In the late spring of 1964 the two of us sat alone in his austere corner office on the twenty-fourth floor of Twenty Broad Street in New York City while I tried to persuade Mr. Nixon that only he could save the Republican Party from the debacle that would surely follow a Goldwater nomination.

"Okay, go ahead," he told me. "Get on the phones and see how many delegates we can count on."

Though he tried to appear casual about it, his eyes lit up at the thought of the campaign. "Johnson would have to debate me wouldn't he, Chuck? I mean, after all, I agreed to the debate with Kennedy." He turned and stared wistfully out of the window at the skyline of his newly adopted city.

Nixon and I understood one another – a young ambitious political kingmaker and an older pretender to the throne. We were both men of the same lower middle-class origins, men who'd known hard work all our lives, prideful men seeking that most elusive goal of all – acceptance and the respect of those who had spurned us in earlier years.

"But it will be tough this year," Nixon mused. "The whole establishment is against us. If we don't go this time, well, there will always be. . . ." His voice trailed off.

And of course there was no way that year to stop the Goldwater nomination and the subsequent November disaster for the Republicans. But for Richard Nixon and me the dream remained vividy alive.

I was, predictably enough, in the middle of his 1968 campaign, much to the distress of my clients and the law firm from which I took a four months' leave of absence. "This race is too important to the country. The country needs Nixon right now. I will be back after the election," I promised my partners, yet knowing in my heart where my deeper interest lay.

At the beginning of the Nixon Administration my old friend, John Volpe, former governor of Massachusetts and now Secretary of Transportation, asked me to take a post in his department. Under Secretary of State Elliot Richardson asked me to become an Assistant Secretary. I hedged. I was waiting for the one call, the one telling me that the *President* needed *me*.

It came in the late fall of 1969 – a call from the White House.

"Right this way, Mr. Colson." A tall ramrod-stiff Navy commander with a gold-braided aiguillette draped around his shoulder, was beckoning me toward what appeared at first to be the white plaster wall of the office occupied by the President's appointment secretary. Then I saw the faint outline of a small door etched in it; a piece of the wall itself, moulding, chair rail and all, forming a private entrance used only by the staff into the President's formal Oval Office.

As I stepped for the first time into the sun-filled, stark-white, curving walled room, my heart was beating so hard I wondered if it could be heard. I walked over a huge blue and gold oval-shaped rug, the Great Seal of the United States colourfully embroidered in its centre, directly beneath a matching white plaster seal moulded in the ceiling. In front of the floor-to-ceiling windows looking out across the South Lawn, the President sat at a large mahogany desk.

He was leaning back in his chair, sun streaming in over his shoulders revealing the first specks of grey in his hair, intently studying the pages of a large brown leather folder propped in his lap. He glanced up, peering over reading glasses I never knew he wore, and flashed a broad, quick grin: "Sit down, boy. Good to see you again. I'll be with you in a minute." With that his eyes returned to the brown notebook on which I could read in gold embossed letters: DAILY INTELLIGENCE SUMMARY and below that simply: THE PRESIDENT.

The President. Not the person I'd known for so many years, but *the* President – and in this room constructed during Theodore Roosevelt's Presidency, where so much of the high drama of the twentieth century had been enacted. Just to be in the room was exciting enough, but now I was here alone with *the* President, the single most important man in the world, and here as a member of *his* staff. My life, the whole thirty-eight years of it, was about to be fulfilled.

3

"Break All the — China"

To most of the White House staff, I was suspect from the beginning, Ivy League educated, and from the citadel of liberalism, Boston. To make it worse, I was the original booster of Ed Brooke, the only black then in the Senate. Bob Haldeman's Orange County California Conservatives therefore regarded me as just another "Eastern lib." An early interview with a young reporter from the *Boston Globe* didn't help.

One of the questions asked me was about Attorney General John Mitchell and his southern strategy for selection of Supreme Court Justices. Having had a run-in with Mitchell in the 1968 campaign and some questions about his judgment, I effusively praised Nixon and "no commented" Mitchell.

The resulting headline was a minor disaster: *Mitchell No Hero: Colson.* For months after the story appeared, the Attorney General would not return my phone calls. No one in those days challenged Mitchell privately, let alone publicly; one word from Mitchell and men were summarily dismissed. Perhaps Mitchell was so taken aback by my brashness, which he didn't know was unintentional, that he failed to call Nixon to have me unceremoniously dumped out onto Pennsylvania Avenue. By the time he did try – a year later in the fall of 1970 – I'd become firmly entrenched. For years afterwards at the mere mention of my name, Mitchell would grunt and puff furiously on his pipe until the bowl glowed red-hot.

On the job I began doing what I'd always done in politics

and government – jump into the middle of situations. First the postal reorganisation plan which was pigeonholed in Congress, later a threatened postal strike. The key union man was a friend; we hammered out compromise legislation and I brought him in for an off-the-record chat with Nixon cementing the deal and incidentally planting the first seeds of a new political alliance with labour.

One Friday afternoon early in 1970, Nixon flew into one of his angry tirades against the federal bureaucracy. For a year he had been asking for a simple executive order to create a commission to study ways to help Catholic schools. It was a campaign pledge. Several aides had been stalling on it. Mitchell questioned the constitutionality. The public-education lobby was death on the idea. I had brought in a group of Catholic-school educators to meet Nixon that morning; they told him of their needs and reminded him of his campaign promise. A few hours later I was summoned back to the Oval Office.

"Chuck, I want a commission appointed *now*," he told me. "I've been thinking about what those men said this morning. I ordered it a year ago and no one pays any attention. You do it. Break all the —— china in this building but have an order for me to sign on my desk Monday morning."

It was now 5:00 p.m. Friday. "I don't know where to start," I confessed to my secretary, Joan Hall. My staff in those days was just the two of us. John Ehrlichman, Nixon's chief domestic aide, was off skiing that week; Bob Finch, head of the Department of Health, Education, and Welfare, was vacationing in the South. One of Finch's assistants found the file for me; it had been buried under a stack of papers on a mid-level career man's desk.

I called the Department of Justice first; all executive orders are drafted and cleared there. But the assistant whose office handles such things curtly told me the department was closed for the weekend; he could not put anyone to work until Monday. No wonder, I thought, *the President explodes in frustration. He probably thinks he's running the government.* I thought about calling Mitchell, but even if he took my call he'd probably refuse to help.

And so on Friday night, digging out some old orders to use

as models, I dictated the document to Joan, the beginning of a frantic two days.

The next morning I reached Finch. "That's the thing the boss has been asking about, isn't it?" he asked, confessing he hadn't been able to locate it for months. When I told him the file was now on my desk, he gave me his approval. Then the White House operator found the budget director, calling him off a golf course. In an exasperated voice, he approved the money. Ehrlichman was on a Colorado slope and didn't return my several calls; his assistant was travelling and also unavailable. A strictly worded White House staff order required that Ehrlichman pass on all domestic matters. But the President had said Monday morning, and so Monday morning I placed the order on his desk.

When Mitchell and Ehrlichman discovered what had happened they were furious. It set off a minor uproar within the staid offices at 1600 Pennsylvania Avenue. Richard Nixon loved it. He had found someone to cut through red tape and "break china." Soon I was doing it in other areas, winning a vote for the ABM missile programme by finding a job for a senator's friend, arm twisting, making deals, leaking stories to cut down opponents and promote friends.

It wasn't long before I was very much a part of the workings of the Presidency. Soon after the "executive order" weekend a black limousine was assigned to me. It was a heady experience to speed through the streets of Washington in my first motorcade, close behind the sleek bulletproof limousine with Presidential flags flying from small staffs on the front fenders, on our way to the Capitol. On this occasion the chamber of the House of Representatives was packed – the Cabinet, the Supreme Court, the diplomatic corps and 535 elected members occupying every seat on the floor, the galleries overflowing.

I took my place standing along the wall just to the side of the Speaker's rostrum as the voice of Fishbait Miller, long-time doorkeeper of the House, bellowed through the chamber, "Mr. Speaker, the President of the United States." A thunderous, almost deafening applause began and went on. And on. My boss made his way down the crowded aisle, smiling, shaking hands with old colleagues, then up onto the platform to begin his constitutionally mandated duty to "give to the Congress [and, nowadays, millions of Americans watching on television] information on the State of the Union."

But mostly there was gruelling hard work, dizzying rounds of meetings, and mounds of option papers detailing the conflicting views of government agencies on policy questions. *Nothing that gets this far is simple,* I remember discovering. Each paper demanded an opinion, a careful recommendation, but some days there was scarcely time to do more than react. Pressures were unrelenting, days vanishing into night, passing by like wisps of smoke. I never once doubted that I could get the job done, whatever it was. It was just straight ahead, pushing and driving, the simple formula I had followed all my life.

There were times, however, when I did have doubts – anxieties and even deep fears for the country and the government we were trying to run. It was in the aftermath of Nixon's controversial decision in the spring of 1970 to order an invasion – "incursion," we preferred to call it – of Cambodia that I first felt the full weight of being part of the Presidency. The President was convinced that the action was necessary to relieve the pressure on our armed forces in Vietnam and was also aware that such a decision would provoke a fresh round of domestic dissent and political backlash. "We'll catch unshirted hell, no matter what we do so we'd better get on with it," Nixon told Ehrlichman and me when we warned him that an all-out assault, as distinguished from more limited military operation proposed by the Pentagon, could inflame the country.

Nixon's speech to the nation the night of April 30 gave our critics no quarter. "The U.S. would not be a pitiful, helpless giant," he argued. Expressions of shock and outrage swept across the country from governors to local church leaders. Four senators – Mark Hatfield of Oregon, George McGovern of South Dakota, Harold Hughes of Iowa, and Charles Goodell of New York – bitterly assailed Nixon's decision and introduced legislation to cut off all funds for Vietnam.

But it was an event that took place on a sleepy college campus nestled in the hills of Middle America which set off shock waves around the world. On the afternoon of May 4 came the first flash bulletins from Ohio's Kent State University – the National Guard had fired on a student demonstration. Grim-faced White House aides, haunted by memories of the domestic violence which erupted after Martin Luther King's shooting two years earlier, clustered around the chattering ticker-tape machines in Ron Ziegler's press office as the ugly story unfolded : four dead, eleven wounded.

I was working late that evening and went to the White House staff mess for a quick dinner. In a corner of the small oak-panelled dining room on a large colour-television set were scenes of National Guardsmen advancing through tear gas, volleys of shots fired, bleeding bodies of college students lying on the ground. There was the horrifying picture which remains in my consciousness, as vivid today as it was then, of a young girl screaming in anguish, kneeling over the body of a friend.

I looked around the crowded room. Like a scene from a stop-action camera nothing was moving : dinner plates were untouched, red-jacketed stewards stood frozen in place, White House staffers sat in stunned silence, their eyes fixed on the grisly tragedy being replayed before them. Then on the screen appeared a sobbing grief-stricken face, the father of Allison Krause, who was dead. "The President is to blame!" he cried out.

My first reaction was : How unfair ! What a terrible thing to say. The President didn't have anything to do with Allison's death. And then I thought, *Supposing it were my Emily?* I, too, would lash out at the leader of the government, the symbol of authority against which my daughter was protesting. Maybe I'd do more.

Then the sickening thought crossed my mind that if his accusation was fair, even in part, then I, too, was responsible; I'd helped the President make the Cambodia decision. For one awful instant I felt that Mr. Krause was right in that room, that his tear-filled eyes were looking straight into mine, and I felt unclean. I skipped dinner.

I learned in time that if I was to remain in the White House, advising the President on decisions which meant life or death to real people, I could afford no personal feelings. How easy it used to be to read history, to study someone else's decisions, to ponder the merits with detachment – how different to make and live with those decisions. When word came of prisoners taken in a raid we had ordered, the picture would flash into my mind of a man crouched in a bamboo cage, rats and spiders picking at his flesh; I could actually hear his cries of pain. They were daytime nightmares, real as life.

Soon I forced myself to think only in numbers; the larger the numbers, the more impersonal it all seemed. Comparative statistics were anaesthetising, too: only ten U.S. servicemen killed in Vietnam last week compared with fifty the same week a year ago.

In the wake of the Kent State shooting, student and faculty strikes erupted on scores of campuses from Stanford to the University of Maryland. Two black students lay dead at Jackson State campus in Mississippi, shot by state police. Mirroring a fear-gripped nation, the stock market plummeted 100 points. Independent-minded Secretary of the Interior Walter Hickel released a private letter to Nixon, chastising his chief for turning a deaf ear to the student protesters Nixon had in an unguarded moment labelled "bums." Publicly Nixon praised Hickel as "courageous," privately vowing to fire him.

The Secretaries of State and Defence leaked to friends in the press the stories that they had opposed the President's decision. Some of Henry Kissinger's most valued brain trusters resigned, including longtime Vietnam expert Morton Halperin who with his close friend, Dr. Daniel Ellsberg, drafted Nixon's first top-secret option paper on Southeast Asia, "National Security Study Memorandum Number One."

There were public calls for Nixon's removal from office by student leaders and the head of the Wholesale, Retail, and Office Workers Union. In the Capitol cloakrooms the first impeachment murmurs could be heard. Nixon had been President slightly more than fifteen months.

On the weekend of May 9 throngs of students, estimated at over 150,000, descended upon the nation's capital. Streets surrounding the White House that Saturday morning were cordoned off several blocks in all directions. My car was met at a checkpoint at Nineteenth and E Streets and escorted in by helmeted police. As an emergency precaution several hundred D.C. Transit buses were strung out, end to end, around the White House, blockading Pennsylvania Avenue to the north and the Ellipse to the south. Riot-squad police were stationed at key points behind the buses; in the E.O.B. basement was a battalion of troops from the Eighty-first Airborne Division, soldiers in full combat dress with field packs and camouflage-covered helmets.

As I walked through the basement chatting with the troops, most of them bright-faced kids, some sprawled on the cold marble floor sleeping, others reading or playing cards, it was hauntingly reminiscent of what I had seen twice before in Central American countries: uniformed troops guarding the palace against its enemies. But here – in the strongest democracy in the world?

Later from an upstairs window as I watched the crowd filling the streets, I struggled with my thoughts. What holds our society together is not force or even laws but moral suasion. Presidents rule not by fiat, but by the sufferance of free men. Without the collective goodwill of 200 million Americans, glibly called "public confidence," government is impotent, anarchy – or worse – inescapable.

Yet as far as I could see in every direction were angry citizens shouting defiance. Whatever was right or wrong in our foreign policy was irrelevant if moral leadership could not be regained. Maybe we were the "pitiful, helpless giant" Nixon spoke of – not our armies in battle as he meant it – but right here as the delicate fabric which binds a free people together was being stretched to its breaking point.

As the day passed the anxious expectancy inside the besieged White House mounted. In mid-afternoon a warning was flashed from the command post in the White House basement: a large gathering of demonstrators was moving toward the northwest corner of the grounds. Several rocks were thrown, shattering bus windows. I could hear the rustling of the troops in the basement – loosening rifle straps, fixing bayonets, laying out ammunition clips.

Suddenly there was the muffled thump, thump, thump of tear-gas guns firing canisters into the crowd, great puffs of smoke billowing in the air. Two of the buses crashed over on their sides. Police wearing gas masks and steel helmets began moving into the crowd – clubs swinging, men running, some falling. There were shouts and screams, the shattering of glass and steel. A gentle breeze from the west swept a mist of tear gas through the White House windows; I felt the acrid, burning sensation in my eyes and nose. Then all was quiet. The alarm ended as quickly as it had begun; the crowd routed, dispersed into small groups.

Nixon's tough decision to go all out to rout the North Vietnamese from their sanctuaries in "neutral" Cambodia, and then his steadfastness in the face of mounting congressional protests and public demonstrations, seemed to pay off when great caches of enemy supplies were captured and destroyed. Hanoi's forces were badly crippled, American casualties reduced, and troop withdrawals speeded up.

In late May more than 100,000 construction workers and longshoremen marched through the streets of New York bearing placards urging "support the troops," their hard hats covered with Nixon stickers. Despite the opposition of most White House staffers, who saw the hard hat as the symbol of student oppression, Nixon had me telephone the march organiser, a burly two-fisted Bronx Irishman named Peter Brennan. Two days later a procession of hod carriers, bricklayers and ironworkers, wearing hard hats and flag pins on their coats, paraded through the Oval Office to meet a grinning, appreciative President. Photos of that meeting – which signalled an unprecedented political alliance between a Republican President and organised labour – flashed across the country.

Within days, telegrams of support were flooding the White House. Spirits buoyed, Nixon continued the momentum by inviting fifty Wall Street leaders to an elegant dinner in the State Dining Room. In two days the market jumped fifty points: stability seemed to be returning to the country, fears receding.

But the memory of May 9 would not be erased. Within the iron gates of the White House, quite unknowingly, a siege mentality was setting in. It was now "us" against "them." Gradually as we drew the circle closer around us, the ranks of "them" began to swell.

Nowhere did our animosity run deeper than toward the media. Responding to what we viewed as the daily attacks of TV news commentators, the *New York Times*, and the *Washington Post* cryptic memoranda were circulated containing as one did in 1971, the blanket order: "No one on the staff is to see any reporter from the *New York Times* for any purpose ever."

One day I made the mistake of accepting an invitation to lunch with Joseph Kraft, a liberal syndicated columnist. Lyn Nofziger, a hard-line conservative on the White House staff, spotted us at the posh Sans Souci. Nofziger came by our table and with a churlish smile berated me for having lunch with a "flaming liberal." I thought it was in good fun, a little joshing for Kraft's benefit, until I was summoned to Haldeman's office that afternoon and dressed down: "If you want to stay around here, stay away from that ——," he snapped. Stunned, I did.

In the fall of 1970 the President dispatched me to conduct "quiet" visits in New York with the presidents of the three networks simply to discuss regulatory matters and the fairness of network coverage. All-powerful within their own corporate domains, but with their economic fortunes held on a tight tether by the Federal Communications Commission, the three men were unusually accommodating. The significance of my visit was not lost on them. We engineered a successful legal challenge to a "loyal opposition" series giving free TV time to Democrats, and believed we had tamed our foes.

Vice-President Agnew's verbal assault on the press rallied the silent majority but unfortunately solidified the antagonism of most journalists toward us. As the networks became merciless in their nightly barrages against the Vietnam War and Nixon policies, we in turn lost our capacity to be objective, seeing ourselves more and more the victims of a conspiracy by the press. Our attitude hardened newsmen's convictions that we were bent on destroying the free press. Thus the cycle continued.

Early in 1971, after a year of meticulous staff work by John Ehrlichman's domestic council, the President launched, under the banner of the "new American Revolution," the first cohesive domestic initiative of the Nixon Administration. Revenue sharing, welfare reform, and government re-organisation turned out to have all the crowd-drawing power of a last-place baseball club in September. The quick demise of this ballyhooed domestic programme merely confirmed to us that Mr. Nixon's Presidency would ride or fall on foreign policy.

The blueprint for realigning world power which Mr. Nixon and his adviser, Henry Kissinger, conceived soon after the election was ambitious and farsighted. The President would announce at Guam in July 1969 that the United States could no longer be policemen of the world, and would help other nations only if they would help themselves. The speech's significance was understood in Moscow and Peking; there would be no more Vietnams. But Mr. Nixon was also saying privately that he would begin squeezing the Soviet Union for an arms agreement and détente. By driving a wedge into the Communist world, pushing the Soviets, tempting the Chinese, he would strive for a new tripartite balance of power in world politics, one that would maintain its own peace-keeping equilibrium. Linkage was the key phrase; everything was interrelated, nuclear arms agreements, tensions in the Middle East, trade, and of course, the one big open sore – Vietnam.

To engineer the design from its first ingenious blueprint was quite another task and may, when the passions of this era subside, be recorded as one of the great diplomatic juggling acts in history. "Buying time" for an honourable solution in Vietnam, as the President often described it to me, was critical to America's bargaining position in secret negotiations with China and Russia. The talks themselves had to be managed in utmost secrecy. Leaks were more dangerous than the skills of our adversaries. It was nerve-racking business.

In May 1971 the Kremlin relented on one key sticking point that had kept strategic arms negotiations deadlocked for over a year. A private message from Brezhnev was delivered to Nixon in mid-May, concluding four months of secret negotiations between Kissinger and Soviet Ambassador Anatoly Dobrynin. Both sides were serious now. An arms agreement could be concluded before year's end. Simultaneous announcements were scheduled for May 20 in Moscow and Washington. The wording was to be guarded, but even the fact that the United States and Soviet Union could agree on issuing statements was significant.

To celebrate this breakthrough the President invited Kissinger, Ehrlichman, Haldeman, and me to join him for dinner on the Presidential yacht *Sequoia* the night before the announcement. Cruising the gentle waters of the Potomac was one of the few ways Nixon had discovered to escape the crushing weight of the Presidency.

I rode with the President to the Navy Yard. In the soft-grey-velveted comfort of the big Cadillac, he talked steadily from the minute we left : how this strategic arms agreement would be the first building block of the new order. More was to come, peace in Vietnam within a few months – Henry was about to deliver a generous offer at the secret Paris negotiations – then détente, a new understanding with the Soviets and the Chinese, bright promises for America. Dreams coming true – and – for a change – good news to announce.

Twelve minutes later we were inside the grounds of the historic Naval Gun Factory, pulling up to a heavily guarded pier, the stately old yacht tied up alongside. Sailors in crisp starched whites snapped salutes. Nixon stopped at the head of the short gangplank, returned the captain's salute, then turned, faced the ship's stern, and with obvious feeling, saluted the flag. It wasn't a politician's showmanship; nobody but a few stone-faced sailors and his closest confidants would see him. But respect for the flag was deeply ingrained in the man. Later that evening, precisely at 8 : 00 p.m., Nixon led us all to the foredeck to stand at rigid attention while the colours were lowered at Mount Vernon in the distance. The *Sequoia*'s ship's bell rang in salute.

It was a balmy evening, the air clear; even the polluted brown water of the Potomac looked refreshing as it rippled past the long, narrow white hull of the Presidential yacht. We sat on the top deck; Nixon, Kissinger, and I sipping Scotch and sodas, Haldeman and Ehrlichman drinking ginger ale. I proposed the toast to the President, then to Kissinger, who smiled appreciatively. It was a moment to savour.

Thoughts of triumph, however, brought to mind the critics who had been snapping so furiously at the President's heels. "Maybe those —— in Congress will give us a little time now," Nixon mused. "Do you suppose they will understand the meaning of this, Chuck?" Then before I could reply: "No, I suppose not. All they can see is Vietnam. They'll never see what's at stake. Peace, real peace – an end to the arms race – hope for your kids and grandchildren."

It was well after seven when we went below to the mahogany-walled main cabin to take our seats around the long table, the Navy's best sterling glistening on the stiff linen tablecloth. Nixon tucked his napkin into his collar and took his seat at the end of the table. I looked at him in surprise. *Why should a President care if he spills something on his tie?* I wondered, until I realized that this, too, like saluting the flag, was a part of the man. It was a vestige of his plain middle-class background, a habit from years of sitting at the kitchen table with Pat and the girls.

Over tender New York strip steaks and fresh corn on the cob, the President outlined his plans for détente with the Soviets. It was an extraordinary recitation, lucid despite the freely flowing wine, coldly analytical, brilliantly conceived. All at once he turned with a wink at me: "Do you think, Chuck, you'll get me an SST to fly to China?"

It was a needling reference to my unsuccessful effort to mobilise public pressure on the Congress to fund the supersonic jet passenger plane. But Kissinger blanched, fearful that Nixon, his guard relaxed, was about to blurt out the details of the plans to visit China, fully known only to Kissinger and Haldeman. Nixon turned on Kissinger: "Relax, relax. If those liberals on your staff, Henry, don't stop giving everything to the *New York Times*, I won't be going anywhere. The leaks, the leaks; that's what we've got to stop at any cost. Do you hear me, Henry?"

Kissinger, who often did not know when he was being kidded, launched into an impassioned defence of his own office. It was all coming from "disloyal bureaucrats" in the State Department. Haldeman smiled. He and I knew, as did Nixon, that Henry himself was often the major source of leaks; not the serious ones, not ones that compromised security, but those that made Henry look good in the press, often at Nixon's expense.

The President continued to return to the subject of his critics. "Chuck, your job is to hold off those madmen on the Hill long enough for Henry to finish his work in Paris. Then we go for the big play – China, Russia."

One of the "madmen" most nettlesome to Nixon was a freshman senator, Harold Hughes. The brawny ex-truck driver and self-confessed alcoholic was a particularly vocal leader of anti-Administration forces in the Senate and a candidate for the Democratic nomination to oppose Nixon in the next election. In March he had bitterly assailed Agnew as the "most divisive man" in American politics. He was in the forefront of each new anti-war demonstration and a leading sponsor of every end-the-war amendment. On April 7 he had been one of six Democratic senators to participate in a nationally televised denunciation of Nixon's foreign policy, and two weeks before in a Law Day speech he'd accused the Administration of "repression, wiretapping, bugging . . . surveillance . . . and attempts by government to intimidate the communications media." Unaware of the Sony tape recorders hidden throughout the White House and the FBI wiretaps spread throughout the city, I dismissed Hughes's accusations as the paranoid prattlings of an ambitious politician.

The President's finger circled the top of his wineglass slowly. "One day we will get them – we'll get them on the ground where we want them. And we'll stick our heels in, step on them hard and twist – right, Chuck, right?"

Then his eyes darted to Kissinger. "Henry knows what I mean – just like you do it in the negotiations, Henry – get them on the floor and step on them, crush them, show no mercy."

Kissinger smiled and nodded. Haldeman said not a word, but the look on his face was one of hand-rubbing expectation. I spoke for all three of us: "You're right, sir, we'll get them." Only Ehrlichman, expressionless and often a lonely voice of moderation, jerked his head back and stared at the ceiling.

And so on the *Sequoia* this balmy spring night, a Holy War was declared against the enemy – those who opposed the noble goals we sought of peace and stability in the world. *They* who differed with *us*, whatever their motives, must be vanquished. The seeds of destruction were by now already sown – not in them but in us.

4

The President's Night Out

Not that the job of a President's assistant was concerned exclusively with matters of national and international policy. I remember a night in early October 1971 when I was working late with Budget Director George Shultz, preparing for delicate negotiations with union leaders over wage-and-price-control policies. By 9:00 p.m. we had papers strewn all over Shultz's office.

The President had just finished a television address to the nation on the economy, which we had watched. I expected his call. He always wanted reactions from me and it was a part of my job to be on the alert for this and anything else twenty-four hours a day, seven days a week.

A few minutes after nine the phone rang. "Well, what did you think of it, Chuck? How did you like the point I made about public co-operation? Remember, that's what you were so concerned about." We rambled on. About four minutes into the conversation, he asked, "Where is Eugene Ormandy tonight?"

"I don't know," I answered, wondering what the conductor of the Philadelphia Symphony Orchestra had to do with an economic speech.

The President explained that Julie had been to the Kennedy Centre a few days earlier for an Ormandy performance which she highly recommended. "Find out if Ormandy is still at the Centre and call me back," he asked.

Simple enough, I thought. But through the White House operators I discovered that staff members who usually handled such details had left for the day. Shultz's secretary, Barbara Otis, began thumbing through newspapers. There were performances listed for the two other theatres in the Kennedy Centre – the Opera House and the Eisenhower Theatre – but none for the Concert Hall nor any mention of Eugene Ormandy.

I was becoming a trifle concerned; four or five minutes had passed and the President would be getting restless. Recognising my distress, Shultz had abandoned the complex option papers that were spread out on his desk. All three of us – the director of the Office of Management and Budget, his secretary, and the President's Special Counsel – were flipping through newspapers and weekly entertainment magazines.

White House operators, who had never failed us in reaching anyone, anywhere, anytime, were frantically now trying every conceivable number at the Kennedy Centre: backstage phones, listings for the manager's office, emergency numbers – all to no avail. (We learned later that the Centre did not answer its phones after 9:00 p.m. when its box offices closed.)

Six minutes had elapsed since the President's call. As I feared would happen, he called again. He was very pleasant. "Just wondered if you have found whether Ormandy is at the Kennedy Centre?"

"Not yet, sir. We're still searching."

He made one of those indistinguishable muttering noises, cleared his throat, and suggested I call him back when I had the information.

I was getting nowhere in Shultz's office and decided to return to my own. My resourceful secretary, Joan Hall, would surely be able to handle this. Joan came up with a reasonable idea. She placed a call through the White House switchboard for Eugene Ormandy at his home in Philadelphia.

"Mr. Ormandy, this is the White House calling."

"Really."

"Yes, the President is trying to find out if you are at the Kennedy Centre tonight."

Long pause. "No. I am here at home reading a book."

"Oh. Well, thank you. Sorry to have disturbed you."

Joan hung up a bit sheepishly. I have often wondered what

thoughts went through Mr. Ormandy's mind that evening about the President, and how well we were managing the nation's affairs.

Always before, in handling sensitive, special tasks for the President, I had remained cool. And never before had I been given such a simple request, although anything to do with his travel had always been handled by someone else. But in those few moments after his second call – it was now about 9:25 p.m. – I found myself on the verge of panic. What if he decided to go? Oh, no! How would I handle it?

At this point Patty called. "When are you coming home?" she asked.

"Get your copy of the newspaper and find out what's playing at the Kennedy Centre," I shouted into the telephone. "Don't ask me any questions, just find out and call me. I'll explain later."

I don't think she even replied. Patty would assume the worst, I knew. She had been urging me to take a rest. Meanwhile Joan continued making calls to the Social Office, the newspapers, the military aide's office, and elsewhere, trying to find out what in fact was playing at the Concert Hall. Harried, frustrated, I decided to send a message to the President through Manola, his valet.

"Manola, this is Mr. Colson."

"Yes, sir. Do you want to speak to the President?"

"No, no. Has he – er – retired for the night?"

"No, Mr. Colson. He is walking around the Lincoln Room. He seems restless, sir."

"Manola, please take him a note. Tell him that Mr. Ormandy – Yes, ORMANDY – is not playing at the Kennedy Centre."

I hoped that the note from Manola would satisfy the President. After all, it was now 9:30 p.m., really too late to go anywhere. Maybe – I hoped – he would just decide to read a good book. But it was not to be.

At 9:35 p.m. the President called again, his irritation quite evident in the tone of his voice. "Well, Chuck, you found out that Ormandy wasn't at the Kennedy Centre, eh?"

"Yes, sir."

"That's very good, Chuck, very good," he replied. There was a short pause and then came the question I dreaded, "Do you suppose, Chuck, you might find out what is playing there?"

I explained to him that none of the papers had been any help to us.

"Have you thought about calling the Kennedy Centre, or should I?" the President asked, deliberately measuring each word.

I told him that I had tried that, but the phones didn't answer, that I would keep trying and call him back.

He said, "That is very good. You do that," and hung up.

By now my tie was down and I was perspiring. My assistant, Dick Howard, was also in the office calling friends, seeking their help.

Then Joan signalled me. She had on the phone the head waitress from the Kennedy Centre restaurant, La Grande Scene. The young lady, Raquel Ramirez, was Spanish and did not speak very good English. Would I talk with her? Yes, I sure would.

"Miss Ramirez, my name is Charles Colson – Colson – COLSON. Yes, I am Special Counsel to the President. The President of the United States, that is – Yes, that's right – Mr. Nixon."

I loosened my tie further.

"Now, Miss Ramirez, the President would like to come to the Concert Hall tonight. But we cannot seem to discover what is playing there. Would you be kind enough to walk over to the Concert Hall and find out what is going on?"

This is utterly ridiculous, I thought to myself. *She will think I'm a nut, that this is a practical joke.*

"The President wants me to go over to the Concert Hall?" a wee voice said incredulously.

Carefully I went through it again. "I'll wait on the line until you come back," I said desperately.

La Grande Scene is on the fourth floor of the mammoth building at the far south end. Fortunately – the only break so far in the evening – the Concert Hall is also on the south end. It is a good ten-minute walk from one end of the Kennedy Centre to the other.

For some inexplicable reason that waitress believed me. I waited for what seemed like an eternity. Within a few minutes, she was back, explaining in broken English that the Concert Hall seemed to be filled with military officers in dress uniforms and a military band was playing. I asked her for one other small favour : to go backstage, find someone who looked like he might be in authority, and tell him that the President might be coming and to make necessary arrangements.

With this clue, Joan reached the duty officer at the Pentagon and learned that this was a formal black-tie affair for senior officers, plus a performance by the four military bands. With a sigh of relief I called the President at 9:53 p.m. to tell him it was a military concert, private, by invitation only.

"These are the same bands you hear at the White House, sir; I don't think you are missing anything. These bands will come and play for you any time you like."

"Marvellous," he replied, to my consternation. "That is just what I feel like hearing tonight, but I'm not dressed. If it's black-tie, I'll have to change."

"Do you really want to go to all that trouble – I mean, you must be tired," I suggested meekly. I should have known better. That was the surest way to guarantee that he would go.

"Have the car at the South Entrance in five minutes, Chuck."

I sat for a long instant in frozen horror. How did I start this process by which the President could have a night on the town? There were Secret Service men to notify and the problem of carrying that vital little black briefcase housing the nuclear-alert device. Doctors, the press, radio hookups. For the President to walk across the street involved assembling a small army. I'd never had anything to do with arranging his travel.

Fortunately, my assistant had been an advance man for a year and a half. He called W-16, the Secret Service control office in the White House basement. He would take care of getting the President to Kennedy Centre, Dick told me as he pushed me out the door. "You get down to the Concert Hall and let someone know that the President is coming."

Dashing out of the door like a scalded bird, I jumped into a

White House limousine which Joan had called. "Come on, step on it. The President is right behind us," I shouted to the driver, forgetting to give him directions. The driver looked startled, then suspicious; for a moment I thought he was trying to get a whiff of my breath. Finally, when I told him our destination, we shot out of the driveway.

As we sped down Virginia Avenue toward the Kennedy Centre at seventy miles an hour, I could listen on the two way radio to the frantic calls from W-16 summoning agents back to the White House, calling for the President's car and an accompanying Secret Service car. All but two agents had retired for the night, I later learned.

For a few reflective moments, I thought about the silliness of the whole business. Over the years a system of total and unquestioning loyalty to Presidents had grown up. General Eisenhower's hard-nosed chief of staff, Sherman Adams, tolerated nothing less than heel-clicking obedience from a small, tightly disciplined staff. The era of the "Imperial" Presidency came to full flower with John F. Kennedy who trusted only family and long-time Camelot worshippers around him. Stories still circulate about Lyndon Johnson's gruelling demands on his men who were drummed out for the slightest transgression and forever banished from the court.

I didn't have a chance to pursue these ruminations because of a sudden and sickening thought. *What if the Concert Hall performance was already over?* I had forgotten to check that. A cringing sensation began to rise from the bottom of my stomach as I imagined the President arriving at the Kennedy Centre only to find the crowd pouring out. We had been unable, except through the very accommodating waitress at La Grande Scene, to let anyone know that the President even might be on his way. Would they believe her? As I thought about it, I became even more mortified. Why should they believe her? I wouldn't have.

When we arrived at the southern entrance to the Kennedy Centre, I was relieved at least to see one of the President's own Secret Service agents there with a radio plug in his ear. The professionals had taken over! Backstage were a collection of stagehands, a tall and very distinguished man standing in the shadows, and the red-tunicked conductor of the Marine Band. Cheerily I gave him the news: "The President is on his way to listen to your concert."

He turned pale. "It's too late. Tell him not to come. All four service bands are now playing together on the stage. It is the final medley. In six minutes the programme will be over."

"The President will be here any moment. You'll have to play something. Play the medley over again," I said firmly.

Marines follow orders. The conductor took a full breath, stared at me for an instant, still ashen, then turned and marched onto the stage. He began whispering into the ear of the Army conductor. It was like watching a silent movie.

The Marine nodded his head up and down vehemently.

The Army musician shook his head stonily from side to side.

More whispers. The same thing all over again. One head bobbing up and down – the other shaking side to side. *This whole performance will wind up in an interservice melee*, I groaned to myself.

Suddenly there was another flurry of whispering. Then the Army conductor began nodding his head up and down. I sighed in relief.

As the pantomime on stage was going on, I peered around the curtain into the cavernous, elegantly decorated Concert Hall. Men were in dark blue dress uniforms, bedecked with gold braid and colourful ribbons; women were in long flowing gowns. The reflection of the stage lights on the glittering braid against the darkened backdrop of the hall was a magnificent sight. Then I began to think about the puzzlement that would soon sweep over the crowded hall when the exact same medley was replayed. It was the first humorous thought I had had all night.

The Marine conductor was now backstage with his colleagues from the Navy and Air Force, working out additional numbers that would extend the programme another half hour. It was then I recognized the tall, distinguished man nearby. He was William McCormick Blair, director of the Kennedy Centre, former ambassador to Denmark during the Kennedy Administration, married to Danish nobility and a prominent Washington socialite. He, along with much of the Washington establishment, viewed us Nixon men as uncultured intruders at *his* Centre.

I introduced myself to Blair, who dilated his nostrils and said, "This is highly irregular, you know." I explained that the President had a regular box at the Kennedy Centre. It was *the* Presidential Box and the President's prerogative to use it whenever he wanted. In the future some better communications should be arranged in the event the President again had a last-minute desire to attend a performance.

"I have had a very clear understanding with the White House that the President will always give us twenty-four hours' notice before he attends," he said testily.

I decided I didn't have time to stand there arguing and was afraid, in my distraught condition, I might commit some violent act – like punching him in the nose. I did think about it, but only for a fleeting moment.

Expecting the President at any moment, I sped back down the passageway to the double fire doors which led back into the main lobby. I was running and there was no point in slowing down. So I hit the two bar-type release handles at full speed. *Pow!* The doors exploded open. Barely a foot away was a startled President and an agitated Secret Service man who had started for his gun. I had nearly knocked the President down !

"Well – Chuck !"

Recovering my composure, I noticed that the President was wearing a red smoking jacket with black lapels. I started to tell him he had forgotten to change, but wisely thought better of it. "Everything is in order," I said breathlessly. "You can go directly to your box."

"Where is the box ?" the Secret Service agent asked.

"I'll lead the way," I said nonchalantly, not knowing the location but hoping that I could bluff it through.

Halfway down the long passageway leading to the back of the hall, the President turned and said, "Have you made arrangements for them to play the you-know-what, Chuck ?" He tried to slough it off with a wave of his hand, not wanting to come right out and say, "Hail to the Chief." According to protocol, it had to be played when he entered the hall. Once more I sped backstage to find my good new friend, the

Marine conductor, grateful that the Secret Service agent would now have to find the entrance to the President's box.

The Marine bandleader did not seem happy to see me. "Watch for the President. When he appears in his box, have the band play 'Hail to the Chief,' " I panted.

The conductor looked startled. "The four bands are still on stage. They have never played 'Hail to the Chief' together, and I don't see how they could do it without rehearsing."

I must have looked on the verge of apoplexy because he raised his hand. "Wait a moment." Another consultation. More pantomime. Then he was back. "We'll have the Marine Band play it alone," he said.

Back down the long hallway I loped until I found the President's box. To my relief, the Secret Service agent was guarding the door. The President was standing alone in the small anteroom which is between the open entrance hall of the mezzanine and his box. It is a lovely room with red velvet-covered walls, a private bath, and a refrigerator for use between the acts.

The scene is forever engraved in my consciousness. The President was standing facing the wall, about a foot away from it. He was staring into the red velvet, his arms hanging limply by his side in the most dejected posture I have ever witnessed. I imagined that he was either counting to ten or else repeating over and over to himself, "Colson must go – Colson must go."

I went into the box, brought out General Haig, who was using it that evening, opened the door wide so the Marine conductor would get the signal, and ushered the President in. The Marine Band then struck up "Hail to the Chief" and the President began waving to the cheering crowd.

Slowly I returned to my waiting limousine. My legs were weak. On the way home I advised the Secret Service command post by radio that the President was in his box and they should do whatever they normally do to take the President home after the performance. I also left word that if he were to ask for me – a possibility I considered quite remote – I would be at my residence.

At home, halfway through the second Scotch, it did occur to me that I should let someone other than the Secret Service

know that the President was at the Kennedy Centre. I called
Press Secretary Ron Ziegler and crisply gave him the news.

"The President couldn't be there," he said stiffly. "Otherwise I would have been notified."

When I briefly explained the rather unusual circumstances, Ziegler sputtered, "The press corps will be very upset
that no one let them know."

I hung up with a rather terse parting two-word epithet
which I thought a fitting ending to the evening.

The next day Haldeman summoned me to his office and
dressed me down for breaking every rule in the book. "You
know, Chuck, this isn't funny. You could have put the
President's life in jeopardy. The Secret Service wasn't
prepared. It was a thoroughly stupid thing for you to do."

I agreed it certainly had been stupid, but I asked Bob what
I should do if it ever happened in the future.

"Just tell him he can't go, that's all. He rattles his cage
all the time. You can't let him out." While I pondered this
startling metaphor, the usually stern Haldeman softened.
"The President enjoyed himself and it came out well. I guess
that's what counts."

The next time the President called me, to my relief it had
to do with the war in Vietnam, inflation, and negotiations
with Russia.

5

Hatchet Man

Dear Chuck:

Of course you know how proud I am of all that you are doing. If that old Swede, my Dad, should come to life, he would almost bust with pride over the success of his grandson. Only in America could such a thing happen.

I put down the letter from my dad and turned slowly in my chair to look at the view from the window. The long shadows of the December afternoon fell over the tailored shrubs of the South Lawn. From my room in the Executive Office Building I looked across at the west wing, the large glistening glass windows of the Oval Office curving outward.

When I had first come to the White House staff, an old friend, who had been President Eisenhower's appointments secretary, gave me a piece of wise counsel: "Once in a while just walk around, look at the beauty of the grounds and the buildings, take deep breaths and sniff in the history. It will help you to remember where you are and keep things in perspective."

I was aware of where I was, all right, but somehow the perspective had not come. The past months had been too frantic. There wasn't time to think much about anything beyond postal strikes, Cambodia, student protests, the cliff-hanging battles with Congress over the Supreme Court nominations, and the 1970 congressional elections. I'd found myself in the thick of each one as the President's trouble-shooter. We were too busy making history ourselves to think about the history that had been made here – sometimes too busy to think at all.

I could tell how impressed my dad had been when he visited here, two weeks before. My office had been redone for me by GSA, the Government housekeeping agency. The bright yellow draperies and deep-pile navy carpet was the same colour scheme as the Oval Office; massive, historic paintings from the National Gallery of Art adorned the white walls. It was a huge cubelike room with twenty-foot-high ceilings. Sometimes the wasted space bothered my Puritan frugality. The doors, ten feet high, were heavy hand-carved mahogany with gold-leaf hardware, forged with the seal of the agency first occupying the office. Mine had an old Navy Department crest.

Most important, my office was next to the President's working office, separated only by bookshelves constructed to wall off what had once been a doorway. I'd seen him there almost every day now, sometimes several times a day. The new office was only part of what had come with my promotion the end of the first year. I had been assigned a large staff of twenty people and was attending Cabinet meetings and early-morning senior staff meetings with Kissinger, Haldeman, Ehrlichman – the men who ran things in the government. Heady stuff for one whose grandparents had come to this country as immigrants.

I'd taken Dad to the ceremony in the State Dining Room when the President personally decorated the heroes of the Sontay raid, the daring but unsuccessful attempt to rescue prisoners of war behind North Vietnamese lines. He was dazzled by all of it, the President standing under the grand portrait of Abraham Lincoln while military bands blared martial music, the magnificent chandelier glittering in the bright lights of the TV cameras.

On our way back to my office I was showing Dad the Rose Garden when Steve Bull came running up. "Mr. Colson," to my father, "the President would like to see you."

Mr. Nixon had spotted the white-haired man with me and sent for us. We were ushered into the Oval Office, where Dad told the President he had voted for every Republican candidate since Coolidge, having been too young by one month to vote for Harding. The President, with his impressive knowledge of history, talked in depth about Coolidge and then told my dad how much he relied on his son's counsel. I thought my father's chest would explode. The White House photographer was summoned and that picture, Dad assured me in the letter, was now his most treasured possession.

Abruptly, I picked up the letter and thrust it into a drawer. I knew, as Dad did not, that if I was as valuable to the President as he said I was, it was because I was willing at times to blink at certain ethical standards, – to be ruthless in getting things done. It was earning me status and power, as this quote from *Newsweek* (September 6, 1971) indicated:

> . . . when the President walked from the Oval Office to his helipad to begin his trip. . . . the figure talking rapidly into his left ear at every step was Chuck Colson. Washington hostesses have begun to reckon with his name, the mere mention of which "makes the tensions come in like sheet rain" in the words of one government wife.

But that same drive – getting the job done for the President whatever the cost – earned me also the dubious title of Nixon's "hatchet man." The *Wall Street Journal* had this headline on October 15, 1971: NIXON HATCHET MAN CALL IT WHAT YOU WILL, CHUCK COLSON HANDLES PRESIDENT'S DIRTY WORK.

Buried in the *Journal* account was a seemingly tongue-in-cheek quip attributed to an unnamed former staff member of Senator Saltonstall: "Colson would walk over his own grandmother if he had to." At the time it had seemed to me good for a passing chuckle; I was to hear a lot more from it in the years ahead.

As troubleshooter – or hatchet man – my axe-wielding skills were often called upon to deal with government officials who leaked classified information to the press while so many secret negotiations were going on with Hanoi, Peking, and Moscow.

On Monday, June 14, 1971, when I arrived at the White House for the early-morning briefing, Henry Kissinger was pacing the floor as angry as I had ever seen him. "There can be no foreign policy in this government," he began. "No foreign policy, I tell you. We might just as well turn it all over to the Soviets and get it over with. These leaks are slowly and systematically destroying us." He pounded his outstretched palm on the antique Chippendale table, rattling pencils and coffee cups. "Destroying us," he shouted again.

I had seen Kissinger angry before, sharp flashes of temper which, like summer cloudbursts, quickly passed. But never like this. He turned to glare at Bob Haldeman. "I tell you, Bob, the President must act – today. There is wholesale subversion of this government under way."

Kissinger was referring to the leak of the top-secret Pentagon Papers, the first instalment of which the *New York Times* had published the day before. I had read Sunday's account, and it looked to me to be nothing more than a compendium of old memos, position papers, and cables detailing how John F. Kennedy's New Frontiersmen had gotten us involved in Vietnam in the first place. But as I listened to Henry roar on, I realized that the material being disclosed could torpedo our secret negotiations.

"I tell you, gentlemen, there are forces at work bent on destroying this government. Look at this." He sent three single sheets of paper spinning across the table. "Cables from Australia, Great Britain, and Canada. All the same – protests. They can't trust us. Why should they? If our allies can't trust us, how will we ever be able to negotiate with our enemies?"

Later that morning I met with Ehrlichman who was receiving similarly alarming reports from the Justice Department. Continued publication could seriously compromise vital national security secrets and U.S. decoding capabilities, the National Security Agency warned. The identity of CIA agents in the field might be revealed. Reports of U-2 flights over China were contained in some of the as-yet-unpublished documents. While the Chinese knew of the flights, the disclosure would publicly embarrass them and force Peking to save face by cancelling Nixon's visit – then in the most delicate stage of final preparation.

What began in the morning as familiar Kissinger fulminations exploded by late day into a full-scale governmental crisis. The decision was made that afternoon to seek a court order to stop publication.

On Tuesday a federal district judge in New York ordered the *Times* to discontinue the series, but on Thursday the *Washington Post* picked up where the *Times* left off. The *Boston Globe*, then the *Los Angeles Times* followed. Copies of the Pentagon Papers were by now popping up everywhere, including, we learned to our horror, at the Soviet UN mission in New York. A few days later, a red-faced Ambassador Anatoly Dobrynin, anxious to avoid any incident that might upset the budding courtship between Nixon and Brezhnev, returned the set of papers to Kissinger's office. Why not? He could read it all in the *Times* and *Post*.

Next, a copy of "National Security Study Memorandum Number One," the highly classified document outlining strategy for Vietnam, turned up in a senator's office. We feared that the floodgates were about to swing wide open, that this was only the beginning of a campaign by dissidents to leak all manner of classified documents.

Behind all the mischief was one Daniel Ellsberg, the enigmatic young man who had worked for Kissinger in 1969, drawing up contingency plans for Vietnam. A former Marine officer and avowed hawk, who by his own admission once experimented with LSD, Ellsberg became overnight a folk hero of the anti-war movement. The press hailed him as a courageous champion of the "public's right to know."

The Attorney General concluded from FBI reports that Ellsberg was part of a Communist spy ring. The President viewed Ellsberg's conduct as nothing less than treason. "I want him exposed, Chuck. I want the truth about him known. I don't care how you do it, but get it done. We're going to let the country know what kind of 'hero' Mr. Ellsberg is." Nixon was pacing in front of the doors to the Rose Garden, jabbing his finger in the air and repeating, "Do you understand me? That's an order."

"Yes, sir, it will be done," I replied. I needed no coaxing. As far as I was concerned, Ellsberg stood in the way of ending the war. Friends of mine were in Vietnam, like Bill Maloney, who had talked me into the Marine Corps and was now flying rescue missions behind the lines, shot at day and night.

Our effort to stop publication of the papers was eventually thwarted; happily the newspapers refrained from printing some of the most sensitive documents, and others did not follow Ellsberg's example, as we feared would happen. The Chinese and Soviet talks continued. But the controversy, set against the backdrop of a sagging economy and a seemingly endless war, cost us dearly. Gallup and Harris polls reported the lowest rating yet for the President. Ellsberg's actions gave fresh heart to the anti-war forces, too. New hearings were held; and on June 22 the Senate by a 57-42 vote for the first time adopted an end-the-war amendment, calling for unilateral withdrawal in nine months. Four days later North Vietnamese negotiators in Paris rejected the peace proposal Kissinger had left on the table in May, more than just an unhappy coincidence, we concluded.

Ellsberg himself was only a name to me, a symbol of the villainous forces working to undermine our goals for peace in the world. So it was that I gathered my staff together one July day and told them to nail him in the press. Then with Nixon's words ringing in my ears, I happily gave an inquiring reporter damaging information about Ellsberg's attorney, compiled from secret FBI dossiers. Later I was to learn that the FBI had released the same information to a national news service which published it. This was a not uncommon use of the media by the bureau when they were investigating someone.

Next I called in friendly congressional staffers and urged a full-scale, well publicised investigation of Ellsberg, his motives and associates. I gave not a passing thought to the effect the hoped-for publicity might have on Ellsberg's up-coming trial on charges of stealing government documents.

During a late-night meeting with Haldeman and myself, Nixon for the first time was showing signs of personal strain. He exploded, pounding his fist on his desk and leaning forward in his chair, his face flushed. "I don't care how it's done. I want these leaks stopped. Don't give me any excuses. Use any means. Bob, do we have one man here to do it? I want results. I want them now."

At the time there did not seem to be overly much signifi-cance to the outburst. Richard Nixon had simply blown his top. Presidents are human and most do it once in a while. Yet it was at that moment that the Nixon Presidency passed a crossroads of sorts.

The "one man" Mr. Nixon wanted for the job of nailing Ellsberg turned out to be an ex-CIA operative by the name of E. Howard Hunt. Debonair, smooth talking, unobtrusive, Hunt was an ideal candidate. He knew foreign policy, but more important, was a conservative true believer, fanatically loyal. I met him when we worked together on Brown University alumni affairs.

Ironically, Hunt's name was at the bottom of a list of six candidates I myself had given Haldeman; the other five were unavailable or unacceptable. Hunt was hastily interviewed by Ehrlichman and hired as a $100-per-day part-time consultant. Little did I dream of the far-reaching role he was to play when I assigned him a tiny cubicle office in a remote third floor corner of the E.O.B. "Howard, your job will be to research the Pentagon Papers – beginning to end. Analyse the political opportunities we can salvage now that we've taken all these lumps. Work with the congressional committees investigating the leaks and this madman Ellsberg."

Hunt, dressed in a sporty tweed jacket, just properly baggy, sat across from my polished rosewood desk, winking knowingly as I spoke. *What a relief, I thought, to get a professional in here to deal with such matters.*

I should have been wary of the spy business after Hunt's initial assignment, an interview with a CIA operative who'd been involved in the ill-fated Diem coup of 1963 which had plunged the U.S. into Vietnam. A tape recorder was set up under a couch in a vacant office and the CIA man invited there for a Friday afternoon meeting. He would talk more freely, Hunt suggested, over a bottle of Scotch; it was standard procedure in the intelligence game, I learned. For two hours the two men guzzled a fifth of the White House's best, while I awaited the results in my office.

It was after six when Hunt reported, blurry-eyed, his tie loosened and stammering an apology. He'd taken no notes, and there was no tape. Secret Service had placed the recorder under a couch which Hunt by mistake had sat on, crushing the sensitive equipment.

In a few weeks Hunt was assigned to the special investigative unit set up under Egil "Bud" Krogh, an intense, no-nonsense young assistant to John Ehrlichman. Hunt was joined by a steely-eyed ex-FBI agent named G. Gordon Liddy – like Hunt, fervently loyal. The unit, later to be known as "the plumbers," was given wide latitude to plug leaks of secret government information.

In late summer the Hunt-Liddy team burglarised the offices of a Los Angeles psychiatrist, seeking information that might be used against a former patient, Daniel Ellsberg. With our sense of fair play gone, there was no check on the methods of these two political idealists whose misguided adventures would soon explode into bizarre headlines.

Our fortress mentality plunged us across the moral divide, leading to "enemy lists," a new refinement on the ancient spoils system of rewarding friends and punishing enemies. Other excuses came, as the shadowy form of the demon which would strike down the Thirty-seventh President of the United States was now slowly taking shape – like a genie drifting out of a bottle.

Meanwhile, with his trip to China announced and the peril of leaks averted for a time, Mr. Nixon turned his attention to the nation's economic woes. Though the President was soon to reverse field on the government controls he'd spent a lifetime opposing, in late July he was still trying to rally public belief in an imminent upsurge of the economy. Nixon's Cabinet dutifully followed orders, speaking publicly in glowing terms about the recovery just around the corner.

Arthur Burns, however, long-time Nixon friend and adviser and now chairman of the prestigious Federal Reserve Board, refused to go along. He testified before the Joint Economic Committee of the Congress that the Administration's lack of progress in fighting rising wages and prices was a "grave obstacle" to the hoped-for recovery.

The press played up Burns's implied criticism of Nixon, who lamented during a session with several of us that day, "Why can't Arthur ever give us a little boost? We've got to pick up people's spirits; that's what the country needs – confidence. Arthur can be so dour at times."

One official present, opposed to Burns's policies, said slyly,

"You know, Mr. President, about Arthur's plan to increase
the salary of the Federal Reserve Board chairman to the
level of Cabinet officer?"

"What did you say?" Nixon demanded, sitting upright
in his chair . "You mean Arthur is preaching wage-and-price
controls and he wants a pay raise?"

The official nodded.

"Well, how do you like that?" Nixon said, half-bemused,
half-angry. Somehow I knew what was coming even before
he turned to me. "Get that out, Chuck. Get that into the
papers."

Mr. President, you don't really mean it, I thought. Wall
Street was shaky enough; we had to present a solid front to
the public at least. Shooting at Burns in the papers was risky.
I glanced at Haldeman and raised my eyebrows to ask
whether to write it down or forget it. Haldeman nodded
affirmatively.

The official later pointed out that Burns was recommending
the increase to be effective for his successor; he would not
personally profit. But it was too late for that minor detail
now. The enthusiasm for "knocking Arthur off his high
horse" was not to be contained. I passed on the instructions
to a staff member who dutifully relayed to a *Wall Street
Journal* reporter that Burns was publicly pushing wage controls while privately seeking a raise in salary.

As happens with most bad ideas, a disaster of sorts followed.
Burns shot a strong complaint to the White House about
the dishonest report. Haldeman shrugged his shoulders, assuring the kindly one-time professor that "no one around here
would ever do such a thing." Ziegler reported he had no
knowledge of discussions between Nixon and Burns over a
pay raise. *Time* magazine, acting on a tip from a White
House source, reported that the villain was Colson. Ziegler
advised newsmen off-the-record that Colson had been acting
on his own. Meanwhile, as feared, the ruckus sent tremors
through Wall Street and the rest of the financial community.
At his next press conference President Nixon praised the
"most responsible and statesmanlike" leadership in fiscal
policies of his "very good friend, Arthur Burns."

The Burns fiasco touched off a new round of Colson-the-

hatchet man stories, reviving old tales especially involving
the rough tactics of the 1970 campaign for which I had been
responsible. The welter of articles brought new demands
for interviews. I turned them all down in the misguided
belief that by avoiding reporters I'd discourage publicity.
Actually, the more I evaded the press and shunned the social
circuit, the more curiosity I aroused. Unwittingly I was
becoming a mysterious, shadowy figure and incurring
reporters' hostility to boot.

Through 1971 the White House staff was divided over
political strategy. Ehrlichman, Mitchell, speech-writer Ray
Price, and others argued for an appeal to traditional Republican suburbanites and to the liberal, uncommitted voters. An
opposing group – speech-writer Pat Buchanan; Mike Balzano,
a talented young member of my staff; and I – argued the
case for capturing the Middle America-Wallace vote. The
winds of social change sweeping across the country were, we
felt, changing minds and hearts to our position.

In August 1971 the President promised federal aid for
parochial schools to a cheering, foot-stomping crowd at a New
York Knights of Columbus dinner. Nixon's stand against
liberalised abortion toughened; the crackdown on drugs
intensified. We rode the issue of bussing for all it was worth,
stealing the issue which propelled George Wallace to smashing victories in the Florida and Michigan primaries. Amnesty
for draft dodgers became anathema to our new majority.
Slowly we inched upward in the polls.

The law-and-order standard which Richard Nixon and his
men first unfurled in the 1968 campaign was now as
American as wearing a flag pin on one's lapel, while the "era
of permissiveness" became the enemy. Our Democratic con-
tenders, their party machinery captured by reformers and
liberals, were forced to equivocate over bussing, compromise
on abortion, duck amnesty, and as we charged, go "soft" on
criminals and pot smokers. We were seizing the high ground,
politically speaking, and what's more, believed in the rightness of our cause with a religious fervour.

In part, the choice of issues was hard-nosed politics, as I
suspect it has been in varying degrees with most of the tough-
minded men who make it to the top of the political heap. But

beneath it were deeply held convictions. The President thirsted for a restoration of the old-fashioned values, something a restless nation could rely on and believe in. He once told me in the summer of 1970 : "If I do anything else as President, I'm going to restore respect for the American flag." And in the fall of 1971, after a long arduous session with his domestic advisers, in which aid to parochial schools was again debated, Nixon confided a secret longing for something of "enduring spiritual value."

"You know, Chuck," he said earnestly, "I could be a Roman Catholic." Just the two of us sat alone in the Oval Office; it was close to seven; we were tired, the President's dinner was waiting, but he seemed in no hurry. "I honestly could. Except if I converted, everyone would say it was some political gimmick – Tricky Dick making a pitch for the Catholic vote. But you know," he mused, speaking softly, wistfully, "it's beautiful to think about, the fact that there is something you can really grab hold of, something real and meaningful. How I wish sometimes we could all have it – something really stable. All this business about Catholic schools, you know, it's not politics. I believe, I believe . . ."

By the autumn months of 1971 the campaign strategy for 1972 was firmly set : the Middle America appeal. The President had phoned me at home just before the last weekend in September. "Chuck, get your wife and let's take a long weekend in Key Biscayne."

It wasn't a command, but rather a personal invitation, a warm one at that. I rode for most of the flight with the President in his handsome private compartment on *Air Force One*, sitting across from one another with his folding desk between us. Later Mrs. Nixon, Julie, Patty, the President, and I sat together in the forward section of the helicopter which whisked us from Homestead Air Force Base to the Key Biscayne helipad. Our Pats chatted away like any two housewives, while the President and I stared silently at the bright lights of Miami swiftly passing only a few hundred feet below.

As the steady thump, thump, thump of the giant bird's mighty engines pounded in my ears, I couldn't help but recall that day on Vieques when I'd clawed my way up an impossible cliff. Gone now was the anger and confusion of the past summer. Richard Nixon was at peace with himself and confident of his place in history. At long last we were in control of events. And Nixon's gesture – seemingly so casual – the two families riding together – was a signal to the staff and the press travelling with us: I was to be in charge of the political game plan. At that moment I felt a sense of victory and even immunity from the petty bickering and infighting in the White House. It was the last time I was to feel that kind of elation.

We entered election year 1972 neck and neck with Democratic front-runner, Edmund Muskie, the gangling senator from Maine. Catholic, articulate, handsome, he had earned plaudits as the Democratic Vice-Presidential candidate in 1968. Since then he had carefully straddled most issues, leaving him in the "centre" of the Party. Having worked with him when he was a junior Senator in the late fifties, I knew his one vulnerability, a low flash point. It's a popular myth that Muskie's high-flying campaign collapsed with his own emotional response in the closing days of New Hampshire's primary after newspaper smears on his wife and the publication of the famed and apparently phoney Canuck Letter accusing him of an ethnic slur against French Canadians. (A member of my staff, Kenneth Clawson, was accused of originating the Canuck Letter in a banner headline in the *Washington Post*. If it was a White House inspired trick, it was never proven. I knew nothing of it and the Watergate Special Prosecutor, after the most exhaustive investigation, apparently found no evidence linking it to the Nixon campaign, since charges were never brought.)

Actually, the deathblow to Muskie's candidacy was administered in January, the result of good old-fashioned slug-em-in-the-gut politics, the kind I had learned in earlier Massachusetts brawls. On January 25 Nixon, convinced that the North Vietnamese would not agree to a negotiated peace, gave up on the secret Paris negotiations. In a half-hour telecast he stunned the nation by disclosing one of our best-kept secrets, that for thirty months Kissinger had been journeying secretly to Paris making peace offers more generous even than those doves in Congress were pushing. Nixon announced a new proposal and publicly invited Hanoi to accept it and end

the war. The President came off triumphantly as patient and
long-suffering, enduring in statesmanlike silence the attacks
of smaller men.

We looked eagerly about for some way to capitalise on
this dramatic turn of public opinion and incredibly the usually
cautious Muskie provided it. He interrupted his campaign to
fly to Washington and laboured with his staff late into the
night over a speech which he delivered early the next morning to an anti-war gathering at a local church. In it he bitterly
denounced Nixon's proposals, then offered his own peace plan,
even more generous to Hanoi. John Mitchell, still Attorney
General but readying himself to take over the campaign,
sent instructions through Jeb Magruder, a young ambitious
Haldeman aide: ignore Muskie, any attack will only build
him up. The President and I believed otherwise.

I phoned Bill Rogers, the amiable, dignified Secretary of
State: "Bill, you've got to take Muskie on for sabotaging the
peace talks." It has been a time-honoured unwritten rule that
Secretaries of State stay out of partisan politics; but what
Muskie had done went too far, I urged. The Secretary agreed,
unprecedented though it would be.

The next morning Bill Rogers walked unannounced into
the State Department press briefing room. The assemblage of
staid old-time diplomatic correspondents sat in stunned
silence as Rogers attacked Muskie's speech as "harmful to
the national interest." His voice rising in anger, finger jabbing
in the air, he charged that Muskie was undercutting our
bargaining position. The North Vietnamese had not
responded to Nixon's offer and would now be encouraged to
wait out the election; after all, they would get a better deal
if Muskie were elected.

It was tough stuff, all right, from such a usually mild-
mannered gentleman. Rogers's blistering of Muskie was
reported in every foreign capital of the world. Reeling from
the blow, Muskie was alternately self-doubting and then
self-justifying to the press, so much so that political pros began
to wonder aloud whether Muskie had the internal strength
to be President. Muskie must have wondered, too; his next
speeches were flat and bland.

Mitchell called me in a rage: "I'm going to the President

unless you promise never to attack Muskie again. Do you?"

"Of course, John," I assured him. "It won't be necessary."

And it wasn't. That one episode, more than all the dirty tricks combined, started Ed Muskie's toboggan ride down from his position as the top Democratic Presidential contender.

Though it eliminated our chief rival, the incident deepened the rift between the Colson men and Mitchell men. Magruder, now at the campaign committee, protected his territory – as he later wrote – "for fear Colson would take it over." I kept Mitchell and Magruder out of the inner councils. The split was to cause much of our later grief.

Muskie's decline was accompanied by Nixon's visit to China. Televised live and watched by millions, the modern-day Marco Polo journey was a political as well as diplomatic tour de force. Our fortunes were rising fast.

Then came the spring offensive of the North Vietnamese which threatened not only the South Vietnamese Army but also the sixty thousand American troops still remaining.

With the election coming up, delicate negotiations going on with Peking, and a Moscow Summit Conference weeks away, the President faced the toughest decision of his Presidency. To do nothing might result in the collapse of South Vietnam and a President humiliated, bargaining in Moscow from a position of near impotence. To react could put the Summit in jeopardy, maybe risk a widened war. He made the hard choice: mine the Haiphong harbour and launch an all-out bombing attack right up to the China border.

When told the decision would infuriate the American people and perhaps cost him the election, now only five months away, I saw the President's jaw tighten. "So what!" he snapped. "It's the right thing to do. If I didn't do it, the Presidency wouldn't be worth getting re-elected to."

Later he confided: "Only Al and John understand. [Al Haigh, then Kissinger's deputy, and John Connally, Secretary of the Treasury.] They're the only ones in the whole government, besides you and Bob, who favoured this decision." Then wistfully he added, "You know, Chuck, those are the only two men around here qualified to fill this job when I step down." *

Sick of the Vietnam situation as I was, feeling from the beginning that the whole Asian venture had been a dreadful mistake, seeing my election plans being knocked askew, still I admired the President for a decision based on principle. To me, it was one of Richard Nixon's finest hours.

Criticism was heaped upon us from the press, television, and Capitol Hill, but the events of the next months not only vindicated Nixon's judgment but produced a windfall of dividends. The mining and bombing stopped the North Vietnam offensive, the Summit Conference took place as planned, and the public – our "silent majority" – rallied behind the President so solidly that political analysts later described the decision as the pivotal turning point in the election. Certainly Nixon's courage and tough foreign-policy stand (along with our careful wooing) were big factors in bringing endorsements from scores of labour leaders and unions who had never before supported a Republican president.

By late May, with Alabama Governor George Wallace paralysed by a bullet wound and out of the race, with Senator George McGovern's long-haired supporters wresting the Democratic nomination away from the party regulars, and with Nixon riding the crest of his diplomatic triumphs, the President's re-election was all but wrapped up. Only the close circle inside the White House could not see it, so haunted were we by the memories of the close campaigns of 1960 and 1968, when early leads had slipped away.

On a sunny Saturday afternoon in June, I was about to take a quick swim in our pool at home when the White House

* *Editor's Note:* On May 1, 1973 the day after Haldeman's resignation, Charles Colson wrote President Nixon to recommend that he bring in General Haig as chief of staff. On May 4, 1973, Haig was named to replace Haldeman. Colson also negotiated John Connally's switch to the Republican Party, pledging to him early in 1973 Richard Nixon's support for the Republican nomination for President in 1976. Connally was indicted by the Special Prosecutor's Grand Jury in July 1974 on charges of bribery in the milk scandal, then acquitted in March 1975.

phone rang. It was John Ehrlichman. "Where is your friend Howard Hunt these days?" he asked.

"Working at the Re-election Committee, I think." Hunt had gone off the White House payroll months before. "Why?" I asked Ehrlichman. It seemed to me a curious question. On the car radio that day I caught a minor news item about a robbery at the offices of the Democratic National Committee located in a complex of offices and apartments known as Watergate. I'd been mildly amused, thinking of the disappointed expression when the thieves discovered an empty safe. Everybody knew the Democrats were broke.

Ehrlichman pressed the question. "You are sure he is not working for us?"

"Positive," I replied. "Why do you ask?" It must have been the tone of John's voice, because I remember all at once something that felt like an iron hand clutching at my stomach.

"You've heard about the robbery at the Democratic Head-quarters?" Ehrlichman asked. "Well, one of the burglars had something in his pocket with Hunt's name on it. I'll let you know if I learn anything further."

I walked away from the phone and sat alone at poolside, terrible thoughts racing through my head. One of the last times I saw Howard was when he had come by my office with Gordon Liddy some months before – was it in February? He and Liddy were working on an intelligence plan and trying to get Magruder to approve it. *But it couldn't be this, it just can't be,* I thought. Surely Hunt was too smart for anything this stupid. If Hunt should be involved though, the press would quickly draw me in since I was his sponsor and friend.

The next morning the *Washington Post* bannered the story: FIVE HELD IN PLOT TO BUG DEMOCRATIC PARTY OFFICE. There was no mention of Hunt. But by Monday, speculation about his involvement was being widely reported. The telephone lines into my office were flooded with press calls. White House Counsel John Dean was tensely looking for information about when Hunt had left the White House, and the President was called from Key Biscayne, furious that anyone connected with the campaign would be involved in anything so idiotic. The news plunged Nixon into such a fit of temper that he hurled an ashtray across his Key Biscayne living room.

By Tuesday the trail led from Hunt to me. The *Star* ran the headline in bold black type right across page one : COLSON AIDE – BARKER TIED. The Colson aide, of course, was Hunt; Barker was the Cuban who had led the break-in.

The President must have known how low I felt because he called me into his office that afternoon to reassure me. "Don't let them get to you, Chuck. It is me they're after, not you."

I told the President that I would like to give a sworn statement to the FBI and suggested that everyone in the White House do the same.* I never suspected for a moment that anyone in the White House, least of all the man I was talking to, would for a moment tolerate or cover up such bungling incompetence. This was not a moral judgment on my part; the burglary seemed too stupid by the standards we set.

The Democrats shouted and screamed about it; the press made the most of each new morsel of circumstantial evidence, inferring that Hunt shared my office and was my closest friend. Larry O'Brien brought a civil suit hauling many of us before the Democrats' lawyers for depositions – each one giving rise to a new round of publicity. Yet to the nation in the summer of 1972, Watergate was no more than a nettlesome distraction. Campaign spying was, as one analyst put it, "like trying to steal the other team's signals from its huddle."

Everything else, however, was breaking our way. Along with foreign policy glories, the economy was surging. Our opponent meanwhile was thrashing helplessly, undercut on Vietnam by Nixon's bold stroke in May, stunned by the AFL-CIO decision not to endorse him, embarrassed by his Vice-Presidential selection and forced to change running

---

* *Editor's Note:* The actual White House transcript of June 20, 1972, quotes Colson addressing the President as follows : "Everybody [in the White House] is completely out of it. . . . This is once when you'd like for our people to testify." This tape was subpoenaed by the Special Prosecutor but not introduced in the Watergate trial. The transcript was made available for inspection by attorneys in the case.

mates in midstream. By September McGovern was reeling from our blows, defending his hastily conceived $1,000-per-person welfare plan against steady attacks from Cabinet members whom I scheduled for press conferences each day. Nixon meanwhile remained safely perched on the Presidential pedestal. Victory was not to be denied by one campaign gaffe like Watergate.

But the Watergate break-in sent reporters digging into the newpaper morgues for old clippings about Mr. Nixon's hatchet man. Most stories contained a rehash of all the old dirty-tricks charges and that I had once boasted I would run over my grandmother if necessary to elect Nixon. I tried to steer a few reporters back to the original *Wall Street Journal* article. "I never said it," I protested, but it made such colourful copy no one heard me.

It was late August when Granny, in fact, became something of a minor campaign issue. I returned from the Republican Convention on a Friday morning, discovering to my dismay that about half of my staff had apparently decided to take a long weekend. I kept a huge poster in my office with a dial showing the exact number of days until the election. I glanced over at it – seventy-one days left. We were well ahead in the campaign, but I was not one to take anything for granted. How could anyone take a long weekend this close to an election?

The more I thought about it, the angrier I got. Then a little genie with a pitchfork prodded me. I called into my office one of my junior secretaries, Holly Holm, a bright, attractive twenty-four-year-old from a small town in Indiana. "We'll put an end to this nonsense," I muttered, and my scorching series of instruction went something like this: "No one is to leave town without my permission. There are only seventy-one days left and every one counts. Ask yourself every morning what you are going to do to help re-elect the President today. A campaign is a twenty-four-hours-a-day, seven-days-a-week job. If I hurt anyone's feelings, I'll apologise after the election."

Having said this, I concluded by poking a little fun at myself. "More erroneous things about me have found their way into print lately – but last week's UPI story that I was

once reported to have said that 'I would walk over my grandmother if necessary' is absolutely accurate."

I felt better now and even managed a smile. Those who
worked for me knew my penchant for sometimes outrageous
statements to make a point. But my quiet young secretary
was ashen-faced, her hand shaking as she wrote down these
words. Then with a deep breath, Holly asked, "Mr. Colson,
you don't really want this to go to all the staff, do you?"

"Of course, Holly. They'll know most of it is tongue-in-
cheek, but it will make the point."

It did all right – halfway around the world. Within twenty-
four hours a copy was leaked to the Washington Post and
printed in full, the whole bombastic memo. It was picked up
by the networks, re-printed in scores of papers across the
country, and even in the Paris Herald Tribune. It was the
subject of a Sevareid commentary and two Art Buchwald
columns.

My mother failed to see the humour in the whole affair,
convinced that I was disparaging the memory of my father's
mother. I received a flood of angry mail from grandmothers,
some of whom threatened to form an organisation to protest.
Even though both of my grandmothers had been dead for
more than twenty-five years (I was very fond of both), two
press conferences were called during the campaign by
"Charles Colson's grandmother" to announce her support
for McGovern, one by an elderly black woman in Milwaukee
who managed to draw a large crowd of newsmen before the
joke was discovered.

Not surprisingly, the furore the memo kicked up served
only to reinforce Nixon's respect for my loyalty. "Colson –
he'll do anything. He'll walk right through doors," the
President would brag to others.

In our small White House circle, machismo and toughness were equated with trust and loyalty; these were keys
to the cherished kingdom guaranteeing continued closeness
to the throne.

Hubris became the mark of the Nixon man because hubris
was the quality Nixon admired most. Small wonder that
ambitious young men like Magruder and Haldeman's other
eager, unquestioning young lieutenants sought through

tough talk and derring-do to prove their political virility to Nixon and those of us around him.

Maybe it was bald stupidity to expect to get away with breaking into one of the most heavily guarded office buildings in Washington, but it sure was *hubris*. As in time I was to realise, whether we – Colson, Mitchell, Ehrlichman, Haldeman, yes, even Richard Nixon – knew about Watergate in advance, might later be important as a legal distinction, but it made little moral difference. We had set in motion forces that would sooner or later make Watergate, or something like it, inevitable.

6

"Exhausted Volcano"

In the weeks following his smashing re-election victory Richard Nixon withdrew to the seclusion of Camp David. Haldeman and Ehrlichman also moved their offices there. On the windswept Catoctin mountain-top they would plan for the four years ahead.

On the Monday following the election I joined them at Aspen, the rustic Presidential lodge nestled under tall pines. During a sumptuous dinner the President toasted me again with his best vintage wine for my election strategy, while Haldeman and Ehrlichman sat in stony silence.

"Stay with us for the next term, Chuck," the President asked genially. "There'll be increased responsibilities – great things to be done."

To the visible relief of my colleagues at the table, I declined again. "I'm one of those burned-out volcanoes you talked about, Mr. President." Nothing had really changed in my thinking. I did agree to stay on for several months into the new year to help staff the new Administration and also, important to me, avoid the appearance that I was leaving because of Watergate.

Dick Howard, my shrewd young assistant, had picked up shoptalk among the lower-level staffers that Ehrlichman was telling friends the White House Watergate woes would go with Colson when he departed. The eagerness of Bob and John to see me leave led to the uncomfortable suspicion that I was to be the scapegoat. The way I'd been targeted in the press, it was plausible enough.

Meanwhile, Haldeman and Ehrlichman were embarked

on the most ambitious White House reorganisation in history, which not only streamlined the government's decision-making machinery but also drew all executive power into a tiny circle of six White House super-aides. The two men controlled all access to and from the President, summoning those Cabinet members to be removed, determining those whom Nixon would interview as their replacements, and keeping him away from such "interferences" as demanding senators or staff members with contrary views. Nixon was rarely seen; the press camping on Catoctin Mountain in makeshift trailers began to complain. At the nearly abandoned White House the favourite gag, though repeated with a touch of bitterness, was that the President, now re-elected handsomely, had been kidnapped.

It was during a trip to the mountaintop late in November when I realized that my inner malaise needed more than just a few days rest. Peter Brennan, the hard-hat union leader from New York whom I had recommended for Secretary of Labour, joined me aboard one of the President's choppers for the trip to Camp David. We climbed to 1,000 feet, following the Potomac River west, then once outside Washington headed north for the mountains. The pilot, a Marine veteran, kept his craft low as long as possible to reduce the buffeting from gusty head winds. It looked like we were headed right into a forested mountainside until the pilot pulled up sharply. We climbed the side of the mountain like a tram car on a cable, then roared over the peak, and quickly settled down into an open field cut into the dense forest.

Armed Marines dressed in combat fatigues were stationed as always on the outer edges of the landing area. A Navy commander opened the door of the chopper a second after the wheels hit the asphalt, snapped a salute, welcomed Brennan, and quickly walked us to a waiting limousine which sped us through the narrow tree-lined roads past more armed sentries, to one of the small guest cabins.

The commander instructed us to wait until Mr. Haldeman arrived. "No one without an escort is to walk outside," he politely explained for Brennan's benefit. A cheery, white-hot fire was burning, warming the comfortable sitting room. Brennan was impressed, not only with the obvious comforts of Camp David, but the military split-second efficiency. "This is really something," he muttered, peering out the window for a look at the other buildings scattered through the woods.

"It's something all right, Pete, something right out of 1984," I replied. Brennan and I had become good friends following those fearsome days in the spring of 1970 when he paraded his flag-bearing carpenters and ironworkers through the streets of New York – and later into the Oval Office.

"This place is not for me," I said. "I feel like I'm being watched all the time, guards everywhere, even hiding behind the trees. It's like one of those secret hideaways in a James Bond movie – eerie! I can't wait to get back to the city."

Brennan was staring at me. "Chuck, you need a rest. Something's bugging you."

Something was bugging me all right. But what was it that I resisted here? There were Navy officers saluting every time I stepped out of the door, luxurious quarters, beautiful scenery, gourmet meals, power to order anything I wanted. But the only thing I wanted to order, despite Nixon always urging me to stay overnight, was a helicopter to take me home. Pete was right; something was wrong, and by now I was beginning to wonder what I'd have to do to shake it off. It should have been the most triumphant time of my life; yet inside I was miserable.

Haldeman soon joined us and we walked together to Aspen for a relaxed hour with Nixon. As soon as Peter accepted the position of Secretary of Labour, I asked for a chopper to take me back to Washington.

A new crisis in Vietnam that December took our minds off Watergate and the second term. When Henry Kissinger had returned from Paris on October 24 with a tentative peace agreement in hand, his feet were hardly touching the ground. Ending the war, Henry believed, would sew up the election. But the President had been convinced there should be no announcement before the election lest it be labelled by the press as a political gimmick.

"I gave just a little background information to Max Frankel," Kissinger offhandedly told the President that next afternoon, referring to his friend on the *New York Times*.

The three of us were sitting alone in Nixon's office. I glanced at Nixon as Henry was talking. He did not explode as I feared, but I could tell the President was seething. He spoke slowly through clenched teeth, glaring at Henry. Henry seemed not to notice.

The next morning, Paris time, the middle of the night for us, the North Vietnamese announced the agreement. Whether the result of inquiries by the *Times* Paris Bureau or a conscious decision by Le Duc Tho to complicate our lives just before the election, the damage was done and the next morning after frantic briefings by the President, Haldeman, and me, Kissinger walked into the Press Room to deliver what Nixon insisted be a down-played explanation. But buried in his long monologue was the phrase "peace is at hand" which, predictably enough, was bannered around the world. We worried for a few days that the overstatement would boomerang. Nixon in his next televised speech toned down Kissinger's words. To our pleasant surprise hardly anyone viewed it as a last-minute gimmick; even the sceptics knew we needed no desperation effort to rescue an election in which we were already twenty-five points ahead.

After the election in November the agreement had begun to come unstuck. Hanoi hedged on key provisions. President Thieu of South Vietnam demanded more assurances. In December when Kissinger returned to Paris, hopefully to conclude the agreement, he was given an icy rebuff. The first day he fired back an angry cable recommending that negotiations be broken off, massive bombing resumed, with Mr. Nixon going on national television to explain it to the American people.

The President called me into his office to read the cable. "Well, what do you think?" he demanded.

I studied the three-page document carefully while Nixon sat tapping his fingers impatiently. "I'd tell Henry to keep negotiating; they are just trying to test us," I finally answered.

"No, no," Nixon interrupted, obviously not interested in my foreign-policy judgment. "What do you think about going on TV?"

"I wouldn't advise it. It will look like the October

announcement was a phoney. The country will never take it."

Haldeman joined us shortly and echoed my sentiments. Later that morning Nixon cabled instructions back to Kissinger: " Keep negotiating."

Kissinger stayed at the table, but the North Vietnamese remained truculent and on December 14 Henry broke off negotiations, returning to Washington. The next day Nixon fired off a strongly worded cable to North Vietnam : return to the Paris negotiations in seventy-two hours or else. It was no bluff. When the ultimatum expired, wave after wave of B-52s began raining hundreds of tons of bombs on North Vietnamese targets. Nixon made no public statement for fear of hardening the negotiating position, making it tougher for Hanoi to come around.

The public reaction was predictable shock and outrage, followed by a torrent of editorial denunciation, all directed at Richard Nixon. Kissinger's friends in the Washington press corps simply could not believe that Henry would be party to what the *Washington Post* labelled "the most savage and senseless act of war ever visited . . . by one sovereign people upon another."

The reaction from the Congress, happily for us then out of session, was the most vitriolic. Sentiment began to mount on both sides of the aisle for a resolution terminating all funds for military operations in South East Asia. We took the threats from Congress seriously; we knew we were racing the clock. If the North Vietnamese did not cave in and agree to return to the conference table by the time the new Congress got under way in January, we faced stern action.

The President got less and less sleep as he took almost the full weight of the criticism. Physically, he was drained before the crisis. He had taken only one brief weekend rest after the election. Now I saw him ageing right before my eyes. Many days his speech was not entirely clear, a sign of the total exhaustion I had come to fear. The President always drove himself hard, but except in periods of tremendous stress his speech remained clear, his voice strong. When his words slurred, as they had two or three times in the past, I knew that he was pushing himself beyond the point of even his extraordinary endurance. He was giving little or no attention to other matters, such as restaffing the second Administration, a fact that was to plague him in the months ahead.

With Haldeman and Kissinger vacationing in California, the President and I maintained the vigil alone. I remembered tales of Lyndon Johnson getting up in the middle of the night, putting on bathrobe and slippers and walking down to the Situation Room, the National Security Council headquarters in the White House basement, to read the latest military reports from Vietnam. Johnson became so totally immersed in the battlefield situation, his intimates later reported, that he began to lose his perspective and aged visibly. Richard Nixon learned from Johnson's mistake, and to my knowledge never once visited the Situation Room. But I could understand what had happened to Johnson, because for a brief time in December it started to happen to Nixon. Hard as he tried to discipline himself, there was no way to escape the anxiety of awaiting each report from the military command in Saigon – how many bombers shot down, how many men killed and captured – while Hanoi remained stubbornly silent. The strain weakened him physically and mentally. He was limping badly from a toe he cracked on the edge of the swimming pool at Camp David; like the hay fever he would never admit he had, Nixon refused to let the doctor treat his injured foot.

At 4:30 in the afternoon on December 28, the President summoned me to his working office next to mine, greeting me with the kind of smile he usually saved for mass television audiences, "Sit down, Chuck," he said. "I have something to tell you, but not another person in this building can know. This must not leak. The North Vietnamese have agreed to go back to the negotiating table on our terms. They can't take the bombing any longer. Our Air Force really did the job." The smile never left his face and there was boyish excitement in his voice.

The bombing was to cease the next day – Friday. On Saturday a very low-keyed announcement was to be made by Deputy Press Secretary Jerry Warren that the bombing had ended and that negotiations would resume the following week. Nixon's instructions to me were precise: we must not

crow over our success as this might give Hanoi a reason to
back away.

The helicopter was already waiting on the South Lawn
to take the President to Camp David for the New Year's
weekend; his being away from Washington would help us
underplay the big news. Henry had wanted to return for the
announcement but Nixon insisted that he not, fearing such
an action would signal more than we wanted to signal. It was
best for Henry to remain in Palm Springs, out of reach of the
press. The President wanted no repeat of the October gaffe.

"Walk with me to the chopper, Chuck," he said, bounding
out of the easy chair. I helped him into his overcoat and we
walked briskly to the South Lawn where Mrs. Nixon joined
us, wearing slacks and a beige car coat. It was the first time
I had ever seen her dressed casually, looking like any other
housewife off for a weekend in the country. Nixon repeated
his instructions about Saturday's announcement, then took
Pat by the arm and started for the chopper. All at once she
turned around, walked back a few steps, and saying not a word
gave me a big hug. She knew her husband's agony was over.

The President's helicopter lifted slowly into the air, banked
sharply to the right, and headed up the river. I stood alone
for a few minutes in the cold, dry winter air. I longed to tell
someone the news I had just heard, maybe the guard at the
door, or John Scali of my staff, who had been very much a
part of the long ordeal, but I knew I could share that moment
with no one.

Warren's Saturday announcement was terse and press
reports which followed were restrained. The President and
I talked by phone several times that afternoon and evening.
His spirits were high. He and I had both talked with Kissinger
who assured us he would talk to no one in the press.

I was up early Sunday morning anxious to read the full
press coverage. Before nine the calls started, the first one
from Scali, a long-time journalist himself. "Have you read
Reston's column?" Scali roared. "It's a disaster. It can scuttle
the negotiations before they even start."

I flipped quickly to the editorial page. Whatever James
Reston, senior eminence of the *New York Times*, said soon
became gospel among the rest of the pack. Reston painted a

reluctant Kissinger, opposed to the bombing, ready to have settled for the October 26 agreement, dragged along by a President who had capriciously decided to bomb Hanoi to try to get a better deal. Was this an attempt by Kissinger friends to salvage Henry's good-guy reputation? The danger was that Hanoi might misread it and hang tough on their November demands, believing there was some split between Nixon and Kissinger.

I made the first mistake of the day by reading it to Nixon when he called half an hour later. He exploded, ordering me to call Kissinger at once. (It was then 6 : 30 a.m. in California.) "I will not tolerate insubordination," he barked into the telephone. "You tell Henry he's to talk to no one, period ! I mean no one. And tell him not to call me, I will accept no calls from him." With that he slammed the receiver in my ear. Henry, when I got through to him, promised not to talk to anyone in the press. I relayed his assurance to Nixon.

Nixon normally could cool off in a hurry, but not this day. By nightfall he was still brooding, so glum, Manola told me later, that he couldn't even enjoy the Redskins' championship football game. During the last call of the day, he ordered me to have the Secret Service keep a record of all incoming and outgoing calls from Kissinger's heavily guarded villa in Palm Springs.

I carried out that order and that was my second mistake. Secret Service learned – and I reported – that after trying to reach the President unsuccessfully, Kissinger proceeded to call his old friend Joe Kraft, whose column in the *Washington Post* three days later described Kissinger's valiant role in opposing Nixon's "twelve days of murder bombing." Kraft charged that Nixon "compromised" Kissinger's honour and unless Nixon now gave him "a new mandate . . . like being made Secretary of State," Kissinger should quit. (Two years later Kraft explained that he'd been misled by Kissinger.) That did it. Stories and rumours of a Nixon-Kissinger rift were by now running rampant through Washington. Most people thought the rift caused by disagreement over the bombing decision. It wasn't. It was over the rash of news stories by which Henry or his friends tried to extricate him from the unpopular decision. Either way, it was damaging.

The President remained angry, counting the days until Henry left to return to Harvard. He had told me one November night at Camp David, after an especially unfortunate egocentric interview which Henry gave an Italian journalist, "Kissinger will be leaving in six or eight months; it's not good for a man to stay too long in that position; it will be better for Henry. Time for him to get back to other things." I thought in November that Nixon was merely piqued over one column and in time would forget it. In January I knew better.

In its "last hurrah," Vietnam managed to poison the relationship between these two unusually gifted men, a relationship which had led to some of the most spectacular American foreign-policy achievements in decades. Ironically, it would take the catastrophe of Watergate to force the two men back together, when Nixon would see in Kissinger's unsullied reputation with the Krafts and Restons a desperate last-resort weapon. Watergate would force Nixon's hand; by September of that year instead of shipping Henry back to academia, Nixon would make him Secretary of State, just as Kraft had demanded.

Thus it was that a small band of tired, dispirited, sometimes mean and petty men, bickering among themselves, wary and jealous of one another, launched the Thirty-seventh President's second term. The inaugural festivities were fittingly regal, even by Nixon and Haldeman standards. The President, moreover, thoroughly enjoyed his own party, dancing late into the night at one of his own jam-packed balls, calling me in at two in the morning to read some last minute changes he'd penned in his inaugural address.

Then, only three days later, came the final announcement that "peace with honour," a phrase borrowed from two Nixon favourites, Disraeli and Woodrow Wilson, had been achieved. This was the moment Nixon had longed for more devoutly than even his own re-election. We lunched together in the privacy of Nixon's private office that day, indulging ourselves to the extent of two Dubonnets on the rocks before the standard fare of cottage cheese and pineapple. Why not? The speech wasn't to be until evening and he'd rehearsed its lines in dream after dream over four long years. "It's been a tough road, Chuck, but we've come through it," Nixon said, but without the exhilaration I had expected. He was subdued as he recalled one agony after another, once staring pensively into his glass as if seeking in the reflection the response that would tell him it was worth it all.

He added, his voice even softer now, "How rough it's been. No telling how long this peace agreement will last – a year, two years maybe, who knows. But we kept our word, we'll get our prisoners home and well, the South Vietnamese – at least those poor devils will have a fighting chance."

Quiet and fatalistic, those were the inner thoughts of a man who recognised full well that little had been achieved for all the turmoil, blood, and sweat. It was no triumphant V-E Day; there'd be no flags waving, no ticker-tape parades for the returning heroes. A warm welcome, surely, for the POWs but it would be followed by a great sigh of relief and 200 million Americans would turn away, erasing the past decade of riot and war as quickly as possible from their minds.

There were long creases in Nixon's face and the dark shadows under his eyes had deepened since the early days of December. The day in-day out pressures of the Presidency had taken a fearful toll even on this remarkably rugged man. Always before I'd marvelled at Nixon's resilience, the way he usually brought himself back, tougher and stronger than ever, after each gruelling experience. Not now. He was tired this time and there was no hiding it. It was on his face, in the melancholy of his voice, in the new specks of grey in his hair glistening in the midday sun that poured through the tall windows of the old Victorian building. I thought then that his worst problems were behind him.

Nixon talked on wistfully : "Some day, people will understand why it was so important for us to do it this way. Somebody in this chair some day will surely understand." With that, Nixon got up, walked across the room to the fluffy sofa, loosened his tie and stretched out: "Ask Manola to pull the drapes, Chuck. I need a little sleep before tonight. A big night."

"Get some rest, Mr. President. You deserve it."

History will doubtless show that the President's gritty

stand in December 1972 and the peace accord that followed
was just another grizzly chapter in North Vietnam's unrelenting thirty-year drive to take over South Vietnam. At
the time it seemed a major breakthrough in America's ten-
year war in Asia, worth all of the President's mind-and-body-
sapping efforts. But the more significant consequence of this
stressful time was that it consumed so much of Richard Nixon
and his Presidency as to wound him mortally for the greatest
crisis yet to come.

As a final official act, the President asked me to travel to
Moscow in February to pry open slightly, if I could, the
jammed doors that were blocking the emigration of Jews
from the Soviet Union. Congress, under pressure from labour
and influential elements of the American Jewish community,
was threatening not to approve the Summit trade agreements
until the Russians relented. Détente was again in peril, this
time over an issue the Soviets indignantly told us was none
of our business.

I knew the President picked me to go in part because he
thought the change would be good for me and Patty, who
was accompanying me. When we returned, my resignation
would become official and I could return to my law office, only
a block away. We would remain close; he wanted me to head
his "kitchen cabinet" of outside advisers and friends.

One could not be mawkish and still part of the machismo
cult we so fervently worshipped in the White House, yet I
found myself close to tears as we said good-bye the day I was
to fly to Moscow. He spared us both by thumping me on the
back, saving his good-bye for a letter delivered later. (*See* next
page.)

Richard Nixon is a man of many parts, at times brutally
cold, calculating, a manipulator of power as so many great
leaders in history have been. But he is other things, too – at
times an intensely compassionate human being who all his
sixty-plus years held up his own mother as a saint and could
never bring himself to point out to a secretary her mis-
spellings. I once saw him re-dictate a letter to eliminate a
troublesome word, rather than embarrass the secretary.

A very excited Patty was waiting in a White House

THE WHITE HOUSE

WASHINGTON

March 10, 1973

Dear Chuck:

It is with deepest regret that I now officially accept your
resignation as Special Counsel to the President.

I shall not dwell on my reluctance at seeing you go, for
you know how highly I value your remarkable record of
achievements during the past four years. Let me simply
say that our Administration has been served by many
outstanding men and women, but few can match -- and
none exceed -- the skill and dedication you brought to the
post of Special Counsel.

Our association over the past years has been marked by
a deep and abiding friendship. Even more gratifying,
however, has been the knowledge that we share a common commitment -- to make these years the very best
in our Nation's history. I shall always cherish your
loyal friendship, and in equal measure, I shall always
treasure the superb work you did for our Party, our
Administration, and the people of this good land.

It is good to know that we may continue to call upon you
from time to time, and you may be certain that we will
take advantage of your generosity. As you return to
private life, Pat and I extend to your Pat and you our
heartfelt good wishes for the success and happiness you
both so richly deserve.

Sincerely,

Honorable Charles W. Colson
The White House
Washington, D. C.

limousine. As I held her hand in the back seat, she bubbled over with questions. Would someone meet us at the Moscow airport? How cold would it be? Was she wearing the right outfit?

I tried to share her excitement, but the familiar inner deadness was asserting itself once more. What challenges did life hold, now that I was leaving the White House? Was I perhaps afraid to slow down, afraid to get off the twenty-four-hours-a-day, seven-days-a-week merry-go-round, for fear of coming face to face with a certain inner poverty? Did I really know what was important?

Although the plane was warm I found myself shivering. There was a point only months ago when I would have been as thrilled as Patty about a trip to Russia. Now I found it hard to pay attention to the briefings of Steve Lazarus, the brilliant Soviet expert accompanying us.

It was shortly before 11 p.m. when our 707 touched down at Moscow's Sheremetyevo Airport. We were, the pilot told us, the only flight to make it in through the fog that night. As the plane taxied toward the terminal, at first I could make out only occasional lights through the thick grey mist. Then all at once in the middle of the runway appeared a landing ramp, bright lights, a swarm of people, dressed in fur hats and long bushy fur coats.

"What do I do now?" I asked Steve.

"This is very good. The brass is here, which means they're going to treat these meetings seriously. Very interesting," he muttered, staring out of the window.

"But what do I say?" I persisted, this being my first venture in international diplomacy.

"Anything," Steve replied calmly, his eyes fixed on the crowd. "At this hour it won't matter. Just smile."

I took a deep breath and stepped into the cold, dank night. The Russians – the officials they sent to the airport anyway – weren't the lean steely-eyed Communists I'd expected, but warm, outgoing people, pleasantly plump most of them; with their great fur coats and generally round faces they looked like big friendly teddy bears. I even managed to get out a phrase or two of Russian I'd learned during cram sessions at the State Department.

But on the ride into the city, Acting U.S. Ambassador "Spike" Dubs, a hard-nosed Midwesterner and career State Department officer, leaned toward us. "Never say anything anywhere, including in this car, that you don't want *them* to hear. Remember everything is bugged, even the ambassador's residence where you'll stay. Everything you say is recorded, that goes for you, too, Mrs. Colson," he stared unsmilingly at Patty.

Spaso House, the official residence of the United States ambassador, is a large white Victorian building on an out-of-the-way side street, surrounded by forbidding dirty brick buildings and equally forbidding Soviet soldiers in their long brown coats, red epaulettes, black boots, and fur hats. Inside the darkened house were only two servants, one smiling old Chinese man, Yang, who'd worked for our embassy since we recognised the Soviet Union in the thirties, and one hefty Russian butler.

"Agatha Christie would have a field day here," I whispered to Patty as Yang led us through long dark corridors, floorboards creaking with each step, up a rickety old elevator and into the tastefully furnished guest suite. Along with Steve, we were the only occupants of the house. Dubs, as acting ambassador, lived in the apartment building connected to the embassy. We stared at the radiators, ceiling mouldings, paintings, wondering which concealed hidden microphones. Little did I dream that I'd been working daily for over three years in a building similarly equipped.

From Spaso House early next morning began a dizzying week; for me a steady series of meetings morning and afternoon with various Soviet officials, for Patty a grand tour of Moscow in the company of a smiling but muscular blonde, Mrs. Ulyanova (whom we later learned was a KGB officer). "The Colonel," as we called her out of her hearing, never once let Patty out of her sight, even for the necessities of life.

The preliminary meetings were but the prelude to my scheduled encounter with Vasiliy Kuznetsov. Dubs, Lazarus, an Assistant Secretary of State, some other functionaries, and I were escorted into a cavernous conference room on the top floor of the towerlike Foreign Ministry. Kuznetsov, a tall gaunt man with deep penetrating eyes, entered a moment later trailed by a bevy of aides in dark suits, all wearing the same solemn expressions. Kuznetsov took his seat in the centre of the table across from me, our respective delegations flanking us in precise protocol order.

After brief amenities, Kuznetsov, speaking flawless English, said that the Soviets were not interested in the domestic political problems of the United States; that Congress' threat to nullify the trade agreement between the two countries was our concern, not theirs. The Russians *knew* Nixon could handle his part of the bargain, couldn't he? He was staring at me, waiting for my response. *Not a very agreeable fellow,* I thought. I took a deep breath to try to slow down my racing heartbeat.

"Mr. Minister, your confidence in President Nixon is well founded. But you don't understand the American people. We are all immigrants, a whole nation of them. One of my grandfathers came from Sweden, the other from England – you see, to us the right of a person, Jew or Gentile, white or black, to emigrate is a fundamental human right. We can't bargain it away; it's non-negotiable. It's God-given to everyone."

For an instant I thought I detected the hint of a smile in the leathery face of this old-line doctrinaire Communist. I pressed on, explaining how deeply our labour unions felt about the issue. Kuznetsov then launched into a tirade, right out of the Communist handbook. I came back with a civics-class lecture on human freedom. More than an hour of the give-and-take passed, then Kuznetsov raised himself up in his chair, his shoulders braced back, glanced at his colleagues to either side, and announced: "Mr. Colson, we will do our part. You can tell the President." Curtly he shook hands with me, turned, and strode out of the room, the procession following.

"Did he mean something by that last statement? Did I hear him right?" I asked Steve.

"You sure did. Wow, I've sweat right through my shirt, but it was worth it. We got what we came for!"

Kuznetsov's parting words, brief though they were, had great meaning to seasoned diplomats in our group who watched for nuances of words and even the inflection of a voice; the world of diplomacy turns on such things, I learned.

(Following later visits by the Secretary of the Treasury and others, the quotas for emigrating Jews were increased; more than 30,000 Jews left the Soviet Union in the next year. The Soviets never gave in all the way, however, and in late 1974 the Congress, over Kissinger's vehement objections, passed an amendment restricting U.S.-Soviet trade relations until the Soviets eliminated all Jewish emigration restrictions. The Soviets predictably renounced the trade agreement, unwilling to allow their internal policy to be decided by an act of the U.S. Congress.)

My first solo flight in the rarefied air of foreign affairs jacked up my spirits – until our last day in Moscow when Spike Dubs scheduled a press conference open to Western newsmen, about thirty hardy souls who endured Spartan life within the Soviet Union in order to report to the world outside. After my guarded, watered-down account of the meetings and several general questions about the trade bill and Jewish emigration, a reporter fired a question I was not prepared for: "Mr. Colson, there is a report from Washington that you sent Howard Hunt to Denver to interview Dita Beard during the ITT affair. Is this true?"

I felt like the quarterback all set to pass who was suddenly hit from the blind side. Watergate had followed me halfway around the world. There had not been a single word about the scandal in the Soviet press and the Soviet officials who were aware of it were perplexed; wire-tapping and bugging is a way of life in their country. One or two indeed had told me to express their private sympathies to President Nixon that so much was being made of nothing. But the free-world press corps stationed in Moscow followed every unfolding revelation with keen interest. I tried to get rid of the question with a quip answer, but other Watergate questions followed. Dubs shrewdly and mercifully terminated the press conference.

Any elation I had felt over the success of my mission evaporated. Despite an interesting visit to Rumania, a courtesy call on President Ceausescu who had helped us open relations with China, and pleasant days in Vienna, the nagging restlessness returned. I just couldn't shake off persistent forebodings.

It was during a carefree afternoon in Vienna that Patty noticed the latest European edition of *Newsweek* in a tiny shop window. I made the mistake of purchasing it and there to my horror was a full page entitled "Whispers on Colson," an article charging me with every imaginable Watergate misdeed, including many I'd never heard of. (See page 220 for explanation of the source of this story.) As I stood on the crowded street corner in Vienna, reading each poisonous accusation, Patty looking on with sorrowful eyes, I could feel the noose tightening. There was no way to escape the demon. We cut the rest of our trip short by two days; I had to get back to Washington.

My forebodings were justified. It was not the same White House I had left three weeks earlier. Haldeman seemed distracted and preoccupied. When I told him of my concerns over Watergate and the need to clear it up, he tried to shrug it off with a flip remark; yet he was obviously worried. I met with John Dean the same day I returned, hoping to track down the sources of the *Newsweek* article. He barely gave me a chance to begin talking.

"Chuck, you wouldn't believe what's happened around here since you left. *He*," gesturing deferentially towards the Oval Office, "has been calling me in every day. I guess I've kind of picked up where you left off."

I looked more closely at John. He had been one of the more obscure members of the staff handling all the knotty, small legal problems. Far from a Presidential confidant, his long hair, occasionally loud dress and bachelor's life-style never fitted him into the Nixon mould. Now he'd been asked for a photograph by *Time* magazine; he spread some glossy prints across his desk top and told me to select the most flattering one.

"Don't worry about the *Newsweek* article," he said off-handedly. "That's only a drop in the bucket. We're getting clobbered from all sides on this Watergate thing now ... Do you like this picture?" Excited about his daily visits to the Oval Office and rising status, he was unable to pay much attention to the concern I expressed. I knew the feeling only too well.

Anyway, there was nothing left for me to do at the White

House but pack up my personal files, dash off the final trip reports and thank you notes, and with Holly Holm, who was now my top secretary, move "across the street" to the plush suite of offices my law partners had provided for me.

It would be good to be back with my close friend Charlie Morin; I'd missed him. And the new partners, including a gregarious, heavy-set Brooklyn-born trial lawyer of some renown – Dave Shapiro – had opened their hearts as well as their pocketbooks. The name of the twenty-five man firm was changed to COLSON AND SHAPIRO, and as a coming-home present they'd purchased a Lincoln Continental and hired a driver for me.

Clients were lining up at the doors, the result of a rash of articles like the feature piece in the New York Times describing "the first bona fide member of the President's inner circle – well on his way to becoming one of the busiest and best-paid lawyers in Washington." All of this, the warm welcome, plenty of money; surely, I thought, would give me a new thrust.

During my last meeting with the President as his Special Counsel, he was leaning back in his chair, crossed legs resting comfortably on his massive carved mahogany desk. We talked of the trip to Moscow and other things. Then I came to Watergate. "Whoever did order Watergate, let it out!" I said emotionally. "Let's get rid of it now, take our losses." *

I barely had the words out before the President dropped his feet on the floor and came straight up in his chair. "Who do you think did this? Mitchell? – Magruder? – " he was staring intently into my eyes, face flushed, anger in his voice. I had struck a raw nerve, but I was convinced at that moment that he was as much in the dark as I was.

For reasons I could not then fathom, Richard Nixon seemed almost paralysed by Watergate, unable or unwilling to face harsh realities as the net was being drawn tighter around all of us.

*Unpublished White House Transcripts of February 13, 1973, subpoenaed by the Watergate Special Prosecutor but not introduced in the trial. (Expletives deleted.)

7

The Long Hot Summer

A few weeks after my return to law practice, I was in New
York to meet with the producers of a promising TV system
which might in time give the networks tough competition.
With me was a bright young lawyer, Fred Lowther, whom
we had hired away from the government. A healthy fee was
on the line.

We met in the offices of one of New York's old-line invest-
ment banking houses. Soon the company's president, chairman of the board, three vice-presidents, and two bankers were
seated around a long boardroom table, peppering Lowther
and me with facts, figures, statistics, information about their
plans for the multimillion-dollar investments. They needed
a competitive break against the networks which would come
if a government study, soon to be approved and released by
the White House, were to recognise their industry.

Lowther was eagerly taking notes. I could not. For the first
time in my life I was not able to concentrate in a meeting; it
was all I could do to appear interested, nodding, I hoped, at
the right times.

Am I having a blackout? I asked myself. Something serious
must be wrong with me physically; I can't still be tired. Once
I imagined that someone had drawn a soundproof glass
window right across the table, leaving the mouths on the
other side moving soundlessly. At the end of the day I was
exhausted from struggling to maintain a pretence of alertness.
The company's president came to the point: "Will you
represent us, Mr. Colson?"

"We'll be happy to," I responded, naming a six-figure amount.

"It's a deal," he grinned, then happily shook my hand and instructed a vice-president to have his limousine drive us to La Guardia where the company's corporate jet would whisk us back to Washington.

"Fred, did you take good notes?" I asked my young associate as we leaned back in the plush seats of the four-million-dollar Gulfstream II.

Lowther assured me he had.

"Would you write up a complete memo and have it on my desk Monday? I'm still a little tired from the trip to Europe, I guess." With that I turned and stared out of the window, alone again with the same doubts and worries that had been my unwelcome companions for five months. In the old days, landing a big account was exhilarating, a cause for taking Patty to dinner to celebrate. *Where was the old competitive zest?* I asked myself.

Many men I knew encountered periods like this in their lives, especially in their forties – fears about the future, about self-worth. "Male menopause" it's often called. Having read some about this subject, I went through a quick checklist. Marriage – happy. Alcohol – no problem. Career – fulfilled. Health – good. Still puzzled, I decided that the decompression from the tension-packed White House years to law practice was an adjustment that simply would take time.

There was one client I'd represented before whose return I welcomed: the Raytheon Company, an electronics manufacturer and the largest employer in New England. In mid-March I flew to Boston for all-day meetings with the company's top executives. The executive vice-president, Brainerd Holmes, who once headed the government's manned-space programme, was an old friend. His boss, Tom Phillips, the company's president, had climbed to the top by shrewd wits and raw ability.

I met Brainerd first in the company's modern brick and glass headquarters overlooking Route 128, the busy beltway around Boston. Holmes, bubbling over with enthusiasm for Raytheon's new programmes and my return as their legal adviser, ran me through a series of meetings with engineers and vice-presidents. Later in the day Tom Phillips left word that he, too, wanted to see me before I departed.

As I started for the president's office, Brainerd stopped me. "Chuck, maybe there's something I should tell you about Tom before you go in there. He's had quite a change – some kind of religious experience." Brainerd paused, searching for the right words to explain it. "I don't really understand it, but it is quite important to him. He – he might come on – well, you know, maybe a little strong." Brainerd concluded with an embarrassed smile.

This was surprising news. Tom Phillips had always been such an aggressive businessman; it was hard for me to see him teaching Sunday school. Once he'd told me he was Congregational in the same way I labelled myself Episcopalian. Nothing important – just another membership. I thought that he might be involved in church fund raising, as the top executive of the state's biggest company would be expected to do for church and community.

When I entered his office it was the same old Tom, jet-black hair, athletic build, stripped down to shirt-sleeves as always. But the smile was a lot warmer, radiant, in fact, and he looked more relaxed than I had ever seen him. In the old days though always genial, he had had a harried look – with phones ringing, secretaries running in and out of the office, his desk piled high with paper. Now there was something serene about his office as well as about Tom.

"Tell me about yourself, Chuck. How have you been doing?" he began.

An honest answer would have been, "Thanks, I feel rotten," but instead I said, "I'm doing fine, a little tired." I had to maintain a strong front; Tom was an important client.

"You really should get some rest, Chuck. It's important after what you've been through," he said, and I had the curious sensation that rather than being surface talk, he genuinely meant it.

We reminisced about old times, then it was back to me. "About this Watergate business, Chuck, are you okay? It looks to me like people are trying to drag you into it."

I told Tom that I had no direct or indirect involvement in the burglary – despite the heat from the press. I was launched into a lengthy defensive explanation when Tom cut me off. "Don't explain. If you tell me you weren't responsible, that's all I need to hear."

We had talked for twenty minutes and nothing at all had been said about religion. Yet Tom was different. There was a new compassion in his eyes and a gentleness in his voice. "Uh – Brainerd tells me that you have become very involved in some religious activities," I said at last.

"Yes, that's true, Chuck. I have accepted Jesus Christ. I have committed my life to Him and it has been the most marvellous experience of my whole life"

My expression must have revealed my shock. I struggled for safe ground. "Uh, maybe sometime you and I can discuss that, Tom." If I hadn't restrained myself I would have blurted out, *What are you talking about? Jesus Christ lived two thousand years ago, a great moral leader, of course, and doubtless divinely inspired. But why would anyone "accept" Him or "commit one's life" to Him as if He were around today?*

The conversation turned to more comfortable subjects and then Tom walked me to the door of his office, his long arm around my shoulder. "I'd like to tell you the whole story some day, Chuck. I had gotten to the point where I didn't think my life was worth anything. Now everything is changed – attitude, values, the whole bit."

Phillips was boggling my mind. Life isn't worth anything, he says, when you're president of the biggest company in the state, have a beautiful home, a Mercedes, a great family, probably a quarter-million-a-year salary . . .

But he had struck a raw nerve – the empty life. It was what I was living with, though I couldn't admit that to Tom. I went back to Washington to struggle with my inner malaise – and Watergate – and Phillips's astonishing words.

Weeks before, John Dean had asked me to see Howard Hunt and find out his attitude toward the White House. Dave Shapiro shrewdly vetoed it and saw Hunt himself instead, learning on March 16 for the first time that Hunt was demanding money to remain silent. Hunt wanted me to pass his demands on to the White House. When Shapiro and I met to discuss Hunt's startling disclosures, he said, "Chuck, you stay away from this or I'll break your neck. If you pass that message on, you are involved in an obstruction of justice. This is serious business and our friend the 'Trick' is in deep trouble."

Shapiro, a liberal Democrat, had no use for Nixon. Coming from a pro like Shapiro, the words *obstruction of justice* were ominous. I had never thought of Watergate in that light. I should have, of course, but in my mind the crime had been ordering the stupid break-in, whoever had done that. By now a Select Committee, headed by Senate-dean Sam Ervin, was gearing up for a full-scale investigation. The *Post* had been waging a ferocious campaign to unearth Watergate skeletons and federal agents were digging intently.

"If you want to help your friend, we'd better get him the best criminal lawyer in the business," Dave concluded.

I passed the suggestion on to the President during a mid-March phone conversation. A week later Bob Haldeman called me. Could I come over to the White House? Bob was waiting for me in his office. "Let's sit here," he said, walking toward the comfortable chairs in front of his fireplace.

This was a switch. The crew-cut, stern-faced Haldeman never relaxed; he was always brusque, all business. I'd been in his office hundreds of times and almost always sat at his conference table under the windows.

"How's the law practice?" he asked, smiling warmly. This wasn't the Haldeman I knew. He detested small talk. Was Bob worrying about me, doubting my loyalty, afraid of my new partner Shapiro?

"Chuck," he continued, "we have got to get rid of this Watergate mess. It is hanging like a dark cloud over the President. He trusts you and needs your best advice. What can we do? What are we doing wrong?"

"Bob, I told the President last week to hire a criminal lawyer, someone who can get all the facts, piece the whole mystery together and give the boss cold-blooded, hard advice. Then get rid of the culprits. It's the only way."

Haldeman's expression never changed, although I now realise that with what he knew, my proposal was like suggesting he hire his own executioner.

"You lawyers are all alike," he laughed. "This is a public-relations problem. We've got too many lawyers now."

Just then the phone rang and as Haldeman jerked the receiver towards him, he missed his ear and cracked the hard plastic against his forehead. It was the action of a man under tremendous pressure. *He's powerless,* I suddenly thought, *right in the midst of all this power.*

Later walking across the lawn toward the sentry box at the Northwest Gate, I felt a curious sense of relief at being out of the White House. In spite of exhaust fumes from the rush-hour traffic, the spring air felt wonderfully fresh as I smiled at the guard and passed through the massive iron gates.

A few days later the headline in the *Washington Post* ended my smugness. It read: MCCORD LINKS MITCHELL AND COLSON TO WATERGATE BUGGING PLANS. I scanned the story with sinking heart. It was based on a leak from testimony given to the Ervin Committee by James McCord, one of the Watergate burglars. McCord had heard through Hunt, it was reported, that Colson was "knowledgeable" about Watergate. The article was written by the *Post's* crusading Watergate hunters, Bob Woodward and Carl Bernstein.

Across the breakfast table Patty looked up. "What's the matter, honey?" she asked.

"Look at this." I slapped the paper on the kitchen table. "A man I've never met, never laid eyes on, has tied me right into the break-in. I didn't even know a James McCord existed until the Watergate burglary."

It was a rotten way to begin what shaped up as a rough enough day as it was. A debate on "Government and the Press" was scheduled during a National Press Club luncheon between myself and a bitterly anti-Nixon, prizewinning reporter, Clark Mollenhoff. National television was to cover it. When I arrived at the Press Building, reporters and a TV camera crew were waiting.

"Mr. Colson, you have been named by James McCord as the man responsible for the Watergate break-in. Do you have any comment?"

I denied it but my words sounded hollow. The question made it headline news. No one paid any attention to denials.

During the debate Mollenhoff, with arms waving wildly in the air, and voice reverberating through the high-ceilinged ballroom, indicted Nixon and his men for every high crime short of treason. I roared back. The heated exchange delighted the packed hall, five hundred of the most influential newsmen in America. But no matter what I said, I was on the defensive, parrying the attacks on Nixon and myself.

As press assaults mounted over the next days, I found myself once again *the* prime Watergate culprit. One evening Dave Shapiro came up with a suggestion. "Take a lie-detector test, Chuck, with all the junk in the press it could help, might keep the prosecutors off your back."

I shook my head. "That's black magic. I'm not putting my life in the hands of some quack." I had nothing to hide about Watergate, but I was getting so jumpy on the inside that I feared my collywobbles would show on the machine.

Over the next weekend, however, I studied material Shapiro gave me about polygraph tests and the impressive qualifications of Richard Arther, the New York specialist he wanted to use. "It might be the only way to clear yourself," Dave argued. Then with a smile, "If you don't pass, no one would know. The test results are confidential."

By Monday morning I had reluctantly come around. Both *Time and Newsweek* on the news stands that day featured the McCord charges prominently. I knew I was telling the truth. I only hoped that the machine would know it as well. Shapiro scheduled us for Arther's first available time, Wednesday noon.

New York's skyline was eclipsed by a low-hanging grey sky that morning as blinding sheets of rain angled in from the north east. Shapiro had taken a flight up the night before. I came in on the last shuttle before the airport was closed. We had agreed to meet at Arther's office.

As I climbed into a cab a man asked if he could share it with me. It was, of all people, a reporter from ABC news, Bill Gill. Though Bill was a friend, I dared not let him know even the address I was heading for, so I asked the cab driver to let me off at Fifty-fifth and Fifth Avenue, four blocks from Arther's office. I made it the rest of the way through ankle-deep puddles, dodging the outward spears of passing umbrellas. At one point I caught sight of myself in a store window; collar turned up, rain-drenched hat pulled down over my eyes. This whole episode was turning me into a criminal.

Arther's office is located in a run-down building on the edge of the theatre district, surrounded by old movie houses, delicatessens, and flashing neon lights. It had been years since I'd ridden in such an antique elevator, which the operator opened by pulling down on a large metal bar stretched across the inside of the grated door. We clanged and shook our way to the eleventh floor, stopping at each level to discharge short frizzled-hair ladies carrying shopping bags.

On the eleventh floor at last I walked down a long brown-and-black-tiled corridor, past rows of oak doors, each with lettering on a frosted glass window: SYDNEY FAYNE/ PODIATRIST – WALTER RUBENSTEIN, D.D.S. It was straight out of a 1940 detective movie. The black lettering on the door to Arther's office read SCIENTIFIC DETECTION SERVICE, INC.

The door was locked. After I'd twisted nervously on the handle several times, a small man opened it, introducing himself as "Mr. Arther's assistant." I was told to sit on a straight-backed chair in the tiny windowless reception room. What had I gotten myself into? Moodily I remembered that this was our tenth wedding anniversary. I should be home with Patty.

In a few minutes Dave Shapiro and Richard Arther, a smiling, round-faced man, came out of a back room. The two of them burst out laughing at the sight of the forlorn and very wet figure of the former Special Counsel to the President of the United States.

I drew Dave aside: "I'm not going to do this. I didn't sleep last night. My stomach is turned inside out. I couldn't eat this morning, and this place . . ."

Shapiro's hefty jowls were still shaking with laughter. "Dick is the best in the business – and don't worry if you fail." His expression turned serious now. "I'll still represent you. I've gotten guilty people off as many times as I've lost innocent ones."

That hurt. So even Shapiro didn't believe me. Never before had I felt the awful frustration of knowing in my own heart what was true but being unable to persuade anyone, not even my lawyer.

"Wiring up" for the test was enough to start adrenalin flowing even if I had been relaxed at the outset. The victim is seated in a dentist-type chair while narrow strands of wire running from a big grey metal box are taped to each fingertip. Next a rubber pad is strapped around the left arm and inflated. A large metal chain was fitted around my chest, connected by another set of wires to the same grey box, on top of which little pencils suspended from metal arms would record a series of wavy lines on a moving roll of paper.

Arther did his best to relax me with small talk and calm reassurances about the reliability of the test, a statistical record of only .03 per cent. error. If a person had sensitive reactions, particularly a hypertense individual like me, the test was unfailing. "Tell me every lie you've ever told and anything you've done you are ashamed of," Arther began.

"You're kidding. We'll be here all day."

"No, it's important. You must begin with a clean slate, holding back nothing from your past."

I would have gotten out of the chair except I was fearful of electrocuting myself.

"I have a graduate degree in psychology," Arthur volunteered, apparently bewildered by my reluctance to bare my soul in an unfamiliar confessional. The preliminaries took an hour, with my recitation of prior indiscretions going back before college days, and Arther monitoring test runs on the machine. To demonstrate the sensitivity of the machine, he gave me plastic cards numbered one to fifteen, and told me to note one number to myself and answer falsely when he read the number I picked out. I did, and Arther, by checking his machine, pinpointed the card.

"Not bad," I admitted. This eased my anxiety slightly, but I could feel my heartbeat pick up, my hands start shaking, when Arther began the critical questions.

"Did you order the Watergate break-in?"

"No."

"Did you know about it in advance?"

"No."

Six key questions. As each one was asked I felt a surge in my heart and a flush in my face. My skin was icy-cold. I imagined the little pencils bouncing all over the charts. The tests completed, I waited numbly while Arther disconnected me.

"I failed, didn't I?"

He was passing the long sheet of paper which had now spilled out on to the floor through his hands, staring thoughtfully at the chart of wiggly lines.

"Dunno, I'll have to study this and let you know."

But of course my nervousness had ruined the test. Shapiro wanted me to wait, but I was going to catch the next train back to Washington. "Call me when you find out, Dave."

On the street the rain was still coming down in torrents. I didn't care. I stood waving vainly at passing cabs imagining the headlines once Messrs. Woodward and Bernstein heard about the results, as they somehow would. A cab was pulling over at last when I heard Shapiro's booming voice, "Chuck, Chuck – stop."

Shapiro in his shirt sleeves was lumbering toward me. "You passed – flying colours – Dick just had to double-check the control question. No doubt that you are telling the truth."

I stood there hugging Shapiro, a 250-pound hulk of a man, right there on the crowded corner of Fifty-seventh and Broadway. It was raining so hard he couldn't see the tears rolling down my cheeks.

Passing the lie-detector test gave me a feeling of confidence for a few weeks. Shapiro, with my consent, leaked the story to the *New York Times* and on Sunday, April 8, it ran on page one under a three column headline: COLSON REPORTED PASSING A LIE TEST ON WATERGATE. For a while at least I believed that truth could be found in little grey electronic boxes.

But my sense of security was short-lived. Within a few weeks the press found a way to use the tests for their own purposes. The *New York Times* on April 19 observed: "Charles Colson, formerly a special counsel to the President, took a lie detector test two weeks ago to certify that he had no foreknowledge of the Watergate plot – *the first overt sign of continuing concern about guilt and possible recrimina-*

tion within the President's close circle of advisers" (italics added).

On April 27 the *Post* headline bannered: AIDES SAY COLSON APPROVED BUGGING. It was a devastating and untrue story reprinted in hundreds of papers and leading the network news shows. "Charles W. Colson, former Special Counsel to President Nixon, knew of the Watergate bugging plans before they were executed and urged that the electronic surveillance be expedited, Federal prosecutors have been told by two top officials of President Nixon's Re-election Campaign Committee," the article began. The Woodward and Bernstein story, later discredited in the Watergate testimony, was based on an innocent phone call I made to Jeb Magruder at campaign headquarters early in 1972 – before the Watergate scheme, according to testimony, was even conceived. And I had been the one to report this conversation. It is almost impossible to counteract an untruthful press report that circulates the nation – like trying to retrieve feathers shaken loose from a pillow in a high wind.

My misery deepened as I remembered the untrue story I had leaked about Arthur Burns.

Camera crews now began to surround our quiet, secluded home in McLean almost daily. We were, as one ABC cameraman sheepishly explained, on their "stake-out" list. Morning after morning we would be awakened by the sound of cars and camera trucks crunching down our gravel driveway, doors closing, metal cases being opened, stage whispers of reporters instructing cameramen where to set up their equipment. Then always the same tiresome questions – the same wearisome answers.

If we slept late on a weekend morning reporters would often tire of waiting and knock on the door until we answered. Only Patty's love of people and unfailing sense of humour saved us. She would offer the cameramen coffee, kid me, break the tension. One morning as I was about to swing the front door open wide, stomp out in my nightclothes, and tell them all where to take their cameras, Patty began to giggle. "Smile, you're on candid camera." I laughed with her, got dressed, and gave the umpteenth interview.

Then John Dean began to talk to the prosecutors, and

the White House went through another convulsion. The "resignations" of Haldeman, Ehrlichman, and Attorney General Richard Kleindienst, and Nixon's half-hearted effort to placate the nation on April 30 did nothing to slow the onslaught.

To the outside world I preserved the tough-guy façade, but there were moments when my own weakness now surprised me. I often woke up in the middle of the night with a sick feeling in my stomach, my heart beating rapidly and wild fantasies racing through my mind – scenes of jail, cold cement floors, iron bars, and men in grey denim marching along steel walkways.

One day outside the Senate Office Building I was stopped and interviewed by a man from CBS News while the camera ground away. At the end, the reporter shook his head. "I don't know how much of this you guys can take. I told my wife last night one of you is going to crack or commit suicide before this is over. Keep your chin up, Mr. Colson." There were days – and nights – when those words would return with a dreadful chill.

In late April Shapiro and another partner, Judah Best, began meeting with the prosecutors. The U.S. Attorney's office for the District of Columbia labours under a hefty caseload of shoplifting, narcotics traffic, rapes, and murders. Probing into the affairs of the President and his men was as unfamiliar territory for Chief Assistant Earl Silbert and his two harassed aides as it was for us who were their targets.

Best and Shapiro escorted me for a face-to-face confrontation one evening. Silbert tried to compensate for his lean boyish appearance by scowling constantly, peering owlishly through huge horn-rimmed glasses. The grilling lasted four hours. Point by point I answered his questions. "You, of course, wrote the Canuck Letter which ruined Muskie's campaign," he accused me at one point.

"No, I didn't, Mr. Silbert. I had nothing to do with it."

The prosecutor, his brow now furrowing deeper, sat staring at me in disbelief. When the questioning was completed, Dave and Judd asked me to wait in an adjoining office while they talked to Silbert. It was a bare-walled room crammed with steel government desks, their tops piled high with newspapers, Watergate clippings, assorted writs, complaints, warrants, and mounds of court documents. Like a hundred other rooms in the massive courthouse, it housed the clerks and court officers who each day handle the cumbersome mechanics that keep the wheels of justice slowly grinding. As a lawyer I'd often been in the high-ceilinged, austerely elegant courtrooms, the warmly furnished judges' chambers, the handsome lawyers' libraries, lined with neat rows of books and portraits of judicial greats – where the eloquent arguments are made over abstract legal principles. For the first time I was inside the drab quarters of the army of marshals, clerks, and investigators who enforce the law – where the law touches lives. I was beginning to sense how it felt to be personally caught in the cumbersome machinery.

The minutes dragged by. I paced about, stared at the misty black night outside, thought of Patty home alone and worried, flipped through the papers, then stared at the desks and saw in my mind the pathetic human problems which parade through this room every day.

Eventually Dave and Judd came out all smiles – the prosecutors believed me. But the trapped sensation I had felt in that room persisted for days, even after I was officially notified that I was not a target of Silbert's grand jury but would be a government witness.

It was an important night. I now had Mr. Arther's grey box and three Washington prosecutors on my side. But it was not to last. The appointment of Harvard Professor Archibald Cox as Special Prosecutor changed everything. Cox, a long time friend of the Kennedy family, immediately suspended the original prosecutors.

In their first meeting Silbert presented to Cox a detailed eighty-page memorandum on the status of the investigation. Among other things, it exonerated me. Cox skimmed through it, listening attentively to the young lawyer's briefing. When Silbert finished, I was told later that the thoughtful grey-haired professor, peering over his glasses, inquired, "Is that all?" Silbert nodded it was. "But where's Colson?" he asked.

Then in his first press conference Cox announced that a

more exhaustive investigation was necessary into the role
of Charles Colson. I was back on the griddle.

Patty and I were in New York during the first weekend
in June attending the wedding of Charlie Morin's son when
a call came from the President. "Well, boy, how are you
holding on?" It sounded like the old Nixon, firm, confident,
deep, resonant tones in his voice, reassuring. "I hear you are
considering some TV interviews. You'd be tremendous – no
one any better. Just be careful. Don't get caught in the line
of fire yourself."

I knew he was coaxing me on even as he spoke. Yet I felt
a sudden surge of excitement – back in the fight. The President
needs me.

"Howard Smith wants me to do a half-hour special," I
told him. "I'll really give it to Dean." I was sitting on the
hotel bed Indian-style, with Patty watching, her face troubled
as her warrior suited up for battle. I was positively obsequious,
so thrilled was I that Nixon had called and needed my help.

"Chuck, you are still serving the Presidency," he continued. "Bring the truth out. Dean is lying. I am innocent.
These are terrible things he is saying. You know that."

"Yes, sir," I replied. We talked for forty minutes. He was
preparing me for combat and I was dutifully rehearsing my
lines. It would be like the old days, the days of glory, fighting
for a cause, believing in something. "Hail to the Chief" might
well have been playing in the background. That's what had
been wrong these past months. I needed a cause and Nixon
was my cause. There was the appeal to pride, too. I could
defend the President. I would turn the tide.

For weeks I gave it everything I had. ABC ran a special
half-hour broadcast on June 5. "I know the President of the
United States was not involved in the Watergate," I affirmed
as Smith nodded benignly. "I know the President of the
United States was not involved in the Watergate cover-up."
I was as emphatic in tone as I was in my heart; after all,
he had told me so.

The President called to tell me that Julie had watched the
Smith show and it was "the best job she'd ever seen. Keep it
up," he added. Nixon would never – even to me – admit

to watching television, but Manola later told me he'd wheeled a television set into Nixon's office so the President could view this one. Nixon's encouragement spurred me on.

The interviews continued through June. A full hour on CBS morning news – more ringing, unqualified defences of Richard Nixon, coupled with increasingly vigorous attacks on his chief accuser, John Dean. Spot interviews before the camera in my front yard, on the steps of my office building; lengthy newspaper interviews. At least twice, sometimes three times a week, I was on national network programmes. Meanwhile Shapiro kept calling the Ervin Committee demanding – to no avail – that I be allowed to appear.

Then came a gruelling full-hour interview with NCB's crack Watergate reporter, Carl Stern, on the "To-day" show as I continued the assault on Dean and the stout defence of Nixon. On "Face the Nation" I said more prophetically than I knew, "What happens to Charles Colson or Bob Haldeman or John Ehrlichman or John Mitchell or any of the others who served the President, is really very secondary. There is a fundamental question that is before the American people, and that is, was the President involved or wasn't he? I think it's imperative that the American people know immediately the truth about the President of the United States." I was *the* Nixon defender.

Meanwhile, John Dean stepped up the attack, five days of testimony carried live by all three networks and watched by eighty million Americans. Dean's drumbeat was precise, almost mechanically so. His emotionless monotone ground away, ticking off dates of key meetings – March 13, March 21 – and accusing Nixon of being in the cover-up of Watergate from the beginning, of ordering the truth withheld. Specific charges which demanded specific answers.

But Nixon remained in silent seclusion, succumbing to pneumonia, the first illness of his Presidency, and thoughts of resignation which he discussed with me in a late-night phone conversation in July. It seemed he would not defend, he could not resign. Quitting was the act of ultimate dishonour in Nixon's book. There was another factor known only to a few of us – a local Baltimore prosecutor, Mr. Nixon, my partners, and me. At the President's request we were handling a "small" legal matter for the Vice-President. Spiro Agnew was being threatened with criminal charges and might not be around much longer to succeed to the Presidency. My mind grappled with the enormity of the crisis – a President and Vice-President crippled. But the thoughts were so horrendous I quickly blocked them out.

Though convinced of Nixon's innocence, I was forced to admit to myself that I had not been present at any of the meetings Dean testified about. The doubts were fleeting ones, however. Even if Dean *were* telling the truth and Nixon were lying (inconceivable though that was), did it really matter all that much? Not really. Nixon was the President and it had always been my duty to defend him. That's what being a White House aide is all about – loyalty is the one imperative. Presidents couldn't survive without loyal aides – and I'd been blindly so all along. There the gospel began, there it ended – with one simple and unchallenged message. Dean had broken the commandment; I was still living with it.

The possibility of misleading Smith, Stern, and millions of Americans (as events of the next year proved that I did, unwittingly or not) never crossed my mind. The immorality of that was in time to burden me with a sense of guilt and shame far greater than any of the assorted misdeeds of which I was accused while in the President's service.

As the President's chief defender, the opposition aimed their guns at me. Charges, real and imagined, were making daily headlines. June 9, *Washington Post*: COLSON SAID TO URGE BREAK-IN, ARSON – June 12, *Post*: COLSON ORDERED TO TESTIFY ON SEC – June 13, 14, *Washington Star*: COLSON PARTNER REGRETS MEMO – June 15, *Post*: COLSON SAYS HE ORDERED HUNT TRIP – June 15, *Times*: COLSON SAYS HE PUT HUNT ON I.T.T JOB – June 21, *Post*: HUNT SAYS COLSON ORDERED BREAK-IN OF BREMNER HOME – June 30, *Times*: COLSON CONFIRMS BACKING KENNEDY INQUIRY BUT DENIES KNOWING OF HUNT'S CIA AID.

In July the Ervin Committee's televised hearings reached their crescendo. On Monday, July 16, Washington was buzzing with rumours of a bombshell to explode during the hearings that day. Dave Shapiro and I were huddled before the television set when Alex Butterfield, Haldeman's deputy, made the startling admission – all the President's conversations – in both meetings and on the telephone – had been secretly tape-recorded since 1971. The existence of the taping system was known only to Nixon, Haldeman, and several of Bob's aides.

Shapiro turned to me, scowling suspiciously.

"I didn't know it," I muttered, the colour draining from my face.

Dave's eyes were filled with disbelief at first, then sympathy. "Some friend you've got," he snorted.

Shock gave way to hurt. I could hardly believe the President would have hidden from me the existence of a taping system. Then I remembered occasions when I should have been suspicious: the time at Camp David when he walked from his office to the corridor to whisper to me sensitive information about another staff member; then once during a telephone conversation with the President there had been a clicking sound, probably the changing of tape reels. I had been so naive and blindly trusting.

Then hurt turned to sudden relief. The tapes will prove my non-involvement in Watergate! The tapes will show that I'm right and Dean is lying! My euphoria was short-lived. When I visited the White House the next day, the worried expressions indicated more and greater troubles were ahead. The tapes would be the subject of a new controversy. All the while, the President's credibility was going down every day.

Now Watergate's hateful venom was rushing through the veins of Washington. There was a pervasive fear, a sense of impending doom, an atmosphere of recrimination reminiscent of McCarthy days. Usually-smiling secretaries were harried and irritable. White House staffers were worried and fearful. Tempers quickly flared even among friends who could normally discuss their differing views on controversial issues with civility. The press reporting was harsh, attacks personal and bitter, political rhetoric increasingly shrill. As the debate became more rancorous, thoughts of violence were spawned in a few warped minds. The FBI was called in to investigate three bomb threats against my home and car which followed TV appearances.

The workings of government were becoming paralysed; senior policymakers were without direction; option papers went to the White House, but no decisions were returned. There were few in Washington not absorbed in the drama being played out in the Senate Caucus Room; TV sets were on all day in many government offices.

Late one afternoon Holly summoned me to the TV in our law firm's reception room. The scene, as every day, was the Senate Caucus Room. The cameras were trained on Connecticut Senator Lowell Weicker, junior Republican member of the Ervin Committee. "Efforts are being made to pressure this committee," he charged furiously, and then proceeded to read verbatim the text of criminal statutes that he told his national TV-viewing audience I *had violated* by planting stories about him in the press. The senator's face was flushed with anger and the students packed in the Caucus Room to watch Nixon's men be skewered one by one burst into thunderous applause at the end of Weicker's ten-minute-long harangue.

"What is he talking about?" Shapiro was ashen-faced.

"I don't know," I stammered. "Weicker is a beer-drinking buddy and neighbour of John Dean's. I've never met Weicker, but from all I know he's a reasonable fellow." I recalled an interview I had with a *Star* reporter a week earlier. Weicker's name came up but nothing had been said to hurt him.

"Come on, Dave, only one thing to do. We'll call him, explain the misunderstanding, and I'm sure he'll retract this."

The senator, however, would not take the call, insisting through his secretary that I appear in his office at 8 a.m. the next day. I knew the instant that Dave and I walked through the senator's door that trouble was ahead. There were five men in the large office, seated on both sides of the senator's desk. Weicker is a big man, 6'4" and 250 pounds, and he looked even angrier than he had on television, leaning forward across his desk on his elbows, fists pressed into his cheeks.

"Sit down, Mr. Colson," he said, barely rising enough to shake my outstretched hand.

I began with as cheery a voice as I could muster that early in the day. "Senator, I appreciate your seeing me. I think there has been some mistake. I'm not the fellow who tried to stir up stories about you in the press." Already that morning the newspapers had reported that the "smear" Weicker accused me of was attempted through another former Nixon aide.

The senator brushed this off and tore into me about other White House actions. We had an exchange of words that increased in its intensity. Finally, leaning across his desk, he shouted, "You guys in the White House make me sick. I don't know you – but I do know what you stand for, Mr. Colson, and we live in two different worlds. I deal in hard-nosed politics; you deal in ——————. You make me so mad I'd like to break your —————— nose."

With that he came around the desk and stood not six inches away, like a baseball manager trying to provoke a fight with an umpire. "You make me sick," he roared. "Get your ————— out of my office." Hastily I followed Dave out the door.

Shapiro and I headed for the cafeteria in the Senate Office Building. Dave spilled his first cup of coffee, stuck his finger in the second. The sight of Shapiro unstrung by the encounter cheered me up momentarily. But within hours someone in Weicker's office distributed to the press a verbatim transcript of our meeting and that weekend produced a fresh torrent of devastating headlines and articles.

In the whole sordid Watergate struggle, the Weicker episode for me was the most unpleasant; being falsely accused before millions on national TV, then coming almost to blows with a United States senator. I was used to playing as rough as the next guy, but Watergate was creating a madness I had never witnessed in twenty years in Washington, reducing political morality to the level of bayonet warfare. I cancelled the balance of my scheduled television shows. The feeling of emptiness was back as well, the questions about myself, my purpose, what my life was all about. The doubts which had invaded my consciousness in February hung over me like shroud.

The meeting in March with Phillips, meanwhile, had remained vivid in my memory. His warmth, his kindness, the serenity of his face, the startling words, "I have accepted

Jesus Christ and committed my life." I hadn't understood them, but they had a ring of simple, shameless sincerity. Tom represented everything Watergate and Washington were not: decency, openness, truth. I thought often of Tom's words during this stormy time; even more often I recalled the expression on his face, something radiant, peaceful, and very real. I envied it, whatever it was.

When my efforts to appear before the Ervin Committee were rebuffed again and the committee recessed on August 7, Patty and I decided to get away for a week on the Maine coast we loved so much. It would enable us to make a stop en route to visit my parents in Dover, just outside of Boston. Mom and Dad, now both in their seventies, were bewildered by all that was happening in Washington. Our visit might ease their apprehensions.

At the time I was not sure why I called Tom Phillips to seek another get-together while I was in Boston, but he welcomed the call. We agreed to meet Sunday night, August 12, at his home. I was surprised at how much I looked forward to seeing him again.

8

An Unforgettable Night

It was eight p.m., a grey overcast evening, when I turned off the country road connecting two of Boston's most affluent suburbs, Wellesley and Weston. The towering gentle pines brought sudden darkness and quiet to the narrow macadam street. Another turn a few hundred yards later brought me into a long driveway leading to the Phillipses' big white clapboard Colonial home. As I parked the car I felt a touch of guilt at not telling Patty the truth when I had left her alone with my mother and dad in nearby Dover.

"Just business, honey," had been my explanation. Patty was used to my working at odd times, even on this Sunday night at the start of a week's vacation.

The Phillipses' home is long and rambling. I made the mistake of going to the door nearest the driveway, which turned out to be the entrance to the kitchen. It didn't bother Gert Phillips, a tall smiling woman who greeted me like a long-lost relative even though we had never met before. "Come in. I'm just cleaning up after supper."

Supper. Such an unpretentious New England word. Gert escorted me into a large modern kitchen. "I'll call Tom," she said. "He's playing tennis with the children."

Tom arrived a minute later along with son Tommy, sixteen, and daughter Debby, nineteen, two tanned, handsome young people. Gert fixed us all iced tea while Tom mopped himself dry with a towel. If Gert was aware of the importance of her husband's position as president of the state's biggest company, she certainly did not show it. In fact, she reminded me of a favourite aunt we used to visit in the country when I was

118

a boy, who always wore an apron, smelled of freshly made bread and cookies, and had the gift of making everyone feel at home in her kitchen.

"You men have things to talk about and I've got work to do," Gert said as she handed us tall glasses of iced tea. Tom, towel draped around his neck, led me through the comfortably furnished dining and living rooms to a screened-in porch at the far end of the house. It was an unusually hot night for New England, the humidity like a heavy blanket wrapped around me. At Tom's insistence, first the dark grey business-suit jacket, then my tie came off. He pulled a wrought-iron ottoman close to the comfortable outdoor settee I sat on.

"Tell me, Chuck," he began, "are you okay?" It was the same question he had asked in March.

As the President's confidant and so-called big-shot Washington lawyer I was still keeping my guard up. "I'm not doing too badly, I guess. All of this Watergate business, all the accusations – I suppose it's wearing me down some. But I'd rather talk about you, Tom. You've changed and I'd like to know what happened."

Tom drank from his glass and sat back reflectively. Briefly he reviewed his past, the rapid rise to power at Raytheon: executive vice-president at thirty-seven, president when he was only forty. He had done it with hard work, day and night, non-stop.

"The success came all right, but something was missing," he mused. "I felt a terrible emptiness. Sometimes I would get up in the middle of the night and pace the floor of my bedroom or stare out into the darkness for hours at a time."

"I don't understand it," I interrupted. "I knew you in those days Tom. You were a straight arrow, a good family life, successful, everything in fact going your way."

"All that may be true, Chuck, but my life wasn't complete. I would go to the office each day and do my job, striving all the time to make the company succeed, but there was a big hole in my life. I began to read the Scriptures, looking for answers. Something made me realise I needed a personal relationship with God, forced me to search."

A prickly feeling ran down my spine. Maybe what I had

gone through in the past several months wasn't so unusual after all – except I had not sought spiritual answers. I had not even been aware that finding a personal relationship with God was possible. I pressed him to explain the apparent contradiction between the emptiness inside while seeming to enjoy the affluent life.

"It may be hard to understand," Tom chuckled. "But I didn't seem to have anything that mattered. It was all on the surface. All the material things in life are meaningless if a man hasn't discovered what's underneath them."

We were both silent for a while as I groped for understanding. Outside, the first fireflies punctuated the mauve dusk. Tom got up and switched on two small lamps on end tables in the corners of the porch.

"One night I was in New York on business and noticed that Billy Graham was having a Crusade in Madison Square Garden," Tom continued. "I went – curious, I guess – hoping maybe I'd find some answers. What Graham said that night put it all into place for me. I saw what was missing, the personal relationship with Jesus Christ, the fact that I hadn't ever asked Him into my life, hadn't turned my life over to Him. So I did it – that very night at the Crusade."

Tom's tall, gangling frame leaned towards me, silhouetted by the yellow light behind him. Though his face was shaded, I could see his eyes begin to glisten and his voice became softer. "I asked Christ to come into my life and I could feel His presence with me, His peace within me. I could sense His Spirit there with me. Then I went out for a walk alone on the streets of New York. I never liked New York before, but this night it was beautiful. I walked for blocks and blocks, I guess. Everything seemed different to me. It was raining softly and the city lights created a golden glow. Something had happened to me and I knew it."

"That's what you mean by accepting Christ – you just ask?" I was more puzzled than ever.

"That's it, as simple as that," Tom replied. "Of course, you have to want Jesus in your life, really want Him. That's the way it starts. And let me tell you, things then begin to change. Since then I have found a satisfaction and a joy about living that I simply never knew was possible."

To me Jesus had always been an historical figure, but Tom explained that you could hardly invite Him into your life if you didn't believe that He is alive today and that His Spirit is a part of to-day's scene. I was moved by Tom's story even though I couldn't imagine how such a miraculous change could take place in such a simple way. Yet the excitement in Tom's voice as he described his experience was convincing and Tom was indeed different. More alive.

Then Tom turned the conversation again to my plight. I described some of the agonies of Watergate, the pressures I was under, how unfairly I thought the press was treating me. I was being defensive and when I ran out of explanations, Tom spoke gently but firmly.

"You know that I supported Nixon in this past election, but you guys made a serious mistake. You would have won the election without any of the hanky-panky. Watergate and the dirty tricks were so unnecessary. And it was wrong, just plain wrong. You didn't have to do it."

Tom was leaning forward, elbows on his knees, his hands stretched forward almost as if he was trying to reach out for me. There was an urgent appeal in his eyes. "Don't you understand that?" he asked with such genuine feeling that I couldn't take offence.

"If only you had believed in the rightness of your cause, none of this would have been necessary. None of this would have happened. The problem with all of you, including you, Chuck – you simply had to go for the other guy's jugular. You had to try to destroy your enemies. You had to destroy them because you couldn't trust in yourselves."

The heat at that moment seemed unbearable as I wiped away drops of perspiration over my lip. The iced tea was soothing as I sipped it, although with Tom's points hitting home so painfully, I longed for a Scotch and soda. To myself I admitted that Tom was on target: the world of *us* against *them* as we saw it from our insulated White House enclave – the Nixon White House against the world. Insecure about our cause, our overkill approach was a way to play it safe. And yet ...

"Tom, one thing you don't understand. In politics it's dog-eat-dog; you simply can't survive otherwise. I've been in the political business for twenty years, including several campaigns right here in Massachusetts. I know how things are done. Politics is like war. If you don't keep the enemy on the defensive, you'll be on the defensive yourself. Tom, this man Nixon has been under constant attack all of his life. The only way he could make it was to fight back. Look at the criticism he took over Vietnam. Yet he was right. We never would have made it if we hadn't fought the way we did, hitting our critics, never letting them get the best of us. We didn't have any choice."

Even as I talked, the words sounded more and more empty to me. Tired old lines, I realised. I was describing the ways of the political world, all right, while suddenly wondering if there could be a better way.

Tom believed so, anyway. He was so gentle I couldn't resent what he said as he cut right through it all : "Chuck, I hate to say this, but you guys brought it on yourselves. If you had put your faith in God, and if your cause were just, He would have guided you. And His help would have been a thousand times more powerful than all your phoney ads and shady schemes put together."

With any other man the notion of relying on God would have seemed to me pure Pollyanna. Yet I had to be impressed with the way this man ran his company in the equally competitive world of business : ignoring his enemies, trying to follow God's ways. Since his conversion Raytheon had never done better, sales and profits soaring. Maybe there was something to it; anyway it's tough to argue with success.

"Chuck, I don't think you will understand what I'm saying about God until you are willing to face yourself honestly and squarely. This is the first step." Tom reached to the corner table and picked up a small paperback book. I read the title : *Mere Christianity*, by C. S. Lewis.

"I suggest you take this with you and read it while you are on vacation." Tom started to hand it to me, then paused. "Let me read you one chapter."

I leaned back, still on the defensive, my mind and emotions whirling.

There is one vice of which no man in the world is free; which everyone in the world loathes when he sees it in someone else; and of which hardly any people, except Christians, ever imagine that they are guilty themselves. I have heard people admit that they are bad-tempered, or that they cannot keep their heads about girls or drink, or even that they are cowards. I do not think I have ever heard anyone who was not a Christian accuse himself of this vice ... There is no fault ... which we are more unconscious of in ourselves. And the more we have it ourselves, the more we dislike it in others.

The vice I am talking of is Pride or Self-Conceit .... Pride leads to every other vice: it is the complete anti-God state of mind.

As he read, I could feel a flush coming into my face and a curious burning sensation that made the night seem even warmer. Lewis's words seemed to pound straight at me.

... it is Pride which has been the chief cause of misery in every nation and every family since the world began. Other vices may sometimes bring people together: you may find good fellowship and jokes and friendliness among drunken people or unchaste people. But Pride always means enmity – it *is* enmity. And not only enmity between man and man, but enmity to God.

In God you come up against something which is in every respect immeasurably superior to yourself. Unless you know God as that – and, therefore, know yourself as nothing in comparison – you do not know God at all. As long as you are proud you cannot know God. A proud man is always looking down on things and people: and, of course, as long as you are looking down, you cannot see something that is above you.

Suddenly I felt naked and unclean, my bravado defences gone. I was exposed, unprotected, for Lewis's words were describing me. As he continued, one passage in particular seemed to sum up what had happened to all of us at the White House:

> For Pride is spiritual cancer: it eats up the very possibility of love, or contentment, or even common sense.

Just as a man about to die is supposed to see flash before him, sequence by sequence, the high points of his life, so, as Tom's voice read on that August evening, key events in my life paraded before me as if projected on a screen. Things I hadn't thought about in years – my graduation speech at prep school – being "good enough" for the Marines – my first marriage, into the "right" family – sitting on the Jaycees' dais while civic leader after civic leader praised me as the outstanding young man of Boston – then to the White House – the clawing and straining for status and position – "Mr. Colson, the President is calling – Mr. Colson, the President wants to see you right away."

For some reason I thought of an incident after the 1972 election when a reporter, an old Nixon nemesis, came by my office and contritely asked me what he could do to get in the good graces of the White House. I suggested that he try "slashing his wrists." I meant it as a joke, of course, but also to make him squirm. It was the arrogance of the victor over an enemy brought to submission.

Now, sitting there on the dimly lit porch, my self-centred past was washing over me in waves. It was painful. Agony. Desperately I tried to defend myself. What about my sacrifices for government service, the giving up of a big income, putting my stocks into a blind trust? The truth, I saw in an instant, was that I'd wanted the position in the White House more than I'd wanted money. There was no sacrifice. And the more I had talked about my own sacrifices, the more I was really trying to build myself up in the eyes of others. I would eagerly have given up everything I'd ever earned to prove myself at the mountaintop of government. It was pride – Lewis's "great sin" – that had propelled me through life.

Tom finished the chapter on pride and shut the book. I mumbled something noncommittal to the effect that "I'll look forward to reading that." But Lewis's torpedo had hit me amidships. I think Phillips knew it as he stared into my eyes. That one chapter ripped through the protective armour in which I had unknowingly encased myself for forty-two years. Of course, I had not known God. *How could I?* I had been concerned with myself. *I* had done this and that, *I* had achieved, *I* had succeeded and I had given God none of the credit, never once thanking Him for any of His gifts to me. I had never thought of anything being "immeasurably superior" to myself, or if I had in fleeting moments thought about the infinite power of God, I had not related Him to my life. In those brief moments while Tom read, I saw myself as I never had before. And the picture was ugly.

"How about it, Chuck?" Tom's question jarred me out of my trance. I knew precisely what he meant. Was I ready to make the leap of faith as he had in New York, to "accept" Christ?

"Tom, you've shaken me up. I'll admit that. That chapter describes me. But I can't tell you I'm ready to make the kind of commitment you did. I've got to be certain. I've got to learn a lot more, be sure all my reservations are satisfied. I've got a lot of intellectual hang-ups to get past."

For a moment Tom looked disappointed, then he smiled. "I understand, I understand."

"You see," I continued, "I saw men turn to God in the Marine Corps; I did once myself. Then afterwards it's all forgotten and everything is back to normal. Foxhole religion is just a way of using God. How can I make a commitment now? My whole world is crashing down around me. How can I be sure I'm not just running for shelter and that when the crisis is over I'll forget it? I've got to answer all the intellectual arguments first and if I can do that, I'll be sure."

"I understand," Tom repeated quietly.

I was relieved he did, yet deep inside of me something wanted to tell Tom to press on. He was making so much sense, the first time anyone ever had in talking about God.

But Tom did not press on. He handed me his copy of *Mere Christianity*. "Once you've read this, you might want to read the Book of John in the Bible." I scribbled notes of the key passages he quoted. "Also there's a man in Washington you should meet," he continued, "name of Doug Coe. He gets people together for Christian fellowship – prayer breakfasts and things like that. I'll ask him to contact you."

Tom then reached for his Bible and read a few of his favourite psalms. The comforting words were like a cold soothing ointment. For the first time in my life, familiar verses I'd heard chanted lifelessly in church came alive. "Trust in the Lord," I remember Tom reading, and I wanted to, right that moment I wanted to – if only I knew how, if only I could be sure.

"Would you like to pray together, Chuck?" Tom asked, closing his Bible and putting it on the table beside him.

Startled, I emerged from my deep thoughts. "Sure – I guess I would – Fine." I'd never prayed with anyone before except when someone said grace before a meal. Tom bowed his head, folded his hands, and leaned forward on the edge of his seat. "Lord," he began, "we pray for Chuck and his family, that You might open his heart and show him the light and the way . . ."

As Tom prayed, something began to flow into me – a kind of energy. Then came a wave of emotion which nearly brought tears. I fought them back. It sounded as if Tom were speaking directly and personally to God, almost as if He were sitting beside us. The only prayers I'd ever heard were formal and stereotyped, sprinkled with *Thees* and *Thous*.

When he finished, there was a long silence. I knew he expected me to pray but I didn't know what to say and was too self-conscious to try. We walked to the kitchen together where Gert was still at the big table, reading. I thanked her and Tom for their hospitality.

"Come back, won't you?" she said. Her smile convinced me she meant it.

"Take care of yourself, Chuck, and let me know what you think of that book, will you?" With that, Tom put his hand on my shoulder and grinned. "I'll see you soon."

I didn't say much; I was afraid my voice would crack, but I had the strong feeling that I *would* see him soon. And I couldn't wait to read his little book.

Outside in the darkness, the iron grip I'd kept on my emotions began to relax. Tears welled up in my eyes as I groped in the darkness for the right key to start my car. Angrily I brushed them away and started the engine. "What kind of weakness is this?" I said to nobody.

The tears spilled over and suddenly I knew I had to go back into the house and pray with Tom. I turned off the motor, got out of the car. As I did, the kitchen light went out, then the light in the dining room. Through the hall window I saw Tom stand aside as Gert started up the stairs ahead of him. Now the hall was in darkness. It was too late. I stood for a moment staring at the darkened house, only one light burning now in an upstairs bedroom. Why hadn't I prayed when he gave me the chance? I wanted to so badly. Now I was alone, really alone.

As I drove out of Tom's driveway, the tears were flowing uncontrollably. There were no street lights, no moonlight. The car headlights were flooding illumination before my eyes, but I was crying so hard it was like trying to swim under water. I pulled to the side of the road not more than a hundred yards from the entrance to Tom's driveway, the tyres sinking into soft mounds of pine needles.

I remember hoping that Tom and Gert wouldn't hear my sobbing, the only sound other than the chirping of crickets that penetrated the still of the night. With my face cupped in my hands, head leaning forward against the wheel, I forgot about machismo, about pretences, about fears of being weak. And as I did, I began to experience a wonderful feeling of being released. Then came the strange sensation that water was not only running down my cheeks, but surging through my whole body as well, cleansing and cooling as it went. They weren't tears of sadness and remorse, nor of joy – but somehow, tears of relief.

And then I prayed my first real prayer. "God, I don't know how to find You, but I'm going to try! I'm not much the way I am now, but somehow I want to give myself to You." I didn't know how to say more, so I repeated over and over the words: *Take me.*

I had not "accepted" Christ – I still didn't know who He was. My mind told me it was important to find that out first, to be sure that I knew what I was doing, that I meant it and would stay with it. Only, that night, something inside me was urging me to surrender – to what or to whom I did not know.

I stayed there in the car, wet-eyed, praying, thinking, for perhaps half an hour, perhaps longer, alone in the quiet of the dark night. Yet for the first time in my life I was not alone at all.

9

Cottage by the Sea

Mother and Dad were up early the next morning to see Patty and me off on our Maine vacation trip. Dad's worry-filled eyes told me what was coming when he suggested the two of us walk alone behind their house.

"You're positive, son, that no one told you anything about the break-in before it happened" he asked. We had talked about Watergate Sunday afternoon, but his lawyer's mind was still probing.

"Absolutely, Pop. I've thought back to every conversation. Nothing."

Dad's steps were flagging as we walked up the gently sloping lawn. For the first time I realised how fast the years – seventy-three now – were overtaking him. Beneath his pure-white crew cut glistening in the morning sun were new furrows in his brow, deeper lines on his face.

"I read through all the Watergate material last night and I just don't see how you can be dragged in. You're sure you've told me everything?" he pressed one final time.

When I assured him I had, his warm grin returned. He and Mother hugged us and Patty and I backed our car out of their driveway and headed toward the Maine sea coast. Wearing a sweater, slacks, and an excited smile, Patty began chatting eagerly about lobsters, clams, and the scenes flashing by. It was our first time alone in months.

But I was too preoccupied to be good company. My thoughts were not on Watergate but on my visit with Tom Phillips the night before. I had expected to awaken feeling embarrassment for my uncontrolled outburst of emotion. Not so. The sense of freedom in my spirit was still there. Something important was happening, but what? Perhaps I'd find the answer in *Mere Christianity*.

What better place to search for answers than by the ocean. From boyhood when I used to walk the stony beach of Winthrop, Massachusetts, the sea had been important to me. Rejuvenation always came when I lost myself in the sea's vastness, feeling its power as the waves crashed in great sprays of foam on to moss-draped rocks.

When combined exhaustion and anxiety nearly paralysed me one day late in the 1960 Massachusetts election campaign, I left the campaign office and drove to a favourite spot in Gloucester. There on an overhanging cliff I felt renewed as I watched the raging seas smash against the rocks, then subside into a cluster of small eddies. I'd gone there later to be alone when I was searching for answers about my first marriage. Faced now with a major decision, the sea would again help me find the strength and clearness of mind I needed.

After a four-hour drive Patty and I arrived in Boothbay Harbour, a lovely old fishing village and sailing port 180 miles from Boston. The narrow streets of the village are lined with steep-roofed, grey-shingled houses nestled together. Cool breezes from the east fill the air with the briny odour of fish and sea peculiar to New England coastal towns. Old as it is, everything about Boothbay looks freshly scrubbed, even the native fishermen who walk through the streets in heavy slickers, high boots, caps shielding their leathery, wrinkled faces from the glare of the sun and sea.

Having made no reservation, we skirted the main part of town, driving along a winding coastal road looking for an out-of-the-way spot. We were twelve miles from town when Patty spotted a small inn at the end of a long, narrow point of land jutting straight out into the Atlantic. "Maybe no one will recognise us here," I agreed, weary of curiosity seekers, autograph collectors, Nixon partisans and adversaries who were always happy to tell me exactly what they thought, often at length and with passion.

Cautiously we drove on to a narrow dirt road atop a man-made causeway built over the sea ten feet below. The causeway connected what was once a small rocky island to the mainland. The innkeeper was a stony-faced young man, tall and gaunt, who gave us the quizzical once-over so typical of cautious Down Easters and then showed us the one cottage which surprisingly was available for the week. It suited us perfectly. One huge room and a great open deck were suspended over the rocks and sea below.

Patty began unpacking, gleeful over our discovery, and I returned to the office. As I signed the register and waited, the innkeeper conferred in a corner with one of his employees. He returned and looked at me curiously. "Colson, eh?"

"That's right."

"From McLean. That near Washington?" He looked suspiciously at the address I'd scribbled. My heart sank; Watergate was following us all the way to this craggy little spit of land.

"Friend here tells me you're famous." He wasn't smiling.

"No, not really."

"You been on TV?"

"Well, yes, a few times. This Watergate business, you know," I admitted. *What was the sense in trying to hide it?*

"Eyuh," followed by a pause and a stare. "Watergate still going on?" The word *eyuh* is generally spoken by Down Easters with a heavy nasal twang and means "Yes," "Maybe," "I don't know," "That's interesting," and scores of other interpretations.

"Yes, it's still going on."

"Well, I'll be – thought t'was over in June. My TV's been busted." With that, still unsmiling, he handed me my key.

I couldn't wait to tell Patty. Hallelujah! We had found a spot where the TV was out of order. And the sea, the beautiful green-blue ocean, was roaring in under our picture window." What a great time to relax," I told Patty. *What a great time to think about God,* I told myself.

That first night I unpacked Lewis's book and placed a yellow pad at my side to jot down key points, not unlike the way I prepared to argue a major case in court. In a moment of emotion the previous evening I had made a surrender of myself to something – or Someone. Now the habits of a lifetime rose in protest. All my training insisted that analysis precedes decision, that arguments be marshalled in two neat columns, pros and cons. I wondered if I could overcome my intellectual obstacles so as to believe in my mind what I had felt in my emotions.

On the top of the pad I wrote : Is there a God?

As I probed back in time, I remembered the night twenty years before when I stared into the vast darkness from the rail of the U.S.S. *Melette*, cruising off the coast of Guatemala. There was no possible explanation for how this whole magnificent universe, the glittering array of galaxies and stars, could remain in such perfect harmony without the direction of some awesome power which created it all in the first instance. That there is such a force greater than man seemed indisputable to me. And I had no trouble calling this force God.

Then I found myself remembering a curious shining moment seven years before. In the summer of 1966 I had bought a fourteen-foot sailboat for my two boys and hauled it to a friend's home on a lake in New Hampshire to teach them to sail. Christian, then ten, was so excited over having his own boat that even though a gentle summer rain was falling the day of our arrival, he was determined to try it out.

As the craft edged away from the dock, the only sound was the rippling of water under the hull and the flapping of the sail when puffs of wind fell from it. I was in the stern watching the tiller, Chris in the centre, dressed in an orange slicker, holding the sheet. As he realised that he was controlling the boat, the most marvellous look came over his cherubic face, the joy of new discovery in his eyes, the thrill of feeling the wind's power in his hands. I found myself in that one unforgettable moment quietly talking to God. I could even recall the precise words: "Thank You, God, for giving me this son, for giving us this one wonderful moment. Just looking now into this boy's eyes fulfils my life. Whatever happens in the future, even if I die tomorrow, my life is complete and full. Thank You."

Afterwards, I had been startled when I realised that I had spoken to God, since my mind did not assent to His existence as a Person. It had been a spontaneous expression of gratitude that simply bypassed the mind and took for granted what reason had never shown me. More – it assumed that personal communication with this unproven God was possible. Why else would I have spoken, unless deep down I felt that Someone, somewhere, was listening?

Perhaps, I thought, *it is on this intuitive, emotional level that C. S. Lewis approaches God*. I opened *Mere Christianity* and found myself instead face-to-face with an intellect so disciplined, so lucid, so relentlessly logical that I could only be grateful I had never faced him in a court of law. Soon I had covered two pages of yellow paper with *pros* to my query, "Is there a God?"

On the *con* side were listed the conventional doubts so prevalent in our materialistic, science-has-all-the-answers society – we can't see, hear, or feel God.

Or can we?

What happened to me on Tom Phillips's porch? What was the emotion I had felt? Love? Some unseen force had stirred inside me. And I had always felt that unseen forces were more powerful than visible ones.

A piston engine with 280 horsepower can move a precise number of pounds against the calculated resistance of friction, but not one pound more than known physical laws prescribe. The engine is made of hard steel, its existence evident to every sense. Yet love, which no one sees or touches, moves men and nations in limitless ways. Love caused one man to renounce a kingdom in my lifetime. Another kind of love causes a soldier to hurl his body over a grenade which has fallen into the midst of his buddies. Love has incomparably greater force than any engine of known horsepower.

I struggled on with this thought. A law is tangible in the sense that it is recorded somewhere on a piece of paper, but it exists only to the extent it causes men to do or not to do certain things. Its real force is then beyond the reach of that which we see or touch, made real by the extent people accept and believe.

As a lawyer I was impressed by Lewis's arguments about moral law, the existence of which he demonstrates is real, and which has been perceived with astonishing consistency in all times and places. It has not been man, I saw for the first time, that has perpetuated moral law; it has survived *despite* man's best attempts to defeat it. Its long existence therefore presupposes some other will behind it. Again, God.

I was back with Lewis, my yellow pads, and my questions early the next day. Patty was beginning to eye me a little strangely. Usually when we travelled to new places, I was active, restless, eager to see the sights; here I was sitting quietly engrossed in a book.

If there is a loving God, the automatic next question was, of course, "If He is good, why does He preside over such an evil world?" Again my legal training suggested a useful parallel. In the beginning, God gave to mankind dominion over the earth He created (*see* Genesis 1 : 26–30). In other words, He made us, in lawyers' parlance, His agents.

The theory of *agency* in the law suggests a freedom of action, something beyond being a servant or mechanical robot. The agent is given the power to act within the *scope*, lawyers say, of authority – within certain set limits. The limits of this authority – the delegation as we call it in the law – God also laid out in Scripture.

But at the same time, He gave us free will. That is the point, of course; give someone less and he is no agent; the giver ends up doing it all himself. With a free will we can defy those limits and His instructions to us as readily as any agent exceeds the scope of his authority in civil law. And that happens each day; there are hundreds of law suits going on to prove it. As with the failure of agency in the law, so man often fails in discharging our Creator's agency.

History supports this view. Down through the years it has been man's abuse of God's authority, his malice toward his fellow men, which has created the preponderance of human grief. And probably we will go right on abusing it.

To understand this I came back to where Tom Phillips started: pride and ego. As Lewis put it, "The moment you have a self at all, there is a possibility of putting yourself first – wanting to be the centre – wanting to be God ..." How devastatingly I now saw that in my own life.

It was during this second day that I was emboldened to begin to tell Patty of the journey I'd begun. "You believe in God, don't you, honey?" I asked. We were both sitting on the deck reading. Patty had inquired once about my little green and white paperback, which I explained merely as a book Tom Phillips had given me.

"You know I do," she answered, with a hint of suspicion in her eyes – the latent, never spoken concern, perhaps, that some day I'd try to talk her out of her Roman Catholicism.

"But have you ever really thought about it – deeply, I mean? Like who is God and how does He watch over each of us and why did He create us, things like that?"

Patty's look of suspicion changed into one of pure bafflement. "What's in that book you're reading?"

In the ten years we'd been married, I realised, we'd never discussed God; religion once in a while, what Patty felt about confession and Communion, the significance of the Mass. But these are procedural points. We'd never gone right to the substance, the living God, the faith down deep inside either one of us. We had done so much together but never touched on the essence of life itself. How much on the surface are even the closest of human relationships!

"I guess I'm looking for something," I continued. "I'm trying to find out what's real and what isn't – who we are – who I am in relation to God." Then I told her something about my evening with Tom Phillips – not the tears, but the dismal self-discovery, all quite clinically, not wanting to admit how much my emotions had been touched. She looked dubious, but was fascinated by the story.

"You see, I'm looking for answers and this little book is terrific."

"Maybe you should talk to a priest," Patty suggested, now wanting (I could see it in the compassion in her eyes) to help me, knowing the struggle was genuine, no flip remark or banter to pass the time. Patty is the gentlest, most caring person I've ever known, taking others' problems as her own, feeling the full weight of every burden I ever had to bear. She hadn't quite expected this one – a search for God – but I sensed she was ready to share it with me.

I checked myself from voicing the critical statement, "No priest or minister these forty years has ever explained any of this to me." Who was I to point an accusing finger? I had never been looking, probably never really listening. Now for the first time Lewis's explanation and Phillips's example were opening a whole new world.

We talked into the night, while the bell buoy clanged, guiding the lobstermen through the early evening fog, and the waves slapped against the rocks beneath us. It was a relief to have Patty know of my search to find new peace within myself, and to acquire an antidote for the disease inside which had been sucking life out of me, vampire-like, for eight long months ever since election night the year before. We ended by deciding to get out the family Bible when we returned home and begin reading it.

It was during the next morning, as I went on reading, underlining, making notes, that another important question was resolved for me. If God is listening to my prayers, how can He hear those being uttered at the same time by many millions of others?

That is a question which boggles the finite human mind. The difficulty is the same as when we try to understand where the universe ends, and if it does, what is beyond. Lewis shed light on this in a chapter entitled "Time and Beyond Time": "God [is] beyond all space and time." And there is now a respectable body of scientific knowledge to establish that time is indeed relative, not the absolute measure we know.

Since the Creator of an infinite universe has no limitations in terms of hours or days, the fact that He could listen to four billion prayers at once was suddenly not the dazzling feat I with my limited mind had made it out to be. It was hard for me to accept this only so long as I struggled with my finite mind to understand a concept which is beyond finite limits. I can't explain it any better than I can explain what is beyond the stars, but simply knowing that man can't, provides an important answer.

All of this added to my conviction that there is a loving, infinite God, but left unanswered the question of what Tom really meant by the words *accept Christ*. How does Jesus Christ figure into all this? Hindus believe in God and that He can be worshipped in almost any way anyone pleases. All my analysing so far had only gotten me to Hinduism.

The central thesis of Lewis's book, and the essence of Christianity, is summed up in one mind-boggling sentence:

Jesus Christ is God (see John 10 : 30). Not just part of God, or just sent by God, or just related to God. *He was* (and therefore, of course, *is*) God.

The more I grappled with those words, the more they began to explode before my eyes, blowing into smithereens a lot of comfortable old notions I had floated through life with, without thinking much about them. Lewis put it so bluntly that you can't slough it off : for Christ to have talked as He talked, lived as He lived, died as He died, He was either God or a raving lunatic.

There was my choice, as simple, stark, and frightening as that, no fine shadings, no gradations, no compromises. No one had ever thrust this truth at me in such a direct and unsettling way. I'd been content to think of Christ as an inspired prophet and teacher who walked the sands of the Holy Land 2,000 years ago – several cuts above other men of His time or, for that matter, any time. But if one thinks of Christ as no more than that, I reasoned, then Christianity is a simple palliative, like taking a sugar-coated placebo once a week on Sunday morning.

On this sunny morning on the Maine coast with fresh breezes picking up off the ocean, it was hard for me to grasp the enormity of this point – that Christ is the living God who promises us a day-to-day living relationship with Him and a personal one at that.

Each of the steps I'd laboured through was an essential building block to get to this point, but once I had, the others seemed almost irrelevant. Lewis's question was the heart of the matter. The words – both exciting and disturbing – pounded at me : Jesus Christ – lunatic or God ?

Even atheists concede that Christ's coming changed the course of history. The year in which we live, for example, is based upon the date of His birth. He was a man without power in any worldly sense, no money, no armies, no weapons, and yet His coming altered the political alignments of nations. Millions upon millions of men have followed His promises and words. No work of literature has even begun to approach the endurance of the Scriptures which record Christ's life and have the same vitality to-day as they did nearly two thousand years ago. Magnificent churches, in which are invested centuries of labour and treasure, have been built as altars to Him. Could all this be the result of a lunatic's work, or even the result of one man's work? – The weight of evidence became more overwhelming to me the more I thought of it.

My legal training led me to another parallel. Our system of law is founded on the principle of *stare decisis*, that is, a court decision stands as a precedent with the same force of law as if it had one time been enacted or decreed; the whole system is built on precedents and presumptions which rest upon the foundation of earlier decisions. It is the key to giving stability to the law, a validation of history.

The most important decision of the Supreme Court, for example, studied intensively in law school, is *Marbury* v. *Madison*. Nowhere in the Constitution did the founding fathers give the Supreme Court the right to pass on the constitutionality of Acts of Congress. The Court acquired that power years later as a result of this famous case.

Today no one questions the Court's power of judicial review which it has exercised with dramatic effect thousands of times since. Even a neophyte law student would prefer to argue the validity of the case for *Marbury* v. *Madison*. There isn't much going for him with a contrary position, because of the way in which the doctrine has become so well established by its long history of acceptance.

So why should I worry as I once did about being accused of mindlessly following the pack by accepting Christ? And why struggle so hard with concepts about God when I wouldn't question legal principles which have far less historic validity than the one we have laid before our eyes in the life and impact of the Carpenter of Nazareth?

Once faced with the staggering proposition that He is God, I was cornered, all avenues of retreat blocked, no falling back to that comfortable middle ground about Jesus being a great moral teacher. If He is not God, He is nothing, least of all a great moral teacher. For what He taught includes the assertion that He is indeed God. And if He is not, that one statement alone would have to qualify as the most monstrous lie of all time – stripping Him at once of any possible moral platform.

I could not, I saw, take Him on a slightly lower plateau because it is easier to do so, less troublesome to my intellect, less demanding of my faith, less challenging to my life. That would be substituting my mind for His, using Christianity where it helped to buttress my *own* notions, ignoring it where it didn't.

I realised suddenly that there is less heresy in rejecting Him altogether, dismissing Him as a raving lunatic, to use Lewis's word, than to remake Him into something He wasn't (and isn't). Jesus said take it, all or nothing. If I was to believe in God at all, I had to take Him as He reveals Himself, not as I might wish Him to be.

Patty and I decided to spend Thursday evening in Boothbay Harbour. It was band-concert night on the steps of the town library, a venerable and colourful institution of the New England summer. The music might have sounded to Arthur Fiedler like someone scratching a fingernail across a blackboard, but we loved every discordant note blaring forth with mighty gusto.

The band came in all sizes and shapes – from a tot with a trumpet who couldn't have been more than twelve, to a sweet-faced teenage girl in pigtails on the drums, her face pockmarked with acne, wearing a straight, flowered dress which mostly covered her knobbly knees, to a man of eighty or more at the bass trombone, pure-white hair, a wrinkled, unsmiling face, and denim coveralls hanging from his rounded shoulders. Fifteen band members in all were lined along the wide wooden steps of the white clapboard building, the panes of its tall windows etched with century old swirls and bubbles shimmering in the glow of two big floodlights.

It was a Norman Rockwell *Saturday Evening Post* cover come to life, a priceless piece of rich Americana, unspoiled and untouched by what modern society calls progress. There were tourists sprawled on the green lawn, kids with spun candy on a stick, and a large number of townsfolk for whom the concert is the major outing of the week.

The strains of "As the Saints Go Marching In" mixed with the fresh smell of salt in the night air. As I surveyed the faces in the crowd, something about them looked altogether different. Each one, including the kids with sticky sugar on their cheeks, looked like an individual, a separate human being, a child of God. Always before I'd seen crowds as blurs, a mass of humanity blending into an indistinct mosaic. Perhaps this new perception came from another Lewis passage, one that sent many of my cherished political ideals scattering like tenpins hit by a perfect strike:

And immortality makes this other difference, which, by the by, had a connection with the difference between totalitarianism and democracy. If individuals live only seventy years, then a state, or a nation, or a civilisation, which may last for a thousand years, is more important than an individual. But if Christianity is true, then the individual is not only more important but incomparably more important, for he is everlasting and the life of a state or a civilisation, compared with his, is only a moment.

The lowliest individual was more important than a state or nation! I had to take a lot of deep breaths after that one. Yet I had always thought of myself as a Jeffersonian conservative, one who believed fervently that the state exists only to serve the individual, created and maintained only with the individual's consent. What had happened to me was obvious; everyone who spends time in government becomes to some degree a "statist," dedicated to preserving the institutions of the state, often at all costs. Thus the paramount place of the individual in the scheme of things is gradually, unknowingly subordinated. Law-and-order legislation, for example, is aimed at maintaining the stability of the state – even if a few individuals have their rights trampled on in the process. Then, hard as it was to stomach, I had to admit that Dr. Daniel Ellsberg's rights were more important than preserving state secrets.

The political convictions I had developed from reading Locke and Jefferson had proved pliable guidelines, subject to tempering adjustments as "governmental crises" required, bending in the winds of the moment. But if Christ is real, if that fundemental decision is once made, then I am face-to-face with the very core of life itself, and with that I cannot

tinker. Was Christ to change my view of life – and my
neighbour, enemy, friend, and stranger alike – so drastically?
My mind was whirling. Maybe it was the music, the nostalgia
of the moment, the escape from the rest of the world one
finds in Boothbay Harbour, Maine. Yet deep down I knew
forces were at work which were demanding that I rethink
every facet of my life.

Back at the inn doubts about my motives continued to
nag at me. Was I seeking a safe port in the storm, a temporary
hiding place? Was that what happened in Tom Phillips's
driveway? Despite the arrow to the heart and my awakening on the Maine coast to the incredible realisation about
Jesus Christ, was I somehow looking to religion as a last-
gasp effort to save myself as everything else in my world was
crashing down about me?

Did I hope that God would keep my world intact? Legitimate doubts, I suppose. Certainly many people would accuse
me of copping out in time of trouble. But could I make a
decision based on how the world might judge it?

No, I knew the time had come for me: I could not sidestep
the central question Lewis (or God) had placed squarely
before me. Was I to accept without reservations Jesus Christ
as Lord of my life? It was like a gate before me. There was
no way to walk round it. I would step through, or I would
remain outside. A "maybe" or "I need more time" was
kidding myself.

And as something pressed that question home, less and
less was I troubled by the curious phrase "accept Jesus
Christ." It had sounded at first both pious and mystical,
language of the zealot, maybe black magic stuff. But "to
accept" means no more than "to believe." Did I believe what
Jesus said? If I did, if I took it on faith or reason or both,
then I accepted. Not mystical or weird at all, and with no in-
between ground left. Either I would believe or I would not –
and believe it all or none of it.

The search that began that week on the coast of Maine,
as I pondered it, was not quite as important as I had thought.
It simply returned me to where I had been when I asked
God to "take me" in that moment of surrender on the little

country road in front of the Phillips's home. What I studied so intently all week opened a little wider the new world into which I had already taken my first halting, shaky steps. One week of study on the Maine coast would hardly qualify, even in the jet age, as much of an odyssey, but I felt as if I'd been on a journey of thousands of miles.

And so early that Friday morning, while I sat alone staring at the sea I love, words I had not been certain I could understand or say fell naturally from my lips: "Lord Jesus, I believe You. I accept You. Please come into my life. I commit it to You."

With these few words that morning, while the briny sea churned, came a sureness of mind that matched the depth of feeling in my heart. There came something more: strength and serenity, a wonderful new assurance about life, a fresh perception of myself and the world around me. In the process, I felt old fears, tensions, and animosities draining away. I was coming alive to things I'd never seen before; as if God was filling the barren void I'd known for so many months, filling it to its brim with a whole new kind of awareness.

I wrote Tom Phillips, telling him of the step I had taken, of my gratitude for his loving concern, and asked his prayers for the long and difficult journey I sensed lay ahead.

I could not possibly in my wildest dreams have imagined what it would involve. How fortunate it is that God does not allow us to see into the future.

10

Washington Revisited

At 7:30 a.m. I heard the crunch of tyres on gravel outside our home in McLean. As I opened the front door to greet our law firm's chauffeur, the smell of the Maine sea coast seemed far away. It was Monday morning and time to go to work.

Stocton Von Black flashed me a big grin. "Good morning, Mr. Colson. Good to have you back." Stocton was always cheerful but I had never before noticed such warmth and kindness in his eyes. In my preoccupation I had usually managed only a "grumph" in reply.

As he drove into the city, I found myself asking about his life and family. I also noticed how green and beautiful were the trees and shubs lining the sides of the George Washington Parkway, how clear and blue the sky. The outline of the city was suddenly before us as we rounded the great curve following the Potomac River: the white marble and glass of the buildings glistening in the sun, with the majestic Capitol Dome perched atop a knoll as a backdrop.

"That's quite a sight, isn't it, Stocton?" I remarked and then noticed the puzzled expression on the chauffeur's face as he glanced back at me through the rear-view mirror. It was precisely the same view that had been there every morning all the months Stocton drove for me.

When the traffic closed in, bumper to bumper, I managed to get all the way through the *Washington Post* without a single profane outburst. If enjoying the green trees and the skyline was unusual for me, not crumpling the *Post* in an angrily clenched fist at least once was really a change. Even the people in the lobby of my office building seemed friendly,

143

probably because I really looked at them for the first time.
One can almost always spot a VIP in this city of power and
protocol – the determined stride and the air of studied concern as he passes unseeing through the crowd signal the importance of the problems he shoulders.

Ordinarily I would have concluded that the week of vacation had rested me, provided renewed energy and a better
outlook, but I knew, in fact, that it was much more than
this. Everything *was* different, much different, from before
– before Watergate, before any time I could remember.

One morning later that week Holly buzzed me on the
intercom. "There's a Mr. Coe here. He wants to see you but
he won't identify himself. He's probably a reporter; those
guys are really something." I remembered Tom Phillips had
said a man named Doug Coe would be contacting me. He
certainly hadn't wasted any time; Tom would barely have
gotten my letter.

Holly, protective as Washington secretaries are trained
to be, wanted to turn him off. "You'll get yourself into something, if I don't." I wanted to tell her that I'd already gotten
myself "into something".

Doug Coe moved into my office as if we had known each
other for years. He greeted me with a wide, friendly smile
and had one arm around my shoulder before I could even
invite him to sit down. "This is just great, just great, what
Tom has told me about you," he said.

New Englanders are natively cautious about complete
strangers. I usually took the first few minutes of any
encounter to feel my way slowly and keep idle chatter going
while I took full measure of a visitor – a little like the family
dog circling around a new animal in the neighbourhood. But
Doug in those first minutes broke through the usual amenities, tossed a rumpled raincoat on the corner table, plopped
his gangling 6'1" frame into one of my leather chairs, draping
one leg over its arm, and smiled continuously.

As we chatted I saw a strikingly handsome man, with
short-cropped, curly black hair, dark dancing eyes, glistening white teeth, and always that instantly contagious smile.
Within minutes I realised it was the same radiance and
unpretentiousness I felt with Tom Phillips.

"Tom called me and – I hope you don't mind – read me your letter." Doug Coe was studying my reactions.

I *do mind*, I thought. But there was such kindness in his eyes my resistance began to melt.

"So great to have it happen that way," Doug said with a warmth that filled the room.

Still, what had happened was between me and God, I thought. You don't go around talking about such things, at least not with people you hardly know. But Doug Coe suddenly didn't seem to be a stranger. As we talked on I learned that Doug had come to Washington with Senator Mark Hatfield, an old friend from their Willamette University days in Oregon. He now worked with the Prayer Breakfast group in Washington, of which former Senator Frank Carlson of Kansas had been the prime mover. I should have known Doug; he'd been around the Senate for years. I did not. Still I felt as if I'd known him always.

Soon I found myself with growing excitement relating the story of my experience in Tom's driveway and the follow-up intellectual quest at a Maine cabin hideaway. "And so, Doug, I've asked Christ into my life. Nothing held back."

It was the first time I had articulated my commitment aloud to another person and the words startled me with their strangeness. Coe's smile broadened and his eyes shone as he repeated the words, "That's so exciting, just tremendous ..." Then Doug shifted ground. "You'll want to meet Senator Hughes. Harold is a tremendous Christian."

I laughed. "Harold Hughes won't want to meet me. From what I've heard, he considers me the number-one menace to America. He's anti-war, anti-Nixon, anti-Colson and we couldn't be farther apart politically."

"That doesn't matter now," Doug continued with unabated exuberance.

"You are telling me that because I've accepted Christ, Harold Hughes, just like that, wants to be a friend?" I shook my head in disbelief.

"Wait and see, Chuck. Wait and see. You will have brothers all over this city, hundreds of them, men and women you don't even know who will want nothing more than to help you. Some of them know we are meeting and are praying for you right now."

I stared at Doug. For months I had been battling Cox's army investigators, the Ervin Committee, a dozen other congressional committees which were joining in the Watergate spectacular, plus hordes of newsmen and 90 per cent of the Washington establishment – or so it seemed. No one in the long months ever once asked if I needed anything – not even my old friends in the White House. Now Doug was telling me that perfect strangers cared about me. The idea almost paralysed my mind.

Then Doug suggested that we pray together at my desk. At first I was concerned what my partners would think if one of them burst through the door. But Doug was so natural and relaxed that I relaxed, too. He thanked the Lord for bringing us together in the bonds of fellowship, for letting us know His love. I stumbled and stammered through my prayer; it was the first time I had prayed aloud with anyone in my life.

My new friend then handed me a copy of the Phillips version of the New Testament, inscribed: *To Charles – It is better to fail in a cause that will ultimately succeed than to succeed in a cause that will ultimately fail – God bless you! Doug. Matthew 6:33.* How those words were to haunt and then lead me in the days to come!

Doug recovered his balled-up raincoat, gripped my hand, stared knowingly into my eyes for a long moment and then, as quickly as he had come – with a cheery "Bye, brother," was gone. Gone with him was the presence, the warmth that had filled the room. The white-walled office looked sterile, cold, businesslike again.

"Well, you certainly spent a long time with him. Who is he, Chuck?" Holly, arms folded, was standing in the doorway, mildly annoyed at the intrusion into our busy day. I hadn't realised that over an hour had passed. "A friend, Holly – a good friend. He'll be coming by often, I hope. Yes, he will be, I am sure."

Doug meant it when he said that I had unknown friends in the city. The next day Under Secretary of State Curtis Tarr whom Nixon brought to Washington from the presidency of Lawrence University, a strong personality whom I admired greatly although I had met him only once, called. "Anything I can do for you Chuck, just call. I'm with you all the way. Just keep it in mind. You've got a friend here."

I was so taken aback I hardly knew how to answer. Some of my erstwhile colleagues in the Nixon Administration, even men I had placed in their high positions, had grown more distant as the accusations increased. Men in politics always watch their associations carefully and Watergate's ugly stain was being spread on a lot of bystanders with a broad brush. Yet in the days that followed, men whom I hardly knew did not hesitate to ally themselves with me, each with the same message spoken in a dozen ways: "As brothers in Christ we stand together." There was, I discovered to my astonishment, a veritable underground of Christ's men all through the government.

The moral support could not have come at a better time, since my blunt talk and outspoken defence of the President had made me a prime target of the forty-odd lawyers, mostly liberal, Democratic, and honour graduates of Harvard, now part of Professor Cox's office. Dave Shapiro and Judd Best from our office gently broke the news to me one evening: the grand jury investigating the break-in at the office of Ellsberg's psychiatrist was hearing evidence on me.

"Let's go see them. Let me tell them what really happened," I suggested with what now seems incredible naiveté.

"Okay, if you're sure you want to," Shapiro said, "but the orthodox way is to stay a mile away from a grand jury when you're a target; all you can do is give them more to use against you later in the . . ."

Dave stopped and I finished the sentence for him. "Trial, Dave – okay, I understand but I'll never be happy if I don't try. Get me a chance to testify and there won't be any trial, you'll see."

Dave, Judd, and I sought a hearing. A week or so later we climbed to the sixth floor of the U.S. Courthouse, walked the dimly lit corridor past large menacing signs which warn: "General public and media personnel not permitted beyond this point," and entered bare-walled rooms where the Watergate special grand jury was meeting. We waited in an outer office while the Special Prosecutor's ace assistant, William Merrill, briefed the grand jury on the evidence it might expect from one Charles Colson. I had once met Merrill, a mild-mannered man in his late forties, at a conference in his office. Having been a Democratic candidate for Congress in Michigan and state chairman for the "Robert Kennedy for President" campaign, his political sympathies obviously were not with me.

As I moved about the room restlessly, I reviewed what I remembered from law school about a witness coming before a grand jury – he appeared alone without counsel before some twenty-three citizens selected from the community. The sole function of a grand jury is to decide whether evidence presented by government prosecutors is sufficient to support charges against an individual and thus warrant a court trial. In theory it is to protect an individual against reckless or capricious prosecution.

Finally a young man emerged from an inner room and beckoned for me to follow. I walked through what appeared to be a metal-detection device, past a sleepy-eyed uniformed guard slumped in a chair at the door, and into Grand Jury Room No. 2. To the right was a benchlike table at which were seated two young assistant prosecutors. Immediately before me was another small table with a microphone, obviously for the witness. Beside it sat a court stenographer, her hands poised over a little black stenotype machine. In the rear were six rows of chairs, six abreast, each tier slightly elevated above the one before it. With a sinking feeling I could count only three white faces among the twenty-three representative citizens of the District of Columbia. The blacks had not exactly been Nixon supporters.

William Merrill stood in shirt-sleeves before the grand jurors, reminding me of a kindly schoolteacher addressing his flock. "If you are ready," he said, smiling and peering over his half-moon reading glasses, "we can now begin the questioning of Mr. Colson." The foreman of the grand jury administed the oath and Merrill turned to me.

"I should tell you for the record that you are here before this grand jury which is inquiring into the possibility of violations of the federal law relating to the break-in of Doctor Fielding's office in Los Angeles, Doctor Fielding having been the psychiatrist for Daniel Ellsberg. I think I should tell you also that from evidence the grand jury has heard you are a prospective defendant in the violation of certain criminal statutes relating to that matter, that you therefore have the right to take the Fifth Amendment in answer to any question that I may give to you, that any answers that you do give here can obviously be used against you . . ."*

Under my shirt I could feel cold drops of perspiration forming. I started to reach for the small paper cup of water on the table, but discovered my hand was shaking so badly that I couldn't lift it without making my nervousness obvious.

Merrill turned, smiled at the grand jurors, then continued: "It is also my understanding and should be made known to the grand jurors if it is correct, that you are here at your request. Are the things that I have said – do you understand them and are they accurate?"

"I understand them fully, Mr. Merrill, and I am here at my own request because I have felt from the beginning that I would like to be in a position to tell as much as I know about the events, anywhere I can," I replied.

I was relieved to hear my own words through the speaker, firm and clear; at least my voice would not betray me. After Merrill had dispensed with the preliminary questions – name, occupation, when I came to the White House, what I did for the President – one of the young men at the table beside him, passed him a note and I waited for the main line of questioning to get under way. He began: "Do you ever recall a discussion with Mr Magruder about obtaining one hundred thousand letters for use in the New Hampshire primary to try to persuade Democrats to vote for Kennedy?"

The question had nothing to do with the Ellsberg matter, and I hoped that I did not look as stunned as I felt. No one in all the months since the Watergate investigation began had ever asked me about this mailing, our secret attempt to

*Editor's Note: All questions and answers in this colloquy are taken from the actual transcript of grand jury proceedings.

encourage a write-in campaign in the New Hampshire primary to flush out Ted Kennedy, to force him to declare or disavow his candidacy. It was a campaign "dirty trick" of old-style politics that indeed I had been responsible for.

I tried to collect my thoughts. I had been prepared to give every detail of everything I knew about the Ellsberg case, but I hadn't thought about the Kennedy write-in. Nonetheless, I truthfully answered each of Merrill's questions, aware that the Kennedy family is revered by the vast majority of blacks in the District of Columbia. If the question was designed to put me on the defensive, it succeeded.

The morning questioning dealt almost entirely with the 1972 campaign, other non-Ellsberg matters and my attitude towards the Kennedys. Merrill pressed on : "Did you ever have any knowledge or suggestion of an effort to recruit either individuals or a group of homosexuals to indicate support for McGovern?"

"No, sir," I protested, while one of Merrill's young men shook his head in disbelief, to the obvious delight of several of the jurors. There was not a shred of truth to this well-publicised accusation. Merrill's assistants then took turns in the interrogation, each one seemingly competing to ask the most difficult and embarrassing question. I felt like I was facing a wall of angry faces.

At the lunch break Shapiro and Best tried hard to buck up my flagging spirits. I was both outraged and dejected; during two hours in the grand-jury room there had been hardly any questions about the case I volunteered to testify about.

After Shapiro had a talk with Merrill, the questioning focused on the matter before the grand jury, the Ellsberg break-in. As Merrill laboured over each piece of evidence, much of which I had earlier turned over voluntarily, the interest of the grand jury waned. Several jurors, I noticed, were reading newspapers. One very heavy-set woman in a starched-white maid's uniform seated in the front row kept dozing off, her head falling forward and chin thumping against her breastbone. Just as I thought I was making a particularly telling point, she would reach the bottom on this seesaw and a titter would ripple through the room. Another man in the second row fought to stay awake, moaning loudly each time he yawned.

At one point Merrill did manage to get their attention: "Did you ever tell anybody that you wanted to *paint Ellsberg black*?" Groaning to myself, I admitted using that phrase once in a memo. It was useless to plead that I meant no racial slur; merely by asking the question Merrill scored.

The next day was almost a repeat performance, the questions just as piercing, my attempts to get exculpatory matter into the record thwarted. With the novelty of my appearance gone, many of the grand jurors either left midway through the session or slept unashamedly.

Shapiro, Best, and I concluded that evening that I should stop the voluntary appearances. Whatever I said could not possibly help me with the grand jurors. Merrill knew the evidence; he was either going to recommend my indictment or not. And indeed, two days later Merrill contacted Shapiro: "We are going to indict your client, probably next week."

Late that same afternoon I sat alone in my office staring moodily out the window. How would I explain it all to Patty and the children? The stigma would be on them forever. Strangely though, the fears of early summer were gone. There would be a trial and if I lost I could go to prison. But somehow that thought, grim and black though it was, no longer seemed to be the end of life.

What bothered me most was the inner knowledge that events were moving inexorably forward, that bitterness and anger now tended to tip the scales of justice, and that there was no way I could turn back the onrushing tide. The evil of my pride had been exposed that night with Tom Phillips, but the process of ego slaying was still going on.

Just at that moment Doug Coe burst into my office with his usual, "Hi-ya brother – just passing through the neighbourhood." His sense of timing was uncanny. He always arrived, it seemed, when my spirits most needed a lift. As I explained the impending indictment, Doug listened with a look of growing concern.

"It's tough on you, Chuck – really tough," he said. There was a period of silence. "What really matters," he continued, "is not what Mr. Cox or Bill Merrill think or do, but what

God knows. He knows your sins; He knows mine. And He's always ready to forgive us. That's the beauty of having a loving Father. You can be open with God no matter what you've done."

As we talked, the truth of Doug's point became clear. God does not promise to spare us the pain or punishment that comes from our mistakes, but He will always forgive us, love us, and provide the strength to see us through the most difficult experience. Doug's insights and our prayers together lifted my spirits.

Yet in the days which followed I learned how hard it is for a new Christian to turn himself over to God completely. Daily prayer and a study of Scripture helped, but the old self keeps fighting; the old ego and pride die hard. I worried about what others would think of my indictment. How could I ever prove my innocence to my friends? An indictment is a permanent scar no matter what happens in a trial. There were times, too, when I was just plain frightened.

But remarkable things were happening inside me. I felt less of the old animosity and bitterness toward my adversaries. At a dinner party in October with old White House friends I found myself suddenly uncomfortable when the others began to attack John Dean.

"He's got to live with himself," I responded mildly.

Patty looked at me surprised. Previously the mention of his name would bring a hot flush to my face and angry words. I found I could no longer hate so easily and quickly as I once had.

Meanwhile Dave Shapiro became convinced that he and I were too close personally for him to defend me in court. Ethical questions were raised as well, since the prosecutors indicated that Shapiro, who had met once with Howard Hunt, might be called as a witness at the trial. After several long talks, we decided to find a top trial lawyer to assist us if the case came to trial. Both of us agreed on the man – Jim St. Clair, senior partner of a prestigious Boston firm. Twenty years earlier Jim had been the young understudy to Joe Welch, the wily old defence counsel whose homespun barbs made him the hero of the Army-McCarthy hearings. Over the years Jim St. Clair had won the reputation of being one of the ablest trial lawyers in the country, as shrewd and canny as his onetime mentor.

Before agreeing to handle the case Jim insisted on knowing everything. He spent two days interrogating Shapiro and me, interviewing key witnesses, and combing through my files. Late the second day he met with me in my office to announce his decision. "I'll represent you. In fact, I believe you are innocent of the Ellsberg charges. That isn't essential to my decision but it helps. As I see it, you can feel pretty good about this case; we have a fifty per cent chance."

"You believe I'm innocent, and we have a good case, but I've only got a fifty-fifty chance?" I protested.

Jim leaned back in the black leather chair across from my desk, erupting with a low guffaw. "Look, Chuck, when a prosecutor is out to get you – and these Cox guys are out to nail your hide to the wall – it's rough to beat it. The Feds have everything on their side, including sometimes the jury. It's uphill now for all you guys with Nixon."

St. Clair's big toothy grin, greying mane, and stocky frame which moves nimbly in the courtroom earned him the nickname of the Silver Fox. He stared at me, grinning: "All prosecutors are cops, you see." Jim's brutally frank words, the language of the criminal world which even a stuffy Boston lawyer uses after two decades as defence counsel, remained vivid in my consciousness in the months to come. I was fast confronting some of the harsher realities of life – such as how criminal defendants feel – that I had passed right by in my headlong rush for the top.

We were still awaiting the promised indictment when a new crisis was upon me. There was nothing I had wanted more through the long summer of 1973 than my turn at bat before the Ervin Committee. But time after time my appearance was postponed. We suspected that the committee counsel, Sam Dash, had no desire to let a free-swinging Nixon defender before the TV cameras until the case against Nixon was firmly made with the eighty million Americans in the viewing audience. Even in early September, Dash's lieutenants refused to confirm a date for my testimony. But two days after Merrill informed Shapiro of my "imminent" indictment, Dash called to schedule my appearance. Shapiro explained the dilemma : I obviously could not testify about matters – the Ellsberg break-in in particular – that would be included in the indictment. Under committee rules, and with the guideline of a Supreme Court decision, they could not even inquire into those matters.

"But he hasn't been indicted yet," Dash insisted.

"That's a technical distinction," returned Shapiro. "The prejudice would be the same. In the interest of justice the committee should postpone the Colson testimony for ten days. If not indicted by then, well, Colson may have to take his chances and testify."

Dash could not argue the fairness of Dave's position. He would check the committee's desires and call back. Within hours he did; the committee was determined. "Of course," Dash concluded, "Colson can always invoke his constitutional right against self-incrimination . . ."

The Fifth Amendment to me was the scarlet letter of American politics. Nothing creates the aura of guilt and stench of cowardice more than refusing to testify. Those accused of Communist ties during the McCarthy days who invoked the Fifth Amendment might just as well have said, "I'm guilty as charged," as far as public opinion was concerned. No one had done it in connection with Watergate, except Bud Krogh, the youthful head of the Plumbers, who invoked his right before an obscure House Committee.

"I won't do it, Dave. I absolutely will not take the Fifth," I insisted, as Shapiro reported his conversations with Dash.

Shapiro, a lawyer who defended more Loyalty Review Board cases than anyone else in the McCarthy heyday, paced angrily in front of his desk, one moment railing at the committee and the next screaming at me for my stupidity. "Chuck, you stick your neck out now and you're dead. Do you want to commit suicide? Have you got a death wish? The only place you testify now is in court. You can say nothing. We don't know what those guys in Cox's office will use against you and we aren't giving them more ammunition." St. Clair was in agreement with Dave as well as all my partners.

Ervin scheduled my appearance for the morning of September 19, behind closed doors. He was uncertain, as even

Shapiro was, whether I'd testify or take the Fifth Amendment, and should I do the latter on national television, under prevailing Court decisions, that could cause any subsequent prosecution against me to be thrown out.

As the hour approached I was still wrestling with my dilemma. Every instinct within me argued that I should testify. I spent five years working in the Senate, almost four in the White House, over half of my adult life in government or in the military, and all the while believing fervently in what I was doing. Refusing to testify seemed like ducking combat duty, failing to heed "our country's call." Then there was my pride still clamouring to be on stage, to rise to the defence of my commander-in-chief, to carry the battle to our attackers.

Camera crews were stationed at every entrance to the Capitol Building when we arrived. "Let's go in with our heads up," I urged. Shapiro, a young associate in our firm, Ken Adams, and I were met at the car door by a rush of cameramen and reporters, lights flashing, microphones on long poles thrust in our faces. A cordon of burly Capitol policemen rescued us and burrowed a path through the melee, up the short flight of steps, through the revolving glass doors. The crowd inside the building was almost as large as outside.

I struggled vainly to escape the grip of two overly protective policemen clutching both arms; the photo of that would be terrible. Other blue-suited officers were now out front, pressing ahead in a flying wedge. We inched our way through throngs of staring tourists, past rows of rich-brown mahogany doors and paintings of great moments in American history, and into Room S-143.

While waiting in the anteroom, we reviewed our strategy: first, through a series of manoeuvres, try to get the committee to vote a ten-day delay. Maybe we'd get one Democrat – the laconic Georgia senator, Herman Talmadge, to vote with the Republicans, which would carry 4-3. If that failed, Shapiro was adamant about the Fifth Amendment. I wasn't sure I could force the words out even if I agreed.

The chairman opened the session with only the seven senators and a handful of staffers in the room. We were seated at the far end of a long conference table. Shapiro began reviewing all of my voluntary appearances over the prior sixteen months, the dilemma which the threatened indictment posed, deploring committee "leaks," and begging the committee to protect his client's rights to a fair trial.

He pointed out that my appearance this day would be the same as parading us before live TV cameras, that the resulting publicity would be just as damaging. If I were to take the Fifth Amendment, this would certainly influence the grand jury now considering my indictment. If I refused to take the Fifth I was waiving future rights to remain silent, stripping my trial defence. Through the full ten minutes of his impassioned appeal, not a person stirred in the committee room and there was a long moment of silence when he finished.

Dash was the first to speak: "I do want to confirm, Mr. Shapiro . . . on my own inquiry of the Special Prosecutor's office, it is true that the current grand jury . . . does intend to come down fairly shortly . . . and I have been informed that Mr. Colson is a very real target and most likely would be one of those indicted."* It was support we hadn't expected.

Sam Ervin, proud of his reputation as the eminent constitutional scholar of the Senate, seemed affected by Shapiro's argument. "We have granted other witnesses the use of immunity," he mused, looking down thoughtfully at his fingers tapping on the tabletop.

"Mr. Colson has been rather – uh, he has made statements freely and voluntarily and on TV programmes and in press interviews," he said, indicating that my TV appearances had stung him. Although I hadn't criticised the chairman directly, I had knocked the committee's tactics, the torrent of leaks to the press, the berating of witnesses, the exclusion of Nixon defenders. All my efforts had not affected public opinion one whit – Nixon continued to plummet in the polls. But it had succeeded in bruising Sam Ervin who now had me where he wanted me; I was looking right down the barrel of his loaded howitzer – and squirming.

Shapiro and I were asked to leave the room while the committee debated in private. But voices were soon raised until we could hear them even through the closed door. Senator

*Editor's Note: All quoted statements are from Executive Session transcripts of the Ervin Committee.

Baker was in spirited support of my requests for a delay, Senator Weicker shouting opposition. The hands of the clock ticking off ten minutes, then twenty, thirty, forty, gave us hope. If Ervin had the votes to defeat the delay, this much debate would be needless.

After an hour we were called back. The chairman asked us to be seated. Ervin was obviously uncomfortable, his facial muscles twitching continuously, his jowls trembling, deep furrows across his brow as he squinted over his glasses. "The committee has denied the request," he announced. "Stand up and raise your right hand."

Shapiro protested, only for the record now, and then leaned over to me and whispered, "You have to do it or you can get yourself another set of lawyers."

I bit my lip and gripped the underside of the felt-topped table so hard my fingers went numb. Pride, pride, pride ! How I had despised cowardice in any form. How I had scorned those whimpering bureaucrats who invoked the Fifth Amendment during the early fifties and the thugs who did the same thing during Senator McClellan's racket hearings of a few years later. Pride. I had so wanted to ride forth on a white horse and save President Nixon, to hear his grateful voice, "Good job, boy – you really laid them back on their heels."

"Mr. Colson, are you acquainted with E. Howard Hunt?" Dash's words rang in my ears, cutting and sharp. I turned towards the chairman.

"Senator –" I stammered, my voice failing me for a moment, "I wanted more than I can tell you to appear before this committee and to be able to testify. If I believed one-tenth of the things that have been printed about me, I would not deserve to be sitting here. I am proud of the service I have been to my country . . . I never thought I would be in this position where I felt that my own legal rights were being prejudiced and that I had to avail myself of my constitutional privilege. I do not like doing this. I very much dislike it; I hate it. I am going to, Mr. Chairman, follow the instructions of my counsel which I have to say are not the instructions of my conscience."

Then it was over, just three questions, three apologetic, feeble "I decline to answer" responses that I could barely get past the big heavy lump clogging my throat. I wanted to push myself away from the table and run out of the room. For a moment there was an eerie silence. Even Senator Inouye's stern scowl was gone. His eyes seemed to be saying, "I don't like you but I feel for you."

Ervin continued to stare at me with a knowing, fatherly expression; the hurt in Howard Baker's heart was as obvious as the bold pattern of his tweed jacket; all of the venom and outrage was gone from Lowell Weicker as he sat motionless, staring out of the one window in the small room. Men in politics savour their moments of victory, but there is no joy among politicians in witnessing one of their own, even a bitter foe, not just defeated but helpless, shamed, the last vestige of self-respect stripped from him.

As we left the committee chambers, we saw Senator Ervin, surrounded by cameras and reporters, explaining that I had taken the Fifth ! No inferences were to be drawn, he reminded them. But we knew what would happen the next day – and it did.

The *Washington Post* printed, above the fold on page one, a gigantic picture of the onetime "tough guy". Beneath the photo was the headline: COLSON WON'T REPLY TO WATER-GATE QUIZ. One unnamed committee source described me as "subdued and contrite." All three networks and virtually every major paper in the country gave banner coverage to the political obituary of Nixon's last stalwart.

Tom Phillips had begun the process on that still, humid night in August when for the first time I came face-to-face with the person which years of striving for the successes of this world had created. The old was dying, all right, but not without pain, not without resistance, not without tears and sorrow. Though my eyes were being opened slowly to a whole bright world I'd not known before, I was still struggling to save what I should have known must be left behind. For some of us, at least for a while, the struggle continues for the riches of both worlds.

11

Brothers

My encounter with Senator Harold Hughes was arranged for an evening in late September. Harold, I later learned, had stoutly resisted the idea when Doug Coe first called him to suggest it.

"There isn't anyone I dislike more than Chuck Colson. I'm against everything he stands for. You know that, Doug," he protested.

Before Hughes hung up, Doug gently suggested that the senator's attitude was hardly Christlike. The next day Hughes called back and with a weary sigh relented. "All right, Doug. You set it up."

Fearing that a one-on-one confrontation between Harold and myself might be too explosive, Doug decided to make it a quiet evening with wives, at the home of the soft-spoken veteran Minnesota Republican congressman, Al Quie. He invited as well a former Democratic congressman from Texas, Graham Purcell. That made it two Democrats, two Republicans, and Coe.

Harold Hughes is indeed an extraordinary man, I discovered while reading about his past. Raised on a small Iowa farm, he fought his way through the mud of Italy during World War II as an Army infantryman, narrowly escaping death. In the postwar period Hughes became a truck driver and an alcoholic, brawling his way from one bar to the next, sometimes gone from his young family for days on end, and often waking up from a drunken stupor to find himself in a strange hotel hundreds of miles from home. Alienated peri-

odically from family, imprisoned by whisky, he often
thought of suicide.

Alone late one night in 1954 Hughes cried out to God for
help. When the fog lifted the next day from his whisky-
soaked brain, everything around him seemed new. He never
took another drink.

Hughes achieved moderate success with a small trucking
business. He and his wife, Eva, become active in the church.
At first involved in Young Republican politics, the fiercely
independent Hughes switched in 1957 to the minority Democratic Party and was elected state commerce commissioner.
In 1962 he ran for governor. When a whispering campaign
began about his alcoholism, Hughes met the issue head-on.
Politicians didn't usually admit such things but he was what
he was, he explained publicly, among other things a recovered
alcoholic. The state's traditionally Republican voters elected
him governor by over 40,000 votes, and despite his outspoken
liberalism, re-elected him twice, then sent him to the U.S.
Senate in 1968, replacing a conservative GOP stalwart.

Ignoring unwritten traditions that freshmen members of
the Senate sit quietly in the back row to learn from their
elders, Hughes was quickly championing liberal causes and
within a few months became one of the most outspoken ad-
vocates of legislation to end the Vietnam War. This was
when we in the Nixon White House put him high on the
"enemies" list.

Burning with idealism about the need for sweeping social
reforms in American society, Hughes plunged into the race
for the 1972 Democratic Presidential nomination. His charismatic personality won him some pockets of early support,
but with no political base of his own, meagre campaign funds,
and his blunt manner frightening many of the more orthodox politicians in his party, Hughes decided to withdraw from
the race.

Meanwhile the senator was finding the demands of political
life more and more in conflict with his own commitment to
Christ. Though he was virtually certain of re-election,
Hughes, in the summer of 1973 after deep soul-searching announced that at the end of his term in January 1975 he
would retire from the Senate. The announcement left political

observers and the voters of Iowa stunned. Hughes stated that he felt he could do more for his fellowman out of public life, serving only one Master.

After reviewing what I knew about Senator Hughes, I found myself intrigued by his gutsy approach to life. At the same time my political instincts were preparing me for battle.

Doug was on the phone a few days before the planned meeting. "Brother, why don't I pick you up at your office?" he suggested. "Say about eight p.m."

"Sounds good." Patty was to take Doug's wife, Jan, in our car.

At the selected time and place I spotted Doug's battered blue Chevy station wagon. Realising someone was in the front seat, I climbed in the back. The someone was Senator Hughes!

I sat back and studied my longtime adversary. Hughes was dressed in a checkered sport shirt hanging loosely over a set of denim coveralls. His deliberate disdain of the attire considered proper by Washington standards had earned him the title of "worst-dressed senator" in the year's annual poll of Senate staffers. It was this very casualness plus the warmth of his deep resonant voice that made me lower my guard.

Yet I sensed that the senator was not making the same instant re-evaluation of me. Every now and then he would shift his husky frame, turning to stare into the backseat. His sharp features, black hair, and deep-set eyes give him the appearance of American Indian heritage. His scowl as he measured me sent shivers through me. I noticed Doug's eyes glancing nervously first at me through the rearview mirror, then sideways at the senator.

Feeling uncomfortable in my conservative blue business suit, I removed my coat. Conversation fumbled along in safe areas: family and the few mutual friends I could, only with considerable effort, think of. As we pulled up to the front door of Al Quie's white Colonial home nestled among old oak trees, I could sense Doug's relief. So far, so good.

The Quies – Al and Gretchen – greeted us warmly. Al, a tall, rugged, athletic man and a former dairy farmer, flashed a shy smile which gave him the appearance of being younger than his fifty years. Graham Purcell, grey-haired and rangy, and his vibrant, attractive wife, Nancy, arrived a few minutes later. We all gathered before a mammoth brick fireplace in the large panelled family room, its walls covered with trophies and awards won by Al and his prize horses.

It was also the first time that I met Jan Coe whom Doug married when they were both freshmen in college during the late forties. She is graceful and ageless like Doug, with the same effervescent personality. In fact, I was startled by how much they look alike.

Whenever two or more politicians gather together during a Washington social evening, the conversation quickly turns to the latest fight on Capitol Hill, upcoming elections, and the fall from or rise to power of the current political personality. The men congregate together, leaving the ladies to fend for themselves. It is important to get the first cocktail in hand quickly, followed by a second and a third. Each man tries to impress whomever will listen with how close he is to the real source of power. "You know, my friends in the White House tell me . . ." The scene might be cast in Greenwich, Connecticut or Winnetka, Illinois, and the conversation about the latest gyrations of the stock market or who's on the way up the corporate ladder.

This night instead we sat in a large semicircle around the fireplace, sipping iced tea and lemonade. Husbands and wives were together, and the talk was about Al's horses. We might as well, I realized, have been in the living room of the Quie farm 1,000 miles from the hubbub of the nation's capital. I marvelled at the warmth and hominess, all the while keeping a wary eye on Harold Hughes. Gretchen, even more a Scandinavian beauty with an apron around her waist, brought out piping hot, homemade apple pie and ice cream and smiled appreciatively as Harold devoured the first helping and asked for another.

It was all so new to me I found myself squirming in my chair a few times. We had come together for me to meet Senator Hughes and the others. They were also to expose me to the nebulous concept which Doug had called fellowship. I sensed that Hughes was becoming a little impatient, too, since he was not known for socialising, particularly without Eva, who was ill at home.

In one sense, Hughes and I were like two boxers in separate corners, restless, awaiting the moment we knew was coming when we would be sparring together. Everyone there knew the two of us would have our confrontation sooner or later, but I was not prepared to have Harold Hughes abruptly put me on stage.

"Chuck," he said, "they tell me you have had an encounter with Jesus Christ. Would you tell us about it?"

I was not ready for this – to talk about Christ to a roomful of people I hardly knew. Even Doug had not heard in detail what had happened at Tom Phillips's and later on in Maine. For a fleeting moment I considered ducking, then from inside me came reassurance. Harold's expression was open – not warm, not cold. Patty looked nervous. The rest seemed very friendly.

Though I considered myself a veteran speaker in the political arena, this was different. The words came out haltingly. But to my surprise there was no embarrassment, simply a feeling of inadequacy in talking about the most intimate experience of my life. In the middle, I almost bogged down as I wondered, *Are they going to think I'm some kind of nut? Do people really go around talking about their personal encounters with God?* I stopped momentarily and looked around the room. No one spoke but their expressions told me to keep going.

"That night with Tom Phillips broke down some kind of lifelong barrier," I continued. "Yet I had to wonder the next day if all the Watergate unpleasantness had left me so shell-shocked that I was just looking for a way out – any way out. It was the week in Boothbay where I put it together in my mind, not just in my emotions. I really was able to see who Jesus is and my need for Him – then I could give my life to Him." Just saying the words brought the emotion back and I choked up for a minute. "As a new Christian I have everything to learn, I know that. I'm grateful for any help you can give me."

For a moment there was silence. Harold, whose face had been enigmatic while I talked, suddenly lifted both hands in the air and brought them down hard on his knees. "That's all I need to know. Chuck, you have accepted Jesus and He has forgiven you. I do the same. I love you now as my brother in Christ. I will stand with you, defend you anywhere, and trust you with anything I have."

I was overwhelmed, so astonished, in fact, that I could only utter a feeble, "Thank you." In all my life no one had ever been so warm and loving to me outside of my family. And now it was coming from a man who had loathed me for years and whom I had known for barely two hours.

Then we were all on our knees – all nine of us – praying aloud together. As I got to my feet, Harold lumbered toward me, a smile slowly spreading over his face. As he wrapped his arms around me in a great bear hug, I needed no further explanation of what *fellowship* meant or what Paul meant when he wrote, "Let us have real affection for one another as between brothers . . ." (Romans 12 : 10 PHILLIPS).

The others also offered their support and counsel. "Politicians are wary of anyone who faces indictment, but Christians stand together," said Graham Purcell, a judge in Texas before his election to Congress. "That's right," chimed in Al Quie. "We'll be with you. Stand tall."

When Patty and I said good-bye, I was marvelling not so much at what was said, but at the impact of non-verbal communication. Harold Hughes need not have said a word to me. I read him perfectly in my heart through his smile, his bear hug, and the caring look in his eyes.

The only question in my mind about this extraordinary evening was its effect on Patty. She had sat in wide-eyed amazement during much of it. As a Roman Catholic, she found God on Sunday morning in the solemn hush of church. Kneeling at a sofa in a living room was a strange experience for her. During nine years of marriage she had never heard me pray aloud until that night. In fact, it was only the third time I had. Nothing she said that night indicated anything but support for me. The expression on her face, however revealed the inner doubts. Non-verbal communication again. I decided that Patty and I needed to have an in-depth discussion about it as soon as possible. But the events that swirled about us postponed it for weeks.

My indictment did not come as expected in September.

At first my law associates and I concluded that the threat to do so had been simply a ploy to keep me from testifying before the Ervin Committee, and humiliate me in the process. Or maybe it was the valiant defence Shapiro and St. Clair were waging, meeting with Cox and his assistants, even once bringing me in for what turned out to be almost a friendly session.

Shapiro submitted briefs to the prosecutors, arguing that for years the FBI engaged in illegal "entries," a euphemistic term for burglary for national-security reasons, that the Ellsberg case wasn't any different from what had happened hundreds of times. Nixon's lawyers argued that the White House files fully supported the national-security justification.

The President then entered the situation. In a brief bravado moment, his voice surging with confidence during one late-night phone call, Nixon said, "I know they've been after you, Chuck, but it won't work. There is no way I am going to let them do it to you. You are innocent in this. I know that, and from now on the President is in charge."

But events in Washington were now spinning wildly out of control. The President was soon calling me evenings about the problems of Vice-President Spiro Agnew. Serious charges – accepting bribes while governor of Maryland – were now being amassed by a Baltimore grand jury investigation. Our firm, representing the Vice-President, was in the thick of it.

At first Nixon wanted to help his two-time running mate. Then the evidence began to pile up and the President's attitude changed. Pressure from the White House came for me to ask an industrialist not to contribute to the Vice-President's defence fund and to encourage Agnew to resign. This put me in an awkward spot. "He's got to go," General Haig told me one night, "for the country's sake". To whom was my greater loyalty: client or country? What did my new faith have to say about this dilemma? It seemed that every day offered me a new test. I decided not to contact the industrialist. A partial answer to my problem was to step aside, turning the case over to other lawyers in our firm more skilled in criminal law.

Agnew's main line of defence was to force Congress to take

up the charges on an impeachment resolution, thereby blocking a criminal indictment in court. Agnew's men began drum-
ming up support in the House of Representatives.

Then Nixon told me one night, "Both Jerry Ford [then
House Minority Leader] and Carl Albert [House Speaker]
will oppose any impeachment resolution." White House
lobbyists had cut the ground out from under their own
Vice-President! Nixon also informed me that the Justice
Department was prepared to offer Agnew a way to escape
prison if he would resign.

I agreed to present the harsh facts to the Vice-President, a
painful experience for both of us. A proud and erect man, he
sat stoically behind his king-sized polished desk as I pressed
home the points why he should resign. I could see the hurt in
his eyes when he realized that his own President had turned
against him.

The Vice-President rejected the first proposals of the Justice
Department and the pressure of his chief. A few weeks later
he made the decision on his own. Entering the federal district
court in Baltimore on that historic October day, he pleaded
nolo contendere to one count of income tax evasion, while
simultaneously a lawyer in our firm delivered the Vice-
President's letter of resignation to the Secretary of State.

Spiro Agnew received a suspended sentence and a once
powerful man was now disgraced. For the country – a Vice-
President vanquished and a President under heavy assault.
It was mind boggling. Frightening for me, too, since I had
been close to each man.

Then, a few days later came the firing of Special Prosecutor
Archibald Cox and the resignation of Attorney General Elliot
Richardson in what was labelled the 'Saturday Night Massacre.' A storm of public outrage swept the nation. The impeachment machinery was unleashed amidst a rising clamour
for Nixon's resignation. What was happening in the capital
in the fall of 1973 seemed completely unreal.

Very real to me, however, were the discoveries I was making as a new Christian. One statement which Paul made to
the Philippians was especially reassuring:

... I look upon everything as loss compared with the over-whelming gain of knowing Christ Jesus my Lord. For his sake I did in fact suffer the loss of everything, but I considered it mere garbage compared with being able to win Christ.

Philippians 3 : 8, 9 PHILLIPS

I wondered : *Could I really lose all things gladly?* This passage kept coming back to me as I was drawn more and more into the Watergate net.

Then, too, I was learning how little I knew about some of my old friends. Ken Belieu, one of my colleagues in the Nixon White House, for one. When we met one day for lunch at the Sans Souci restaurant, he revealed that ever since 1947 Christ had been first in his life. All of the camaraderie we'd known in the past, working together through two decades at all levels of government, paled into insignificance compared to the bond that Ken and I had from that day on.

Then there was Fred Rhodes, deputy administrator of the Veterans Administration. Our careers had been close – on Capitol Hill, in the Nixon Administration, and over the years in Republican politics. I knew that Fred was vice-president of the Southern Baptist Convention and involved in church activities. Close as we had been, however, he never discussed his religion with me.

It was during a lunch at the Lawyer's Club that I decided to have some fun with my old friend. In the middle of a conversation about how badly the White House was handling the impeachment fight, I asked, "Fred, besides all this Baptist work you do, have you really met Jesus Christ?" The suddenness of the words caused Fred to drop his fork noisily on the plate. He stared suspiciously at me while he groped for an answer.

"Well, you have to appreciate what that means, Chuck. Yes, I have, but you ought to know . . ."

He was winding up for a long ponderous explanation, when I interrupted : "What would you say if I told you I had?"

"I'd shout, 'Praise the Lord'." He was now smiling, though still suspicious. Another Colson practical joke, perhaps?

"Please don't do it here, Fred, or you'll shock some of these stuffy lawyers, but I have. I haven't told many people. It's very personal but I thought you might like to know."

Later that afternoon, a messenger arrived in my office carrying a large box containing a copy of the Living Bible, Fred's own pocket edition of the New Testament, three Keith Miller books, some Baptist literature, and a huge red book containing four translations of the Bible. From that point, our friendship moved forward in ways we could never have suspected.

The seeds planted that sultry night in September when we gathered at Al Quie's home continued to germinate. In late September Hughes, Quie, Purcell, Doug, and myself began gathering for breakfast each Monday morning at 8:30 at Fellowship House. A plain, French Provincial building that might easily pass for just another of the large old residences on Embassy Row, Fellowship House is operated by a group of men and women volunteers who are followers of Jesus Christ. There is no identification on the front of the building, yet for years people in government, in the diplomatic corps, and those visiting from every country in the world have found their way there for quiet prayer and fellowship. In socially conscious, protocol-wise Washington, Fellowship House occupies a unique place. The foreign minister of South Africa may find himself praying with a young black Christian worker whose ministry takes him each day to a nearby Lorton Reformatory. The key to admittance is not politics, but commitment to Christ. Our group was just one of dozens which meet there each week.

The bonds between the five of us grew slowly but firmly. We would spend the first hour gathered around a coffee table in the library sharing personal problems and concerns, then turn to a selection from the Scriptures to read and discuss, ending always with the five of us on our knees praying for each other, our families, and for the men in government whose lives each day we touched. Often the fellowship was so strong, we'd embrace one another after our prayers. If an outsider were to look in on us, he would doubtless consider it a strange sight for a city so torn asunder in the bitterest and most divisive political struggle in a hundred years.

Ironic as it might have seemed, the liberal Democratic partisan Harold Hughes was the one who most often suggested that we pray for President Nixon and the men in the White House. One morning in late October the senator told me, "If the President is innocent as you say he is, Chuck, it's going to shock a lot of my colleagues, but I, for one, will not vote for his impeachment. I'm really going to wrestle with this. The only commitment any of us have here is to God, and God is the Truth." Then the wide furrows of his brow seemed to deepen. "I wonder if we could get the President to pray with us."

I agreed to ask the President if he would do so, even though I knew Richard Nixon considered his beliefs a very private matter. He had often spoken disdainfully of men in public life who used their religious affiliation for political advantage. The opportunity came during one of our telephone conversations following the Cox firing when the burdens of the President seemed overwhelming. "Sir, would you consider meeting with a small group of us to pray through some of these problems?" I went on to describe our group.

My suggestion was followed by a long silence – his way of saying no. It was hard for Mr. Nixon to understand that a commitment to Christ transcended all ideological differences, all partisan quibbling, everything. One day I pleaded with his secretary, Rose Mary Woods, hoping that her Catholic roots would produce support for the idea.

"I know this sounds strange, Rose, but trust me. I know what I am talking about. Harold Hughes really wants to pray with the President. He wants to help him. Just man-to-man, to give him some support.'

"You've got to be kidding, Chuck," Rose replied. "After the terrible things that man has said about the President, I'd never want to see them in the same room."

The poison of Watergate had by now infected everything in Washington. So firmly entrenched were both sides, that no one seemed able to understand there was a healing force that might rescue both the nation and the cambatants.

It was Hughes who suggested also that we meet with former Vice-President Agnew, offer him the strength of fellowship, help him perhaps to see that while his old world might have collapsed around him, there was a much more meaningful world that we might help him discover. Our invitation was declined. Agnew was so overcome with humiliation and dejection that he chose instead the isolation of the small community in eastern Maryland to which he had moved himself and his family.

Unsuccessful in getting these two men to join us, we continued to pray for them and all the others in power and out. As we took steps to strengthen one another in our own commitment to Christ, to share our burdens and to love the Lord together, our scheduled hour and a half often stretched into two, sometimes three hours. The Monday-morning session meant so much to me I would never hesitate to change an appointment or cut short a weekend for it. Hughes often missed scheduled business of the Senate, Quie returned early from visits to his congressional district, Purcell postponed business trips, and Doug was always there – patient, teaching, guiding, lifting us in his unobtrusive gentle ways.

We were such an unlikely combination of men, coming from opposing parties, different sections of the country, and widely varied backgrounds and education. Yet each week we drew closer together in Christian love for one another. We thought we knew it fully that fall, but were to discover in the months ahead that events would bring us even closer.

"I don't know what you have found, Chuck, but I sure wish I had it," Dave Shapiro confessed to me after a long day of jousting with press and prosecutors. Dave's voice was hoarse and his face haggard and drawn. "I'm going to pieces over all the heat *you* are taking and there you sit calmly; nothing seems to be bothering you."

Of course it did bother me; the suspense was agony, always expecting to wake up one morning to black headlines announcing my indictment. Or when Prosecutor Merrill called Shapiro as he did from time to time, my heart raced while I waited for Shapiro to conclude the conversation. Each day I'd think, *Maybe today.* But it didn't come, not in October, not in November, not in December.

In fact, all the work of the prosecution was slowed after the Cox firing. At one point we were heartened when Nixon, on the recommendation of his stalwart friend, John Connally, appointed ex-American Bar Association president, Leon Jaworski – like Connally a Texan – as the new Special

Prosecutor. "Unlike Cox, Jaworski is a realist," Al Haig told me in mid-November. "He's got a great respect for the office of President. We have a good understanding; it will be a good working relationship." Haig's voice was buoyant.

Even after the implausible eighteen-and-a-half-minute tape gap was disclosed, Nixon's spirits seemed up. He called me several times those November days, each time expressing his concerns for "poor Rose" so profusely I couldn't help but wonder if his long-time secretary was about to sacrifice herself by taking sole responsibility for a deliberate erasure.

The long vigil was hardest on Patty. One evening sitting in our den before a roaring fire the concerns surfaced. I began talking about my new faith. Her soft skin furrowed slightly. "I think I understand. I – I'm just not sure how I fit into this new life of yours."

"But, honey, you are a complete part of it. We are both Christians now, whereas before you were a Christian and I was not."

'Will you be going to a church?"

"Yes, but I'm not sure which one yet."

Patty's eyes were still cloudy, her voice apprehensive. "Then you don't expect me to give up my Catholic faith to join you?"

So at last the real problem was out in the open. Somehow Patty had identified what was happening to me as a Protestant experience, rather than an across-the-board Christian one. The language of the Christians we were meeting nowadays frightened her, as well it might: "Accepting Christ" – "In Christ." Unintentionally, they were creating a mystique about what is really the simplest decision each man or woman makes in life. But the language which is so meaningful to one who has made the decision can be as scary as the words of a secret-society initiation to those who haven't – and can sound spiritually arrogant. Patty was put off by it.

She mentioned another concern: "What if the press finds out about this change in you, Chuck? Would this help or hurt?"

I had been giving this a lot of thought myself. "I don't know – probably hurt – but I have no intention of telling them. It's not their business."

I stared for a long moment into the crackling fire. I hadn't even told my children or my parents, nor Charlie Morin, my closest and oldest friend. No one but Tom Phillips, Doug, and a few others in the fellowship knew. *Better that way*, I mused. If it was a foxhole conversion, the drowning man grasping for a straw, and I slipped and fell when Watergate passed by – as someday it must – at least it would only be between God and me and a handful of others. That would be bad enough, of course, but I wouldn't be embarrassed in front of the whole world. And if word got out now, it would be labelled a gimmick for sure. "Colson hiding behind God," some wise-guy reporter would write.

Admit it, Colson, you still care about what others think, don't you? I confronted myself in the dancing white and orange flames. Pride? Yes, I suppose. Yet what was happening inside was so real, the prayers, the Monday-morning time with the other men. But private – between my brothers and me and Christ.

"No, honey," I turned to Patty whose blue eyes sparkling in the fire's glow were filled with love. "No, honey, I'm not about to go shouting from the rooftops."

I could almost feel her relief.

But events – God, I believe now – had other things in store.

12

Christ in the Headlines

Each morning shortly after eight, the men of power in the executive branch of government assemble around a long antique mahogany table in the historic Roosevelt Room just across a narrow corridor from the President's Oval Office. For over three years I was always present, listening to Kissinger's briefing on whatever troubled area of the globe demanded our attention, joining in the discussion of pressing domestic issues with John Ehrlichman or George Shultz, jotting down notes about the President's schedule as Bob Haldeman reviewed it.

Small wonder, I suppose, that all through those frantic years I had not known that at the very same time, one morning every two weeks, another group was also meeting around a table in the basement of the White House west wing. Those present would include a departmental Under Secretary or two, sometimes a Cabinet member and a handful of White House staffers sharing their faith with one another, reading from the Scriptures and praying together. Even if I had known there was a White House prayer group, I would have considered myself too busy to attend.

Although President Nixon had refused to invite his arch foe Harold Hughes inside the executive mansion, the small group meeting bi-weekly in the basement was eager for the senator's fellowship. Harold accepted their invitation to attend a breakfast meeting scheduled for December 6. Since he had been inside the White House only once during Nixon's term, and since these were bitter days, with Washington divided into hostile camps, Harold and Doug suggested I go along. Perhaps I could help in case some over zealous Nixon partisan took offence at Hughes's mere presence there.

I arrived a minute before eight, walking briskly through the South-west Gate, past the familiar faces of the guards who waved cheerily. It was such a beautiful sunny day, and I felt so jubilant over the prospect of Hughes praying in the White House, that I even smiled at the sleepy-eyed reporters who were always about, making notes on everyone coming and going.

I walked through the basement door entrance to the west wing, down the low-ceilinged corridor lined with huge colour photographs of Nixon and his travels, past a door marked simply SITUATION ROOM, the nerve centre of the National Security Council, whose offices stretch through a subterranean labyrinth beneath the South Lawn. The breakfast was being held in the panelled Conference Dining Room, reserved for senior White House staffers and Cabinet members. This morning three tables had been pushed together and places set for fourteen. Already seated, with his back to the wall – I thought he chose it that way – was Harold Hughes looking stiff and uncomfortable, surrounded by a half dozen staunch Nixonites.

The senator looked up at my entrance, brightened noticeably, and shouted, "Hi, brother!" I greeted my friends and took a seat at a far corner of the long table. One by one, others arrived, filling all of the chairs except the one immediately to my right. Under Secretary of Labour Dick Shubert was there, as was Ken Belieu, who had been coaxed out of retirement to help new Vice-President Gerald Ford organize his office. There were other old friends; most I had not known to be interested in this sort of thing. The red-jacketed Filipino stewards began shuttling silver pots of hot coffee and trays of buns from the kitchen. We had started to eat when the door swung open and the chairman of the Federal Reserve Board, Arthur Burns, entered.

"What is Arthur Burns doing here?" I asked in astonishment to the man on my left, Father John McLaughlin, the Jesuit priest and staff speech writer for the President. Aware of the "dirty trick" episode several years before when I falsely accused Burns of seeking a pay rise, Father John chuckled. "Arthur is a regular participant in these breakfasts," he told me.

"But he's Jewish," I protested. Not that this really made any difference; it was simply the first thing I could think to say to explain my obvious distress. As I am sure McLaughlin realized, I dreaded the confrontation.

"He is not only Jewish,' McLaughlin went on, "he is the chairman of this breakfast meeting."

Burns looked just as uncomfortable at the sight of me, and even more so at the realisation, as his eyes quickly scanned the table, that the only empty chair was next to me. He hesitated for a moment, then leaned across the table to introduce himself to Hughes, greeted the others, and with the barest nod in my direction sat down.

Hughes proved to be more of an attraction than the organizers of the breakfast had expected. Soon the room which seats fifty was almost full sending the stewards scurrying to the kitchen for additional plates of scrambled eggs. But the turnout, though large, was scarcely welcoming; the atmosphere was charged with scepticism.

At 8 : 20 Burns, who had picked nervously at his breakfast, welcomed the overflow crowd and explained how happy the White House prayer group was to have Senator Hughes present to discuss his reasons for leaving the Senate to enter a full-time lay ministry. Then with none of the flowery superlatives normally passed among politicians at Washington gatherings, Burns turned the meeting over to Hughes.

After a few opening moments of uncharacteristic nervousness, Harold was in charge, his eloquent commanding self. For twenty minutes there was not another sound in the room other than his deep, powerful voice. He spoke with devastating honesty about his past, the power of Christ in his changed life, the conflicts he had faced as a Christian in government, and then for the final few minutes, how he had come to know his brother in Christ, Chuck Colson.

If it had not been such a moving moment, I would have laughed aloud at the astonished expressions around the room. Out of the corner of my eye I saw Arthur Burns sitting absolutely motionless, eyes fixed on Hughes, a soft shock of grey hair hanging over his brow, his mouth open. The pipe he had been smoking furiously at the outset now lay cold in his right hand.

"I've learned how wrong it is to hate," Hughes went on. "For years there were men towards whom I felt consuming bitterness. I wasn't hurting them, only myself. By hating I was shutting Christ's love out of my life. One of the men I hated most was Chuck Colson, but now that we share a commitment together in Christ, I love him as my brother. I would trust him with my life, my family, with everything I have."

When he finished there was a long silence – no one could take his eyes off the senator. Seconds ticked by, a minute perhaps, almost as if the whole room was in silent prayer.

Arthur Burns, who was to close the meeting, seemed unable to find the words. Finally, he very deliberately laid his pipe on the table, stared at it for a moment, folded his hands in front of him, and slowly lifted his eyes. In a voice so low I doubted if those across the room could hear, he began. "Senator – I just want to say – that is one of the most beautiful and moving things I have ever heard from any man."

He cleared his throat and it was plain that he was choking back tears. "I don't want to say anything else," he said. "Just this – on behalf of this group, would you please come back again?" With that he arose, took my right hand in his left and said, "Now I would like to ask Mr. Colson to lead us in prayer."

Everyone in the room joined hands. I was so surprised that it was a moment before I found my voice. There was no time to compose a prayer in my mind; I would have to depend on the Holy Spirit. The words which came out were a plea for all of us in the room, regardless of our position in government, to come before Him in humility and submission, in the knowledge that we were nothing, that He was everything, and that without His hand on our shoulders we could not possibly attend the affairs of our nation. As I ended the prayer, asking it all in the name of our Lord Jesus Christ, I felt Burns's grip tighten.

As many of the men left, they either embraced the senator or gripped his hand warmly, repeating Burns's invitation to return. Many also clasped me by the arm, welcoming me to a fraternal bond much closer than what we knew as White House men standing alone, we thought, against the world. It was an emotion-packed scene; I had never seen anything to match it in all my years in government service.

After saying good-bye to Harold, I jogged toward the basement entrance, hoping to catch Burns before he reached his waiting limousine. I found him in the little coat-room by the guard's desk, wrapping a scarf around his neck. "Doctor Burns, I know you have good reason to hate the sight of me," I said, "but I want to apologise to you for planting that story. Someday I would like to come and see you."

Though soft-spoken, Arthur Burns can be testy and cantankerous; those who challenged his economic policies are often met with fierce scowls, clouds of smoke rising from his pipe, and a stern lecture. This morning I found myself looking into the understanding eye of a patient, grey-haired professor. "You don't need to apologise," he said. "There's no need for that now. All of that is behind us. I would like to see more of you, too." Then he stammered, "I've never, never felt – I've never known – well, this has been quite a morning." With that he squeezed my arm, turned, and walked into the bright sunlight outside.

I walked back to my office praising God.

The regular White House press briefing that morning was slated for 11:00 a.m. Jerry Warren, a former *San Diego Union* reporter and for the past five years Ron Ziegler's chief assistant, strode into the White House Press Room shortly after eleven, braced for the onslaught of Watergate questions. Reporters lounging in easy chairs at the back of the room ambled to the front, notebooks out, as Jerry leaned into the microphone to begin the routine announcements: the President will sign the Veterans Disability and Death Pension Act of 1973, a three o'clock meeting to be held with his economic advisers, a reception is planned for Vice-President Gerald Ford. Then as was customary he opened it up to questions. The following is taken directly from the transcript of the session (White House News Conference

Transcript No. 1869, December 6, 1973) beginning with Dan
Rather of CBS News:

> RATHER: Jerry, what is the President doing continuing to
> see Charles Colson?
> WARREN: I don't think he is.
> RATHER: What was Mr. Colson doing at the White House
> today?
> WARREN: (pause) Well ... (pause) he was attending a
> meeting in the dining room downstairs which is held
> every other Thursday. A group of White House staff
> members get together for a prayer breakfast and Mr.
> Colson was attending that ...
> UNIDENTIFIED VOICE: Prayer!
> ANOTHER UNIDENTIFIED VOICE: Is he going to be the next
> preacher?

Several minutes of the proceedings here became unintelligible because of the laughter which apparently rocked the
room. Jerry told me later there hadn't been such merriment in
the Press Room since before Watergate began eighteen
months earlier.

> RATHER: I would like an answer
> WARREN: That is the answer.
> RATHER: That he was attending a prayer breakfast?

The transcript shows that Warren launched into a lengthy
explanation about Senator Hughes's appearance at the breakfast that morning, those who attended, the frequency of the
breakfasts, and the fact that former staff members such as
myself did attend. The laughter evidently was gone.

> RATHER: Jerry, isn't this a little unusual, to have a full-
> time paid lobbyist for very large occasions and individ-
> uals in and out of the White House to attend things such
> as a prayer breakfast?
> WARREN: Dan, I don't think so at all. I think that is
> stretching it a great deal. When a group of individuals
> who have worked together, sit down together to practise

what they believe in, and that is a prayer breakfast, I see just no connection at all. I think you are stretching it.

RATHER: If I may follow on this, let the record show I am not anti-prayer or prayer breakfasts or anything, but I do think there is a fairly important question involved here. While Charles Colson was, at one time, a member of the White House staff, he is now operating for people such as the Teamsters Union. Now we all know the way Washington works. These people ingratiate themselves with people in positions of power, and at such things as, yes, a prayer breakfast, they do their business. Isn't someone around here worried at least about the symbolism of this?

WARREN: No more than we are worried about the symbolism of Senator Hughes being the main speaker.

QUESTION FROM UNIDENTIFIED VOICE: Is he representing some outside business interest?

QUESTION: What is the parallel?

WARREN: The parallel is that these are human beings who are expressing their belief together, and I see no problem with that whatsoever.

QUESTION: Senator Hughes is going to go into the clergy. Are you comparing that with the Teamsters Union? (laughter).

WARREN: I think this has gone far enough.

With that Warren turned and walked away from the podium, leaving a roomful of bemused reporters and only one news story of the day – Colson at a prayer breakfast.

Shortly before noon every button on my telephone lighted up at once. Nothing unusual. It happened often enough through the long night of Watergate. Whenever a new accusation was hurled my way, reporters reached for their phones to call for my comment, a standard practice. "The *Chicago Tribune*, the *Post*, the *New York Times*, AP," Holly reported. All of them calling at once."

My heart raced. There had not been much about me in the press lately. Could it be the long-expected indictment? I took the *Chicago Tribune* call first, because I liked Aldo Beckman, its Washington Bureau chief who was on the line.

"There's a story moving on the wires, Chuck, about your attending a prayer meeting at the White House this morning, about you and Senator Harold Hughes of Iowa becoming close friends." The scepticism in his voice increased: "And then something else here about your having found religion."

In a flush of anger I protested, "Come on, Aldo, you guys have printed everything there is to print about me. But my religion is my own business and I'm not about to talk about it in the public press. Enough is enough."

"Warren has announced that you were at a prayer breakfast this morning at the White House. It's already public."

"Warren announced it?" I was stunned. "Well, then let Warren tell you all about it." With that I hung up.

By now the calls were coming in a torrent. "What shall I tell them?" Holly asked.

"Tell them to . . ." And then I thought better of it. "Just take down the names. Maybe I'll call back."

I placed a call to Jerry Warren who explained what had happened. "I guess someone saw you come in today, Chuck. These vultures are grabbing for every little straw. They had a field day with the prayer breakfast bit. You should have seen their faces," he chuckled.

"But I've been in the White House over and over these past months, Jerry, and they've watched me come and go all the time. Why should they ask about it today?"

I called Doug Coe, who told me that reporters were calling Hughes and Fellowship House, too, and were piecing the story together. "Just be careful, Chuck. Don't lose your temper," Doug advised.

The question I had asked Jerry Warren began to plague me: "Why today?" Dan Rather might have asked that question almost any day of the week over the prior nine months. There were times just before a major Presidential announcement, or after the "Saturday Night Massacre," or when the Ervin Committee was in full swing when my visits should have drawn suspicious attention. They never had. Why now?

Was it possible that it wasn't chance at all? I was learning that the Lord works in mysterious ways – although it was hard for me to see how His purposes could be served by cynical articles about my conversion. Yet the thought persisted.

Why had not Warren brushed Rather's question aside, said simply that I had not been to see Nixon? Or that he didn't know? Why bring in the prayer breakfast? That wasn't Warren's usual style.

And yet how could this be God's doing? Attention from the press was the last thing we wanted now; the lower my profile the better, my lawyers believed. And the cynics would have a circus; there would be a lot of snickering, especially from old friends. Finally, if the story ever came out with my verification, I'd be locked completely into a new life, no falling back into my old ways.

And suddenly I found myself remembering how Tom Phillips had proclaimed his faith to me. He risked embarrassment in doing so, but his courage helped change my life. The teaching of Scripture was as clear as the sparkle of sun now streaming in my office windows. "Never be ashamed of bearing witness to our Lord," Paul wrote to Timothy (*see* 2 Timothy 1:8 PHILLIPS). We had discussed this recently at a Monday meeting. Not to verify the story would be almost to deny the reality of what had happened to me. There was no other way, I concluded, no way to modify it, condition it, or call it something else, no socially acceptable middle ground.

The decision was made. If Rather's question was the result of a one-in-a-thousand coincidence, so be it. But if it was God's doing, I must do my part. So I called the reporters back and did my best to explain my commitment. Even as I listened to the words coming out of my mouth against the clattering of typewriter keys on the other end of the phone it sounded unreal: "Accepting Christ . . . Jesus Christ in my life." What this was going to look like in the stark black of printer's ink! The occasional titters, the "Would you repeat that – more slowly – this time," confirmed my worst fears.

"TOUGH GUY" COLSON HAS TURNED RELIGIOUS proclaimed the *Los Angeles Times*; COLSON HAS "FOUND RELIGION" in the *New York Times. Time* magazine summed up the press reports the following week (December 17, 1973) under the heading "Conversion":

Of all the Watergate cast, few had a reputation for being tougher, wilier, nastier or more tenaciously loyal to

Richard Nixon than onetime Presidential Adviser Charles W. Colson. The former Marine captain is alleged by Jeb Stuart Magruder to have urged the original Watergate bugging and has been implicated in a host of other dirty tricks, including the forgery of a State Department cable. At the peak of his influence, he proudly boasted that his commitment to the re-election of the President was such that "I would walk over my grandmother if necessary".

At a White House staff prayer breakfast last week, Colson, 42, revealed a new aspect. He said that he has "come to know Christ . . ." Suspecting that his newfound faith may go down hard with some, Tough-Guy Colson had a forthright response for scoffers. Said he : "If anyone wants to be cynical about it, I'll pray for him."

I regretted this widely reported remark – "I'll pray for him." I had not meant it to sound so patronising, so much like the old Colson arrogance. It was simply the first answer that had popped into mind when someone asked what I would say to those who doubted my sincerity.

The *Boston Globe* in a lead editorial entitled "Amen, Brother" recited every real and imagined Colson misdeed and concluded : "If Mr. Colson can repent his sins, there just has to be hope for everybody."

Syndicated columnist Harriet Van Horne was more direct : "I cannot accept the sudden coming to Christ of Charles Colson. If he isn't embarrassed by this sudden excess of piety, then surely the Lord must be."

And a Catholic priest, turned liberal philosopher journalist, Colman McCarthy, likened the Colson conversion to Rennie Davis's profession of faith in Guru Maharaj Ji of India. It was my willingness to speak publicly that offended McCarthy: "In the history of authentic conversion . . . the new members of the faith always kept silence at first." And so it continued for days and weeks to come.

I worried whether there had been something smug and self-righteous in saying "I *have* been converted?" Can anyone really be sure that in fact he has been? Certainly I had accepted and fervently believed certain truths. Yet I was hardly a transformed person. All I could honestly say was that I was seeking, searching, trying, learning, failing and falling short, recovering and continuing to try – all the time reaching for a relationship with Jesus Christ. The change was in my spirit, in my attitudes, in the set of my will. Why should anyone believe me when I described it, and why should anyone accept my word that indeed the conversion was permanent? The sceptics had every right to say. "Let him show us by his deeds not by words."

I've discovered that the term *conversion* is misunderstood by many people. St. Paul's experience on the Damascus Road is the best-known in all of history and books written about other conversions are similarly dramatic. Yet I am sure that most are simple, undramatic, and not newsworthy.

I was troubled, too, by the popular assumption that to be converted to Christ one must be driven to it by the most heinous and sinful past, one's conscience must be so guilt-ridden, his mischief so great that in an act of desperation he thrusts himself upon God's mercy. For days after the initial rash of stories, many, including the prosecutors, believed that I was on the verge of stepping forward to confess to all of the most dastardly sins of Watergate.

In a meeting that took place in Mr. Jaworski's office in late December, attended by Mr. Merrill and several young assistants, the subject of my much-publicised conversion was brought up.

"We've read about your experience," Merrill said. "We believe that you are sincere and that *now* you do want to come forward and tell us everything."

Merrill was sitting across from me at the big conference table in Jaworski's office. He lowered his eyes as he spoke, as if he wanted to spare me the embarrassment of staring at me while I told all. I looked to my left at Leon Jaworski; there was a faint enigmatic smile on his round face.

I knew, of course, what they expected. If my conversion was real I should tell them how guilty I had really been all this time. The only difficulty was that I had been trying to tell them the truth from the outset. They didn't believe it and hoped perhaps that God had now joined the Special Prosecutor's force to open me up. They were also saying, or so it seemed to me, that I could only prove the sincerity of my religious conviction by confessing to something I had previously withheld.

Anger welled up in me. "I didn't seek this publicity about my religion," I responded to Merrill. "And I don't intend to use it, but it shouldn't be used against me." Merrill quickly changed the subject; but I knew then and there that the publicity about my conversion had further eroded what little was left of my credibility with the prosecutors.

The other reactions ran the whole gamut. My mother was irate. "His father and I raised our boy as a good Christian. He was baptised and confirmed in the Episcopal Church. We taught him every Christian principle. Imagine saying he's just now become a Christian!" she lamented to a neighbour.

I tried to explain to my parents that while their efforts had been sincere, nothing had happened to me. It was my fault, not theirs.

One relative believed that the strain of Watergate had been too much. "I'm afraid poor Chuck has snapped, gone over the edge. This kind of religious fervour is often the sign of mental instability," she wrote a mutual friend.

The sharpest blow of all was inflicted on Wendell, then in his sophomore year at Princeton. He was, as he later recounted, studying quietly in his room when one of the girls down the hall (yes, coed dorms at Princeton), an active Campus Crusader, pounded excitedly on his door. "I just saw your father on television!" she exclaimed. "He is one of us; he has accepted Jesus Christ as his personal Saviour!'

It was for Wendell the last straw. It had been hard enough for a nineteen-year-old college student struggling for acceptability on campus to have his father accused day after day of one crime after another. But he was not prepared for this. Slapping his hand against his forehead he sighed, "Oh, no! Dad's a Jesus freak."

Dave Shapiro was predictably irate, storming into my office the morning after the first stories broke. "You've done it this time, Colson, you've really done it. I hope He [I assumed he meant Christ] can save your butt now because I can't."

"Calm yourself, Dave," I said. "I couldn't do a thing about it this time. We should have expected it one of these days."

"Calm yourself!" he screamed, pounding his beefy fist on my desk. "Just when I thought we had the Ellsberg thing licked, just when you've been out of the press for a month, now this. It looks like the biggest 'dirty trick' you've ever pulled, the final big play for sympathy. It probably is. As far as I'm concerned they ought to indict you for this one." With that he stomped out of my office past Holly, whose fingers were plugged in her ears.

Old friends had the toughest time understanding it. Brad Morse, under-secretary-general of the United Nations, who thought he knew me as well as anyone, was visited one day by Jonathan Moore, my assistant in Saltonstall days and best man when Patty and I were married. Brad glared at Jonathan. "What's all this Jesus stuff about Colson: I have only been double-crossed twice in my life, both times by Christians. Do you think Chuck is okay?"

An intensely serious Harvard law student who had worked ed for me as an intern in the White House put it very bluntly: "Some of us knew, admired, and respected the Colson that 'was'. All this conversion talk, in addition to being pontifical, I frankly resent." The young man took it as a renunciation of my past, of which he considered himself a part.

Teamster President Frank Fitzsimmons, himself a deeply religious Catholic, was furious. "Those – in the press, nothing is sacred, nothing. Writing about a man's religion; that is the dirtiest, lowest thing of all."

And yet some of the press coverage was surprisingly sympathetic. Bill Greider, a reporter for the *Washington Post* authored a page-one feature article, detailing the history of my conversion, the relationship with Hughes and the Monday prayer group. The Lord's ways are mysterious indeed: it had to be my sworn enemies on the *Post* who would write the first serious treatment of the subject. "Colson's spiritual awakening may not remedy any of his problems with the Watergate Grand Jury," Greider wrote "but it does satisfy one group, the men who meet with him regularly for prayer at Harold Hughes' home." The understanding *Post* article, along with a sympathetic UPI story written by a young Christian, Wes Pippert, were carried in hundreds of papers across the country.

On Monday, December 17, Eric Sevareid devoted his entire commentary on the CBS evening news to the blizzard which had struck Washington that day – and the Colson conversion. An act of God, the snowstorm, he opined, had done more to save energy and to cleanse Washington's air than all the conservation legislation Congress was then scrambling to enact. As for the conversion, the other act of God he said, "Mr. Charles Colson, once the toughest of the White House tough-guys and a man believed by many to be standin' in the need of prayer as well as a good defence lawyer, Mr. Colson has made page one with the news of his conversion to religion. He is not repenting of any alleged sin of a juridical nature, but he does confess that he was just too big for his breeches. The new Colson does not claim the capacity to walk on water, but he has given up walking on grandmothers. A good many people here, anxious to believe in something, are quite willing to take Colson's change of heart as real. After all, that kind of change is what innumerable critics have been demanding all along ... Mr Colson is clearly on the right track in more ways than one. An act of Congress has its place, but it's a simple act of God that gets results."

The Sevareid commentary, watched by perhaps thirty million Americans, and the *Post* and UPI stories reaching millions more, resulted in a powerful public testimony for Christ. I could never have anticipated such a thing – nor another reaction which for me at least was the most surprising of all.

Almost from the first day, large bundles of letters began to arrive in my office, some addressed to the Ervin Committee, some to the White House, some simply to Washington, D.C., one in care of "Watergate." I tried to answer them all but in time it became impossible. They came from all parts of the country, some from abroad, as far away as Manila and New Delhi. Almost without exception the letters spoke of prayers that were being offered for me, of the writer's excitement over one person finding Christ, of Christian love. Many were from people who confessed their complete disdain for Mr. Nixon's politics and mine, but who in the next breath welcomed me as a brother, pledging their complete prayers for me. Some were from people who said they had never written to a public figure before. All of them praised God.

I'd never thought about how many such people there must be, but the letters piled on my desk renewed my enthusiasm as I pored through them each evening. Late one afternoon, shortly after Christmas, I came upon a letter that was to continue to affect my view of my own goals for months and years to come. It was scrawled on a single sheet of lined white paper:

25 December 1973

Dear Sir:

This may seem to you as an unusual letter, however, after reading an article in the *Charleston Evening Post* on you I gathered that you were (in the past) an unusual person. I'm a S/Sgt. in the USAF. For 19 years I've been trying to find myself. I've went to church on several occasions but they (the pastors) didn't reach me. After reading your article it has helped me more than anything in my entire life. It is Christmas morning. I'm usually drunk or trying to get drunk by now, but here I am watching the children open up their presents and thinking about going to church somewhere, instead of the club or someone's house and get drunk. I didn't even buy any "booze" this year. It's people in positions like you who confess their past (maybe not so good life – wrongs) or whatever it may be called. Sure do help people in a position like me. I truly feel free within my inner self this morning and I pray that God may help both of us in all of our trying efforts.

I am going to try and find that book MERE CHRISTIANITY down here and read it myself.

God blessing you,
S/SGT. NATHANIEL GREEN

I didn't care who saw me in my office as the tears streamed down my cheeks while I read and re-read Sergeant Green's letter. He said it all. For eleven years of my life I'd driven

with every ounce of energy in my body to do the things in
government that I believed might make people's lives better.
But in all that time I could not point to one single person,
not one life, that had actually changed for the better. In
fact, nothing I could reflect back on could compare to the
feeling of joy I felt at the thought of one man re-united with
his family on Christmas Day. And the means of reaching
this staff sergeant had been the press, against which I'd harboured such resentment.

"The individual is ... more important ... for he is everlasting and the life of a state or a civilisation, compared with
his, is only a moment," C.S. Lewis had written.

If – as one of my friends called to tell me, "Everybody in
this town is laughing at you," then le. them laugh. *There
are many Sergeant Greens out there*, I thought as I looked
into the late afternoon darkness beyond my office windows.
And there is also the Master, alive and working in ways that
we never will understand. I thanked Him, thanked Him for
Dan Rather's hostile questions, for Jerry Warren blundering
into the whole prayer-breakfast business, even for those who
had written the barbed and cutting stories.

"It's worth it all, Holly," I said as I passed her desk, watching a bewildered expression come across her face, "worth it
all."

13

The Lonely House

The day after the CBS broadcast by Eric Sevareid, Steve Bull called from the White House: "Chuck, the President would like to see you. Can you come right over?"

Just like the old days, I thought. I felt the same old flutter in the heart, the excitement of going to see the most important man in the world. Although we had talked on the phone regularly, we had avoided face-to-face meetings since I left his staff, nine months before, for fear that the Watergate bad-guy image which clung so firmly to me would be an embarrassment to him.

It must be important, I thought, grabbing my overcoat and excusing myself without explanation from several of my partners then meeting in my office. I made my way the half-block from my office to the Southwest Gate, tramping through the now-grey snow which, along with my conversion, Sevareid had philosophised about the night before.

Steve was at the gate. To avoid the press he led me up the long circular driveway of the South Lawn, across the open, grassed area where the President's helicopter lands and takes off, past Secret Service men stationed around the building, and in through the diplomatic entrance.

"What's up, Steve?" I asked once we were inside the reception room with handsome Early American murals covering the walls and a gigantic blue, white, and gold rug with the fifty state seals woven into its border.

"The boss needs to talk to you, Chuck. Watergate has made things rough. No one knows you're seeing him. He's upstairs in the Lincoln Sitting Room. Safer that way. Can't even trust the staff in the west wing anymore." Steve shook his head in dismay. "It's killing him. He's taking it all so hard. Cheer him up, Chuck, like you used to in the old days."

As I walked up the wide red-carpeted staircase and across the marble-columned centre hall, I felt a chill. The White House seemed deserted. Usually there were Secret Service men around, staffers showing people through, military aides, lines of tourists. But today there was no sign of life anywhere; the only sound was my leather heels hitting the cold marble. For an uncanny moment I remembered the silence of that strange day after the election.

Even the door to the Lincoln Sitting Room on the second floor was unattended as I walked in. The President was slumped in an uncomfortably stiff-looking yellow brocade chair in the corner of the small room crammed with relics of the Lincoln Presidency. "Good to see you, boy, good to see you." Nixon was out of the chair and on his feet, a big grin on his face, grabbing my hand as he had never done before.

After seating me in one of the rosewood chairs purchased by Mrs Lincoln, he offered me one of his pipes. Following an inquiry about my family, Nixon got to what was on his mind. " The lawyers tell me we shouldn't be seen together. This business goes too far. No reason two old friends can't get together. We'll talk about George Meany, labour issues, or something; no one can criticise us for that, can they ?"

We had not been together since I learned of the White House taping system. Half in jest I asked, "Mr. President, is our conversation being recorded?"

"What do you mean, recorded? Who would do that to us?" He sat upright in his chair, the smile gone, a flash of fear in his face. "Would *they* do that ?" he demanded.

I tried to explain that I was only curious as to whether he himself was still taping conversations. But he kept interrupting : "Can I trust the Secret Service, Chuck? I don't know that I can. You don't suppose Jaworski would bug *this* room, do you ?" Again I tried to assure the President that if *he* did not have the room bugged I was certain no one else did. But this did not satisfy him.

"The problem, Chuck, is that I don't think I can trust anybody. Not even the secretaries."

What irony, I thought. For years the President had recorded every unsuspecting visitor to his office; now he was obsessed over the thought that someone was recording him. The man who for four years strode so confidently through the grand halls and offices of the White House, savouring every minute of the unparalleled power he enjoyed, was hiding out in a far corner of the nearly empty mansion, distrustful of everyone around him. I felt a surge of sympathy for my old friend. He looked different, somehow smaller, as if he had shrunk into a protective shell; his skin was sallow, the lines on his face deeper. The fatigue was more apparent than it had been during any of the crises I had lived through with him.

"The tapes," he recounted slowly regaining his self-assurance, "they were all Haldeman's idea. Stupid. I told Bob twice to have the system removed, but you know Bob. I forgot all about them. But there aren't any here now. I ordered every one removed. I saw to it myself. You can be sure of that."

Then the President questioned me about the conversations we'd had together in the early part of 1973. He donned his horn-rimmed reading glasses and began studying a sheaf of papers resting in his lap. Tape transcripts? I decided not to ask. I repeated each conversation as I remembered it, while Nixon nodded approvingly, his eyes scanning one sheet of paper after another. Was he testing me to see how good my recollection was? Now and again he interrupted: "You're sure of that, are you?" Then he'd return to the papers in his lap, puffing again on his meerschaum pipe.

"Are you sure you never asked me to grant clemency to Hunt, Chuck?" he asked when I had completed the recitation.

"Positive," I replied, "I started to once and you cut me off. I remember it well."

"Good, good, so long as you are positive. Well, let's talk about more pleasant subjects." Nixon took off his glasses, slid the papers back into a brown manila envelope and began to smile. *Surely he hasn't called me here for this*, I thought;

we had discussed these conversations three times on the phone. The answers were always the same and he had all the tapes.

"Do you have any reason to think my memory is faulty?" I asked – as close as I dared come to asking him what was in those papers. "No, no, boy. Can't be too careful nowadays, though. Jaworski wants all these tapes; I just have to be sure. Don't you worry about it. That was an interesting article in the *Post* about you."

Now it had come out. This was the real reason, I surmised for the President wanting to see me – my conversion. Was he worried that my commitment to Christ or my friendship with Hughes would turn me against my old leader? Or – could he be looking for spiritual strength himself? Should I recount my experience, as Tom Phillips had with me? If I could speak boldly to sometimes hostile reporters, why would I retreat now?

The silence hung there. And I remained silent – retreat it was. He would not understand, I rationalised. Besides, why should he take sermonising from me? I was no Billy Graham. "The papers will print anything nowadays," I said lamely. "Crazy times, Mr. President."

If the President was giving me the opportunity I'd sought weeks before, to meet and pray with him, I failed him completely. I had always been forthright with the President on on other subjects. Why the timidity about my conversion? It was to haunt me for months.

The rest of the conversation was filled with nostalgic reminiscing. We were back living again in the golden days when the crowds in the streets, roaring their approval, pressed forward for a closer look at *the* President and his passing motorcade. Those were the days of victory when the polls showed us on our way to a massive record-breaking re-election victory, when an American President triumphantly toured the Kremlin and marched atop the Great Wall of China, signalling a new era of American diplomacy. Ending the twenty-five-year cold war, plus the hot one in Vietnam, was to usher in a "generation of peace," Richard Nixon's most cherished dream. "We must have been doing something right, Chuck, no matter what they say now, right?"

"How different the world around me looked . . . with the globe and anchor on my cap." Colson as a lieutenant, USMC, in the summer of 1953, Camp Lejeune, N.C.

"I married Patty . . . whose radiant smile and winsome ways made her one of the best-liked secretaries on Capitol Hill." Patty Colson at work in the 1968 campaign.

At strategy session in library/office at Key Biscayne, Florida, following the 1970 congressional elections are (from left) Nixon, Donald Rumsfeld, John Mitchell, John Ehrlichman, Colson, Bryce Harlow, Bob Haldeman, Robert Finch (back to camera)— *Official White House Photo. Below:* Editorial cartoon by Pat Oliphant. Reprinted with permission. *Los Angeles Times* Syndicate

'YOU'D BETTER CALL THE REVEREND BILLY—COLSON'S GOT RELIGION!'

"Each morning shortly after eight, the men of power in the Executive branch of government assemble around a long antique mahogany table in the historic Roosevelt Room just across a narrow corridor from the President's Oval Office." (Clockwise from top) Henry Kissinger, Peter Flanigan, John Ehrlichman, Colson, Clark MacGregor, Bill Timmons, Bob Haldeman, George Shultz, Ron Ziegler—*Official White House Photo.*

"Charlie Morin had nearly abandoned his law practice, visiting me several times a week and organising a campaign to ask President Ford to pardon me." Charles H. Morin, Colson's oldest friend and longtime law partner. *Cashen/Stout.*

Above: Wendell Colson with his dad —Dover, Massachusetts, summer of 1970.

Below: "Daddy, I'm proud of you." Colson's daughter, Emily, with her dad two weeks before Colson entered prison.

Above: "Thank You, God, for giving me this son . . ." Christian Colson at high-school graduation in Weston, Massachusetts, June 1974.

' COLSON ?! . . .'

Cartoon by MacNelly—*Richmond News Leader,*
© 1974 by *Chicago Tribune.*

Doug Coe—"'Hi-ya, brother . . .' He always arrived, it seemed, when my spirits most needed a lift." *Cashen/Stout. Right:* Harold Hughes—". . . this hulking combat veteran, truck driver, and one-time two-fisted drinker, a flamboyant orator, but a compassionate man whom I had come to love very much." *Cashen/Stout.*

Al Quie, veteran Republican congressman from Minnesota— ". . . a tall, rugged, athletic man and former dairy farmer, flashed a shy smile which gave him the appearance of being younger than his fifty years." *Cashen/Stout. Right:* Graham Purcell, five-term Democratic congressman—"I had long since learned that beneath his hardened Texas-cowboy hide is a heart as big and soft as a ripe melon." *Cashen/Stout.*

Above: "Shapiro continued to negotiate with Jaworski's men, haggling over the kind of plea which both sides could agree to and which would save my license to practise law." David Shapiro, Brooklyn-born trial lawyer and Colson's chief counsel—*Cashen Stout.*

Below: "All the material things in life are meaningless if a man hasn't discovered what's underneath them." The man who led Colson to Christ—Thomas L. Phillips, chairman of the board, Raytheon Company—©*Karsh, Ottawa.*

Above: "Peace. Peace. Serenity." Cleaning up final details before surrendering to prison; at poolside with wife, Patty, and secretary, Holly Holm—*Newsweek/Wally McNamee.*

Below: "Oh, how I love Jesus Christ . . ." Edmon W. Blow, pastor of Trinity Bible Church in Montgomery, Alabama—raw-boned preacher who ministered weekly to Colson and other inmates at Maxwell Prison—here with Colson at Southern Baptist Pastors' Conference, June 1975 —*Biblical Recorder.*

"Right, right, Mr. President," I was saying, though it was only the memories that lived. All else lay crumbled and broken in the wreckage of Watergate.

More than an hour passed before the President looked at his watch. "I'd better get back," he said. "Nobody except Steve knows I'm here. I'll never forget you — the service you've given your country. Someday we'll set all this straight, you wait and see, Chuck." He repeated it, as much to convince himself, so I thought, as to reassure me. "You just wait and see. There'll come a time when we wipe the slate clean. Not yet, but it will come."

I knew, of course, what he was alluding to: pardons for his loyal staff members facing criminal charges, as soon as he regained popular support. Somehow it was not reassuring. Deep in my heart I felt that the Watergate tide would not be turned away. As we walked together through the family quarters I felt the President knew it, too.

We said good-bye at the edge of the Rose Garden. I stood for a moment watching his back slightly hunched, fade into the December grey, two Secret Service men scampering ahead to open the doors to the west wing. For him it was a return to the world of missing tapes, of new accusations, of irregularities in his tax returns, of congressmen calling for his impeachment. For me — a return to grand juries, sessions with my lawyers, the constant probing of Jaworski's men, and the uncertainty of the future.

My phone rang shortly after 11:30 that night, waking Patty and me from a sound sleep. The voice of the White House operator: "Mr. Colson, it's the President." Though I had been unsettled by our meeting, chagrined that I hadn't been bold enough to talk about Jesus Christ and alarmed by the tragic picture that lingered in my mind of my old friend, it had apparently been a tonic for Mr. Nixon. "Sorry to call so late, but it was so good to talk with you today. I just wanted to chat a few minutes longer if you don't mind." It was a continuation of our conversation that afternoon, more reminiscing, more questions about our conversations the prior January, a good report he'd received that day from Kissinger about the Israelis' willingness to make concessions in the

Middle East, how to handle the Ervin Committee demand for 600 Presidential tapes. In the midst of a discussion about the tapes, Nixon suddenly stopped.

"Let me ask you one more time. Why did you suggest today that the room might be bugged? Do you have some information that you didn't want to tell me?"

There was no way I could reassure him. The tone had changed completely! I was no longer listening to the strong, self-assured resonant voice I knew so well. Then he turned to the appeal now before the court over delivering to the prosecutors The White House tapes. "You know, Chuck, I will have no choice but to resign if we lose this case. I simply must draw the line." His voice rose, strong again for an instant, "I will not preside over the destruction of the Presidency."

The prospect of stepping down was weighing heavily on the President's mind as it had the night he called late in July. "What do you think will happen, Chuck, if I stick it out and there's an impeachment? You know that if I am impeached I'll be wiped out financially – no pension – and now with all I owe in taxes. Everybody thinks I've gotten rich, but it just isn't so."

Self-interest? Or high patriotic motive? The two were inextricably woven together in this complex man. I struggled to muster an enthusiasm and confidence which I did not feel. "Stop talking that way, Mr. President, you'll fight and you'll win as you always have."

Then came the question that still rings in my ears. "I know Jaworski doesn't want to hurt the President; he's said so. But you don't suppose *they* would send me to jail do you, Chuck?"

For an instant I couldn't believe he was serious. "Stop it, Mr. President!" I exclaimed. "That's the most absurd thing I've ever heard! and stop talking about quitting. The captain doesn't desert the ship."

"I know all that," he countered. "But maybe the country should be spared all of this. Maybe what the country wants is a nice, clean Jerry Ford – the trouble is, Jerry isn't ready just yet. It would take him a year to get up to speed on all the international issues – and you know Jerry would have a tough time with Kissinger. I'm not sure he could control him, Chuck; you know Henry can be unstable at times – fly off in all directions. You remember what we had to go through last year during the December bombing, holding Henry down. You remember, Chuck. No, Jerry needs more time; he'll have to learn Henry's ways."

The President was using me as a barometer to find out how bad the situation really was. He wanted total reassurance which I tried to give. He wasn't reflecting on Ford or Kissinger, merely assessing realities. Ford had been on the job less than a month and was unfamiliar with the volatile idiosyncrasies of Kissinger's genius. For five long years Nixon and Henry worked together intimately, aware of each other's strengths and weaknesses, dependent on one another like two tightrope walkers – high-powered foreign-policy manoeuvrings are every bit as precariously balanced.

Then Nixon made the most startling statement of the day : "You know, Chuck, I get on my knees every night and just pray to God."

I was stunned. For a man so proud he could never admit human weakness in any form – refusing to acknowledge a common cold even when his chest was so congested he could hardly talk – it was an amazing confession. From the tone of his voice I am convinced he was sincere. The statement came from nowhere, had nothing to do with anything we were talking about, but before I could say a word he leaped back to safe ground and strategy to be employed against House Judiciary Committee Chairman Peter Rodino. Knowing Nixon as I did, I knew he was embarrassed by his own frankness in opening up such a personal topic.

But again that day he had given me the opportunity to speak, to tell him how God could lead us out of this wilderness. And again I kept silent. Was it cowardice? Was it the Lord Himself keeping my lips sealed? All I know is that a second time that day I had failed him.

It was nearly 1:00 a.m. when I put the receiver down, pushed my desk chair back and fell to my knees in the quiet of my library. I asked God to forgive me for my lack of boldness, imploring Him to overlook my weakness and deal with the President in His way. After all, I was still seeking Him myself – He alone knew through what struggle and confusion.

In the weeks that followed I resumed my old battle station, now as the President's impeachment adviser. Of top concern was finding the right criminal trial lawyer. We went through a long list of possibilities. None was right. Most people think that all the President has to do is push a button and he can command the services of top specialists in every profession. It doesn't work that way. The top talent is often hard to find, even for White House service, more so in the shadow of Watergate than ever before. The pay is lower than in the business world, but the real deterrents are the punishment of long hours, a paucity of gratitude, and the ever-present possibility of finding your mistake a national news item.

Late in December I offered him my own lawyer, Jim St. Clair, describing him as tough, adroit in the courtroom, respected. The President interviewed Jim the next day, and two days later St. Clair phoned to ask me to release him. There was no emotion about it. Jim, coldly professional as always, seemed to feel no excitement over going to work for the President who was to him just another client.

The following week St. Clair's appointment was announced with scarcely a word in the press about what I feared might become an embarrassment – the connection between the President, St. Clair, and myself. So little escaped critical examination in the glare of Watergate that it was a rare bit of good fortune for Jim St. Clair to move into the White House untarnished.

For a while it seemed like the good old days, Nixon and me together again for the big fight ahead. But it was not like it used to be. We had both changed. Nixon, flag, and country were no longer one and the same to me. I was beginning to see for the first time Richard Nixon, the man. This individual, the one out of 200 million who rose to the highest office in the land, was great in some ways, weak in others, limited as all mortals are. If anything, I cared more for him in a personal way than ever before, but the awe and reverence were gone.

Nor could I put out of my mind nagging doubts about the President's innocence. Why the curious summer-long silence while John Dean's charges were rocketing off the walls of the Senate Caucus Room? Why the almost obsessive worry over the tapes? Why that eighteen-and-a-half-minute gap and Nixon's protestations about "poor, poor Rose"?

The situation in the White House had become almost chaotic. Petty intramural jealousies dominated the various echelons. Haig told me one night in early January he was quitting unless Nixon demoted Ziegler; I called Nixon to warn him and put myself squarely in the middle of a bitter feud. Young staff members were leaving as fast as they could find jobs outside; those on the wrong side of the warring internal factions soon found themselves forced to look elsewhere. Practically all who had been in the White House during the first term were being summoned regularly before grand juries and Jaworski's prosecutors. Many were gripped with fear that they might be the next target of prosecution; all were in debt, incurring heavy legal expenses.

The White House staff Christmas Party that year was like a wake. Steve Bull took me into a quiet corner to whisper his most private fears that "no one around here is trying to save the President; everyone is knifing him, protecting themselves." Ziegler refused to attend because Haig was scheduled to be there. In the end neither came, a slight the juniors felt. Nixon himself was increasingly withdrawn and reclusive. "We never even see him walking around anymore," a senior staffer complained. One young girl began to cry as I was reminiscing about the exciting, purposeful days of the 1972 campaign.

Gone was the sense of mission, the common dedication to a cause greater than oneself. Never had I seen liquor flow more freely or produce fewer smiles. According to my former assistant, Dick Howard, the White House was like Berlin in the last days when Hitler's once proud and haughty lieutenants, trapped, smelling death and defeat, turned bitterly on one another and indulged every hedonistic desire.

As I began to see the shallowness in my blind and unquestioning approach to the President – to any human being, for that matter – I began to think more and more about the "causes that mattered" in Doug Coe's inscription in my Bible. Some days, in fact, my own thoughts surprised me. I found myself caring more about wanting Christ to come into President Nixon's life than whether he could successfully parry the thrusts of his attackers.

New Year's weekend I found a breath of hope in a small news item from San Clemente, reporting that Nixon was reading a recently published book about Lincoln. I knew at once it was Elton Trueblood's work on Lincoln's spiritual life. Tom Phillips had given it to me in September to read and perhaps pass on to the President. I had found the book spiritually stimulating as it portrayed Lincoln's slow conversion in 1862, his gradual turning to the Almighty for guidance and strength. I had sent my copy to Nixon in November. The President had never acknowledged receiving it, and I had wondered if he felt I was pushing him. Now I knew he was reading it.

It was the evening before the National Prayer Breakfast in late January that Al Quie, Graham Purcell, Doug Coe, Harold Hughes and I met for prayer and dinner in the Capitol with Billy Graham and Senator Mark Hatfield. Mark Hatfield's outspoken opposition to Nixon's Vietnam policy had earned him a reputation as a leading Republican maverick. Mr. Nixon had ranted about him many times and I had joined in the denunciation myself. To Senator Hatfield I was the embodiment of all that was misguided and evil in the Nixon White House.

Yet as we knelt in prayer together at the altar in the quiet of the tiny granite-walled prayer room located just off the massive domed rotunda of the Capitol Building, the animosity drained away. Much of Hatfield's prayer was devoted, in fact, to thanking God for my conversion and for bringing us together in Christ. At dinner we discussed helping Nixon as a human being and as a national leader – Senator Hughes, a political foe; Hatfield, a rebel within his party; Billy Graham and I, his friends – all pledging ourselves to pray for our beleaguered President.

That night the President called to ask me a host of questions about the National Prayer Breakfast upcoming the next morning. Though it was late, and earlier in the evening Nixon had delivered his State of the Union address to Congress over live television watched by millions of Americans, he was alert, probing, obviously preparing his remarks as he talked.

"You know, Chuck," he mused, "I've never been able to talk about my beliefs in God in public and I resent people using religion in politics. That's so hypocritical. Not the kind of thing I've ever done." As he talked on, he was as unguarded as I'd ever known him. He spoke of his devout Quaker mother, and how he himself accepted God when he was a boy and found strength from his faith. I urged him to speak freely at the breakfast.

Billy Graham rode with Nixon the next morning from the White House to the Washington Hilton Hotel; he later told us that he and the President enjoyed the most frank discussion ever about Christ, Nixon's faith, and the need for the Lord's hand in guiding an embittered nation. Nixon's remarks before 3,000 men and women from all over the world left no doubt about the impact Abraham Lincoln's spiritual life had had on him.

> Although he never belonged to a church, he probably prayed more than any man who has ever been in the White House ... He did not have a feeling of arrogance about his side as compared to the other side. He did feel that America was destined to be united ... He did believe that America had something to stand for, something to believe in, and something to do in the world bigger than itself. In other words, there was something other than Lincoln, the politician, the President, and the American people, each individual; there was what he called the Almighty, the Universal Being; sometimes he referred to him as God who guided the destiny of this nation.

As he spoke, Nixon came close to professing his own commitment, speaking more openly than ever before in his long political career.

> When I was eight or nine years old, I asked my grandmother, a very saintly woman, a little Quaker lady, who had nine children – I asked her why it was that Quakers believed in silent prayer. When we sat down to the table,

we always had silent prayers; and often at church, while we sometimes had a minister or somebody got up when the spirit moved him, we often just went there and just sat, and we prayed. Her answer was very interesting, and perhaps it relates to why Lincoln prayed in silence. My grandmother spoke to me on this occasion, as she always did to her grandchildren and children, with the plain speech. She said, "What thee must understand, Richard, is that the purpose of prayer is to listen to God, not to talk to God. The purpose of prayer is not to tell God what thee wants, but to find out from God what He wants from thee."

Watching his face closely as he spoke, I noted the sudden relaxation of all the tense lines and tightly drawn muscles as he said: "Too often we are a little too arrogant [when] we try to talk to God ... [Let's] listen to God and find out what He wants for us and then we will all do the right thing." His voice almost trailed off and he was through. It was not the flag-waving ending he always sought in his speeches, but an awkwardly humble and candid remark that told of the hunger of his heart.

I knew that morning what had happened to the "old fire" inside me, the old drive I could not now muster to lead Mr. Nixon's charge against his enemies. No longer could I be Mr. Nixon's unquestioning political lieutenant, dealing in hand-to-hand combat, and at the same time help him – or anyone else for that matter – find a relationship with Christ. By wanting to do both for my old friend I wasn't doing either one. My causes had been mixed up, I realized, as Doug's inscription in my Bible paraded again through my mind: "Better to fail in a cause that will ultimately succeed ..." And being faithful to Christ I realized, meant living it with everyone I encountered, as well as believing it. For me it could no longer be a private luxury. Nor could I apply it selectively, but universally.

"The one thing I don't want to do, and certainly not for any newspaper story, is try to relate my own beliefs today with Watergate," I had told a UPI reporter only a few weeks earlier. Knowing Christ in my heart, but dealing with the biggest moral crisis in generations as if nothing had happened was, I now knew, trying to straddle two worlds.

What if I were to try to step boldly from the old into the new?

14

Underground Movement

The Cox firing created a temporary lull while the Watergate prosecutors regrouped under Leon Jaworski. For me this time was important, a chance to breathe in the fresh air of the new world I was discovering.

There was a sharp contrast between my hours of tense defensiveness over my past life and the time spent with a whole new set of people I was meeting through taking a stand for Christ. It was like finding shafts of sunshine and blue sky in a murky overcast.

One of my first steps, I knew, was to try and make amends to those I had injured with various "dirty tricks". I had already offered a faltering apology to Arthur Burns as both of us were leaving the prayer meeting in the White House basement – but I owed him a more detailed account.

There was another reason for my seeking him out. His wife, Helen, intensely involved with her husband's career, had also been hurt by the episode. I could tell by her angry eyes which bored holes right through me when we had been seated next to each other at a White House dinner not long after the damaging story about her husband appeared in the newspapers. This, too, needed healing.

When I telephoned him, Burns suggested we meet at his Watergate apartment after work the following Tuesday. It was Helen who greeted me at the door and seated me in a downy corner sofa in the Burns's tastefully furnished, homey apartment. Helen, petite and the gracious hostess, was soon serving Arthur and me hors d'oeuvres as I began recounting everything I could remember about the painful episode in the summer of 1971 when I leaked to the press an untrue item that Burns was publicly pushing wage controls while secretly trying to get his salary raised. Burns's face remained impassive as I spoke, but his penetrating eyes never left mine, even when he reached out to sip his drink.

"And so, Arthur," I concluded, "that is the unhappy story. I can't justify it, and I can never undo the harm it caused, but I thought I owed you this apology. I am very, very sorry."

Burns kept puffing on his pipe, continuing to stare into my eyes. "What hurt me most," he said at last, "is that I have never tried to accumulate wealth or possessions. All I have and all I've cared about is my own good name. The story implied that I was trying to feather my nest and it was the first time in my life anyone had questioned my integrity."

Arthur Burns began to reminisce about his many years with Richard Nixon. There was not a trace of animosity toward his old friend as I feared there might have been. "Political wars are cruel," he said. "I just wish we could find a way to help the President. He needs so much understanding and I don't think those around him are really helping." He brought the subject back to me.

"Tell me about this experience of yours. This is what really matters."

For an hour I shared with him what had happened to me in New England, the changes I was beginning to notice in my values and attitudes. "That's beautiful," he repeated over and over.

It was nearly eight o'clock before I noticed that Helen was preparing something in the kitchen. I apologised for staying so long and talking so much.

"Nonsense," Burns protested. "Have dinner with us." I explained why I could not and stood up.

"Please," Burns persisted. "Sit down for just a minute longer. Perhaps we could have a prayer together."

We did, leaning forward over the coffee table and thanking God for the healing of one ugly sore of the Nixon years. As I was leaving, Helen filled a shopping bag with fruit and insisted I take it to my family. The white-haired chairman of the Federal Reserve Board escorted me to the elevator, gripping my arm as we walked slowly along the carpeted corridor of the world's now most famous apartment building.

"Let's meet again sometime," he suggested. "And be firm in your faith. This has been a wonderful evening for me."

God's Spirit was working in powerful ways all over strife-torn Washington. Each Monday morning when we met – Al, Graham, Doug, Harold, and I – someone would report another miracle, old adversaries coming together as brothers, new fellowships begun, prayer groups revived, unlikely men seeking a relationship with Christ.

Doug Coe, for example, had worked for years to interest a few judges he knew in meeting regularly for prayer and fellowship. Since most judges tend to be independent-minded and wary of efforts to bring God into public affairs, nothing had resulted. But in January a small judicial prayer group was convened. Soon judges from several courts, high and low, conservative and liberal in their personal philosophies, were joining the fellowship.

New prayer groups were springing up in a host of governmental apartments. A small band of young senators began meeting regularly for prayer and fellowship. Several new groups began meeting in the House of Representatives.

Early in 1974 Senator Hughes made his second appearance at a White House breakfast, the meeting this time chaired by Earl Butz, blunt-spoken Secretary of Agriculture, whose Senate confirmation was nearly blocked in 1971 by a coalition of anti-Administration senators led by Hughes.

"If I'd known you then as I do now, brother, I might have led your cheering section," Hughes confessed.

"No regrets needed," Butz replied. "I feel guilty enough for all the negative thoughts I've had about you." The exchange was in good fun – lighthearted banter, some thought – but there was something more behind it. Men of opposing political philosophy were experiencing the camaraderie of their common commitment to God and in the process being released from poisoned memories of past political encounters.

The fiercely conservative speech writer, Pat Buchanan, whose saucy and courageous assault on the Ervin Committee ignited a brief pro-Nixon rally in late September of

1973, also attended. Over the years Pat was the author of the most caustic attacks against Nixon's enemies, prominently including Hughes, yet Harold's second breakfast appearance drained much of the partisan fervour from him.

"What a man! What a morning!" was all Pat could say to me as he left the room, shaking his head in bewilderment.

In a nationally syndicated column on January 13, Washington reporter Nick Thimmesch described the growing number of prayer groups as an "underground movement ... spurred by Watergate, which might surprise some of our jaded folks. ... They meet in each other's homes," Thimmesch reported, "they meet at Prayer Breakfasts, they converse on the phone ... a Brotherhood in belief ... there are many here and more are forming. ... I am not about to say that virtue and nobility are about to envelop the nation's Capital – this is a tough, hard town. But Watergate has created a great introspection, especially over personal values and this underground prayer movement can provide some peace, and a better sense of direction to many afflicted with spiritual malaise."

Early in 1974 I strode up the grey granite steps of the Pentagon, the huge vaultlike headquarters of the U.S. military establishment. A year before, this visit would have seemed ludicrous. In the old days I entered this building to represent the President in political battles, like mapping strategy to rescue the anti-ballistic missile programme when Congress threatened to cut off funds. Now I had accepted an invitation – for a fellowship luncheon!

A veteran civilian employee, John Broger met me at the main entranceway to guide me through the mazelike corridors of the world's largest office building. We stopped to look in on the meditation room, a small windowless cubicle on an inside corridor. Inside, chairs were lined along three walls with a simple altar at the far end.

"This was built on the orders of Secretary Laird," Broger explained.

"Mel Laird!" I exclaimed. "What would that old fox be doing building a meditation room?" Laird was Secretary of Defence in the first Nixon Cabinet, a longtime Wisconsin congressman and House leader. His zest for bureaucratic intrigue earned him the reputation as one of the canniest politicians in Washington.

"Secretary Laird not only ordered the meditation room built," Broger added, "but he was in here often himself." Laird I learned, was a regular participant in a small congressional fellowship which later included among others the then-Vice-President Gerald Ford, Al Quie, and House Minority Leader John Rhodes. But there is a deliberate attempt by the military to avoid publicity about any religious events in the Pentagon for fear it would arouse criticism over motives.

The luncheon was held in a small dining room seating fifty men. I spoke briefly, telling of the changes in my life. At the end we all bowed our heads and prayed aloud or silently as the Spirit moved us, simple moving prayers from privates, lieutenants, and admirals alike. From one jut-jawed Army sergeant – a ranger, I could tell from the insignia and ribbons which stretched from his breast pocket to his broad shoulder – came an eloquent prayer for peace among all men. The Holy Spirit, no respecter of rank or armour, pierced this soldier's tough exterior as no enemy bayonet could.

To my further surprise I learned that this luncheon was a regular event; that there were dozens of early-morning groups meeting for Bible study and prayer before beginning twelve-to fourteen-hour crisis-filled days.

To most people, of course, the sudden popularity of religion in a town like Washington remained a matter of scepticism. In my case, in fact, outright hilarity. "Colson coming to Jesus" quips soon replaced "Colson's grandmother" as fodder for the cocktail circuit. At the annual late-January congressional dinner of the National Press Club, Speaker of the House Carl Albert produced a roar of laughter when he described 1973 as "the year when Chuck Colson joined the Jesus movement ... and his grandmother said a prayer of thanks from her hospital bed."

Art Buchwald, the nationally syndicated humorist, joined the merriment with a column entitled "Getting right with Granny. Step on her hand and help her up." Buchwald spoofed the conversation as follows:

When Charles Colson got religion the first person he wanted to break the news to was his grandmother – the very same grandmother he had vowed to run over in 1972 to get Richard Nixon re-elected President.

He knocked on the door and cried, "Granny, it's me, Charles."

"You go away, Charley," his grandmother said, "and take your car with you."

"Granny, you don't understand. I'm not here to run over you. I've got religion now. I've come to pray with you."

Colson's grandmother opened the door a couple inches. "You're joshing me, Charley boy."

"It's true, Granny, I'm no longer the mean, dirty rotten, unscrupulous trickster you used to bounce on your knee. I've been reborn, Granny."

She hesitated, "How do I know this ain't one of your tricks to get me out in the street so you can go vroom . . . vrooooommm with your motor again?"

"I have Senator Harold Hughes with me. He'll tell you I mean it."

"That's right, Granny," Senator Hughes said. "Charley has made his peace and he's asking everyone to forgive him his sins."

"I ain't so sure I'm ready to forgive him. You know I was flat on my back for six months after the 1972 election."

"Granny, please let me in. I want to show you I'm a new man."

"All right," Colson's grandmother said, "but leave your car keys out on the stoop."

Colson came into the house with Senator Hughes.

"Shall we kneel together?" Colson asked.

"Not me," his grandmother replied, "I haven't been able to kneel since you screamed at me, 'Four more years!' and then put your Oldsmobile into drive. . . ."

Some of the barbs shot at me hurt, yet a Watergate-weary Washington needed some laughs. Through it all was the issue of "How much can a man change?" – and maybe an unintended witness.

Among the many calls for interviews and TV shows was one from Mike Wallace, the sharp-questioning host of the CBS popular "Sixty Minutes" Sunday-evening documentary. Wallace wanted to interview Hughes and me together.

We discussed it one Monday breakfast. Doug saw it as a rare opportunity for a powerful Christian testimony to millions of Americans: two political opposites, brought together by Christ's love at a time of unprecedented national division. Hughes was dubious; a tough, probing newsman, Wallace might turn it into a political circus. "I told Mike," Harold reported back later after one of Wallace's insistent calls, "we'd do it with him if he would spend the necessary time with us to see what our fellowship was all about."

Hughes went a step further: "I'll work with you, Mike. We can meet for prayer. I'll even help instruct you if you are serious." People had asked for large fees to appear on Wallace's programme, but this was surely the first time anyone had set such an unusual condition – that Wallace seek a closer relationship with God. That might have ended all discussions with anyone less persistent than Wallace; but after recovering his composure he agreed to try – and along with his producer, a pert redhead named Marion Goldin, actually began meeting with Hughes. The rest of us waited in ill-concealed suspense for the outcome.

And meanwhile every day was bringing its new encounter – some as humorous in their own way as anything appearing in print. I remember the middle-aged waitress at the stately old Sheraton Carlton who learned I was in the hotel's basement barbershop and came down to find me. Interrupting the chatter of Milt Pitts, my longtime friend and barber, she asked me to explain to her how she could "find Christ." While Milt's electric clippers droned on and the rest of the customers stared bewildered, I did my best to outline for her what I knew of the steps in salvation.

Or the night when I participated in a young people's Sunday-evening fellowship at Washington's Fourth Presbyterian Church. The first fresh scents of early spring 1974 were in the air when Patty and I arrived shortly before 8:00 p.m.

at the entrance to the massive red-brick church. As we were exchanging greetings on the front steps with Pastor Dick Halverson and some of his parishioners, I noticed a beat-up white Buick convertible, fenders dented and rusting and canvas top flopping, pull over to the curb nearby. A long-haired young man in an open shirt and dungarees flung open the door and dashed towards us. Nervously I thought of the protesters who were again carrying placards on Pennsylvania Avenue.

I nudged Patty. "Watch out, honey. This could be trouble." With the impeachment drive building to a fever pitch, the streets of Washington were again being visited by carloads of young demonstrators. Bumper stickers like HONK IF YOU THINK HE'S GUILTY were sprouting like spring leaves. Was this guy going to start an argument here in front of the church?

"Mr. Colson, Mr. Colson," the young man shouted, brushing past the others. "I want to talk to you a minute." Then he grabbed my hand and wrung it vigorously. As I listened with growing amazement, he stated that he worked in the dissension-ridden Department of Labour. "It's fantastic the way you and Senator Hughes have become friends. It's been a real boost to our morale in the department. It's given us hope that we can work together, too. You can't imagine what's happened in Labour in the past weeks. . . ."

As he talked on, I could only think of the months I had spent in the White House trying to work out a plan for reorganising the Labour Department. This old-line agency was so encased in a mouldy bureaucratic crust it could hardly function. All my fancy charts had produced nothing and were long forgotten. Now it seemed that my goal was being achieved – without my hand being in it in the slightest – another example of Christ's Spirit-sovereignty at work: changing lives, reviving atrophied bureaucracies.

He was at work in our home as well; one evening Patty announced that she had enrolled that day in the Bible-study course a group of women in McLean were organising. I tried not to let my excitement show. I knew this had to be something Patty would come to in her own time and way. I tried to be nonchalant about it, but underneath was a warm joy and a sureness that God was working in both our lives.

To some it may have seemed odd that I could stand up before total strangers and proclaim my faith, while with my own family I was sometimes faltering, always reticent. I didn't understand it myself. I like to think it was the guidance of the Spirit urging boldness at one point and caution at another. More likely, as a new Christian I was just making the bucketful of mistakes which all excited freshmen believers do.

I realize now that those months in early 1974 were a time of spiritual preparation. It was a calm before the gathering storm, a period for re-affirmation of belief, while all around me the forces unloosed by Watergate were moving relentlessly ahead.

Bud Krogh was the first Nixon man indicted. After the Watergate entry was exposed in the summer of 1972, Bud had denied under oath any knowledge of this or of the Ellsberg burglary months before. Then in the spring of 1973 he admitted that he had ordered the break-in at the office of Ellsberg's psychiatrist.

It was a clear-cut case of perjury, against which Bud's only defence was that John Dean counselled him to lie under oath if necessary, for *national security* reasons. Bud, like myself, genuinely believed that the whole Ellsberg affair should have been properly cloaked in the protective shroud of those never-questioned magic words.

While awaiting a second indictment for ordering the break-in, Bud had obviously gone through a long, searching self-examination. In mid-December he stunned Washington with a surprise guilty plea – no bargaining with the prosecutors, no effort to soften the offence, just a straightforward admission of guilt along with sound advice to those who would follow in government service: "Always ask yourself about every decision – 'Is it right?'"

I had known Bud as an influential member of the White House Palace Guard, a heady post for a thirty-one-year-old Navy veteran with only one year of law practice. I also knew that Bud and his wife, Suzanne, had drifted apart, had actually been separated for a time. Now, the family was reunited, bonds between them seemingly stronger than ever as they faced the onslaught of cameras and reporters on the courthouse steps the day Bud pleaded guilty. He was sentenced to six months.

A week before Bud was scheduled to surrender to the marshals and begin his confinement at Allenwood Prison in Pennsylvania, Doug, Harold, Graham, Al, and I invited him to meet with us at Fellowship House. We wanted to encourage him, to let him know that we cared and that we shared the agonies he and Suzanne were enduring.

While awaiting his arrival, I could not subdue my own apprehensions. I was not yet indicted, but each day I lived with the suspenseful torment of expecting it. In this appearance of an old friend — wan, haggard, dejected — I imagined that I might well be looking into a mirror.

The Bud Krogh that arrived at Fellowship House that late January afternoon was not the person I expected to see. Lean and muscular, with strong angular Norwegian features, Krogh had always been a ruggedly handsome man. On this particular day he seemed more vibrant, filled with more enthusiasm than he had been, even in his energetic hard-driving White House days. While relieved, I wondered what his secret was. He did not leave us long in suspense.

"Suzanne and I have been spending several hours each day deep in the Scriptures," Bud explained. "It may sound a bit strange, but we really thank God for what has happened to us."

We all sat in numbed silence. My carefully rehearsed words of encouragement seemed pallid after his. Graham and Al sat staring. Even Harold, who normally takes command of any gathering, was strangely subdued. What do you say to a man who is penniless, jobless, headed for prison, and yet has this kind of faith?

As we talked together, it was Bud encouraging us, just the reverse of what we had planned. "The Lord takes care of things," Bud explained. "As Suzanne and I were praying about how we would make ends meet while I am in prison, she was offered a teaching job at the school the kids are going to. It will be great for her and we have it all figured to the day; with 'good time' I will be home by mid-June. A six months sentence," Bud said, "is not all that bad."

As the six of us prayed together, I could tell that Bud was

not putting on a brave front. The Lord had already responded to his prayers and provided him with the assurance that he would not be alone in prison. I walked with him down the short flight of steps in front of Fellowship House toward his car parked on the edge of the forested parkland which borders Embassy Row. "Bud, please let me know if there is anything I can do for you or Suzanne while you are away."

But what I really meant was, "Please let me know how you can be so sure." The spectre of prison haunted all of us who had been close to Richard Nixon; it even haunted the President, as I had discovered during our December meeting. It was not so much the fear of confinement itself, even the loss of status, career, resources, friends. There was something more that was seldom discussed, but which lay just beneath the surface. Prisons contain violent men, to whom government officials are "the enemy". Officials are part of the system which caught and sentenced these men. Indeed, our particular administration boasted about it; filling up the prisons was the mark of success for Nixon's disciples of law and order.

There is a continuous stream of unexplained deaths in penal institutions which are usually attributed to prison vengeance. Once that was merely a remote fact of life. Now the realisation was personal – and terrifying.

As I watched Bud drive away, the warmth of his faith lingered on for several minutes. Yet with it was a kind of premonition. Could the Lord be using Bud to help prepare for me the path ahead?

15

Accused

"Mr Colson, unless my staff can show me a lot more evidence I would not include you in the Watergate cover-up indictment."

Leon Jaworski, Watergate Special Prosecutor, was smiling now for the first time in our gruelling two-hour session. The one-time Bar Association president was sitting in shirt sleeves at the head of a long conference table in his stark bare-walled office, flanked by Bill Merrill and other assistants. My lawyers, Dave Shapiro, Judd Best, Sid Dickstein, and I had asked for this showdown meeting, a last-ditch effort to persuade the Special Prosecutor and his staff of my ignorance of the Watergate break-in and to avert the long-delayed Ellsberg indictment.

The expression on Jaworski's round face was positively benign. "Of course," he continued after what seemed an interminable pause, "even if you are not indicted for Watergate, there is still this Ellsberg thing."

I stared at Jaworski, breathing easier for the first time, but waiting, pondering his tactics. No one had ever before suggested I might be indicted in the Watergate cover-up. The original prosecutors had cleared me. But for most of the meeting Jaworski was threatening two indictments! Was it a pressure play?

Jaworski looked away for a moment and then turned to Shapiro, "Why don't you, Dave, get together with Bill here," pointing to Merrill, "and see if you can't work it out? I think Mr. Colson really wants to wipe the slate clean, and look forward to a useful career as a citizen and as a *lawyer*."

With that he stood up abruptly as if on cue, leaving Merrill and Shapiro to dispose of my fate while I, no doubt, was supposed to feel gratitude and relief at the fading of the dread spectre of two felony trials. To the man on the street such terms as *felony, misdemeanor,* and *plea bargain* are confusing legalese. But for me these terms were as real as food and water. Without saying so directly, the prosecution was asking for a plea bargain for me : for me to plead guilty to a lesser charge in exchange for my testimony against others. Such a plea would mean my being convicted of a misdemeanor which carries a maximum one-year sentence, usually resulting only in probation, and would enable me to continue the practice of law. Conviction of a felony normally means prison – up to five years – and dis-barment. Jaworski's reference to my future as a lawyer was a deliberate signal.

Jeb Magruder and John Dean, both of whom were slated to be key government witnesses against Haldeman, Ehrlichman, and Mitchell, had both agreed to plea bargains. The prosecution also needed someone like myself who had been in the inner circle, one of the four men who, as columnist Joseph Alsop wrote, held a "dagger to the President's heart".

As I left the Special Prosecutor's office that day, the painful choice was plain enough. To plea bargain meant my stating under oath that I was guilty of conspiring to break into the office of Daniel Ellsbergs's psychiatrist. It also meant offering testimony in advance about other Watergate figures, telling Jaworski's men what they would be getting in return for their leniency to me. How can anyone ever be sure he isn't even subconsciously tempted to offer up testimony more to the prosecutor's liking than the facts really warrant? When a good deal is hanging in the balance, is it not human nature to do so? "Aw, come on," they say, "it really happened this way, didn't it?" And who is strong enough to say *no* when *yes* means staying out of prison? I wasn't sure I was. Krogh had refused to plea bargain on these precise grounds.

But what a relief to get all of this over with, the chance for Patty and me to live a normal life again, to spend time with our children, the end of my parents' agony, especially for Dad whose health I was worried about. Such thoughts, as I drove home that evening, were like a seductive potion. It would be like having a gigantic suffocating cloud suddenly lift and there would be fresh air and sunshine.

That evening I told Patty only a little of what was happening. There was no sense in getting her hopes up, then having them dashed again, the destructive yo-yo cycle she had been through so often in the past year.

Shapiro continued to negotiate with Jaworski's men, haggling over the kind of plea which both sides could agree to and which would save my licence to practise law. Each time he would return with the same report – "We're making progress." Breaking out in an awkward little jig, he'd dance about the office. "C'mon, smile. I'm going to walk you out of this – a free man!"

I could manage a smile, not so much at Dave's report, as at the sight of his ungainly 250-pound frame performing pirouettes like a bear cub being trained for a circus performance. "Dave, I just don't know that I can do this,' I told him the night after his second meeting. My words fell on him like cold rain.

"Chuck, you gotta be off your rocker. You'll do it or I'll have you committed to the funny farm."

"I'm serious, Dave," I repeated. "I just don't know."

The answer, whatever it was, I knew I could not find alone. It was the following Saturday evening I joined Harold Hughes in the basement of his modest brick home a few minutes from ours. Harold and I were now meeting frequently in between our regular Monday breakfasts at Fellowship House.

"Brother, I need help," I said as we sat alone in the basement room Harold had converted into his study. There was a hooked rug spread over the tiles, a crucifix on the mantel over a snapping fire, freshly cut logs piled alongside, big overstuffed chairs pulled close.

I laid out for Harold, step by step, exactly what my choices were. With each point the pain became more evident on his usually stoic face, his scowl deepening as he interrupted with tough questions. It was a bizarre situation. President Nixon's faithful lieutenant was seeking counsel from one of Nixon's most implacable foes about a decision that could seriously hurt the President. For while I still believed the President innocent and had no intention of testifying against him, I knew my action could set in motion other forces which could damage the President's case. By all political standards Hughes would be expected not only to urge me to plea bargain, but also help me sharpen up the stiletto. I doubt if it entered his mind – our duty as followers of Jesus Christ and our love for one another as brothers were the only issues.

"I don't know," Hughes exclaimed when I finished. "What can I say?" There were deep furrows across his brow. "Are you guilty of what you'd have to plead to, Chuck?" he asked.

"Legally, no. I didn't order the burglary at the psychiatrist's. I didn't know about it until it was over. But I'm not sure there's much moral difference. I'd have done anything to stop Ellsberg, anything the President ordered," I replied.

"That's not the point, Chuck. Is what you would have to say in court true in your own heart, I mean between you and God?"

"No," I replied quietly, "the misdemeanour plea would require me to say I knew and approved the break-in. This would not be true." At that very moment I knew that no matter how long we talked, no matter how many different arguments were advanced, this was the central question and Hughes had pounced upon it.

"Well, you are going to have to ask Christ to give you the answer, brother," he continued. "If it were me, with my family involved and all the rest, I don't know if I could turn it down. No one knows until they have to face it. I can tell you the correct answer but I'm not sure I'd follow it myself, so how can I advise you?" Even as he said it I knew the decision was made.

We sat silently with only the sound of the fire crackling in our ears. I looked at Harold, this hulking combat veteran, truck driver and one-time two-fisted drinker, a flamboyant orator, but a compassionate man whom I had come to love very much. His face was buried in his hands. Harold knew, too.

It was important that Patty and the kids understand. Back home that night Patty wholeheartedly agreed that I should make no plea, although a wistful look in her eyes almost betrayed her once or twice in our conversation. The ordeal of anxious days stretching into months, now into its second year, was taking a more brutal toll on her than on me. Wendell was next, through a phone call to Princeton. His answer was as quick and decisive as Patty's. "Do what is right, Dad." Although I was working hard at slaying the dragon of pride, I couldn't help feeling a tinge of it in the character of my oldest son.

Next I flew to Boston. Driving from the airport in Chris's dented old Ford with Emily in the backseat, I broached the subject with a more careful explanation, convinced that a fifteen-year-old girl would not understand the difference between a felony and a misdemeanour. Partway into the discussion I asked Emily if she understood the terms.

"Sure," she replied. "A misdemeanour means only a one-year prison sentence." Having her dad in the middle of Watergate had accelerated this aspect of her education at least.

I explained that one of the dangers of not pleading was that I might not get off so lightly later; indictment and conviction on a felony could mean several years in prison.

"Most of my friends already think you're in jail or are going to be, so that doesn't matter," Chris replied.

"Do they give you a hard time about it?" I asked.

Chris just shrugged his shoulders, but I knew from his silence he was sparing me the hurt of the truth. *How unfair that these two kids are already bearing scars for things they had nothing to do with,* I thought. Chris in his casual way was telling me the damage was already done and to do what I had to.

Emily was slumped in the backseat, looking even more petite than normal, her long blonde straight hair hanging limply over her shoulders. Gone was the pixie's dance from her blue eyes, replaced this day by an unusual look of melancholy. She was following intently every word. "Did you do what they want you to say you did?" she asked crisply, businesslike, as she sat upright and leaned over the front seat.

"No, I didn't," I replied.

"Well, then don't say you did it," she snapped. It wasn't

advice, it was an order, her voice revealing a core of toughness I never realized this sweet, shy little girl capable of. What simple logic and refreshing honesty. "I don't know where these kids got this kind of courage, but thank You, Lord," I said to myself, looking out of the window so they could not see my emotion.

Dave Shapiro was angry, as I knew he would be when I told him my decision. The negotiations between Dave and the prosecutors were terminated, having achieved nothing but more aggravation between us. (The prosecutors later denied that I was ever offered a misdemeanour plea. Literally that is true. The only basis for the extensive negotiation, however, was a misdemeanour plea. My lawyers were left with the clear impression that it would be formally offered *if* I agreed to accept it. Shapiro and Ken Adams later so testified under oath. The question was mooted, however, since negotiations were broken off before they got to final stages.)

I did not feel self-righteous in the slightest about my decision; I simply could not do anything else, certainly not after Emily's reaction anyway.

As my long, anxious vigil resumed, I continued to wish for another way out. I began to see that defending my past day after day would make it increasingly difficult to live a full and free Christian life, especially since mine was so much in the public spotlight. This letter to the editor in the *Philadelphia Inquirer* stung me:

So, Charles W. Colson has had some kind of religious experience, and now says he's "seen the light." I for one find it impossible to believe that he has accepted the spirit of goodness in any form while he still holds the knowledge of crimes in his heart, and remains unwilling to let the truth come to light.

Until he does that, he's no more than a pious hypocrite, braying his prayers in public for no one's good but his own – he hopes they'll save his skin.

Dan Tanner
Debran N. J.

What were the crimes in my heart? In a state of agony I probed every action I had taken in the White House. There were tough ruthless political acts – "dirty tricks," certainly, because they hurt people. Perhaps even worse in God's eyes, there had been arrogance and pride and ego. My all-out loyalty to the commander-in-chief had warped and blurred my sense of right and wrong, no question about that. But actual crimes as defined in the statutes? – no.

I could try, of course, to dismiss Tanner as an anti-Nixon zealot. But if his reactions were typical, wasn't I doing far more harm than good to the Christian cause by publicly taking a stand on my new faith?

The tension mounted. Hardly a day passed without a fresh round of press speculation about the long-awaited indictments – when they would be announced, who would be included, what would be the political impact on Mr. Nixon's embattled Presidency. Richard Nixon's strength was steadily deteriorating while House impeachment investigators were methodically filling their arsenals for the expected summer offensive. Nixon lawyers, St. Clair and Fred Buzhardt, were engaged in an heroic effort to shore up the sagging bulwarks while the rest of the White House staff sank deeper into the morass, quibbling and swallowed up by petty jealousies. Haig was meeting regularly with Jaworski and reported that his attitude, once sympathetic, was souring as the political balance was shifting. There seemed to be an historic inevitability to the process, like watching a Greek tragedy's final act.

There were other shocks in store for me as well – like the day I was called to the White House and shown files on the CIA's involvement in Watergate. "I'd be fired if anyone knew I let you see these," one of the President's lieutenants whispered to me as he handed me two six-inch-thick bound folders with TOP SECRET stamped in bold blue letters across the front.

I sat there for two hours reading the carefully documented, but seldom discussed CIA role in the Watergate scandal. It disclosed that Howard Hunt was working for Robert R. Mullen and Company, ostensibly just another Washington public-relations firm, but which in fact was a CIA "cover" outfit. The CIA had monitored all of Hunt's activities and appeared to be involved in events leading up to and following the Watergate break-in.

What jolted me most was the series of memoranda about efforts by Robert Bennett, president of the Mullen firm, to implicate me in Watergate, reportedly to take the heat off the CIA. Attached to a March 1, 1973 internal CIA memorandum was a Xerox copy of the same *Newsweek* article Patty and I had read in Vienna almost a year earlier. There followed page after page of reports showing how the CIA fed Washington reporters – including Robert Woodward of the *Post* – damaging information about me, much of it false.*

President Nixon discussed this report with me on two occasions and said he was determined to expose the agency's misconduct. Other voices, principally General Haig, later convinced him he should do nothing to injure the intelligence establishment. Shapiro took the information to the prosecutors who assured him it would be investigated. It never was, to our knowledge, until later revelations brought forth full-scale congressional hearings. Robert R. Mullen and Company was later disbanded.

Dave believed that the prosecutors might be persuaded not to indict me in the Ellsberg case if I took another lie-detector test, this time to establish I knew nothing in advance about the break-in of the psychiatrist's office. I trotted back to the dingy New York office of Richard Arther and passed my second test.

Dave was so impressed he arranged a third test, this one to prove I'd never promised Hunt or his lawyer clemency or a pardon to keep him quiet in the Watergate case. This was, Shapiro learned, the one allegation that could cause Jaworski to include me in the Watergate cover-up indictment.

By now I was almost adjusted to sneaking furtively in and out of Arther's building, rumpled hat over my eyes, glancing

---

* *Editor's Note:* Material from this file was later quoted in Senator Howard Baker's supplementary report, filed as part of the Ervin Committee's final findings, July 1974. According to the Baker report, the CIA "took relish in implicating Colson in Hunt's activities .... It is further noted that Bennett was feeding stories to Bob Woodward who was 'suitably grateful' .. and who was protecting Bennett and Mullen and Company."

from side to side. Anyone so close to the criminal world, I realized, quickly gets used to its ways.

Maybe it was the forlorn expression on my face as Arther went through the now familiar ritual of wiring me up for the test, maybe it was my pulse reading which he took three times that day, but after it was over, instead of telling me the results, Dick Arther advised me to take no more tests.

"Why? Did I fail?" I asked, a surge of adrenaline sending my heart racing and a hot flush across my face.

"No, you passed. I don't mind taking your money [$350 per sitting], but you are tested out. I can tell you are telling me the truth without even hooking you up and if the prosecutors can't by now, you're wasting your time and putting yourself through this agony for nothing."

It turned out that Arther was right. Merrill could not bring himself to believe the test results, even dispatching an FBI agent to New York to investigate Arther's test procedures.

And still we waited. I was asked again to appear before the grand jury, refused since I was clearly a target, and was served a subpoena. Shapiro protested the unusual procedure – but to no avail. For a second time I was forced to invoke the Fifth Amendment, this time appearing like a criminal hiding his sinful past before the twenty or so citizens who in a few days would vote on whether to indict me.

At last the Special Prosecutor announced that indictments would be filed Friday morning, March 1. All week long Washington was buzzing with "hot" rumours. Every reporter had a different list. GBS's Dan Schorr called me Thursday evening: "Sorry to give you the bad news, Chuck, you are one of forty-two on the list. Do you have a comment?"

That seemed preposterous – forty-two indicted – none of us could take it seriously. Jack Anderson, the relentless investigative reporter, called Thursday to say there were only five on the list; I was not one of them. My friends in the White House told me I was not on a list Jaworski had "unofficially" reviewed with the President's chief-of-staff, Al Haig.

I could take my pick of these speculations and sometimes I felt I almost did not care. Anything would be better than the suspenseful waiting. Patty accompanied me to the office that Friday to be there in case the worst came to pass. The press would demand a statement; she would be at my side. Deep down I knew I would be among those indicted. Everything that had happened pointed to it, but outwardly I kept smiling, hoping, reading the Twenty-seventh Psalm over and over:

> For in the time of trouble he shall hide me in his pavilion: in the secret of his tabernacle shall he hide me; he shall set me up upon a rock. And now shall mine head be lifted up above mine enemies round about me ... Deliver me not over unto the will of mine enemies: for false witnesses are risen up against me, and such as breathe out cruelty ... Wait on the Lord: be of good courage, and he shall strengthen thine heart: wait, I say, on the Lord.
> Psalms 27:5, 6, 12, 14 KJV

At 9:30 Shapiro walked into my office, lips curled down, eyes filled with sorrow and hurt. "The prosecutor just called," he began, and after a long pause, he simply turned his big thumb down: "I'm sorry, I'm sorry."

Holly began to cry and Judd Best embraced Patty who was fighting back tears, trying as hard as she knew how to keep that big radiant smile from which I always derived such strength.

Seven of us in all had been indicted in the Watergate cover-up case. Two hours later Merrill called: "Next Thursday the Ellsberg indictment will be returned and your man will be in that one, too," he told Shapiro. What began as a pressure play was now reality. Arraignment was scheduled for both cases on Saturday, March 9, at the federal district court.

When Sid Dickstein and I arrived by cab at the corner of the courthouse that Saturday morning we saw a mass of humanity pressing against a roped-off area around the main entrance. Jeering, shouting spectators were held back from the walkway to the court's doors by lines of helmeted police standing in front of ropes and sawhorses. It reminded me of the days when anti-war protesters surrounded the White House. *There are no sturdy iron gates protecting me now*, I thought with a flash of fear.

Television camera crews and reporters spotted us and gal-loped our way, elbowing ahead of each other, some with bright, hot lights held over their heads. A few policemen caught in the rush were running with them, stopping period-ically in a futile effort to slow the stampede. One cameraman took a bad spill, falling over a low hedge on the border of the courthouse lawn. Another was nearly shoved in front of a car pulling up to the curb.

Within seconds we were surrounded, mikes on long booms thrust at us like spears, questions coming from all sides. I thought *it was a wonder that no one gets trampled in these melees*. The spectators, several hundred by press estimate, were angry, waving homemade placards with slogans like: THEY HUNG HORSE THIEVES and NIXON'S NEXT. Some made obscene gestures. One man wearing a giant papier-mâché mask of Nixon's head was arrested for stripping naked from the waist down and "streaking" through the crowd. (He was later identified as the local radio broadcaster.)

The uproar was predictable: the press all week had been overpowering. *Newsweek's* cover contained four large pen sketches of the heads of Haldeman, Ehrlichman, Mitchell, and Colson. Across the top in bold red letters larger than the masthead was stamped like a modern-day scarlet letter the single word: INDICTED. Almost the entire evening TV net-work news was devoted to the story. AP ran a Wirephoto of a smiling Daniel Ellsberg expressing his delight. Many press accounts were laden with the heavy presumption of guilt, all of them ringing with condemnations. Indictment and con-viction were without distinction; we were handy targets for fast-moving public passions.

The quiet inside Judge Sirica's courtroom was a welcome relief to the noisy mob outside. The spectators' benches were filled to capacity with press. As each of the defendants walk-ed in through the side door, whispers filled the room like a great whoosh of air; reporters busily scribbled their impres-sions, the glimpses of colour that would capture the drama of the long-awaited moment. The *Times* reporter saw me as "self-assured," while the *Post* scribe detected in me an "ex-pression of haunted preoccupation." John Mitchell "sagged in his chair . . . face grey and drawn." John Ehrlichman had a "sweet and sour manner," Bob Haldeman wore "a well-pressed and well-tailored light blue suit." Quick, sweeping strokes of crayons on huge white pads created the caricatures that would flash across the screens of millions of TV sets that night.

As I walked towards John Mitchell, seated with his lawyers at a table across the room, I wondered how to be Christ's man. It had been many months since I had seen or talked with Mitchell, my old White House antagonist. The stony-faced ex-Attorney General looked at first stunned and then pleased when I gripped his shoulder, shook his hand, and wished him well. The reunion with Haldeman and Ehrlichman was also warm; no time for bitterness or grudges.

Gordon Strachan, Haldeman's assistant and only twenty-seven, was one of the three minor figures included in the indictment, committee lawyer, Kenneth Parkinson, and former Mitchell aide, Robert Mardian, the others. A tall good-looking lad with long blonde hair and big blue eyes, Strachan was struggling to hold back tears, his eyes glazed with a distant stare. My heart ached for him. Gordon had served powerful men like Haldeman blindly, believing the cause just. It was a feeling I knew so well. Now suddenly, unbelievably, he was standing in a courtroom as a criminal defendant, jostled by an angry mob, the eyes of an outraged nation upon him.

"I understand you are reading the Bible," he said, a quick flash of brightness in his eyes.

"Yes, I am, Gordon," I replied. Just discussing it seemed to steady him.

"I'd like to hear about your experience," he said.

It was hardly the place, standing in that vast open pit with Leon Jaworski and his lieutenants filing in to sit at the prosecutors' table. "I'd like to, when we can talk," I told him. "Hang in there, Gordon, God will give you strength if you ask." Gordon smiled, then bit his lip.

"All persons having business before the Honourable Judge ..." the bailiff's words commanded silence in the crowded courtroom. As we stood up, stern-faced Judge John Sirica in flowing black robes strode across the raised platform to the high-back leather chair from which he would preside. It was only the second time I had ever seen Judge Sirica, who only a few months earlier was named *Time* magazine's "man of the year" after twenty years of obscure service on the D.C. bench. At a small cocktail party in 1971 we had chatted amiably, the judge recalling fondly his own days in Republican politics, telling me of his admiration for President Nixon. The mild man of that conversation bore no similarity to the determined jurist before me now who was so tenaciously prying loose the lid the White House had attempted to clamp on Watergate.

Sirica summoned the seven of us to walk forward, stand at the rail beneath his bench, and answer as the accusations were read against us. The words were chilling: "The United States of America charges John Mitchell ... Charles W. Colson. ..."

All my life the mere words *The United States* had set my spine tingling like martial music. Corny as it may sound to some, I have deeply loved my country, worn the Marine uniform with a sense of honour, and felt pride every time I saw the flag. Now the beloved words were the accuser, striking at me, filling me with shame. It wasn't the United States against me, I wanted to cry out, it was a group of politicised individuals. My own country was not accusing me – but of course it was. That frightful realisation, which until this very moment I resisted, brought a feeling of nausea. Nothing that could be done to me – trials, prison, ruin – nothing would match the dreadful knowledge that the country I loved was charging me with a breach of my trust and duty.

And in other terms there was something almost as sobering. The government has boundless resources and power: forty well-trained lawyers in Jaworski's office with full subpoena power, gargantuan computers recording, preserving, and tabulating great mounds of evidence, armies of investigators all across the country. One hundred investigators were employed by the Ervin Committee alone, and it was only one of a dozen congressional committees digging into every corner and crevice of our lives. Orders went out to the FBI and IRS to check every lead that might give the prosecutors more ammunition.

The lawyers in our firm were no match for all this. We couldn't even keep track of what was being testified by the hundreds of people who'd been involved in the spreading scandal, and my bank account would be gone in a year. I knew now what it was like for one person to stand virtually alone against the vast powers of government. How calloused I'd been all those past years about the importance of one individual's rights.

Of course there would be trials and a chance to prove my innocence, but no vindication could erase the ugly stain of this day. I stared up at Judge Sirica's scolding eyes, his grim face silhouetted against the cold, black marble wall behind him. My mouth was so parched I wasn't certain my words could be heard: "Not guilty to all counts."

I lowered my eyes. "Neither death, nor life, nor angels, nor principalities, nor powers can separate us from Jesus," the Apostle Paul wrote to the Christians in Rome (*see* Romans 8:38, 39). Never had those words been more important to me than that moment in the courtroom. In that instant when I felt the full wrath of the principality I had worshipped now accusing me, I felt His presence, too – utterly dependable, utterly caring.

In the days ahead I was to learn how this reality could make all the difference.

16

Decision

The words of the indictment were still ringing in my ears the following Monday as I drove to Fellowship House for our early-morning meeting. The blast of worldwide publicity in the Sunday papers added to my state of shock.

Doug Coe met me with the usual merry twinkle in his eyes. "Brother, look at it this way. It's good. We've got a Christian in the news."

My return smile was sickly. To the four men gathered in the library, I put the hard question which had troubled me all weekend: "In view of the indictments, shouldn't I withdraw from this fellowship? Two of you are in public office and this thing could hurt you."

"We're brothers," Quie snapped. "If you're indicted, Chuck, we all are. We're together. That's the way it is."

Hughes nodded. For both men such a commitment could be costly. Though Hughes was leaving politics, he was "Mr. Clean" to an enormous following across the country. Quie as a Republican had to stand for re-election in the fall in a Democratic state with all signs pointing to a Democratic landslide. Even though his own law practice could also be hurt, Graham Purcell was the most indignant over the suggestion. "You're stuck with us, podner," he pronounced in his best Texas drawl.

In the discussion and prayer that followed, the despair of the weekend passed as once again I discovered the strength of His presence. When I arrived at the office later that morning, I felt almost serene. Dave Shapiro looked at me through sleep-starved eyes and shook his head. "How do you do it? This has been the worst weekend of my life. Two indictments, a lynch mob at the courthouse, everybody in town howling for your hide and you look like you've just gotten back from a vacation."

I was ready this morning even to take on Shapiro. "If you really want me to explain we'll have to start two thousand years ago. That's where you guys missed the boat."

Shapiro grinned. "Let's get to work. I'm gonna walk you right out of that courtroom, Chuck. Those indictments are paper-thin."

Buoyed up by the prayer session and Shapiro's brave talk, I settled in for a long fight. First I withdrew from the law firm and the name was changed to DICKSTEIN, SHAPIRO, AND MORIN, though Holly and I kept our office there. Then I explained to each of my clients that they had no further obligation to retain me. To my surprise the secretary-treasurer of the Teamsters, Dusty Miller, chose almost the same words Quie had: "In the labour movement, we are brothers. You're indicted – I'm indicted. That's that." Brainerd Holmes and Tom Phillips of Raytheon offered support. "We'll just work with others in the firm until you're back. It'll be soon," Brainerd encouraged. Not a single client took his account elsewhere.

With St. Clair no longer available and most of the best lawyers already committed to Watergate defendants, Dave Shapiro decided to head up my defence along with Dickstein and a bright young associate, Ken Adams. We consulted the Bar Association which gave us permission, since I was no longer a member of the firm and finding new lawyers would work a severe hardship.

Since the two trials were scheduled back to back – Ellsberg in July, Watergate in September – there was no possible way to prepare adequately for both. Besides, the trials would come right during the impeachment hearings, creating the worst possible public climate for our defence. A delay in one or both trials was essential, we felt, but with the rising clamour for "swift justice," Judges Sirica and Gerhard Gesell, who was assigned the Ellsberg case, would be unlikely to grant it.

"We've only got one chance," Ken Adams concluded after

studying the cases. "Let's collect every newspaper article that's accused you of anything over the past two years. We'll package them together, index them, and drop them in the judge's lap. That's the kind of solid proof of prejudice that might persuade him to delay." The law clearly holds such delays appropriate when there is such overwhelming adverse publicity before a trial.

"You've got to be kidding," I replied, "There must be thousands of articles. We'd need fifty people full-time. It's impossible."

Ken Adams began by mobilising most of the office staff. Secretaries volunteered to work without pay in the evenings, clipping articles from great mountains of newspapers piled high on the conference room table. Some of the lawyers' wives pitched in each evening as additional boxes of old *Posts* and *Stars* were opened. The task began to appear more and more hopeless, like shovelling snow in a blizzard; for each shovelful cleared away, two more fell. It was difficult at times even to keep abreast of the current day's rash of speculations about impeachment and the upcoming trials.

The results of a private survey we commissioned added new urgency to the task. According to pollster Albert E. Sindlinger, a staggering 91 per cent of the nation was aware of the indictments, as high a number as can in most national-election polls identify the candidates for President. In publicity- soaked Washington, the total was even higher. Nationally, of those with opinions 75 per cent believed the defendants guilty, 7 per cent innocent; in Washington the ratio was 84 per cent to 2 per cent. In the Ellsberg case the Washington odds were even more overwhelming – 75 per cent to 1 per cent. It defied all laws of statistical probability to think an impartial jury could be picked. Winning a delay or removal of the trial to a city where the impeachment fever was less epidemic was our one hope. The press clippings were crucial to making our point.

Doug learned of our plight and arrived one evening with an energetic young ex-Marine named John Bishop. Bishop took command like the infantry captain he'd been. Two Fellowship House girls manned the phones. The next day they began arriving: secretaries from government agencies, college students, retired couples, a doctor and his wife, a minister, housewives. By week-end almost eighty volunteers had signed on and were crowded into our offices – sitting on desks and tables, squatting Indian-style on the floor, cutting, pasting, and indexing. They divided into shifts, some working days, others evenings – and a late crew which often stayed until the dawn hours. One morning I arrived early to find several young men stretched out asleep on the library floor.

Before devouring the bags of sandwiches and pots of coffee brought into the office three times a day, little groups would gather to ask for the Lord's blessing. Often before beginning their work the volunteers would gather in a circle with hands joined, asking Christ to strengthen their fellowship and help them in their task. Once I joined a group praying in the room where Ken Adams, who is Jewish, and two of the firm's young secretaries were working.

"Sorry, Ken," I said afterwards. "Didn't mean to trap you."

But Ken was smiling. "That's okay. What these people are doing for you is so great I'm glad to be part of it."

Bit by bit the mounds of paper were whittled away, replaced by neat little piles of pages pasted with clippings, colour coded and ready for copying and filing in one of the thirty-nine big black notebooks Adams had organised. The "Christians for Colson," as the volunteers dubbed themselves, cheerfully attacked the impossible and after two weeks victory was in sight.

More important than the job itself, the invasion began to affect the whole law firm, the "healthy infection" which C. S. Lewis writes about. "I don't know what's going on in here," Dave Shapiro muttered one evening, "but whatever it is, it's unbelievable. I just talked with one of those kids. He told me he couldn't stand your politics, but he loved you. Now explain that, will you?"

A couple of secretaries who had been with the firm for years and were chronic grumblers, watched with wide-eyed disbelief as the volunteers dug away at the work, with never a complaining murmur, even when the air conditioning was turned off at night or when the sandwiches ran out or when, as often happened, something was prepared improperly and had to be scrapped and done over. The harder the work and greater the frustration, the more these Christians smiled and toiled on.

Gradually but perceptibly the morale of the busy law firm was lifted. One of the clerks in the office was undergoing personal difficulties at the time and late one evening poured his heart out to a young Fellowship House worker, as the two manned a Xerox machine together. Some weeks later the clerk began attending a Fellowship prayer group and a few months after that left the law firm to take a sales position which would put him in contact with others which he in turn could help. He explained to me that these two weeks had changed his life.

The motions were due in court May 1. On the last day of April it was still touch and go, with papers spread throughout the office and a massive duplicating job still to be done to meet the court's requirement of four copies of everything. Forty blurry-eyed volunteers worked feverishly through the final night and by early the next morning the bound volumes were ready for delivery in the back of a station wagon to the courthouse. Each set of books rose seven feet into the air and contained thousands of clippings.

A few days later Judges Gesell and Sirica dismissed the most impressive research undertaking of the trial, denying our motions. Sirica refused to disqualify himself and assign another judge to the case even though his prior public statements showed a disposition to expose the "higher-ups" now scheduled for trial, and both judges refused to move the trials to another city, an accepted practice to avoid local hostility. It was a bitter disappointment. But for me no outcome in the courtroom could sour the sweet taste of Christ's love from eighty otherwise complete strangers. "Worth it all," I told Holly once again, and this time there was no quizzical look on her face. She was discovering it, too.

Meawhile a half-block away the President was announcing over nationwide television the public release of quite a different set of volumes. These were also dark, bound notebooks, containing transcripts of forty-seven taped White House conversations. "The documents," Nixon assured millions of

viewers, "will once and for all show that what I knew and
what I did with regard to the Watergate break-in and cover-
up were just as I have described them to you from the very
beginning."

He said it with such confidence that I thought it might
be another rug-pulling performance, like the January 1972
bombshell when he disclosed thirty months of secret negotiations over Vietnam. *At long last,* I thought, *he has the
proof he told me he had all along.* As I watched the "old"
Nixon, a sense of elation swept over me. But why in the
world had he waited so long?

Holly obtained an advance copy of the transcripts early
the next morning. As I began eagerly flipping through the
pages of the thick blue-bound book, Dave Shapiro came to
look over my shoulder. The words before my eyes and
Shapiro's loud groans in my ears made my heart sink. "I
don't believe it," I muttered as on page after page the phrase
expletive deleted was carving for Richard Nixon a place as
the most profane President in history.

"He's dead in the Bible Belt," I told Shapiro.

"He's dead, period," Shapiro responded. "And by the way,
faithful Nixon servant, he's lied right through his teeth to
you."

As I read on, the hurt and the feeling of betrayal came.
And with it the memory of a remark by Bob Haldeman near
the end of the 1972 campaign: "Richard Nixon will use anybody. Remember that. When he doesn't need you, he'll dis-
card you."

At the time I shrugged off the remark as an unfeeling
Haldeman expressing his idea of how any President should
handle his staff. Nor did I mind being expendable, I told myself then, if that was the price of serving the man and the
goals I saw as being so noble. Yet the ego in me made me
think I would somehow be immune.

Here in the transcripts Haldeman's words became real.
Shapiro's eyes were piercing through me. There was no time
for bitterness. "Dave, what Nixon must do is resign. Go out
gracefully. I've got to tell him."

Shapiro thought it unwise for me to call; the prosecutors
might make something out of it. Instead he carried my mes-

sage to Jim St. Clair who brushed it aside. The legal case, St. Clair was convinced, would be strengthened by the released transcripts. But it is the ground swell of public opinion, not legal argument, which moves events and nations. The jury was to decide this case on moral issues and Nixon had returned the decisive verdict himself.

Beyond the "expletives deleted," the raw transcripts exposed to public scrutiny an indecisive, vacillating, and shallow man, Richard Nixon's worst side. This was not the leader I had heard making courageous decisions in an effort to end the war in Vietnam, not the man speaking with gentle sensitivity of the feelings of others, not the idealist who dreamed aloud his visions for America and the world.

For a few moments I felt some personal vindication from the tapes. Not included in the transcripts were meetings with the President when I had argued the public exposure of whoever was involved; the President told me he did not know who they were. But now reading the tapes it seemed that he had known much more than he ever let on. While I was urging disclosure, he was telling Mitchell, Haldeman, and Dean to "stonewall" the investigators.

But the more I studied them the more depressed I became. That Nixon had lied to me, that he had not exercised the strength of character I knew in the man was a blow, yet I still cared about him. What hurt now so deeply was the sickening, lead-in-the-stomach awareness that I myself had helped create the demeaned White House which stood exposed to public view.

Not so much the profanity. The tough talk was our way of showing Nixon we were good enough to stand up against the world, lieutenants worthy of front-line service. The real problem was the moral decay inside an office which should have, if not nobility, at least a high sense of purpose. Memories of the selfless and inspiring words of Washington, Lincoln and Jefferson, who sat in those places before us, rendered our conversations shoddy and dirty by comparison. Yet all Presidents had a private side; Ike was profane, Truman salty, others had moral weaknesses; the public is shielded from much of this knowledge, for most of us want to believe the best of our leaders.

And so the devastating truth came home to me. I as much as anyone had defiled my own lofty – maybe unreal – visions of the Presidency, and thanks to the taping system it was recorded for evermore. Confronting that reality was as shattering as hearing the clerk read, "The United States versus Charles Colson." A second body blow in as many months.

On the heels of Nixon's release of the transcripts came yet another shock, this one from an unexpected quarter. "Chuck, I've got to see you." It was Dick Howard's troubled voice on the telephone, the young man who had served for two years as my superbly efficient administrative assistant in the White House. A tall, handsome Californian in his early thirties, Dick was now about to leave the White House to accept a good position in private industry. He and his wife, Marcia, and twin four-year-old boys were almost like family to us.

"I've been told not to talk to you anymore," he explained when we met in my office. Dick, always unflappable even in the heat of the worst crises, was pallid and unsmiling.

"Who said that?" I demanded.

"The prosecutors, They've told me I'm going to be indicted for perjury." There was a quiver in his voice.

"For what?" My own voice was rising uncontrollably, my stomach starting a fast elevator ride down. Howard explained that he had been grilled by the prosecutor's staff about everything which had gone on in my office. It was standard procedure, I suppose, although I strongly questioned some of the tactics used.

One young girl who handled research assignments reported to me that she was considered "uncooperative" when she failed to confirm a theory of the prosecution. The two young lawyers questioning her asked at the end of a long interrogation, "How could a nice young woman like you have worked for such an evil man?" She and others like my White House secretary, Joan Hall, were dragged before different interrogators every few weeks, forcing them to incur thousands of dollars in legal bills.

Holly, the secretary closest to me during the preparation of my defence, was grilled hard one day by three prosecutors.

After hours of going over and over the same questions, gentle, patient Holly finally had enough. "We can sit here all day and do this," she fired back, "but I know what the truth is and that is all you are going to get." She was not bothered again. While the prosecutors were after me, not them, it was costing these people dearly in time, money, and anxiety. As it turned out, the prosecution failed to turn up a single former member of my staff, which numbered close to thirty, who had testimony to give against me.

But now Dick was on the hot seat. An indictment would wreck his career. He had been questioned over and over about one alleged incident where I was supposed to have hired some thugs to beat up Ellsberg. Dick had denied it under oath, but the prosecutors would not believe him. He was told his own indictment would come in two weeks. "Look, Dick, you are telling the truth," I assured him. "Just stick to the facts and you can't be indicted."

But I felt far less confident than I tried to sound. The rest of the day I was unable to work, my mind turning again to Dick and the other innocent people caught up in the gathering storm. I left the office and went directly to Doug Coe's home.

"This certainly calls for some special prayer," Doug answered sombrely after I had explained Dick's problem.

"Doug, I can't let this happen to Dick and his family. He has no money. His new job will fall through. He's told the White House he's resigning. If it will get Dick off the hook, I'll plead guilty. I'll say I did whatever they want me to say." My agitation must have startled Doug.

"No, you can't do that. We must get the Lord's answer to this," he replied. Doug then went on to describe King David's dilemma when God punished him for prideful disobedience by giving him his choice between a seven-year famine, a three-month defeat in battle, or a three-day plague on his people. "The price of leadership can bring on terrible suffering," Doug continued. "But stop worrying about Dick. There are brothers who will help him. You are being tested. Now open yourself and God will supply the answer."

Further help to me came in a letter from Michael Alison, a young member of the British House of Commons whom I

had met at Fellowship House a month earlier. Alison recommended to me a "short, pithy, crisis prayer" like the one
David used in his ordeal with Absalom : "... O, Lord, I
pray thee, turn the counsel of Ahithophel into foolishness"
(2 Samuel 15 : 31 KJV).

"This prayer was instantly and dramatically answered,"
Alison wrote. "It is this prayer which I pray for you and I
hope you will for yourself in regard to those opponents who
are out to discredit you."

Each day thereafter, as more reports filtered back to me of
former staff members one by one summoned before Jaworski's
men, the pressure intensifying, I repeated the same prayer :
"Lord Jesus, please turn the counsel of my enemies into foolishness. Help me find *Your* answers. Show me *Your* will."

Like opening the floodgates for a fast-swelling river, the
release of the White House Transcripts triggered a deluge of
stories, television specials, and new leads for the prosecutors.
Nixon's supporters were embarrassed, his opponents had a
wealth of fresh ammunition. Republican Senate leader, Hugh
Scott, branded the transcripts "shabby." Two House leaders
demanded resignation. Vice-President Gerald Ford claimed
the tapes cleared Mr. Nixon; then as the uproar continued,
back-tracked, acknowledging the "grave situation." On May
9 the gavel struck, opening the formal impeachment hearings
of the House Judiciary Committee. The rush to judgement was
a near stampede.

As the sound and fury of the Watergate investigations
rose, I noticed a new and recurrent theme in my mail.
Although the tone of the letters remained warm and encouraging, there were more and more exhortations to do my
Christian duty. A letter from Dr. Vernon Grose, a strong
Republican and good friend, summed it up this way : "Be
forthright and utterly honest in your legal confrontations re-
garding Watergate and the associated allegations."

Here again was the dilemma I had encountered so many
times since my conversion – of trying to live in two worlds.
As a Christian I yearned to tell all, to testify in the impeachment hearings, but my lawyers – representing the world's
wisdom – told me I had to keep quiet. My freedom was at

stake, they advised; whatever I had to say should be kept for the trial and even then I was to testify only to things that would help my case. To make it worse, my courtroom defence when it came would concern my life *before* Jesus Christ entered it. The old Colson was on trial and there was a lot in this life I did not feel like defending. But how to separate the new and the old? How to live in two worlds?

In the midst of the mounting pressures, Harold announced one Monday morning that Mike Wallace was receptive and sympathetic, thus clearing the way for us to appear on "Sixty Minutes." Doug was elated at the chance for a powerful testimony to millions. I was not so certain, with the doubts now nagging at me about my ability to be a full-fledged public ambassador. The filming was scheduled for May 16 in the Hughes basement.

The very weather that day was ominous : hot and damp. When I arrived at Harold's house, it was already surrounded by CBS camera trucks. Thick black wires stretched across the front lawn, lights on tripods and metal boxes cluttered the driveway, neighbours stared from adjacent yards. Harold, dressed in a checked suit, the most conservative one in his nontraditional wardrobe, was perspiring profusely. Eva bounced up and down the stairs, carrying trays of coffee and cold drinks. Mike Wallace, so fierce on TV, seemed strangely gentle when he introduced himself.

"What you men are doing is great, just great," he said with a disarming smile. I decided that Harold had really reached him.

Harold and I slipped away to his living room for a few minutes together asking God to take charge of the interview. In the basement we found that producer Marion Goldin and the CBS experts had fashioned a makeshift studio. Under the scorching lights Harold sat in his favourite rocker, I on the Early American sofa.

The words of Marion, "Okay, Mike, cameras are rolling," were to Wallace like the sound of the bell for a prizefighter. His lips curled, his eyes became piercing. The soft-spoken, easygoing fellow we had chatted so amiably with was now a snarling tiger about to pounce.

"Twenty million people will see this," Wallace had told

us earlier. *Fine*, I thought. Having made many television appearances, stage fright was no worry. How hot the lights were! Under the blinding white glare I could feel beads of perspiration popping out on my upper lip, like little crystals on the sand, I imagined.

Mike's words shot forth in short staccato bursts: "Senator Hughes, this is the fellow who put you on the White House 'enemies' list and here you are sitting together . . ."

Hughes turned the question to me and I tried to explain that I was not the one who prepared the "enemies" list but that it didn't matter. Christ heals the wounds, He is the transcendent power. Score one for our witness.

Wallace came on hard after that: "Have you done more than pray? Have you made a palpable witness? Have you tried to make it up to those you've hurt?"

"In my own heart," I answered lamely.

"But have you tried to make it up? . . . Have you apologised?"

"There are a couple of instances . . ."

"With whom?" Wallace pressed.

When I didn't respond fast enough, Wallace listed the sins for me: the Burns smear, the effort to intimidate CBS before the Federal Communications Commission, public attacks on Jack Anderson. Wallace leaned back and mused, "A new Christian, besides talking to his God, does he do no penance for deeds like that?"

Score several for Wallace as he drove home his points with sharp, biting words. My answer about Christ forgiving us – that all of us are sinners – seemed limp. Later came the most lethal exchange of the interview.

WALLACE: Let's turn then to the White House tapes. Do they show a morality in the Oval Office?

HUGHES: Not the standards that I would hope to see in the Oval Office, no.

WALLACE: Do they to you, Mr. Colson?

COLSON:; I'm not going to try to characterise how I look at those transcripts, because I don't think you can . . .

WALLACE: Well, wait . . .

COLSON: I've sat in many, many meetings in the Oval

Office, Mike, and I did not know there was a recording
system. I suppose . . .

WALLACE : Is that moral?

COLSON : I'm not going to try to draw a moral judgment
on it . . .

WALLACE : Wait a minute. *Let me understand something
about this new Christianity, then.* You say that you
are a new man in Jesus Christ. It seems as though your
prior faith takes precedence over your new faith.

With a satisfied smile, Wallace leaned back. Score more
points, many more.

HUGHES : Mike, you are placing a burden on a man who
is new in Christ – a baby in Christ is what we say – and
that implies just what it is, a baby, not full maturity,
not full understanding. I would say it's immoral to make
the tapes. I say it's immoral to use the types of language
that were involved, regardless of whether you're behind
closed doors. And yet I would also say that I have been
guilty of similar things in my lifetime while I have been
in public office.

COLSON : I don't believe that when you accept Christ in
your life or when you decide that you're going to live
by the teachings of Christ, that you necessarily should
set yourself up as a judge of others. As a matter of fact,
Christ teaches us exactly the opposite. Only God really
is our Judge.

WALLACE : Well, I confess you leave me somewhat bewildered, then, as to the meaning of your faith.

That was it. I was impaled on the question about the White
House transcripts, driven right through the gut and then
nailed to the wall. I wanted to say, "They are lousy, rotten,
and I was part of many other conversations just like them."
But I did not, for I might have to defend some of them in
court as I tried to wriggle through the maze of legal tech-
nicalities that lay before me.

I made no effort to wipe my face dry as Wallace wound
up the interview. The reality was exploding before me in
the blinding-white camera lights : I could not be a criminal

defendant and a disciple for Christ at the same time. The
painful dilemma of how to live in two worlds had confronted
me again, this time in living colour on national TV.

After the Wallace filming I flew to Boston to be with Dad
in the hospital where he was making a slow recovery from his
second heart attack. For me it was a painful sight, tubes running out of his arms, a small oxygen cap over his nose, and a
frightened look in his eyes. Everyone loved my dad for his
kindness, his concern for others, for the contagious smile
surrounded by pink cheeks and the close-cropped white hair.
This day the smile was still there, but he could not quite hide
his fear. I believed that brave talk would bolster him.

"Don't worry, Dad, we're going to lick these indictments.
The prosecutors won't get a conviction."

It had no effect because the lawyer in him knew better.
"Are you innocent of the charges?" he persisted. It finally
penetrated that what concerned him was what he had taught
me as a boy: *always tell the truth.* My assertion that I had
not known in advance of the Ellsberg break-in gave him
more comfort than the bravado. I had not lied; I had lived by
the code he taught me, I assured him. This was more important to him than a jury's verdict.

I gave him a copy of *Mere Christianity*, which he was eager
to read. We prayed together before I left. I wanted to go
deeper, to tell him about the question I was struggling with
involving my Christian life, but he was in no condition for
it. Someday I'd be able to explain.

The following Tuesday morning I was in Judge Gerhard
Gesell's courtroom for the opening oral arguments on the
critical pre-trial motions in the Ellsberg case. At issue was
whether the national-security argument would be allowed in
the trial. It was a vital line of defence.

Dave Shapiro was soon prancing before Gesell's bench, his
head bobbing up and down to punctuate key points, his
voice rising and thundering through the room. At moments
the judge looked as kind and gentle as my dad. At other moments his stern, squinting eyes pierced the hearts of those
before him.

Suddenly Gesell interrupted. "The whole purpose of this case, beyond its immediate objective," he stated, "is to direct some attention to the desirability of having a government of law, not a government of men. That is what it is about." Then the judge – his white hair so neatly in place it looked like one of those wigs worn by English judges – proceeded to give Shapiro and the other lawyers a scolding lecture on the fundamentals of the Constitution.

It was something I remembered from Civics I in school. These were the cardinal principles of American government, the real bulwark against man-made tyranny. When a man's constitutional rights are in jeopardy, the violation, even cloaked in the time-honoured protective shroud of national security, is simply intolerable. I did not know whether Gesell was a religious man, but while he was speaking, Lewis's words about the individual being more important than the state kept echoing through my head. Lewis and Gesell were singing the same tune. So what if I had not known of the break-in ahead of time? If I could prove that legally, I would be acquitted – but was that the real issue? When I first learned of the break-in at the psychiatrist's office, I believed it was justified – almost anything was, to stop Ellsberg. So why should my guilt or innocence turn on the particular day I first learned of the misdeed? Legal niceties made moral nonsense.

God was dealing with me at that very moment. I went home that evening and fell into the deepest depression of all the dark days and nights that had gone before. Judge Gesell had not ruled on the motions; he would do that later in the week, but now somehow it did not matter. Nothing he would say could alter my own self-judgment. How smug I had been during those years in the executive mansion. What happened around me never bothered me so long as I kept myself clean. I was just another "see no evil, hear no evil, speak no evil," monkey. If I had sidestepped any direct involvement in the Ellsberg break-in, it was pure happenstance. I had tried to smear him just the way I was now being attacked in the press and in somewhat the same way the CIA had leaked stories about me.

If I had gotten away with it from the sanctuary of the

White House, then no one was safe. I had not succeeded, of course, and I was not being charged with character defamation, but was it any less reprehensible than the burglary I *was* charged with? *Hardly,* I concluded. It was worse: damage to a man's spirit as against damage to property.

Dad's question from his hospital bed, the simple idealism in Judge Gesell's impromptu sermon, memories of my White House attitude of "anything goes just short of breaking the law," Mike Wallace's questions and the realisation of my own crippled discipleship were pulling against me like great iron chains. I'd struggle, twist, tear at them, but I could not shake free. I was barely able to hold a conversation with Patty.

"What's eating you, Chuck?" she asked with a trace of annoyance in her voice, as I sat on the desk by our swimming pool gazing vacantly into the blue water.

"I'm just tired, honey," I replied, but I knew it was much more than that. Somehow I had to be altogether free of the past.

As a favour to Doug some while back I had agreed to speak at the annual prayer breakfast in the small central-Michigan community of Owosso. It could not have come at a worse time – Thursday, May 23. Arguments were continuing over the motions. The trial would begin in less than four weeks and every minute was precious now. My lawyers and I could make it only by working day and night, weekends as well.

But I had made the date, so Thursday morning I was sitting in the Owosso YWCA auditorium, located on a quiet, tree-shaded street just up the hill from the centre of town. Friendly open-faced Midwesterners had risen at dawn to sit shoulder to shoulder at long folding tables. There were high-school students, middle-aged couples, older folks, a sprinkling of clergy. Next to the Fourth of July, the prayer breakfast was the most important event in the town. After we had consumed huge platters of baked eggs atop bread, there were official welcomes, an opening prayer, passage readings from the Old and New Testaments and then I was introduced.

I had discovered that when I ask the Spirit of God to speak through me, the pressure leaves. He takes over. This morning the words came out more boldly than ever before. Toward the end of my thirty-minute talk, I thought I owed some explanation for my indictments, that it was important for them to know the truth so they could better accept my testimony.

"I know in my own heart," I explained, "that I am innocent of many of the charges . . ."

The flow of words stopped as my mind took in what I had said. "*Many* of the charges" – *but not all?*

There was an awkward silence. I looked down at the notes before me, but they were no help. I had hardly glanced at my prepared text during the whole talk. The pause must have been as embarrassing to the audience as it was to me. A hot flush spread over my face. *The press is here* I thought to myself. *Better recover fast.*

"Er – innocent of all the charges I stand accused of," I stammered. I continued, but the life was gone from my words.

No one else seemed to have noticed my slip. There was nothing about it in the press. But the words *many of the charges* throbbed with the pulse of the jet engines flying me back to Washington. Was it a Freudian slip? Or was it God using my voice? "Many, *but not all* the charges, Chuck!"

My own words had clinched it. My conversion would remain incomplete so long as I was a criminal defendant, tangled in the Watergate quagmire. I had to put the past behind me completely. If it meant going to prison, so be it!

In his book *The Cost of Discipleship* Dietrich Bonhoeffer wrote of what he called the Great Divide: "The first step which follows Christ's call cuts the the disciple off from his previous existence. The call to follow at once produces a new situation. To stay in the old situation makes discipleship impossible."

It had all looked so simple once, just getting in tune with God, finding out who Christ was and believing in Him. But whether I was ready for discipleship or not, here I was and there was no turning back.

Patty was the first one whose agreement I had to secure. We talked long into the night amid tears that would not stop. She was hurt. We had struggled through so much and now I was simply to step forward, plead guilty, and go to prison.

"Why? Why do you have to do it?" she kept asking. "Dave

says you'll be acquitted. Then our lives will be normal again. you'll be practising law. We can travel."

"It will never be the same again, Patty. Trust me that this is the way things will get better. I just have to do it." It was the most difficult thing I had ever asked her to do, but finally she did, aching heart and all.

Next came Harold. We talked in the familiar surroundings of his basement den, where only ten days earlier we had filmed the "Sixty Minutes" show. "Harold, I've reached a decision," I said. "I'm going to plead guilty to something I did do, smearing Ellsberg while he was under indictment. I assume if I do, the prosecutors will drop the other charges. The plea should be good for the country; it should stop this kind of thing in the future." Even as I spoke I could taste the new freedom that would soon be mine.

Harold's expression was grim. "How much time will you get?"

"Five years is maximum." Somehow the words did not chill me as they always had before.

"That's tough. I don't think I could do it."

"I'm going to, Harold, unless you and the other brothers disagree. I'm convinced I must."

Harold's rugged face relaxed and a wide grin spread across it. "Hallelujah!" he shouted. "I could never have advised you to do it, but I've been waiting for this day. It kills me, it hurts so much, but I'm swelling up with joy."

Dave Shapiro's reaction was predictable and I held the receiver away from my ear as he exploded. "You are nuts, crazy, you've gone *meshuga*, that's what." And then he really let me have it.

"Dave, calm down. It's a decision I've reached and I know what I am doing." I tried to keep my voice down. Dave and I often shouted at each other.

"Well, we'll see if the psychiatrist agrees that you know what you're doing. I'm taking you to a shrink Monday morning."

"Dave, I want you to talk to the prosecutors Monday. See Bill Merrill. Tell him we want no deal, no strings. Just say I'm ready to plead guilty to disseminating derogatory information

to the press about Daniel Ellsberg while he was a criminal
defendant."

"It's not a crime. How can I plead that for you? No one
has ever been charged with that."

"It ought to be. If I plead, it will be a precedent. That will
stop it in the future."

"You are an idiot and you are going to end up in the slammer."

"I know."

"I won't do it."

"Then get me a lawyer who will."

"Colson, you are nuts. I've suspected it all along but now I
know it. Let's sleep on it. We'll talk tomorrow. Right now
I'm going to have a big stiff drink."

Shapiro can't drink. One knocks him flat. The thought of it
provided the first good laugh I'd had in weeks.

17

Guilty, Your Honour

Dave Shapiro appeared Monday morning looking as if he were wearing a rubber mask. There were sagging ripples of flesh under his mournful eyes; his grey-tinted cheeks were in contrast to a stark-white forehead. I knew one reason he was hurting. Dave is usually a winner, especially in lawsuits. To him this was defeat.

"Are you sure you know what you're doing?" he asked one final time. It was the same question Patty had asked when I'd kissed her good-bye at the front door.

"I've never been more certain of anything in my life, Dave," I assured him, discovering a confidence I'd not known in weeks. With that, Shapiro was off to see the assistant prosecutor, William Merrill.

Everything depended on Bill Merrill and Judge Gesell being in agreement. If they were not, there could be no guilty plea and the fact of my offer would hurt me badly in the trial, where it would be viewed as a sign of weakness prompted by the fear that I was going to be convicted. Here again I had to go ahead on faith.

Only Patty, Harold, Holly, and Dave knew what was afoot. Any premature disclosure could cause the prosecutors to back away. We'd consult the other brothers and the rest of the family only when we had the green light from the prosecution. Somehow I would find a way to let my old friend in the White House know, too, but it would be hard to explain. So besieged was the President that he would probably see my act as one of betrayal.

Bill Merrill was as shocked by the decision as Dave had been, I learned from Shapiro. For the prosecutors about to begin a trial, it was welcome news, simplifying the case against the other defendants, particularly John Ehrlichman. The two lawyers immediately placed a long-distance call to Judge Gesell, who was at his summer home in Maine for a week's rest. The judge would make no commitment over the phone.

"You understand, Mr. Shapiro, *if* I accept this plea, that my policy with high government officials is to impose a prison sentence," he warned.

"I understand, Your Honour, and Mr. Colson does, too," Shapiro replied.

"There can be no deal here," the judge continued. "There is no understanding in advance about sentence. You and Mr. Colson are voluntarily coming before me with no limits on what I may do."

Judge Gesell's words had a menacing ring. Bud Krogh, who had admitted responsibility for the Ellsberg break-in, had been given a six-month sentence. What I was pleading to was a lesser offence and should warrant a lesser punishment. But I was a higher-up target and a more likely candidate to be made a public example. On balance, we reasoned, Krogh's sentence would be the logical guideline. Still the judge's tone was ominous. Five years was possible.

Over the phone Judge Gesell also cautioned Shapiro and Merrill that he would have to be convinced that what I was pleading to was, in fact, a crime. The plea would be an important precedent. Shapiro thus began the anomalous task of researching legal arguments to persuade a judge that his client was actually guilty of a crime. Gesell would not make his decision until he returned to Washington the next week.

"Honey, will it really mean prison?" Patty asked on Wednesday evening.

"I'm afraid so," I replied. "But it won't be long, a few months probably, like Bud. He gets home in a couple of weeks. Four and a half months goes by like nothing."

But both of us knew it was not just the length of time, but the element of danger, too. The reports from Bud's friends were mildly reassuring; he had adjusted well, was working hard driving a tractor at Allenwood. There had been no threats on his life that we knew about. Howard Hunt had had a rougher time, was attacked in his cell one night in the D.C. jail, and later suffered a mild stroke, apparently from working in the sub-zero cold shovelling manure at Allenwood's farm. Stories of homosexual rape in the D.C. jail appeared regularly in the press.

"I'm scared, Chuck. I don't know if I can go through with it." Tears lurked behind her wide blue eyes as she gripped my hand. Patty was tough inside, one reason I loved her so much, but we had grown close and were now dependent on one another. Years before, I had decided never to leave her alone in our house which is surrounded by woods and isolated from neighbours. Whenever I travelled Holly stayed with her. Nightly calls kept us close and I never took long trips without her. We had not been apart more than a two-day stretch in our ten years of marriage. Despite her warm outgoing personality and the brave front she struggled to keep, I realised suddenly how frightened she was.

"Honey, let's pray about it; let's ask God to protect us both and help us face what we must."

In Patty's eyes, while Christ was once a threat to our relationship, He was now becoming a source of strength. The months in Bible class had helped. She had also grown fond of the brothers and their families. Yet not wanting to press her into something she was not ready for, I did not ask her to pray aloud with me this evening. We both did so silently. Later we talked about some of the hard decisions ahead – who would stay with her, who would take care of the house, how to tell the children – all of this assuming that Judge Gesell agreed to my guilty plea.

There was a make-believe quality in our talks all week long, as if a miracle would intervene to rescue us. "Well, it's just not going to happen, that's all," was Patty's way of ending each conversation.

The tentative paperwork with the prosecutors was not completed before Saturday. Some of Jaworski's assistants wanted my testimony in advance. We insisted that public testimony be withheld until after sentencing, except for one affidavit which merely re-stated what I had testified to before.

We wanted to do nothing before that final judgement day that could be interpreted as currying favour with the judge.

Notified that we were in accord with the prosecutors, Judge Gesell scheduled Shapiro and Merrill in his chambers Monday morning at 8:30 sharp. If satisfied, at 9:30 he would accept my plea in open court.

There were two important pieces of unfinished business – the first an eyeball-to-eyeball confrontation between Bill Merrill and myself. Dave arranged it for his office Saturday afternoon. Merrill arrived shortly after 3:00 P.M. and thrust out his hand. "Chuck, I admire what you are doing." He was not smiling, there was almost sorrow in his eyes. *The conqueror can afford to be gracious with his vanquished*, I thought, but soon realised it went deeper than that.

"I wanted to see you face-to-face, Bill," I began, "so there would be no misunderstanding later. I'm not trading my testimony for anything. I just want to tell the truth."

"That's all we want, the truth. I wouldn't ask you to do anything else."

I felt a sense of clumsiness as I groped for an important but elusive thought. "Once this is over, will you guys try to do something about the system, not just the people? There are abuses in the CIA and the FBI and the courts, too, as well as the White House. For the good of the country there's a lot of cleaning up to do."

"I know what you're saying, Chuck," he replied with real compassion in his voice. "You think we're just out to get you and Nixon. I can't blame you, but I want you to know that some of us are in this thing because we really do want to make the system better, correct things that are wrong. We're going to stay with it, and what you are doing now is going to help."

In the half-hour that followed, some of the ugly sores laid bare in the past months began to heal. Merrill's relentless pursuit and hard tactics had embittered me, but as we talked this day the anger drained away. He was another human being doing a nasty job, but with a capacity to care about those he felled as much as those he was charged with protecting. Christ, I discovered, was giving me the capacity to see that which the bitterness of the world hides from view.

The second and most important piece of unfinished business was to lay my decision before all four of my brothers. We met in my house on Sunday evening – all but Al Quie who had been speaking in Pennsylvania and was delayed by the storm which had lashed Washington all day.

Graham, Doug, Harold, and I went into my cherry-panelled study and pulled chairs around the ship's-wheel coffee table. Remembering how long and hard those men had prayed, how much Doug's volunteers had done, it was hard to say it: "I have decided, providing Judge Gesell permits it and you all agree, to plead guilty in court tomorrow morning."

Graham, who was staring at the pictures on the wall, wheeled around, "You're what?" Doug was smiling, however, and something told me that he understood immediately. Harold sat there in quiet but obvious agreement.

I reviewed the steps that led to my decision: the slip of the tongue while speaking in Owosso, my frustration over not being able to testify in the impeachment hearings, and above all the realisation of my crippled witnessing for Christ. I could not continue muddling along the way I had during the Mike Wallace interview. "I knew what I had to do after that interview," I told them.

Graham was the first to speak. "But what you are pleading to isn't any crime, nor do they have a case against you in either indictment. You can't just up and decide to go to prison. I don't think being a Christian requires you to do that."

Harold shook his head. "I have been praying all week long this would be the outcome, that Chuck wouldn't waver in this decision because I know in my heart it is right. This may lead others to do the same thing and, God knows, this agony has to end for this country."

Doug concurred wholeheartedly, but Graham winced when I explained the possible sentence and that it would probably mean disbarment as a lawyer as well. "You guys can't expect me to pray for the judge to accept this," he said.

"That is just what I want you to do," I replied, "but only if you feel it in your heart. Shapiro says there is only a fifty-fifty chance that Gesell will go along. We need prayer."

At Harold's suggestion we wrote out on my yellow pad exactly what I would say the next day, assuming the guilty plea would be accepted. Meanwhile Doug finally reached Quie on the phone. His judgment was swift. "I think it's tremendous," he told me. "I have been expecting you to do this, and I'm with you all the way. God bless you, brother."

Graham was the lone holdout, pacing about the room in front of the big stone fireplace, turning away often to conceal his emotion. The onetime Texas district judge could not shake from his mind the horrors of the dark concrete holes into which he himself had once ordered men to spend years of their lives. Finally he nodded his head. "If this is what it takes to give you freedom of the spirit then I'm with you. But it hurts, man, it hurts."

We prayed for a long while.

It was after midnight when the liberal Democratic senator from Iowa mentioned the political implications. "What does this do to the President and his impeachment?" he asked as I walked him to his car.

"Helps some, hurts some," I replied.

"That's what I thought," Harold mused. He gripped my shoulder tightly, climbed into his car, and drove off.

At 9:00 a.m. Monday morning I was pushing papers around on my office desk, re-reading my statement, and staring at my phone waiting for the call. Patty was chatting with Holly in her little office outside. Five after nine and no call. Was Shapiro having trouble with Judge Gesell? Three miles west in the white cement provincial house near Embassy Row, I knew that Harold, Doug, Al, and Graham were praying for the Lord to be in charge of the decision.

At 9:12 the phone rang. Shapiro's voice was serious: "Okay, come ahead; it was close. Now hurry."

It is a fifteen-minute ride to the court downtown, but one call had to be made first. The familiar, cheery voice of the White House operator explained that the President had visitors in his office. "Then get me Fred Buzhardt, please. It's urgent."

Buzhardt was in a senior staff meeting, but in a few seconds he was on the line. "Fred, please tell the President right now so he gets it from me first. I'm pleading guilty this morning, but I'm not turning against him. Only telling the truth."

There was a gasp, a moment of silence, "But why?"

"Just the truth, Fred, I have to. I'll explain later."

The courtroom was filled with the familiar faces of reporters and cartoonists, plus assorted curiosity seekers, as I strode through the waist-high gate into the lawyers' area and to the defence-counsel table where a solemn Shapiro was waiting. Patty slipped unnoticed into the back-row spectators' bench. John Ehrlichman, fingers gently stroking his chin, was standing nearby talking to his lawyers.

Seated at the table was the strangest of all the characters in the Watergate cast: Gordon Liddy, the Kamikaze mentality, ideologue, and original Plumber. Despite months of incarceration in the D.C. jail, and the twenty-year sentence Sirica had hung on him to make him talk, he remained stoically silent, fervently worshipping a self-conceived deity of high authority. At the sight of me Liddy bounded to his feet and saluted snappily. Adhering to his own vow of absolute courtroom silence, he said not a word, but his eyes showed the fire of defiance, sparkling against a drawn, pallid face, To him I was a high priest of the government order he revered because I had not turned on the President. How the demon of Watergate had warped men's values and lives! For only a few more minutes would I have this proud man's esteem.

"This Honourable Court ..." the words of the crier snapped. Judge Gesell strode in from the corner entrance behind the bench. My heart raced. I knew what I was doing, but still it was a wrenching moment. This one man from his commanding perch had my life in his hands to do with as he alone saw fit. Throwing myself on the mercy of the court at that moment was more than a figurative term, so helpless is the defendant before such absolute power.

The judge announced that there was to be a "disposition" before the subpoena issue was argued. The lawyers knew at once that this term could only mean a guilty plea; their eyes quickly scanned the room, speculating. When Judge Gesell ordered Prosecutor Merrill to step forward, there was a murmur of surprise.

Merrill presented the information (the formal term for charges not brought by a grand jury) against Charles W. Colson. Shapiro and I walked to the rostrum, standing just to the side as Merrill handed the documents to the clerk who passed them to the judge. Years of listening to sordid tales of theft, murder, and rape desensitises the dark-suited bailiffs and clerks, who have learned to discipline themselves to conscious indifference. Like mechanical men oblivious to emotion of the human world about them, they move about the court, passing papers, transcribing, escorting witnesses. But this day they, too, stopped and stared at me. In the unguarded moment of her shock, I was warmed by the compassion in one woman clerk's eyes.

The judge began a series of questions to me. Did I waive the grand jury?

"I do, Your Honour," I replied, relieved to hear my own words strong, for my knees were like sponges.

Bill Merrill then read from a document: "We charge here that Mr. Colson is responsible for devising a scheme to obtain derogatory information about Daniel Ellsberg, to defame and destroy Mr. Ellsberg's public image and credibility ..." Only Merrill, Shapiro, and I knew that I had written the script, had supplied the material and asked to be charged with the words now reverberating with such sinister echoes through the room. "... to influence, obstruct, and impede the conduct and outcome of the Ellsberg trial." Obstruction of justice is the charge of maximum dishonour for a lawyer. *Now I can be free from the past*, I had to remind myself as I recoiled with each word.

Judge Gesell turned to me sternly. "With your plea of guilty, you understand that you waive those rights under the Constitution and that all is left is for the court to impose sentence?"

"Yes, sir," I replied. Then came my statement. My voice like the rest of me was shaky now. "I have come to believe in the very depths of my being that official threats to the right of fair trial for defendants such as those charged in this information must be stopped; and by this plea, Your Honour, I am prepared to take whatever consequences I must to help in stopping them."

"Do you still wish to plead guilty?" Gesell asked, the final step in the ritual.

"Yes, I do, Your Honour."

It had taken just under ten minutes. Sentencing was set for June 21. This was hardly enough time to obtain all the letters and recommendations that might help persuade the judge to be lenient. Speed was necessary. I would soon be a witness before the House Judiciary Committee and wanted to be sentenced first so that my testimony – even subconsciously – wouldn't be influenced by the impact it might have on the judge. Judge Gesell ordered me to report at once to the probation officer and with Merrill's agreement freed me without bond.

The press broke loose from the back of the courtroom and raced for telephones. I was the first of the President's inner circle to fall and there had not been a hint of it in advance. Though Washington had become case-hardened to the daily revelations of Watergate, this story I knew would cause new reverberations, hopefully some of them constructive.

Bill Merrill was the first to come over to me as I walked away from the bench. "Good luck, Chuck. I mean it," he said, grabbing my hand. St. Clair was standing only a few steps behind him, the man who months earlier told me that while convinced I was innocent he could give me only a fifty-fifty chance and who now was engaged in a Herculean struggle to rescue Richard Nixon whose chances were even less. "I wish you the best," he said, struggling with his words.

Inside the small plain-walled probation office, the numbness passed and I began to feel the reality of what it was to be a convicted felon. Here a clerk would write up my report just as he did each day for street criminals, rapists, car thieves, and narcotics peddlers. I had put myself here, but that knowledge made it no more comfortable. I would now be in the hands of GS-7 probation clerks, marshals, prison guards. The loss of control of my body and life was a sensation I had not fully understood before.

I had kept myself in tight control, but the sight of Doug Coe, waving to me from the door blocked by two blue-suited officers, choked me up. He was always there, always when most needed. I asked the police to let Doug through and with

him came a small group from the Fellowship, including Dr.
John Curry and his wife, Betsy, who had worked round the
clock for weeks pasting up clippings in our office. As we
embraced I wondered if the spectators could understand what
it meant to have such friends.

18

Awaiting Judgment

As I read my statement to reporters outside the courthouse – that I had pleaded guilty so that I could be free to speak out the truth, whether it helped or hurt me or others – I had a feeling they were scarcely listening. Fred Graham of CBS posed the only question they cared about: "Are you going to testify against the President?" All I could do was try to explain that it would be improper for me to make any statements until after I had been sentenced.

COLSON'S PLEA OF GUILTY SENDS SHUDDERS THROUGH WHITE HOUSE the *Boston Globe* announced the next morning. COLSON'S PLEA WORRIES WHITE HOUSE, reported the *Post*.

Columnist Mary McGrory interviewed Hughes, Quie, Purcell, and Coe, and then wrote of our Sunday-night meeting: "The Prayer Meeting That Led to Guilty Plea." In the last paragraph McGrory, whose vitriolic anti-Nixon reporting once earned her a high place on his "enemies" list, concluded: "To Richard Nixon, Colson's change of heart may be the worst thing that has happened since John Dean told everthing he knew."

The account of the prayer meeting triggered a fresh round of stories and cartoons. Oliphant of the *Denver Post* sketched me, garbed in priestly robes, parading in front of the White House carrying a sign: REPENT! FOR LO, I AM ABOUT TO LAY IT ON THE HOUSE JUDICIARY COMMITTEE.

The prevailing assumption was that my religious conversion had prompted me to tell all, that I had been hiding all sorts of heinous, dark secrets. The validity of my conversion, I feared, would thus be measured in direct proportion to the number and foulness of past transgressions I would now confess.

Those who thought my decision represented a turn against my former chief were the most eager to give purity to my motives. Carl Rowan, for example, rejoiced: "If the devil made Charles Colson do it and the good Lord made him confess, we could be close to the end of the Watergate nightmare . . . I have a sort of gut feeling that the guy we thought was one of the dirtiest characters ever to nest at 1600 Pennsylvania Avenue, just might turn out to be the one who in telling the dirty truth can help make this nation clean again."

The *Boston Globe* which only months earlier harpooned my conversion editorially now welcomed it and praised Jaworski's "skill" in bringing me to his side. Scores of other anti-Nixon papers followed suit.

The week following my guilty plea the House Democrats dispatched a member of the Rodino Committee to meet with a man they believed to be one of their own, Senator Harold Hughes. He would, they reasoned, tell them how they could use my testimony to skewer Mr. Nixon. Hughes, faintly amused, told his colleague: "Colson is not out to nail anyone's hide to the barn door. He is just going to tell the truth. If the chips fall in someone's back yard, that's tough, whether it's the President's or someone else's." Hughes's compatriots in the Congress believed him no more than the press believed me.

When the President dispatched his top field commander, General Alexander Haig, to reconnoitre, I tried to convince him there were no dark motives or intent. "I just want to be free to testify to the facts."

On the day of the plea Nixon sent me a handwritten note (*see* page 258).

But by the next day Nixon's eyes were focused on impeachment strategy. He called me that evening shortly after nine. "Tell your boys that they can be very proud of their father," he began. "It's a crime that Ellsberg should go scot-free while you plead guilty. You weren't involved in these things; you are innocent," he declared.

The President seemed curiously insensitive to the moral forces at work across the landscape of American life, much of which he had unleashed with his own transcripts. I ex-

June 3, 1974

THE WHITE HOUSE
WASHINGTON

Dear Chuck,

I know what a terribly sad
and difficult day this must be
for you and your fine family

I want you to know that in
a very personal way it is
an equally sad day for me.

You must however keep
your faith in the fact
that as time goes on your
dedicated service to the nation
will be remembered long after
this incident has become only a
footnote in history.

Always - your friend, RN

plained that I *had* done what I had pleaded to; each of us had to be guided by his own conscience. Though underestimating the strength of the forces arrayed against him, Nixon was keen and sharp as ever, clicking off each vote he could count on in the House Judiciary Committee considering possible impeachment, then – if need be – in the Senate.

Near the end of the conversation I told him that regardless of any mistakes he had made, it was because of his Presidency that my sons would not have to go to war. That to me outweighed the pain, even of prison. I meant it, too; his moral judgment had been blurred, yet I couldn't forget the courageous long-viewed way in which he set out to create a more stable order in the world. I did not know then that among the miles of magnetic tape stashed away in the bowels of the White House was the proof of deceptions that would soon mean the end for this man and his dreams.

The President took my remarks as a signal that I was still his fighting knight, that my plea was perhaps one last desperate act of loyalty, flinging myself on the sword. The next day White House aides were telling the press that Mr. Nixon had nothing to fear from Colson's testimony.

As an accommodation to the House Judiciary Committee, Shapiro arranged with John Doar and his staff to have informal interviews with me in Dave's office. Question – answer; question – answer. It lasted all day. "When have you last heard from the President?" Bernie Nussbaum, John Doar's chief assistant, asked during the second day of the sessions.

"Last week," I replied.

Nussbaum's eyebrows lifted: "Oh?"

"He called me," I explained and then repeated the substance of the phone conversation. Nussbaum stared at me incredulously. "He also wrote me a letter," I added.

Nussbaum asked to see it and I gave it to him. He stared at it for a long time in silence. Then he put it down on Shapiro's glass-topped coffee table and, looking puzzled, fixed his eyes on mine.

"But – but how can you still be friendly?"

That evening I learned that the Judiciary Committee struck me from its witness list.

When the news of the committee's decision not to use me reached the White House, St. Clair immediately demanded that I be called as his witness. For the next two weeks the committee haggled over whose witness I would be. Meanwhile committee investigators continued to meet with me – over fifty hours – gleaning every last shred of knowledge I had on all the assorted allegations of Nixon wrong-doing. Not until the eve of the final round of hearings did the committee conclude that I should be called, *despite* the friendly feelings I maintained towards the President.

In the midst of my frustration over being pitched back and forth between the warring factions came one bit of welcome news. The prosecutors informed Dick Howard's lawyer that he was no longer a target of any grand jury prosecutions. Marcia Howard's jubilant and relieved voice on the other end of the phone was the happiest sound we had heard in months. One by one the other former staff members phoned to tell me similar good news.

But for me the painful suspense mounted. The suspended sentence given former Attorney General Richard Kleindienst on June 7 was an unsettling development. Kleindienst had lied to a congressional committee, then plea bargained for a misdemeanour. Judge Hart's leniency touched off a small uproar, triggering a wave of editorial denunciations and demands for harsher sentences. Though I was happy for Dick, I'd be the next Watergater up to bat.

Some days my hopes would soar as I heard about the many letters pouring into Judge Gesell, many unsolicited, most urging leniency for me. *Perhaps Gesell would give me a suspended sentence.* One such letter came from a young black lad I'd represented five years earlier as a court-appointed attorney, a copy of which was sent to me:

Dear Judge Gesell:
    Mr. Colson helped me when I was in severe difficulty with the law, and my life was such that I needed guidance. I was charged as a juvenile with breaking and entering into a convent. At that time I was a poor student, took no interest in schoolwork, and had broken the law numerous times.

More important than what Mr. Colson did for me legally (the charges were dropped) is what he did for me personally. After the Court proceedings, he made clear to me, as no one else had done before, that my life was headed to disaster. He spoke of honesty, truth, ambition, and obligation to others, in terms that since then I have heeded. I I have never again been involved with the law. I am now married, gainfully employed and a responsible citizen.

Very truly yours,
Richard Austin.

I was also buoyed up by a draft of the presentence report obtained from the prosecutors which acknowledged that most of the charges against me were based on evidence I myself had supplied: "Colson turned over to the prosecutors a number of documents in spite of the potentially incriminating nature of them ... [which] ... the prosecutors might not ever have received ... if Colson had not provided them." The report concluded that my guilty plea would be "of great national significance in helping to insure the sanctity of the judicial process" with respect to the rights of defendants in celebrated cases. That report almost sent Shapiro pirouetting again.

The prosecutor even acknowledged to the press: "Colson's alleged roles in the cover-up and burglary would have been more difficult to prove than those of the other alleged conspirators ... because this man was outside the main stream of the overt acts." All this was little solace now. My decision had not rested on how good my case in court would have been.

All convicted criminal defendants must submit to interrogation by one of the court's probation officers whose report is supposed to be the foundation for the judge's sentence. The criminal is accompanied to the interview by as much family as he can gather around him. It is part of the ritual and supposed to help. I protested putting Patty through it, but Judd Best, our firm's expert on sentencing practices, insisted.

Patty, Judd, and I were ushered into an austere office occupied by Horace Smith, a ruddy-faced man in his mid-fifties, sitting in shirt sleeves behind a cluttered and scarred oak desk.

We sat in three hard straight-backed chairs while the probation officer rocked back and forth in a squeaky wooden swivel chair. Smith is a big man, a chain smoker, burdened and somewhat stooped from years of listening to tales of woe, exaggerated claims of hardship, and plaintive pleas for mercy.

He went down the list of routine questions. "Describe the nature of the charges against you," he said, coming to one of the blank lines on the multi-paged form. I did my best while Smith sat scratching his head, staring at the page before him, his pencil not moving. "Don't know how to put this one down," he said. "It's a little unusual." Next Patty answered questions about our homelife.

With the form nearly complete, Smith suddenly leaned back in his groaning chair and stared out of the curtainless window. "Although this may seem a little unnecessary, since I've read so much about you in the newspapers – but tell me about your religious experience and Senator Hughes and the fellowship."

There was nothing routine about this question. Something told me he was genuinely interested, but something else told me that I must not use my conversion to try to gain his sympathy. "Well, it's not really relevant to what we're doing here, is it, Mr. Smith?" I asked. "If you're interested, maybe someday I can come back and tell you about it."

"No, I'd like to know right now," he said. "Just explain it the way it happened."

I began a rather abbreviated account, determined to make it unemotional so that I would not in any sense be "using" my religion. When I came to what had happened in the Phillips driveway, Smith interrupted. "Slow down, Mr. Colson," he said, "I really want to know what this is about."

Suddenly there in that bare room a rather strange thing happened. The leathery exterior of this case-hardened bureaucrat softened. The printed form was pushed aside. Here was a thirsty man looking for the Giver of fresh water. My role was to pass the cup. I finished the whole story twenty minutes later, during which Smith's eyes never left mine. "That's the answer," he said. "It's the answer to all the ugly problems we have in the world." His voice cracked as he added, "You see, I understand fellowship. I'm a recovered alcoholic."

The probation officer apologised for keeping us so long, wished me well, then said rather wistfully that he believed Senator Hughes could help him. The next day Harold and Horace Smith spent three hours together in talk and prayer.

Smith's report, as I learned later, contained a strong affirmation of the sincerity of my conversion, along with excerpts from nearly 150 strong and moving letters. The report concluded that prison was altogether unnecessary, but then recommended that because of the international attention focused on the case, defendant Colson should be sentenced nonetheless. My testimony had no effect on Smith's report, but Christ touched one man's life.

The brothers remained closer than ever through the eighteen days of suspense. We met frequently in Hughes's office, at Fellowship House, or individually as the men and their wives dropped by for a few quiet hours with Patty and me. Their prayers and their presence were reminders that the current situation was but a way-stop on the road I had chosen. Soon I would be free, the past behind me and the "victory," as Harold always put it, was with Jesus.

Doug Coe relieved one of the pressing personal problems; his beautiful twenty-three-year-old daughter, Paula, and a college friend would move in with Patty come autumn when our boys would be back in college.

The Colson family closed ranks as well. Wendell, a star oarsman in the Princeton crew, was scheduled to go to Switzerland for the summer to row in international competition. Being chosen was heady stuff and Wendell had been eagerly anticipating the trip. Now without a word from Patty or me, he cancelled out and moved down to McLean for the summer. He would be on hand for the sentencing and whatever happened next, working full-time as a carpenter, taking over my chores around the house at night. Wendell carried a notebook with him, jotting down instructions from me as I thought about things that would need to be done while I was away.

Emily and Chris also flew to Washington. Emily had taken a lot of abuse from her tenth-grade classmates and a few anti-Nixon teachers. A sensitive child, she would be the most vulnerable, I feared. I arranged for her to return to her mother before the traumatic time of sentencing. Before I put her on the airplane for Boston, we walked to a quiet corner of the airport waiting room. "Emily," I said, "I just hope you aren't ashamed of me. Don't let what anyone says bother you. I've done some wrong things, but now I'm sure trying to do what's right."

"Daddy," she snapped, "I'm proud of you." The little girl of fifteen threw her arms around me and for the first time the emotions we had both held in check were shaken loose. A good cry was in order for both of us. Chris, on the other hand, was unusually quiet and subdued, carrying his own hurt inside. While I didn't know it then, he was to suffer the most.

Support and help came from others, some from old friends but some from unlikely sources as well. Ken Belieu, my old political comrade, now a brother in Christ, called one evening: "Chuck, no time to be maudlin. I just want you to know that we have a guest room for Patty, an extra car, and a few thousand in the bank. They are all yours if you want them." I turned it down but the words my heart searched for wouldn't come.

Other friends made similar offers, including my onetime assistant, Mike Balzano, who tried to give me his life's savings.

Arthur Burns took a call from a reporter who was digging around for anti-Colson material for his syndicated column. The newsman wanted to rehash the Colson-smears-Burns episode of 1971 and thought that Burns might cooperate with some fresh new tidbits. Instead he was told of my apologies, our prayers together, our reconciliation, and Burns's opinion that my conversion was sincere. The startled columnist wrote it all, but was quick to add that there was a long list of other apologies still due from the ex-hatchet man. (*See* "Charles Colson: Time for Apologies?" Tom Braden, *Washington Post*, May 18, 1974.)

Jack Anderson had blasted me for years in his syndicated column for all manner of misdeeds. At the White House we considered him our arch nemesis, and I once proposed an investigation of Anderson. Because the money would help, I accepted an offer to debate Jack on television. The debate was standard fare; it was what occurred back-stage that I'll never forget. While I was being pasted with powder and rouge by the makeup man, Jack asked Patty if he could talk to her alone for a moment. "Don't tell Chuck – he's too proud – but while he's away if you need money for the family, just call. The Lord has been good to me. You are decent folks. This could happen to anyone and if I can help, I want to." I did not learn until later what a deeply religious man Jack Anderson is, a side he has kept out of the news.

As the days passed and such episodes multiplied, Shapiro became increasingly optimistic. "The maximun as I see it is six months. It could go to nine, but my money is on six." Patty still believed the sentence would be suspended altogether. No amount of sober talk on my part seemed to deflate her expectations. She was praying this way and I was troubled about what a tough sentence might do to her growing faith.

Bud Krogh was released from prison in mid-June and Patty and Suzanne set up a quiet evening for just the four of us. It was a sultry June night, muggy the way Washington is during most of the summer, when we arrived at the Krogh's Cape Cod-styled brick home on the edge of one of Washington's middle-class black residential areas. When Krogh joined the White House staff, one of his first assignments was liaison with the District of Columbia. With charasteristic idealism Bud believed he should live in the location of his assignment.

Bud trotted down the front steps to our car when he saw us arrive. There was no sign of jailhouse pallor; his eyes were clear and bright, his grip steel-strong. Everything seemed back to normal in the Krogh home. The two children interrupted us at dinner a couple of times to ask permission to play at a neighbour's house, later to be read to by their mother. Suzanne served steak. I felt guilty about it, knowing how deeply in debt the Kroghs were.

"The time apart really wasn't too hard," Suzanne reminisced at dinner. She had been teaching at a local school and writing articles to earn enough to buy groceries and keep the mortgage paid up. Each weekend she and the children had taken the seven-hour round-trip drive to Allenwood in their old Volvo. The fatigue still showed on Suzanne's young face. "Visiting is a strain," she said. "You're constantly being watched and the guards can be abusive. But Bud and I did a Bible course with that time. Each week we'd study the same lesson and then discuss it over the weekend. It really brought us closer."

After dinner while Patty and Suzanne did the dishes, Bud and I sat together in the living room. "Okay, friend, now that the girls can't hear us, tell me what it is really like," I said.

"It's hell, Chuck. But you're tough; you'll do okay. Be careful whom you associate with. You'll see a lot of ugly things going on around you – a guy once had his skull crushed changing a TV station in the middle of a programme. Just stay out of it and keep to yourself. The blacks will test you. Stand up to them if you're threatened; if they find any weakness in you, your goose is cooked."

The prosecutors had told me that I would be kept at Fort Holabird, an abandoned Army base in Baltimore as long as I was needed in Washington to testify. "You'll hate it there," Bud said. "That fence with barbed wire is right up against the building and the place is full of rats – you know, guys who are informers. But it's better than the city jail. I was in the bull pen in Montgomery County for the first twelve days. There were men in there waiting trial for murder, some real tough customers, twelve of us in one cell. I slept on the floor right next to the toilet and one night a dude urinated all over me. Could have been ugly, but I knew I was outnumbered so I just talked to him, and thank God it didn't happen again."

Bud talked openly enough about prison, but was strangely silent on other subjects. It was obvious he had detached himself from the outside world, a kind of self-insulation. When we had turned on the news telecast earlier in the evening, he had left the room. I could not resist the question that was weighing heavily on my mind : "Bud, why is it that you aren't following things on the outside? Seems like you've shut yourself off from the world."

He pondered that for a moment. "For me it seemed the thing to do, Chuck. I looked at prison as a cleansing time – and for self-examination. I needed it. If you look at it that way, it will do you good. But it means cutting off everything you leave behind, except family, of course. For me it was a conscious decision."

Driving home that evening I asked Patty if she'd noticed any change in Bud.

"Sure did," she replied. "He seemed distant, a million miles away."

"That really terrifies me, honey. I can't believe prison can do that in only a few months to a guy with an iron will like Krogh."

It was not as if prison had broken Bud. In some ways he seemed stronger than ever, but it was as if he had drifted off on a cloud to a faraway place and was now living in his own world. Could that happen to me? *It must not*, I told myself.

For me that would be the slow death of soul and spirit. One day years earlier when the thought that I might ever go to prison was beyond my wildest fantasies, a close friend who worked with ex-convicts told me that men are never the same after confinement. "A year does it," he said, tapping his temple. "They go stirry, locked up that way."

That night, bothered as I was by the change I saw in Bud and the fears racing through my mind, I could not know how much of a struggle it would be.

19

Fall of the Gavel

Shortly after 9 : 00 a.m. on the morning of June 21, Patty and I arrived at Courtroom No. 6. An air of expectancy crackled through the room. The press were nearly crowded out by well-wishers, friends, the office staff from our law firm. The lawyer's dock was almost empty since there was to be no combat this day. Dave Shapiro would make one eleventh-hour appeal on my behalf. A few men from the prosecutor's office would listen silently. The judge would then announce his decision.

By arrangement with the clerk, Harold, Al, Doug, and Graham were allowed through the swinging gate into the area normally reserved for lawyers. By 9 : 15 they had arrived and sat solemnly together on a long bench.

I walked down the aisle attempting a cheery greeting to each friend. Some of the secretaries who had worked for me in the White House were there, also many of Patty's friends. Their expressions spoke of anxiety or sorrow. I spoke to Dick Howard and his wife, Marcia, whose dark eyes were sparkling with encouragement. Dick managed a weak smile.

Marion Goldin, Mike Wallace's producer, was seated in the back as a spectator. I wondered why, since she didn't cover news events. Could she possibly have sensed the part her show had played in all this?

Two of Patty's and my closest friends, Tom and Kay Easely from Boston, had wanted to be present, but I prevailed upon them not to come so that Kay could be at the hospital to keep

Dad from learning about my sentence on television. I'd phone her and she could break the news gently.

Patty took a seat in the front row in space reserved for family. *Like the first pew at a funeral*, I thought grimly. Wendell was beside her. My older son had achieved in those weeks a maturity well beyond his twenty years. Dave Shapiro was sitting at the defence table, pawing through a thick black notebook and rehearsing his arguments one last time. Dave was so hopeful that his final words would move Gesell that in his last conference in chambers he had asked the judge not to rule immediately, but to recess briefly after Dave's argument, withdraw from the bench, and weigh the sentence one last time.

After the words of the crier, Judge Gesell strode majestically across the raised platform, pulling his black robe together as he took his place in the judge's high-backed chair. The courthouse gossips had said that much would depend on Gesell's mood on the day of sentencing, that he is volatile and can change his mind even as he walks into the courtroom. If true, we were starting out this day in trouble. The judge was scowling angrily as he took his seat, glanced once around the courtroom, announced brusquely the motions which would be argued later in the morning, and then snapped, "All right, Mr. Shapiro, would you and Mr. Colson come forward?"

I began reading my statement, stating the reasons for my plea which I believed "right as a matter of law, right as a matter of conscience." I reviewed all of the circumstances surrounding the release of the Pentagon Papers, how Henry Kissinger, President Nixon, and I had viewed Ellsberg's conduct as "treasonous," tracing step-by-step the chronology of my actions. Then I came to the act itself.

"The President on numerous occasions urged me to disseminate damaging information about Daniel Ellsberg," I said – which was not exactly news since I had testified to this before. But a murmur from the clusters of reporters rippled through the room. Little did I dream how that statement would rumble through Capitol Hill, bringing forth new cries for the President's impeachment. If I were guilty of this crime, so was Nixon, his antagonists would argue.

I concluded my statement by telling the judge, "I regret

what I have done and I will spend a lifetime trying to be a better man for it."

Gesell nodded as if by reflex, started to smile but stopped, then turned to Shapiro: "I understand that you wish to make a statement and you may now do so."*

I returned to the defence table and sat down. Shapiro began softly at first. I looked at my brothers; their heads were down – in prayer, I hoped.

"I say Charles Colson was unfairly indicted," Dave said, his voice rising with indignation. He argued that a prison sentence would be imposed only because of public expectations which were created in this case by "fraud – fraud, Your Honour – the most pernicious kind of publicity linking this man's name to every conceivable type of act and dirty trick and for the most part they were created by deliberate government leaks – smear stories." Shapiro had prepared a long recitation of every fallacious story that had been printed about me, hoping to persuade the judge that the public demand for a sentence was falsely created.

But Judge Gesell wanted none of it. "You are barking up the wrong tree, Mr. Shapiro," he interrupted. "I am not a bit interested in the public expectations. That has nothing to do with what I am about to do. You are beating a dead horse." My stomach felt as if it were trying to escape through the bottom of my chair. Whatever Gesell was going to do, he had already decided and was plainly annoyed by Shapiro's statements.

Jolted by the judge's assault, Dave placed both hands on the lectern, his body rocking back and forth, his eyes filled with disbelief and astonishment.

Gesell subdued his impatience but not his annoyance. "You may proceed," he continued, "but I want you to understand you are beating a dead horse ... You represent this man and you can do whatever you wish to do – and I will listen – but I simply wanted you to understand."

Shapiro tried to recover, but all passion and feeling had been sucked out of his voice. The last flickering glimmer of secretly harboured hope that maybe there would be no prison sentence was gone. The only question now was – how bad?

*Editor's Note: All quotations are from the court transcripts.

Six months? Nine months? Longer? Ten months was the maximum time Gesell had dished out, and that to a Watergater convicted of two perjury counts after a jury trial. Sentences after trial are usually stiffer than with voluntary pleas.

Yet I was the closest to Mr. Nixon and during the skirmishes over pre-trial motions Gesell had unleashed angry outbursts against the President, charging him one day in open court with near obstruction of justice for failing to make available White House files. Then, too, he was the judge who heard the Nixon Administration's case against the *Washington Post* to restrain publication of the Pentagon Papers. Gesell ruled against us and for the *Post*. Still, he was known as the fairest man on the bench. What had gone on before, I reasoned, would not affect him this day.

Shapiro forged ahead ticking off one by one, clinically now, the false accusations that had been hurled at me day after day in the headlines, including the documented proof that the CIA had planted false stories about me (*see* page 219). He concluded with words that should have been ringing with emotion, but instead were as icy as the chill which had come over the courtroom. "If Your Honour believes with me that the highest duty of this court, indeed, the highest duty of any court, is to stand between the defendant and the mob, let it be known!"

When he had tried his argument out on me the week before, Shapiro had put so much drama into that last sentence that in his imagination there was the thunder of a foot-stomping crowd, trumpet music in the distance, and the judge leaning over the bench to shake his hand. But now there was only a deadly silence in the room. The judge summoned Shapiro and me to come forward again to the lectern. We now simply waited for the dreadful fall of the gavel.

Judge Gesell took no recess before deciding, telling us instead that another case was pending. His voice devoid of feeling, his manner surgical, he stated that the defendant's "deliberate misconduct affected the conduct of a pending federal prosecution." A shudder raced down my spine. I had never even been charged with that; the prosecutors only alleged that I tried to, but acknowledged that I had failed.

"Morality is a higher force than expediency," he continued, glaring at notes before him. "The court does recognise," his tone softened slightly, "that Mr. Colson's public image has been somewhat distorted ... a thorough review of Mr. Colson's life ... show instances of useful public service, often compassion for others in trouble, qualities of the defendant which have rightly endeared him to his family, his close friends, and to clients he has effectively served."

I felt Shapiro's arm come around my back, squeezing me gently and holding on for what was coming. The kind words were to soften the blow. I was taking deep breaths now to control my emotions. *I must show none,* I thought, as my ears detected gentle sobbing behind me. The judge explained that he reached his decision using as his guide all other obstruction-of-justice sentences handed down in the past year.

Gesell lifted the gavel in the air. "The court will impose a sentence of one to three years and fine of five thousand dollars." Hardwood struck hardwood with an ear-splitting whack. A half-muffled scream came from the back of the room, a high-pitched voice crying, "Oh, no!" Then absolute silence again. A tingling sensation swept through my body like needles jabbing into my flesh. Then a sharp feeling of nausea. Shapiro squeezed harder. I bit my lower lip, praying that it was not Patty's voice that had shouted out.

My mind blotted out the rest of the words Gesell now spoke – the penitentiary, date of surrender, dismissal of other charges. Dave kept squeezing as he replied to the judge, his own voice cracking and hoarse. The gavel fell again. Crack!

Judge Gesell strode from the platform. As I turned away, I saw Dornetha, a black secretary from the law office, doubled over in tears. Others were trying to comfort her; she had been the one to cry out. Then I caught Patty's look, filled with sadness but dry-eyed. Wendell's face was frozen in shock. My brothers were still seated with heads down. Others stood motionless.

There was no press stampede this time, the reporters filing out slowly. It would be newsworthy – the longest sentence yet imposed on a Watergate defendant – but a few minutes give or take against the afternoon deadline didn't matter now.

I walked back to the defence table to gather up my papers. Shapiro kept mumbling, "I can't believe it, can't believe it." Patty came through the swinging gate, walking fast, then half-running, trying as she always did to smile even as she was choking up. "It'll be okay, honey, you'll see," Patty said as she threw her arms around me.

The marshals made available to us a small windowless waiting room. The brothers, Patty, Wendell, and I were escorted into it just to be alone for a few minutes. There was little to say; words were not needed. A surprising feeling of love began to fill our hearts. Even Wendell, who before had squirmed when trapped in a praying group, seemed to be lifted as we asked for God's strength in this moment of pain.

Harold's concern that I not be bitter was unnecessary. "For some strange reason I even feel a sense of understanding toward Judge Gesell," I said quietly.

"What are you going to say to the press outside?" he asked.

"I honestly don't know." I had prepared no statement and was not sure I could have read it if I had.

"Then we'll just ask the Holy Spirit to take over," Harold concluded.

As we walked down the long marbled corridor we could see through the glass doors a crowd of people outside — cameras, lights, and an even-larger-than-usual throng of newsmen. The marshals escorting us offered an escape route through the garage, but I knew I must not duck the press now.

The array of microphones, cameras, and inquisitive faces seemed somehow less hostile than before. "What happened in court today," I heard myself say, "was the court's will and the Lord's will — I have committed my life to Jesus Christ and I can work for Him in prison as well as out."

Those were the words given me and with them a whole new chapter was to begin in my life.

20

The Slammer

I was awakened by the sound of camera crews setting up their equipment in the gravel drive in front of our home. It was July 8, the last morning for a year or longer that Patty and I would enjoy the privacy of our bedroom and a quiet breakfast together. Rubbing the sleep from my eyes and opening a front bedroom window, I shouted: "I am not leaving until two this afternoon. Come back then. I won't avoid you. You have my word."

A chubby, friendly faced ABC cameraman with an American-flag pin in his lapel gave me a big smile. "Okay, Mr. Colson, see you at two. Have a good morning."

The crews packed up their equipment and drove off. In past stake-outs these men would have remained rooted to their positions. *Ironic*, I thought, *now that I was a criminal headed for prison, the hard-bitten cynics of the press suddenly believed me.*

We watched the "Today" show during breakfast, the last of a three-part interview I had filmed the week earlier. Barbara Walters came on live at the end: "These interviews with Mr. Colson were filmed in our studios last week when he was here with his wife, Patty, a charming woman, so supportive of her husband. Sometimes we don't think of the personal tragedies involved, but I can't help but think about the Colsons this morning." Looking straight into the camera, she continued: "And so I say to you, Mr. Colson, if you are where you can hear this, and especially to you, Mrs. Colson, we do feel for you."

Patty and I kept our own emotions in check trying to make this morning just like any other, but the compassion in Barbara's face caught us off guard for a moment. My wife had surprised me with her strength over the final days of my freedom, but she was no more stoic than I was.

Graham Purcell had volunteered to drive us to Baltimore where I would surrender to the marshal at the Fort Holabird prison facility. Promptly at the appointed hour he pulled into the driveway, looking drawn and nervous. I had long since learned that beneath his hardened Texas-cowboy hide is a heart as big and soft as a ripe melon. Along with Judd Best who made the arrangements for my surrender, Patty and I piled into Graham's big sedan and headed up the driveway toward the newsmen and cameras now blocking the entrance.

As the questions came flying at me from reporters, humour seemed in order. How did I feel about going to prison? Like the man Abe Lincoln once described who was tarred and feathered and driven out of town. When asked how he liked it, he responded, "If it wasn't for the honour, I'd just as soon have walked."

One reporter shouted, "What books are you taking with you?"

"Just two editions of the Bible," I replied. When that statement was published, it produced a deluge of Bibles through the mail which I later shared with other prison inmates. The exchange was good-humoured; gone was the rancour of past confrontations.

Graham, unnerved by the mob scene and the number of cars now so doggedly pursuing us, sped down narrow Ballantrae Lane at seventy miles an hour right into the middle of Route 123, the heavily travelled east-west artery through McLean. The whole scene was hardly a time for merriment, but we had to chuckle over the thought of this headline in the next day's paper : COLSON IN NINE-CAR PILEUP ON WAY TO PRISON. Gallows humour, I think it is called.

As much as they could, government officials have tried to maintain an aura of secrecy about Fort Holabird, referring to it only as a "detention facility in the Baltimore-Washington area for government witnesses." Since many of the prisoners detained there were crime-syndicate men who had agreed to testify against underworld figures, the need for a safe, secret hiding place was paramount. Holabird was designated as the temporary facility for all Watergate prisoners who would be testifying in upcoming trials.

Four federal marshals met us at a downtown Baltimore motel, where there was one final moment of confusion, picture taking by the camera crews which had followed us, and good-byes to Patty and my two friends. Now officially a federal prisoner under guard, I was squeezed into the back of an unmarked car, which raced through dingy back streets, under an old railroad trestle, and to the once-proud gates of the now nearly deserted Holabird Army Base.

When we drove inside I was reminded of a ghost town in an old Hollywood Western. World War I-vintage red-brick buildings were mixed in with World War II soot-covered green wooden barracks. The vast sprawling base was slowly decaying, windows boarded over with plywood, tall grass and bushes surrounding most structures, including the line of stately old homes which had once been Officers' Row. The streets were empty.

Our car pulled up in front of one of the green buildings which was different from the others in two ways. There was a nine-foot-high chain link fence around it, topped by jagged strands of barbed wire. It was the one island of life in the otherwise deserted base.

From a small sentry booth two heavyset men with .38s on their hips, moved forward to unlock the tall gate. Between the fence and the prison facility was a small twenty-foot area of grass. I remembered Bud Krogh's statement, "That fence keeps getting closer and closer." We alighted from the car, walked through the gate which was slammed behind me. Dave Shapiro always referred to prison as "the slammer." Now I knew why.

The Army-style barracks was as depressing inside as it appeared on the outside. Paint was peeling from the walls, steam pipes ran down the long corridor through the centre of the building which was illuminated only by dim light bulbs dangling every thirty feet from the ceiling. A stale, greasy odour seeped from a tiny kitchen on the right. A small dining room was on the left immediately inside the hole-riddled front screen door.

The chief deputy led me to the Control Room, a glassed-in office in the centre of the first-floor corridor. Processing began : more finger-prints, Polaroid snapshots, inspection of my luggage and personal effects, a thorough shakedown for drugs and contraband, and the filling out of endless forms.

"What is your number?" the deputy asked.

"I don't have a number."

"What do you mean you don't have a number? Every federal prisoner has a number."

"Maybe you're supposed to give me one, sir."

"Those people in Washington," grumbled the deputy. "Don't they know what kind of an establishment I'm running here?"

Then I made the mistake of asking, "I don't. Can you tell me something about this place?"

"No! The important thing for you to remember is that you remember nothing. No one knows this place exists. You will meet some very unusual men here. Don't discuss your business with them and don't ask them about theirs. When you leave here forget you ever met them. You will only know them by their first names anyway. Obey the rules and mind your own business."

I was then turned over to Joe, a swarthy man with shaggy black hair who spoke little English.* He showed me to my room, a nine-by-twelve cubicle tucked under the eaves on the second floor, furnished with a maple bed, a battered dresser, and a small wooden desk. The desk top was etched with graffiti by the generations who had passed through this room – from young Army lieutenants to federal prisoners. The temperature was over 100 degrees. Baltimore was in the grip of the worst heat wave of the year.

As other inmates drifted by, Joe introduced me. Pete, a young Italian, reported that he, too, had been a Marine; Angie, an outgoing, genial sort, was from New York's "Little Italy." Pat and Andy, I learned, were ex-syndicate operatives

*Editor's Note: Here and elsewhere to protect persons involved, names of inmates have been changed except where permission was obtained.

and central figures in a big narcotics ring. I was told that two young men named Eddie and Jimmy were kept apart from the others for the good reason that both were ex-Baltimore policemen. Former cops and gangsters crammed into the same little building made a strange mix.

There was Mike, a muscular brute with long, flowing blonde hair and an unmistakable Boston accent. There were others representing a variety of nationalities: Italians, Cubans, Frenchmen, including one whose hairy body was colourfully tattooed from top to bottom.

When I asked Joe how to lock my door, he leaned back and roared with laughter. "No locks here; just one happy family." I had not seen the movie *The Godfather* – or his term *family* would have been even more unnerving.

There was one man at Holabird I had known before – Herb Kalmbach, the President's personal lawyer, who had surrendered the week before I did and like me was awaiting his turn to testify at the impeachment hearings. Joe pointed out his room. When I looked in, Herb, a tall, urbane, and handsome man in his fifties, bounded from his chair. "Am I glad to see you! Not here, of course, but it's so great to greet an old friend." It was the renewal of a friendship that was to become important to us both.

I took the deputy's warning seriously and suppressed my curiosity about the other inmates. With no facilities for exercise, time dragged. The heat was oppressive. I was beginning to understand why Bud Krogh had made himself an island. Jimmy the young ex-cop who was in prison for taking bribes, helped lift the oppressiveness with his chatter, particularly at meals.

During dinner one night little Pete was quite noisy, his high-pitched voice reverberating through the room that twenty of us were crowded into. Jimmy whispered to me, "Don't fool with him; he goes off his rocker once in a while. He was one of the top narcotics men in New York."

"That little kid?" I asked.

"That little kid," Jimmy responded, "was one of the bosses. They say his testimony will bring down a hundred people. Leave him alone. He would think nothing of putting one of those knives right through your gut." Jimmy nodded to the large bread knife in the centre of the table, glistening in the late-afternoon sun. Jimmy pointed to Mike. "He was one of their 'hit men,' you know."

"That one who never says anything? The big guy from Boston?" Mike across the room ate without expression, his eyes cold and steel-hard.

"I thought you knew all about Mike," he continued. "You're from Boston, aren't you? It was a big thing when he was pinched. They say he's knocked off twenty-eight."

I stared at Jimmy in disbelief. "People — twenty-eight people?"

"That's what a hit man does, you know. Kills people." Jimmy's tone indicated I was not with it.

I had trouble suppressing a grin. The hit man and the hatchet man — what a vaudeville team Mike and I would make! Serious again I asked, "Why isn't anyone with twenty-eight murders on death row somewhere?"

Jimmy shrugged. "They've got him here to protect him. He's more valuable to the government alive than dead."

While trying to keep from staring at Mike, I began to long for a cell with a lock on it.

As the days dragged by, visits by Patty and the brothers were my faith strengtheners, even though the visiting conditions were awkward and restrictive. It was especially hard for Patty and me — the long days of separation interrupted by a few hours of make-believe normalcy, one eye always on the clock, then the pain of parting. Yet slowly over the months our conversations about faith had become more meaningful. We were making progress in our understanding of the Bible, but still I held back from asking her to pray with me.

One day late in July after a tense visit, Patty wrote me a letter: "Darling, I prayed most of the way home for both of us and I think it might be nice if from now on we prayed together before leaving each other in the evening . . ."

I received the letter the next day and wanted to shout for joy! All that night I felt that tingling sensation, the worth-it-all feeling I had known before in some of my darkest hours. From that day forward we held hands and prayed aloud together every time she visited, whether in public or private.

This spiritual unity would sustain us through harder days to come.

The fall of Mr. Nixon's Presidency had been inevitable for many months. The man who stood in a steamy-hot school gymnasium one August day three years earlier, saying with passion, "It isn't losing that is wrong, it is quitting," fought a long and lonely struggle with himself. This was also the man who one night in July 1973 quietly mused about the country being better off "if I step down," and then a few months later, "Maybe America wants a nice, clean Jerry Ford." But the real Nixon was the man in the auditorium; one who was incapable of bringing himself to quit anything.

To me his resignation was not the act of a quitter. He had been gently eased out of his office when all but his own family, and two diehard aides, Ken Clawson and Rose Woods, recognized the imperative pressures which seemed to demand it. Al Haig, his chief of staff, had told me in January 1974, "If impeachment is inevitable, then better we go peaceably. We must not take the whole government down with us." Haig had been preparing for months, hoping for a miracle, but readying himself for the day which finally came in August.

"The system worked," one politician after another proudly proclaimed when Nixon announced his resignation. I am not so sure. At the end, the formal governmental structures were powerless to move decisively, the Senate would have been ensnarled in months of haggling debate, the courts clogged, the Presidency impotent. Never, in my opinion, has the American government been in greater peril, not even when the Capitol was threatened by Lee's forces advancing across the Potomac.

While the entire government was drifting aimlessly, a four-star Army general spent the last days of Mr. Nixon's Presidency taking almost full control of the governmental machinery, negotiating with his chief's successor, asking the Pentagon to disregard any order from its constitutionally designated commander, and in the final hours working sensitively behind the scenes so that the Secretary of State and congressional leaders could persuade the President to step aside. Similar circumstances in other countries have resulted in bloodless coups. Fortunately for America, General Haig is a man of responsibility and integrity.

And so it was that Mr. Nixon, exhausted by his last desperate convulsions, was unable to the end to recognise the lie with which he had lived or the apocalyptic forces it had unleashed. His own perceptions of the great good he had tried to achieve blotted from his mind the transgressions of certain staff members which he believed to be minor. Then like a man clinging to a rock in rushing rapids, his last ounce of strength gone, he heaved one final gasp, relaxed his iron grip, and was washed helplessly away in the swirling waters.

At his first inauguration Richard Nixon's hand rested on the outstretched pages of his family Bible, opened to the Book of Isaiah and a verse chosen as the guide for his peace-making Presidency – *They shall beat their swords into plowshares* (*see* Isaiah 2 : 4 KJV). Tragic that neither he nor those of us who served him could see seven verses later this warning of things to come : *The lofty looks of man shall be humbled, and the haughtiness of men shall be bowed down* ... (V. 11 KJV). We had all failed. Whether Mr. Nixon was purveyor of the evil spell which was cast across his Presidency – or its victim – seemed irrelevant those grim days of August. The grace and dignity with which he fell was fitting testimony to his noble visions for the Presidency and the side of Mr. Nixon's character I so admired.

That the resignation was necessary made it no less terrifying, particularly watching it on a small television set, stockaded behind rows of barbed wire in an improvised prison. I could not help but believe that God's hand was in those final days, for the quirks of history might have positioned a man less honourable than General Haig to achieve far less noble results. I needed no more vivid demonstration that it is the hearts of men which for better or worse change the course of human history, not the man-made organs of government.

Heartsick as I was for the President in his moment of torment, those of us who had served him were going through our own peculiar agony. Many months before he had told me: "The day will come when I will wipe the slate clean." I knew what he meant: a commander doesn't abandon his troops in battle. Once he regained the momentum he would pardon his aides who had been imprisoned for Watergate offences.

Our hopes were dashed when Nixon's helicopter rose from the South Lawn for the last time. Not a word had been spoken about those whose crimes were committed – not for personal profit, but in his defence. I was prepared to serve my time, and take my medicine, but there is a special torture in seeing freedom dangled before your eyes and then pulled away. After President Ford's startling announcement on September 8 that he was granting a full and unconditional pardon for Richard Nixon, rumours began circulating that we were next. Ford's press secretary announced two days later that full pardons for all were being studied.

The pardon of Richard Nixon produced another public outburst, reminiscent of the Cox firing. An instant NBC poll reported that by 2 to 1 the public opposed Ford's action. Our spirits sank. The next poll showed that more than 50 per cent now favoured our release. Our spirits rose.

Patty had never in her life done an interview on TV, but she bravely agreed to go on the "Today" show in my behalf. The pardon issue had completely aroused the country. Friends in the press called – the decision would come in hours: we'd be set free. The press staked out our home day and night to catch pictures of the jubilant homecoming. But the political heat was threatening Ford's one-month-old Presidency; he announced there would be no more pardons. Those in prison would stay, the Watergate trial would go forward. President Ford had not succeeded in putting Watergate behind him.

For Patty and the other wives, the up-and-down cycle was especially tough – excitement, soaring hopes, anxiety, and then crushing disappointment.

In the depth of my despair these words that I read somewhere seemed to leap out at me: *The darker that all around us seems, the greater the despair in our temporal life, the more light that God shines upon us, the more we feel the power of the Holy Spirit within us.*

There it was again – another reference to the power of the Holy Spirit. I knew little about this Third Part of the Trinity, but I was beginning to feel a deep need for this power. Did the Holy Spirit come when in moments of great helplessness I called upon God's help? At times there had been real stirrings inside me since the decision in Maine. Did this mean that the Spirit was already at work? Or was it a new experience I should seek?

My need for special inner strength was heightened by my loneliness, my daily uneasy encounters with members of organised crime, and feelings of despair about the future. Always the threat of physical assault by another inmate hung over me.

One night I was up late preparing for my testimony scheduled for the next day. It was near one o'clock when I staggered into bed, after drawing tight the venetian blinds to keep out the beams from spotlights hanging from the eaves and illuminating the entire yard area all night. Then there came a noise outside my door. As my eyes probed through the darkness I heard the door handle beginning to turn slowly. My heart began to race. A midnight assailant?

"Dear Lord," I remember saying, "spare me from this, or at least give me something to fight with." I reached beside my bed. Patty had bought me a small plastic lamp weighing no more than a pound so that I could read by it at night. It was utterly useless as a weapon, but maybe as a missile it would startle my assailant and arouse the guards.

The door slowly swung open, and now I could see silhouetted against the dim light a hulking form. I was not dreaming; my heart was pounding and the adrenaline was shooting through my body. It was time for a decision. Call for help? Jump him suddenly? Throw the lamp?

The figure moved into the room, stopped for a moment, then started for my bed. I jumped up, grabbed the lamp, and shouted, "Who is it?" The silhouette practically crumbled before my eyes. "Oh, no!" he gasped. "I'm sorry."

I flipped on the light, and there, pale and trembling, stood one of the deputy marshals. In between the deep, sucking noises he was trying desperately to apologise. I had frightened him far more than he had frightened me. The thought must have crossed his mind – what if I had been Mike?

He explained that he was on the night shift, believed my room was vacant, and was trying to find an empty bed in which to catch a short nap. He had been walking stealthily to avoid being detected by the night supervisor. I shared the experience during the next meal with the other inmates. Told with humour, it made a good story with the crime-syndicate men staring at me. I thought a small lie was permissible and pictured myself as unafraid, ready to administer a mortal blow to the intruder.

Word filtered through one of the marshals that John Dean would be joining us at Holabird. Watergate had turned John and myself into arch foes: John, the President's accuser; I, his defender. During the first days of the Ervin hearings, anger would boil up inside me at the mention of his name. Did I still feel that way? As I grappled with Christ's admonition not only to forgive but love my enemies, the anger inside me seemed to leave. The forgiveness part was not too difficult. In fact, I became aware of a gut-level admiration of John's courage in pitting himself against the awesome power of the Presidency. But to love John, that was not so easy.

He arrived one night just after dark. I was in the dining room when John walked by, surrounded by five marshals. Taking no chances with their star witness, the Watergate prosecutors had issued special instructions that Dean was not to mix with the inmates at Holabird, that he was to be kept isolated, confined to his room at all times with a twenty-four-hour guard outside his door.

"They can't keep him in a room all day alone," laughed young Pat. "He'll go bananas."

That thought broke down my last barrier toward John. Late that night Dean came to the kitchen with one pistol-toting marshal. I burst into the kitchen and stuck out my hand. "Whatever's happened in the past, John, let's forget it. If there's any way I can help you, let me know."

Dean was as startled as the marshal and was barely able to stammer a response: "Chuck, I really appreciate that.

Honest, I really do." The marshal quickly separated us, but in those brief moments some old wounds were healed.

John and I began to spend time together whenever a friendly marshal could be persuaded to look the other way. Our conversation was not about the case or about what had gone on in the past, but about our lives and the future. I discovered that he had once worked on a graduate-school project for a modern revision of the Bible, and had read it thoroughly. Furthermore, his belief in God had been strengthened by the tumultuous experiences he was now going through. It was the beginning of a new relationship.

I was startled to find Patty in the waiting room one Monday morning. Visitors are never allowed inside the compound until four o'clock. The look of sorrow in her eyes forewarned me.

"It's Dad, isn't it?" I asked.

"Yes, Chuck, but he went very peacefully – this morning."

I held her tight, fighting my emotions. She knew how close my father and I had been. A hundred thoughts tumbled through my mind at that moment. Grief that he was gone, gratitude that it had been peaceful and painless. Memories of the last time I saw him, when he was in the hospital and we talked about my pleading guilty. Concern for my mother, now all alone. But overall a deep remorse that my dad had left this world knowing that his only son was in prison. What a sharp contrast to that proud moment when he had listened to the President praise his Special Counsel.

He died in my mother's arms as they had been packing – against doctor's orders – for a trip to visit me. The shock of what had happened to me was more of a burden than his weakened heart could take.

The phone lines between Washington and Holabird were humming that day as my request for a furlough to go to the funeral worked its way up and down the bureaucratic ladder. Late in the afternoon Washington denied the request. A father's death notwithstanding, it would be "inappropriate" for a Watergate prisoner to be given a furlough. I could attend the funeral only if it were private and I were kept in constant custody of marshals. Two would be assigned to me, all at my expense.

One marshal travelled with Patty and me on the flight to Boston. At Logan Airport two broad-shouldered men boarded the plane and ushered us off into a waiting car. For the next few days these men were with us at all times, sleeping in our living room, watching us while we ate, and in some ways sharing our grief.

During this time, as I went through Dad's effects I learned more about him. I had worried about his seeing me in prison, fearful of the shock to his sensitive nature. To my surprise I discovered that he had taken great interest in prison reform in the late thirties even while working twelve hours a day to hold his job and still going to night school. In his papers were moving letters he had written to the governor on behalf of men imprisoned for minor offences. In some cases he was successful in getting their sentences commuted.

I was intrigued to find that he was responsible for the plan whereby debating societies were formed in a number of prisons. He was active in the reform-minded United Prison Association. As I looked through his files my mind leaped ahead. I certainly had every reason to carry on this part of his work, which for some strange reason we had never talked about much during his life.

The tragedy also helped my mother and me to become closer as we worked out the details of the funeral and planned for her future. The services were held in St. John's Episcopal Church in Winthrop, the same church in which my dad and his sister and brother had been baptised. The small church was a little piece of New England – with elegant stained-glass windows, rugged stone sides, brown shingles, and the weathered look of the seacoast. It was tucked away on a narrow street in an old part of town between two- and three-storey frame houses.

My mother and I prayed together before my father's casket. In it I placed Dad's Masonic apron and the American flag which faithfully each morning he had raised in front of his home and lowered at sundown. Following the simple service my mother, Patty, and I stood by the graveside surrounded by a few close friends and the two marshals. We watched silently as the casket was lowered within sight of the high school my Dad had attended, and the baseball field on which he had starred as a youth. The gentle breezes brought fresh salt air off the nearby sea which had been so much a part of his life and mine. The closest friend I had known in life was gone, to a "room in the Lord's mansion," I believed.

That night I was back in prison, reflecting on what the Apostle Paul meant when he warned his disciples against despair: "... it is 'through many tribulations' that we must enter into the kingdom of God" (Acts 14:22 PHILLIPS). I felt close to those words. My beloved father was gone, the man I almost worshipped for four years had been forced out of office, and I was about to be transferred to a much tougher prison facility in Alabama.

I should have been utterly miserable, yet there was a surprising lightness in my spirit. Patty and I were closer than ever before, John Dean and I had become reconciled, and I sensed that in some way the Lord had a plan for my life which He would gradually reveal to me.

21

"Don't Get Involved"

My transfer from Fort Holabird to the prison camp at Maxwell Air Base went smoothly. The two marshals and I were met at the Montgomery airport by the local U.S. marshal. I breathed more easily when I climbed into the back of his car and he made no effort to handcuff or chain me – the painful, animal-like process which prisoners endure when travelling. Our drive took us through the Montgomery Air Force Base, past several golf courses and a desolate wooded area up to a group of low stucco buldings. A large sign with white letters read, FEDERAL PRISON CAMP.

Outside the prison there was an open feeling, with attractive plantings, rosebushes, tall shade trees. Inside the administration building stern-faced, blue-shirted guards took charge marching me past two black steel doors, each with a small square opening covered with a steel mesh grille. A quick glimpse inside revealed dark bare-walled cells empty but for a bench and toilet. This was the "hole," I was told, into which prisoners are thrust for disciplinary purposes. The sense of openness was gone.

Our destination was a sterile and windowless receiving room a few feet beyond the hole. In one corner was a shower; all new prisoners were scrubbed down to eliminate the lice they so frequently carried from local jails. In the other corner was a Polaroid camera. More mug shots and fingerprints followed. Across a wooden counter was a genial, smiling man, the clothing officer, Mr. Bleven.

"Strip down," he commanded. Narcotics smuggling in prison is rampant and prisoners have a knack for concealing "junk" in the most obscure crevices of their bodies. Bleven

started through each piece of clothing and every personal
article I had carried with me. "This goes, this goes – this –
this," he said, listing items which were to be shipped home.

"No," he said after deliberating a moment with himself
about a pair of my shorts. "You can't bring these in, you can
wear them only if you can't find a pair around here." The list
was now two pages long. Next came my wallet, all personal
identification, pictures of Patty and the kids. How I hated to
part with identification! "All jewelry must be removed,"
Bleven said almost apologetically now, looking at my class
ring.

"I wear it as a wedding ring and I'm not sure I can get it
off," I protested. Patty had given it to me.

"Sorry. Regulations. I'll have to have it."

I did not offer up the silver cross and dove, hanging from
the chain on my neck. He didn't ask for them.

"Try these." Bleven tossed me a pair of well-worn under-
pants with a series of numbers that had been stencilled across
the front and crossed out. I tried not to think about how many
men had worn them before me and was so glad to put something on that I said not a word about the shorts being too
tight. Next came well-worn socks, a handkerchief, and finally
a set of ill-fitting surplus Air Force work clothes, dyed
chocolate-brown. The first step in the deliberate de-individual-
ising process was complete. More was to come.

"Out here, Colson," a voice from the hall commanded and
I was led back into the Control Room, from which all corners
of the prison can be surveyed at a glance through thick glass
windows arching outward, turret-like. I had to wait now for
assignments which would thereafter govern my daily life :
Dormitory G and my prison number : 23226. The guard on
duty, a massive man by the name of Prather, was busily
barking out orders over the camp public-address system.

For a moment I had a chance to look through the windows
into the prison compound. Various grassy areas were bor-
dered by concrete walks and two rows of one-storey dormitories. At the far end was the mess hall. Two hundred and
fifty men lived here, but watching them through the
window was like watching a silent movie in slow motion.
Droop-shouldered, sticklike figures of men were drifting

aimlessly and slowly in the open area; others were propped up against the buildings and a few sitting in small clusters on benches. The figures just seemed to be floating ever so slowly. I was soon to learn that no one walks fast in prison.

Not only were all uniforms the same drab brown; so were the expressions on the faces. *Something strange here.* Then it struck me – *no one was smiling.* Although it was a clear day, there seemed to be no sunshine in the compound. All of the colours, like the expressions on the faces, blended into one sandy haze.

Prather's booming voice broke the eerie silence. "Colson, put your address on that package," he snapped, turning in his chair to point to my suitcase now covered in brown wrapping paper and lying on the floor behind me. I knelt over it, carefully spelling out Patty's name and our address, trying not to think about her or our home.

"Colson, you'll be okay here," he said. "Just take my advice. Keep your mind where your butt is. The time will go fast if you do; if you think of home and outside things, this place will be hell."

I could only nod as a chill swept over me. Prather's advice, standard for new inmates, had come in a different way from Bud Krogh. Don't think. Conform. Build an island around yourself. *No, thanks, Mr. Prather,* I thought. *My mind will stay alive.*

Walking across the compound, I sensed that advance word about the Watergate personality had preceded me. As I passed little groups, conversation stopped; men stared. My halfway attempts to smile at the faces I passed were met by suspicious glances. I would have to earn my way.

On the outside, Dormitory G was like all the other buildings at Maxwell, a cream-coloured stucco structure with red-shingled roof, outwardly well maintained. Inside, the stench of body odours and stale tobacco struck me first. Dust was everywhere. The walls inside the narrow entranceway were lined with two tiers of small lockers for those few personal items prisoners were allowed. On one side were two dayrooms, one for reading and card playing, with tables piled high with girlie magazines and cleansing equipment stacked in the corners. The other was a larger room full of broken-down vinyl-covered chairs and one old black-and-white television set.

Past the cluttered entranceway was the open dorm area itself, with two rows of steel cots lining the walls and two rows head to head up the centre with a four-foot-high partition in between. Each bunk was separated by a metal nightstand. The open toilet area was in the far end.

At minimum-security institutions like Maxwell, inmates are now housed in dormitories instead of cells. This supposedly makes for more comfortable living, but I was soon to hear many prisoners disagree with this. In cells there is privacy and a degree of quiet. In dormitories there is constant noise and crowding together. Recent studies have concluded – correctly – that prison dormitories do not offset the disadvantages. Dormitory living can be a "horror to inmates," according to *Struggle for Justice*, published by the American Friends Service Committee.

It was laundry day and the mattresses were stripped bare. A few men were sprawled on bunks, some sleeping, others staring blankly. A large whirring fan overhead in the centre was stirring more dust than air. On the grimy yellowish walls and ceilings were blotches of peeling paint, cracks running out from each like tiny rivulets. This would be my home for the next year or so.

Jimmy, a friendly young black, introduced himself as the "houseman," a title covering a variety of supply and janitor functions. While helping me find my bunk, he began handing out friendly tips: "The commissary is only open on Wednesday, so stock up. Never leave your watch out. Keep anything valuable locked in your locker." Jimmy spotted the Bible as I unloaded my few personal effects. "That's safe. Ain't nobody here gonna steal that from you." He grinned, the first smile I had seen.

"Colson, Colson, report to Control," a rasping voice over the loudspeaker commanded. Prather had warned me that failure to respond immediately could create an instant crisis: a special count of inmates would follow to ensure that no one had escaped. The detested loudspeaker screeched incessantly. I rushed across the compound to the Control Room and was told to wait on a bench; the warden would see me shortly.

Glad for the moment's rest, I began to try to sort out the bits of advice thrown at me.

"You're Colson?" Standing beside me and thrusting his hand forward was a tall, balding man with a strong, self-assured look about him. But for his brown dungarees I might have mistaken him for the warden. Smiling, he introduced himself as "Doc" Krenshaw. I had heard about him, a former official of the American Medical Association, serving time for securities fraud. He had been in prison nine months, he told me, but it had not beaten him down.

Doc's smile suddenly vanished: "Prison will be hard on you for a while. Gotta be a man here. I'm getting 'short' [meaning a sentence is almost over], but let me give you some advice," he said, squinting through thick glasses. "Just expect anything. You will probably see a man die here. Have you ever seen a man die before?"

"Yes," I told him, "I've seen most everything in life."

"Well, you haven't seen prison, Colson. You're going to be shocked by some of the things that happen to you and others. Remember one thing – *don't get involved*. Don't complain. Tend to your own affairs and you'll be okay. I've made it that way."

"This way, Colson," the guard was signalling me to the front office. I stared at Krenshaw for a moment and then trotted towards the administration building. Doc's words were still ringing in my ears: "Don't get involved." Krogh's warning had been to mind my own business. Inmates at Holabird had told me: "Trust nobody with nothin'." Prather said it the same way with reference to my anatomy, and now Doc had added his chilling words.

The advice was more than a prison cliché, it was obviously the formula for survival. I was up against violent men with a code of life all of their own. If I wanted to get home and re-build my own life, I'd better listen to those made wise by the ways of prison.

I expected the warden's office to be as drab and cold as the rest of the prison. Not so. Neither Robert Grunska nor his office fitted the prison scene. A handsome, athletic man in his mid-fifties with greying hair, the warden greeted me cordially. "Sit down here, Mr. Colson – er, Colson – and make yourself comfortable," pointing to a cushioned straight-back chair just inside the door of his panelled office.

"The count is low here now," Grunska lamented, sitting erect behind his desk, fidgeting with a pencil in his hands. "We have a contractual obligation to the Air Force to provide a hundred and fifty men per day for base labour in place of military personnel – grass cutting, clean-up details, that sort of thing."

Grunska was groping for some common point of identification between us. An explanation of the prison's function, its relationship to the Air Force base, and the warden's role seemed good starting points. I was later to discover that Maxwell is little more than a work camp, and that prison policies, furloughs, work programmes, and education – so important to inmates and their rehabilitation – are secondary to the base's need for 150 free labourers a day.

Then with a friendly smile he said, "I want you to know I have an open-door policy. Any time you need to see me, you just let me know – come right in."

I don't know what caused me to do it – the man was being quite decent with me – but I blurted out, "Does that apply to all inmates?"

The warden looked surprised and shifted restlessly in his chair. "Why, of course. I see anyone who wants to see me – as much as I can – this is a busy place."

I explained that I would have a hard enough time being accepted by the inmates and that I wanted to be treated like everyone else. The conversation rambled on, more awkwardly now, with more explanations of prison functions, the moral problems, particularly over furlough policies. "You'll hear a lot of grumbling over furloughs," he said. "Pay no attention. They are the same here as everywhere. If men need furloughs they get them. Now if you need one, when you have to make a court appearance, you . . ."

Grunska caught himself in mid-sentence. "Don't worry; I will see that you are treated like everyone else. The press will be asking about you and that's what I'll tell them. We have very uniform regulations here. Only way you can run a place like this, you know."

The conversation ended and the warden walked me to the door. He was nattily dressed in a freshly starched, blue-striped shirt, a bright blue tie, and creased knit trousers: I was trying to keep closed my tattered brown shirt with two buttons missing, tugging down on the brown pants which were two inches too short. He reached for the door handle and then stopped. "A lot of people ask me about your Christianity – all the stories they've read. Anything you want me to tell them?" I had noticed that he was wearing a silver tie clasp in the simple outline of a fish, symbol of first-century Christians. He seemed pleased when I called attention to it.

I then explained that what he had read was true, that I considered myself a born-again Christian. "I assume you have Bible-study programmes for the prisoners."

"Yes, and you can help with these things," Grunska replied. (During my first weeks at Maxwell, however, the only planned Christian activities I found were church services conducted twice a week by visiting ministers.)

While the warden appeared to me as a kind and gentle man, I had already heard him described as "heartless," a "cold-blooded tyrant," and a "sadist." I had also learned that while inmates tend to hate all prison officials, the warden is their main target. They see only a distant commanding figure strutting about the camp on daily inspections, a symbol of total authority over their lives. The human qualities of prison administrators which vary, as they do among any group of individuals, are irrelevant. "They" – or the system – include lawyers, prosecutors, judges, juries, probation officers and finally – prison administrators. The system punishes, inflicts pain; it is "out to get" the accused. Resentment is a powerful mortar for building the invisible brick wall separating inmates and officials.

Certainly I had more in common with the warden than most of the inmates but at the slightest suggestion of "fraternising with the enemy" I knew I would be in deep trouble: "rats" are dealt with harshly. From what Grunska had said I sensed that I could work as a clerk in the front office. I need only ask. But something inside told me *no*, to seek no special favours.

From the warden's office I was taken to one of the two

harried caseworkers who handle the administrative and personal problems of the entire population. Ben Brown, a stocky, smiling man, gave me rapid-fire instructions and one emphatic warning: "Don't practise law." As one of the two lawyers in the prison, I'd be besieged by requests for help, he told me, but regulations forbid it. Brown's order seemed further confirmation of all the advice I'd gotten to keep a quiet low profile.

As I left the administration building, I noticed a young black inmate, a wide grin on his face, clutching a single sheet of paper. He was pacing back and forth while a secretary busily typed out for him a set of forms. No one in prison smiles like that, I discovered, except when he is being released. I learned later that this young man had that day been freed by President Ford's executive order discharging from prison all men convicted of desertion or draft evasion. Their cases would be reviewed by the Clemency Board, part of Ford's amnesty plan.

I was glad for the young man, happy to see anyone leave, but the irony hurt all the same. A former Marine captain who had spent half of his adult life in military or government service was replacing on the rolls of the Maxwell prison a deserter freed by Presidential order!

Outside, a hazy dusk was falling over the compound, the sultry heat of the day giving way to gentle breezes coming from the banks of the Alabama River which form one boundary of the prison. To learn more about the area, I walked past a softball field and then along a high chain fence behind the dormitories, ending up behind the administration building in the visiting area, a fenced-in yard under tall shade trees with metal tables and chairs arranged in neat rows. I was staring into the yard, my thoughts hundreds of miles away when the silence was shattered. "Colson, get away from there." A tall, scowling, blue-shirted guard was jogging toward me. "Get out of here. The visiting area is out-of-bounds."

At first I thought he was joking. No one had told me about areas out-of-bounds. The look on his face convinced me. "Get out of here – now," he snarled as he steered me back toward the compound. The regulation, I later learned, was to prevent prisoners from ogling the visitors' area, a temptation for inmates who yearned for contact with the outside world. I apologised for my mistake, but the guard was still scowling. "Read the regulations, Colson," he growled and turned away, shaking his head as he walked slowly back to the Control Room.

An inmate who had watched the encounter ambled over: "Don't let that rotten 'hack' bother you. He is one of the worst – in this place." I had heard the term *hack* used for a prison guard, but thought it an unnecessary put-down. From then on I called them hacks, too. Inmates and guards alike are soon trapped together in ugly demeaning practices.

When night fell the full weight of what it really means to be imprisoned settled upon me. I felt closed in and fearfully alone even though surrounded by forty other men. I had known loneliness before – a brief stint in boarding school when I was twelve, long days and nights as a Marine in a far-away land, once when I thought I was lost in the woods. It was not homesickness which weighed on my heart, but the barrenness all around me, the empty shells of men, the pervasive feeling of despair that, like the stale air, filled the dusty dimly lit dormitory.

Men lay on their bunks with glazed eyes, staring at nothing. There was some idle chatter, but unlike any group of men I had been with before there was no laughter, no jokes nor good humour. A harsh epithet, an angry outburst, or the sounds of locker doors being opened and closed were the main sounds above a few pockets of conversation and the steady whining of the fan.

I sat on the edge of my bunk trying to describe it all in a letter to the brothers at Fellowship House. While I knew that the stark drabness of my dormitory would be burned into my consciousness forever, in time as my sensitivities dulled I would get used to it. "I want you brothers to read this back to me when I am out of here and inclined to forget what the initial shock was like," I wrote. "I want to be reminded how great the need is for prisoners to establish their identity and dignity as human beings. My heart aches . . ."

After the letter was written, it was time to meet some of

the men. The clothing officer, Mr. Bleven, had given me some friendly advice: "Find an old moonshiner, a 'country fella,' and talk to him the first night." Word would then spread that I wasn't the arrogant big-shot type they had expected me to be. One young lad named Paul Kramer was in a bunk near the door. A clean-cut type, he wore a large cross around his neck, the mark of a Christian. I had talked with him briefly. I sensed we were to become friends but not this night. He was not the "country" type.

Most of the blacks were gathered in the corner of the dorm nearest me, but they had not acknowledged my smiles. The head-on approach with them would not be safe; they would be distrustful. The older man in the next bunk was a likely prospect. White-haired, a strong, craggy face, rough sinewy hands, he was probably a bootlegger. Earlier he had firmly gripped my hand and told me that his name was Homer Welsh. Homer seemed wary or very shy, stepping backwards as we had spoken. Now he was asleep.

Across the dorm were some men whom I approached. They seemed open, particularly the wiry younger man named Jed who wore an old dirty cap tilted forward over his brow. Jed stood out from the others because he never stopped grinning at me, revealing some missing front teeth. With his tiny chin, he looked for all the world, smile and all, like Mortimer Snerd. We soon were deep in conversation and I found myself fascinated by his mountain stories. (Bleven's advice was good; the next day when the story of my talk with Jed circulated through the prison, there was less hostility toward me.)

Sleep was fitful. The snores, groans, and other body noises of the men continued throughout the night. Many prisoners have trouble sleeping and are up and down, some chain-smoking. There was a constant shuffling in the darkness. The air reeked of smoke, sweat, urine, and dust.

During the first night I was awakened every two hours by the guards clattering through the dormitory, flashing a bright beam in my eyes. It is part of the ritual of body counts which continues day and night; a whistle shrieks, all inmates return from wherever they are to their bunks, each dormitory is counted, a report made to Control and the loudspeaker announces "count cleared." At first it was merely an annoying disruption. Soon it was part of the nerve-chafing tedium, like the Chinese water torture; one drop is nothing, but when it goes on day after day, each drop is like a thunderclap.

Once that first night I awoke totally disoriented, thinking it was all a bad dream. Only later did I discover that some men continue for months to experience this sudden bewilderment as they struggle with reality, waking up abruptly in the darkness believing that they are suddenly free.

There was one welcome break in the routine, the regular Tuesday-night visit of Brother Edmon Blow, a local Southern Baptist preacher. Thirty of us gathered in the auditorium where a portable red vinyl-covered altar was wheeled up to the front of the large barren room; on top of the altar was a lopsided steel cross with the words U.S. GOVERNMENT etched onto the crossbar. An old piano was moved alongside.

Brother Blow is a tall, rawboned man who accepts literally the Scriptural instruction to speak one's faith boldly. There were more *Amens, Praise the Lords,* and *Hallelujahs* in that one hour than I'd heard in a lifetime. But to my surprise I found myself singing loudly and loving every minute of it.

"Oh, how I love Jesus Christ," Brother Blow shouted at the top of his lungs, thrusting his arms upward in an outstretched position, his jacket, which looked too small to begin with, drawn tight across his chest. "He is *my* Saviour – our Saviour." His voice reached a trembling crescendo as he proclaimed, "Thank You, Lord Jesus, for saving this poor wretched sinner."

Then he dropped his arms limply to his side and bowed his head in silence, tears rolling from his closed eyes. *This man actually seems to be talking to Jesus,* I thought to myself. I had never seen the dignified pastors of my church do it this way, but before that hour was over I found myself shouting *Amen* right along with them.

As I was leaving, Brother Blow caught my eye. To my astonishment he charged over and gave me a bear hug "Hallelujah, of all the men to be here," Blow exclaimed. "Hallelujah and praise the Lord." He drew the word *praise* out as long as I'd ever heard it. His protruding cheekbones highlighted his leathery face, the weathered look of rural Alabama, but his eyes were filled with warmth and love.

Brother Blow was to have a part in the surprising things that would be happening in the weeks to come. For this night it was enough that I found a brother when I needed him most.

22

No Favours, Please

There were plenty of jolts those first days, but the biggest was yet to come. As I was passing through the cafeteria line later in the week, one of the messmen named Jerry leaned across the counter, glanced sideways, and whispered, "I need to see you – for your own good."

Something told me he was sincere. When I met Jerry outside the mess hall right after the noon meal, he pointed towards the softball field, one area where inmates could be sure that their conversation would not be overheard. As we began walking slowly in that direction, I studied him. Jerry was a slight, balding man perhaps in his late thirties; he said New Orleans was his home.

Once we were at a safe distance, Jerry slowed down his walk and asked, "Do you have any enemies here?"

"I don't know. Why?"

"I mean someone who is really out to get you?"

"You mean kill me?" My heart was racing, that prickly feeling again attacking my spine.

Jerry nodded. "It's none of my business and I don't know why I'm doing this, but you seem like an okay dude, better than we thought you'd be."

I wondered if this was some kind of set-up. A way of testing me? Prisoners make a fetish of not getting involved. Why was Jerry doing just that?

As if he sensed my thoughts, Jerry shrugged, "I'm a dope to stick my nose into something like this, but anyway – I overheard this dude say to his friend that he wants to kill you. Guys talk like this sometimes, but this one sounded like he really meant it."

"Can you point him out to me?" I asked.

"No way. I'm no rat."

I had kept my eyes on his during the whole exchange. He seemed dead serious. If he was testing me, I'd best appear nonchalant. "If I report this to the hacks, will you back me up?" I asked coldly.

Jerry looked unhappy, then he began kicking the sand underfoot. "Look, Colson, I really could care less about you. I just felt I ought to warn you. That's it. You take it from here and I bow out. Okay?"

I smiled at him for the first time. "Thanks, Jerry, for doing this. I know how to take care of myself." As we silently walked back to the dormitory I wished I felt as confident as I had tried to sound. Who was it? Someone who felt violent toward Nixon? Shades of Mike, the hit man! Now I had another killer to think about. If Jerry was to be believed, this one was in earnest – and about *me*.

It was late afternoon before I was free from a temporary work detail and could get off by myself to think. I sat on the grass by the side of the dorm, my mind thrashing about restlessly. What was I to do about Jerry's warning?

I could talk to the lieutenant on duty right then, or sweat it out this night and see the warden the next day. But what could they do? Jerry would not talk. If it was a gag and I went running to the guards, the next year would be living hell for me. The guards could not protect me anyway; there was nothing to prevent any inmate from quietly coming into a darkened dormitory at night in order to finish off a man in his sleep. I had heard tales of it happening at Maxwell and elsewhere. There were plenty of opportunities to get your victim, even during daylight.

What good would reporting the threat do, anyway? The most likely result would be to ship me somewhere else. It was now in the press that I was at Maxwell; how would they explain my transfer? The Bureau of Prisons would probably be accused of favouritism, that I didn't like Maxwell and had pulled strings to get transferred. Worse yet, I might be put in a maximum-security prison under constant surveillance. That would be one way to get protection, but at what a cost!

There were no options I concluded. I'd have to gut it out and hope that the Lord would guide me. Once again He was making me turn to Him for help. Before attempting sleep that night I prayed for Christ's presence and protection. My faith obviously was still weak, for though physically exhausted I tossed and turned all night long, drifting into a light slumber only to awaken at the slightest noise. For tense moments, I would stare into the blackness, then close my eyes and try again. In the morning I was bleary-eyed and edgy.

To make it worse, the ever-probing eyes of both prison personnel and 250 inmates were constantly on me. I sensed it wherever I was. How was I reacting to the food which I found surprisingly good? Whom did I seek out as friends? How much mail did I receive? Were my letters opened and inspected like everyone else's? (They were.) What work assignment would I draw? This would indicate if I was man-oeuvring for special treatment. The slightest sign of favourit-ism would be seized upon gleefully, for it would prove what most believed anyway, that the system is unfair, or that those coming from important positions can't take it, or both.

There was surprise when word spread that I had not asked for one of the sought-after inside jobs. It had been deliberate. I knew it was expected of me since all prisoners jockey for the better jobs, the prime objective to avoid heavy, outside work details and kitchen duty. Whenever the prison's classi-fication committee met to hand out assignments, there were near epidemics of chronic back disorders, mysterious pains, and other debilitating ailments; otherwise-lethargic men could rise to heroic thespian performances.

I tore into each temporary work assignment, waxing floors, raking leaves, emptying garbage containers as if my life depended on it, which in some ways I thought it might. Win-ning "acceptance" and proving myself was as important now, incongruous though the comparison might seem, as it had been thirty years earlier assaulting the Brahmin bastions of Boston, or later when I sought to be "good enough" in the Marines. I'd have to earn my way – and this time it would be tougher than ever before. For it meant overcoming not only my press notoriety, but penetrating the stifling dense air of mistrust which pervades every prison.

Prison life is often compared to the military. There are certain similarities – the close barracks living, the group standards, the feeling of oppression by authority. But there are sharper differences. In prison the man you befriend may steal your clean socks. Inmates seldom relax their guard even with those they know well.

The sole aim in prison is to survive, make time pass, avoid trouble, and get out. Getting out is the most treasured goal of all and that is very much an individual proposition. Fellow inmates can interfere with a man's chances to win his freedom by involving him in their misconduct, but there is little they can do to help him get out. Men in the armed services, by contrast, are trained to work closely together. In battle they must rely on one another. Staying alive depends upon your buddy.

"Colson, you still don't want to tell us where you'd like to be assigned, eh?" Ben Brown, the caseworker with the round face and a perpetual half-smile was staring at me intensely from behind the conference table. He was flanked by the education officer, two lieutenants, and the other case-worker. The time had come for the classification committee to make its decision on me.

"No, sir. Wherever you decide."

"This is your last chance to make a request."

"I understand."

Brown then asked me to wait outside. In a few minutes I was called back in. "Colson, you will work in the laundry." Then came instructions on what I could and could not do.

I was tempted to ask the education officer whether there was any connection between this assignment and the two days of aptitude tests I'd taken as all new inmates do. I had never even run our washing machine at home and anyone who had even seen me trying to lift the hood of a car knew I was a disaster around things mechanical. The more I thought about it, however, the more I was delighted. The prison administration had struck a compromise between a cushy front-office job and the hated garbage detail. My fellow inmates would now know, at least, that I was not one of the warden's pets.

The laundry was located in a big warehouse-style building which was ferociously hot in the summer and where there was endless sorting of sweat-soaked underwear and brown work uniforms, running washing machines, and handing out clean clothes each day to the inmates. But there were advantages: I would be working for Mr. Bleven, the friendly man who processed me into the prison, and I'd be able to keep myself in clean clothes, an important factor in maintaining good health. On some days work details were called out into the compound to stand in ankle-deep water for up to ten minutes in driving, semi-tropical rains. Prisoners were issued no rain gear and only one towel, T-shirt, and pair of socks each day. One such drenching the second day gave me a severe cold which lasted two weeks.

As a laundryman I could also wash my own socks and underwear; other prisoners had to take what was handed to them each day. Such small benefits could be very important. My assignment to the laundry was also, I'm convinced, another step in my ego-busting process. There was a certain lesson in humility in washing the clothes of other people, not too far removed from washing their feet.

While this work assignment should have been a step forward in overcoming the hostility of inmates to me, if I was any closer to being accepted, I could not tell it from their reaction. The quips flew about my head: "That White House big shot is washing my socks now," was a typical rejoinder. There were a few new overtures of friendship, but most of the men were still wary of me. Starved for the fellowship and warm support I had experienced at Fellowship House, I remembered the young lad with the cross and sought him out.

Paul Kramer at twenty-seven was forthright, muscular, the star second baseman of the prison softball team. After a hitch with the Marines in Vietnam, he had attended college in his native town of Atlanta, Georgia. To make up for lost time and meet expenses, Paul tried to handle two jobs. There were domestic problems, too, with his young bride and in time all of it was too much for him. Paul started using and then selling narcotics, lasting four months in the business.

Caught and arrested, he was sentenced to three years. While in the Texarkana prison, he told me he had faced up to his messed-up life and had "accepted the Lord."

"Paul, I wish we could start a little group here," I suggested. "Couldn't we get a couple of other Christians and meet a few times a week just to share our problems and pray together?"

Paul pondered this suggestion, "I don't know, Chuck; they laugh at 'Jesus freaks' here. You can't carry a Bible around without people ribbing you. There just isn't anything like that here."

"Come on, Paul, let's try," I persisted. "You'll have to start it. I'm new and I don't want people to think I'm trying to take over. How about it?"

But he shook his head. "No, it's not the kind of thing you organise. Maybe we should just pray about it and see what the Lord wants."

I was surprised at the rebuff, but did not press it further. Together we prayed that night, the two of us alone in the darkness just outside Dormitory G, prayers for God to bring men together in prison, prayers which were to be answered in a way that was to shake me to the depths of my being.

All week long I had looked forward to Saturday and Patty's first visit. I was out of my bunk before 6:00 A.M., knowing that Patty would be standing at the visitors' gate when it opened at 8:00. After an extra-close shave, I laboured over the wrinkles in my set of borrowed browns. Helplessly, I kept pulling down the too-short green T-shirt as I stood in the open toilet area, staring into the mirror. Behind a week's accumulation of toothpaste and shaving-soap splatter was the image Patty would see. I hoped the worry lines on my face would not be too obvious.

Only three or four of us were up preparing for visitors, and I was a little self-conscious. Other men had been here for months, even years, and dreaded the weekends when time passed so slowly. Some prisoners actually preferred not to have visits from family and friends, not wanting to be seen in the dreary garb and surroundings of prison. Others believed that time passed faster without the emotional drain on them of the anticipation, the break in routine, and then the trauma of having to see loved ones depart. But for most prisoners the obstacle was economic: their families simply couldn't afford the cost of travel. These inmates had no choice but to glide along in their routines while minutes drifted into hours, hours into days, days into weeks – like one long night of sleep.

Patty and I had decided to spend every possible minute together. Maybe it was easier to adjust to confinement by not living on the emotional roller coaster of weekend peaks and weekday pits, but I was far from ready to become a prison robot. A full hour before visiting time I was pacing about in the courtyard.

Visitors first checked into the outside entrance of the main administration building. There, according to regulations, each one was to be searched (although many were not). Visitors must have been approved in advance, each inmate submitting a list of those he would expect. Prisoners were allowed to take nothing into the visiting room without special permission and could accept nothing but four packs of cigarettes from a visitor. Nothing could be exchanged. There were two pages of rules and regulations for conduct in the visiting room, including an admonition against embracing, except upon arrival and departure. Once a prisoner was inside the visiting area, he could not return to the prison; if he did the visit was terminated. Visiting hours are over at 4 : 00 p.m.

Precisely at 8 : 00 a.m., the loudspeaker called out, "Colson, Colson, you have a visitor." As eager as a first grader on his way home from school. I ran toward the auditorium, forgetting to check in at the Control Room. An exasperated guard called me back and chewed me out, hands on his hips, drill-sergeant style.

Wearing a vivid green sweater and green slacks, Patty was radiant when I came bounding into the auditorium. Both of us had to fight back our emotions, as we did for the better part of that day. I told her nothing of the discomforts, or of the threat against my life, only that most men seemed to be like all other human beings we had met, victims of circumstance. Patty could not take her eyes off my ragged clothes, and I knew her heart was aching.

Later that morning one of the female visitors was asked to leave and the prisoner involved told to report to Control. "What happened?" asked Patty, her eyes troubled.

"Hard to say. Probably caught trying to smuggle something inside."

"What will happen to him?"

"He'll probably go in the hole."

"The what?"

"It's a small cell – for solitary confinement."

Patty was subdued for a while, but soon she brightened – there was so much to cover about our home, friends, the fellowship, Patty's Bible class. By afternoon we had met a number of other inmates and their wives and were joking about my green underwear and old brown khakis.

Even though an early fall chill was in the air, we sat outside all day at one of the round tables. We might have forgotten where we were but for the guards pacing back and forth through the visiting area. It was a relief to be with Patty those two days and a joy to attend church services together in the prison on Sunday morning. At the same time we were fast discovering the emotional strains Bud and Suzanne had talked about. Sunday night back in the dorm, and feeling the awful loneliness again, I wondered how many week-ends like this we could take.

I would in time become used to many things: the roaches noisily flapping about inside the locker beside my head while I tried to sleep, the ever-present stench which permeated one's clothes after a few days, rats, both kinds – rodents and informers. But when I watched Patty's car pull out of the parking lot that Sunday afternoon, there was no way to avoid the depression of the aftermath. While Patty was only a few miles away in a motel, if she needed me I could not be with her. I could not reach for her and touch her, and I had to spend another week in the dismal unreality of prison, waiting expectantly for another weekend.

During the visit with Patty, we had read some Scripture together – the first time I had opened the Bible since entering prison. Feeling convicted about this, I arose early Monday morning determined to begin the Navigators' "Design for Discipleship" Bible course which Doug Coe had given me.

The first suggested reading was Hebrews, chapter 2, for what was described as "valuable information about the humanity of Christ."

What we see is Jesus, after being made temporarily inferior to the angels and so subject to death, in order that he should, by God's grace, taste death for every man, now crowned with glory and honour. It was right and proper that in bringing many sons to glory, God (from whom and by whom everything exists) should make the leader of their salvation perfect through his sufferings. *For the one who makes men holy and the men who are made holy share a common humanity. So that he is not ashamed to call them his brothers* ... [italics added].

Hebrews 2:9–11 PHILLIPS

It is plain that for this purpose his concern is not for angels but for men, the sons of Abraham. It was imperative that he should be made like his brothers in every respect, if he were to become a High Priest both compassionate and faithful in the things of God ... For by virtue of his own suffering under temptation he is able to help those who are exposed to temptation.

Hebrews 2:16–18 PHILLIPS

As I read these words over and over for the first time ever, I had the conviction that God was speaking to me. I was in prison because I had to be there, an essential step, a price I had to pay to complete the shedding of my old life and to be free to live the new. He was preparing me, chastening me for the future perhaps, but for what purpose *now*? Then something inside of me in the most unmistakable terms told me that it was right there before my eyes – *Read it, think about it, it means something about how God came to understand His children, how He became for a time in the flesh of Christ a human so that He could know His sons as brothers. The example means something to you.*

All at once something wonderful and beautiful appeared to me from the words on that page. God, I had already reasoned, had created us as His agents, in His image. We were to be His instruments. But following the original act of disobedience in the Garden of Eden and through all of human history recorded in the Old Testament, men continued to fail to reach His expectations. So instead of inflicting His wrath upon them as He had in olden days, or revoking the agency relationship altogether, God became one of us. He lived among His agents, so to speak, so that He as Jesus could for a time be flesh, understand our sins and temptations, feel our fears as we feel them. He could speak to us in our own language, forgive us, and offer us the way of salvation. What an awesome thought – knowing God as our *Brother* through the Person of Christ! What incredible personal fellowship He made possible! Just the thought of it sent chills through my body.

For the first time the Trinity began to come alive for me. God was first the Creator and Father; then as Jesus – the Son – He lived with us; finally, experiencing our needs in the flesh, He gave us the Holy Spirit, as Christ's replacement, to remain with us as a Comforter and Helper. Up to now I had merely accepted the Trinity as gospel – the way it was – but I had only sampled this Third Part. Now I saw it more and more as the source of strength and power, very real and part of God's logical plan. Before, I had asked the Spirit to lead me and I felt He was, not really understanding what was happening to me. How clear it now appeared.

Then another even more personal thought struck me. Just as God felt it necessary to become man to help His children, could it be that I had to become a prisoner the better to understand suffering and deprivations? If God chose to come to earth to know us better as brothers, then maybe God's plan for me was to be in prison as a sinner, and to know men there as one of them. Could I ever understand the horrors of prison life by visiting a prison? The voice inside of me answered: *Of course not.* No one could understand this without being part of it, feeling the anxieties, knowing the helplessness, living in the desolation. On a tiny scale, it was the lesson of Jesus coming to us.

Of course, of course, of course, I thought to myself. *There is a purpose for my being here, perhaps a mission the Lord has called me to.* As a Christian I fervently believed in Lewis's point that one individual is infinitely more important than the state. This certainly includes the individual in prison.

For the rest of my life I would know and feel what it is like to be imprisoned, the steady, gradual corrosion of a man's soul, like radiation slowly burning away tissue. Just as God in the Person of Christ was not ashamed to call us His brothers, so it was that I should not be ashamed to call each of these fellow inmates my brothers. Furthermore, I was to love each one of them. And would I – if I had not been here? *Never*, I admitted to myself.

Out of these startling thoughts came the beginning of a revelation – that I was being given a prison ministry, both inside while serving as a prisoner and then someday later on the outside! Already I could see and feel that prison life did not provide the creative correction and training needed for a man to be able to make a new beginning on the outside. Instead it was geared to use the men as labour, punish them if necessary, and disregard their inner spirits as of no consequence.

The reading in Hebrews had jolted me, made me re-examine the involvement dilemma. It was the same conflict I had faced when I agonised over whether to plead guilty: the world's way or Christ's? At that point I had chosen the latter. Was I now slipping back to using the world's methods? Doc Krenshaw's advice did make sense, but was it a rationalisation on my part?

Then I remembered the words I had been given on the courthouse steps after Judge Gesell's sentence: "I can work for Him in prison as well as out."

If that was His direction – and it seemed this day unmistakable – I would have to be willing to become involved and trust Him for the wisdom and courage I would need.

23

When Two or More Gather

At 6:00 a.m. shrill bells and crackling loudspeakers pierced the pre-dawn silence. The prison camp seemed to heave and groan, slowly coming to life; lights flickered on from one dormitory to the next, men crowded into shower stalls, sleepy-eyed messmen turned up the steam in cafeteria serving counters, blue-shirted guards paced concrete walks in the compound.

It was the same each morning, but on Monday of the next week the camp seemed stiff and brittle with tension. It was in the air like static electricity, evident in the taut expressions and unnatural silence in the dorms and mess hall. What conversation there was concerned only one subject: the parole hearings scheduled to begin that day.

Once every two months three examiners, mid-level civil servants from Atlanta, spend four days at the camp to make decisions about the forty or so men eligible for parole. One by one in assembly-line fashion, prisoners are paraded past the examiners for interviews, and with the stroke of a pen three-year sentences are cut to one, men with five-year sentences are told to "continue to expiration," as the dreaded term is officially known.

There is good reason for anxiety. Under the general practice of indeterminate sentencing, a man is given both a minimum and maximum term – in my case, one to three years. Parole statutes prescribe that a prisoner be considered for parole at his minimum-sentence date, the intent being to release men who have good prison records and are not considered dangerous to society. But like every bureaucracy, the Parole Board has adopted a complex patchwork of standards – guidelines – setting minimum periods of confinement for specific offences. As a result, parole hearings can be a second sentencing, with parole not often given after one-third of the sentence. Standards constantly change, making the parole process one great guessing game, an excruciating uncertainty for every prisoner and a major cause of prison resentment and anxiety.

In the days before the arrival of the examiners, all attention is focused on upcoming cases. Inmates are remarkably well informed about the particulars of each one. The results are important, not only to those whose freedom is at stake but to the others who will in time be affected by the pattern of decisions.

When the examiners arrived that Monday and began the hearings, bits of information flashed through the prison network: "The first three cases rejected; Pop is getting another hearing; Smitty was given only five minutes and rejected. The —— guidelines are still fouling us up."

By 4:00 p.m. the first day's results cast a dark pall over the prison. Only two of the first twelve men heard were granted parole. The forebodings of morning turned to despair of evening. I was shocked, for like 99 per cent of my profession, I had blithely assumed that parole was virtually automatic, particularly for the kind of "light" offenders which populate a minimum-security institution.

If the dormitory was dark and depressing on my first night, that evening it was a black hole. Everything in the prison, including most of the men's nerves, seemed to be gripped in the same tense vice. It took little to unleash frayed nerves into swinging fists. A large number of men, even in places like Maxwell, have records of violence. Most fights are over such things as the programme to be watched on television, the distance between bunks, since space is such a precious commodity, even the slamming of a locker door while another man is trying to sleep. Fights occur over petty thievery. I once listened to a huge strapping convict shriek that he would "kill" the man who had stolen soap from his locker.

While I was packing things away in my locker that very night, a fight broke out between two young inmates nearby. I later learned that both had long criminal records. These young toughs, heavily tattooed, teeth missing, had plenty of scars to show for previous battles. It started with some friendly pushing and shoving, but soon they were swinging for real. I watched for a moment, frozen on the edge of my bunk. When the blows came vicious, I jumped between them. Instantly both turned on me. Both raised their fists. I smiled; they snarled.

A hush fell over the dorm, the other men sensing gore as sharks do – by vibrations in the water. Blood – mine – was about to be spilled. One spat on the floor, and rubbed his hands together. A shudder ran through me. Could one of these be the man who had threatened to kill me? If so, I had given him a perfect opportunity.

"What's the matter with you guys?" I snapped, hoping they couldn't hear my heart pounding against my rib cage. Nobody moved. No one was going to rescue me. "Didn't you see the hack just outside the window? You'll both be in the hole tonight." It was a lie, a purely self-protective device.

As the words rolled out, tightly clenched fists relaxed, both men's arms dropping limply to their sides. "Why didn't ya tell us?" one asked as I stepped out of the middle. The fight was over. Both of them walked off, arms around one another, their heads shaking in bewilderment over my strange conduct. I returned to my bunk, knees trembling.

Why had I done it? It was instinctive – a direct violation of the don't-get-involved principle. Did my act spring from the Spirit within me urging to prevent bloodshed? If so, it was hardly the Spirit which had me tell a lie to protect myself from injury. I reasoned that God would hardy violate the principle of truth.

The more I pondered the scene, the more I felt that my motive had been right in trying to prevent violence, but that I relied on the old Colson craftiness to get me out of trouble. The right way to have handled it, I concluded, would have been to trust God at the moment of danger by being completely honest with the two antagonists.

Trust. How much I had to learn about this principle. This

would be the key to my getting released from anxiety-filled nights – trust in the Helper. He could help me throw off the fear of sudden attack from the unknown threatener. He could help me resist the temptation of daytime sleep, replacing fatigue with strength.

Sleep was a trap for many prisoners. One young lad near my bunk had a pathetic routine. He arose at the last possible moment in the morning. He would be back sprawled on his bunk after lunch until the afternoon work call at 12 : 30; he would again return to his bunk after the 4 : 00 p.m. meal, sleeping until perhaps 7 : 00. Then he might spend an hour or two reading pornographic magazines before dozing off for the night.

While marvelling at his ability to sleep so much, I saw that his strength was being sapped with each passing day. His walk slowed, his shoulders were hunched, and seldom did his sallow face reveal any emotion. When released from prison, I wondered if he could ever regain the ambition needed to cope even with the everyday necessities of life, let alone a job and family responsibilities.

His was not an isolated case; others in the dorm spent their idle hours simply lying in their bunks, if not sleeping, staring trancelike at the ceiling. Some spent hours on menial tasks, like shining a belt buckle over and over. "Building time" it is called, the ways men find to pass their hollow days. Walking slowly, too, was part of prison life; particularly the "sleepers" shuffling about as if acting out some role in slow motion. Like an invasion of locusts, the empty hours eat away at a man's very being. Soon there is near-total disorientation : staring at the clock, its hands never moving; losing track of time and place.

One sleeper was in the bunk by the entranceway. His name was Lee Corbin and he was assigned to one of the toughest grass-cutting details, swinging a heavy scythe all day and arriving in the dorm each night soaking wet and exhausted. When I saw him reading the Bible one evening, I introduced myself.

"I know you," he replied. "That was good about your conversion. I was a Christian once myself."

"*Was* a Christian?"

He leaned his head back, a wide smile covering his round ruddy face. "Ha, if you only knew. I really fell, man – there's no way for me to get back."

I wanted to pursue it. It seemed hard to imagine that this genial, hardworking man could have committed the unforgivable sin. "Let's talk about it sometime," I suggested.

"I don't think it's worth your time, but I'd like to talk," he replied. Yet each night when I passed his bunk, he was asleep. There would be a time, I knew.

As I watched those who appeared to be almost sleep-walking about the prison, somewhat like men in space, I made the conscious decision never to lie down during the day. I would get what sleep I could at night. There were days when I fought back heavy eyelids and the urge simply to fall into my bunk and let an hour or two pass. But I resisted, even when I knew I needed the sleep.

Later when I read Dietrich Bonhoeffer's *Letters and Papers From Prison*, I discovered that he had made the same decision. He wrote of his rigidly self-enforced schedule to awaken each morning early, take a cold bath, and work all day without sleep. When put into solitary confinement, he determined not to succumb to the reclining position, aware that doing so would aggravate his disorientation and bring him to the "first stage of capitulation."

The man who refuses to be a part of the system, however, and struggles instead to preserve his own identity, all too often can end up fighting everything simply for the sake of fighting. This usually becomes rebelliousness which then hardens into hatred, infecting the man's entire value structure, first about the prison system and then about society as a whole.

It takes only a slight provocation to tip such men over the edge; the inner turmoil can stretch to a snapping point the cords which bind a man together as a rational being. I saw it happen. His name was James Howard, a handsome man in his early thirties, with sparkling blue eyes, reddish blond hair, and an unusually bright, alert manner. Out of prison garb I could see him as a stockbroker or an enterprising young IBM executive. Since Paul Kramer and I had been having Bible talks together he asked me one evening to pray for Howard.

"He just hasn't been himself for a few days. Terrible burdens. Won't say much either," was all Paul told me.

When I saw Howard sitting alone in the mess hall the next noon I sat with him. After the idle chatter and get-acquainted questions, there were long awkward lulls in the conversation. His one show of emotion was when he vigorously protested his innocence of stolen-car charges. I had the uncomfortable feeling through lunch that my words were going right past him, that his thoughts were completely disoriented.

Howard lived in Dr. Krenshaw's dormitory. When I asked Doc about him, he gave me that don't-get-involved look : "It's better not to talk about it, Chuck," he said. "It will be bad for him if the word gets out and people start ribbing him."

"But I only want to help."

With that, Doc looked pained and then explained that in his opinion Howard had suffered a nervous breakdown. Receiving bad news on parole and a "Dear John letter" from his wife on the same day was too much. "Chuck, it could happen to anybody. I'm trying to get Hart [the prison paramedic] to admit him to the hospital just for observation, but Hart can't tell if a man has had a nervous breakdown. He thinks we're all crazy and he's probably right."

Doc related that three nights earlier Howard awoke in the middle of the night screaming. No one paid any attention; nightmares were common in the dormitory of forty men. From then on, Howard had been in a daze, listless as if all life had been sucked out of him. "What the man needs, Chuck, is psychiatric treatment, but that's not going to happen. They don't move anybody out of here unless it's feet first, or unless they cause trouble. Forget it. Just be kind to him."

Some days later Howard was admitted to the two-bed infirmary. His condition was not diagnosed and he was returned to his dormitory. Again at lunch I tried to talk to him. Once he leaned across the table and whispered, "What did you find in my files?"

I was startled : "What files, Howard?"

Looking about cautiously, he whispered again, "You know, the other night when you were up in the office and had my folder out. All of you guys were talking about it. What did you find?"

"Honest, Howard, I have never looked at your file. I swear to you I don't know anything about it."

He nodded with a smug, knowing expression: "I understand. You can't talk about it, can you?" My heart sank; paranoia possessed him. Krenshaw could do nothing; the administration would not. I vowed somehow to help Howard, but it was agony to watch this young man's body and mind drift further apart each day.

Very few prisoners, I discovered, were able to maintain a sense of personal identity, without becoming resentful of the injustice they saw about them. The causes of bitterness went beyond prison life and were deeply rooted in the system of criminal justice itself. For all my years at the bar, all my study of the ideals of the law, I was now coming to perceive the law's workings in an entirely new light. Prisoners exaggerate, of course; I was prepared to discount many of the stories I heard. Yet I had discovered to my dismay that many of the tragic tales from inmates were all too true.

There was a lad from rural North Carolina, for example, who years before had purchased an old tow truck. With that start, he had built a thriving auto-repair and gas-station complex. Late one night he cashed an eighty-four-dollar government paycheque for a customer. After the cheque bounced, the FBI visited the garage and warned him of his rights. It turned out that the cheque was stolen. Though this young businessman had never before been in trouble, he was convicted and sentenced to six months in prison. Gone were six thousand dollars in legal fees paid to a lawyer who confessed that he had never before been in federal court, eighty-four dollars from the bad cheque, and six months of his life.

The case is extreme but not unusual. One of my dormitory mates, a South Carolina small businessman, was convicted of three misdemeanours for failure to file excise-tax returns. He had, I learned, infuriated the trial judge with one defiant remark. This offence, which seldom if ever results in prison, cost my friend eighteen months in jail, with the judge writing the Parole Board to recommend denial. The board did so.

Another man whom I later befriended was doing three

years for a four-thousand-dollar tax evasion. The IRS offered him a chance to plead guilty and accept a fine, but my friend insisted on his innocence. After years of trials and despite acquittal on most of the charges, an exhausted judge gave him a stiff sentence.

There may have been other factors involved in these cases – and many men who should be punished go free, I realise. But as the stories accumulated and I checked them out as best I could, it was easy to see why sentencing disparity is the chief cause of the pervasive bitterness in prison. The injustice of the system, so painful when one comes to know the victim face-to-face, spawns contempt for the law, even among those receiving deserved punishment.

I especially yearned to help the illiterate men with their pleas, but remembered the stern admonition not to practise law in prison. Lawyers who do this, I was told, are transferred immediately to other prisons. Krenshaw was not allowed to practise medicine even though there was a shortage of doctors on the base nearby and no doctor in the prison. Regulations are strict. I was soon to be tested on this as well.

To escape the depressing dormitory atmosphere on the first day of parole hearing, I headed for the library located in the rear of the Control Building. A small room, the library has one wall lined with tiny stalls for writing, while the other walls contain bookshelves crammed with old paperbacks, a tattered dictionary, outdated volumes of the criminal code, newspapers, and old newsmagazines. Inmates usually congregated around two large tables in the centre of the room, chattering about writs and appeals which some enterprising prisoner was preparing, playing cards, or reading. Even so, it was quieter than the dorms, more brightly lighted, and the white walls somehow made it seem cleaner. As the library clerk, Paul Kramer spent most of his evenings there.

When engrossed in my writing I could usually shut out the din of conversation around me. But this evening I became aware of a small group of men gathering around Paul in the corner of the room. Doing most of the talking was a man named Tex, a flamboyant character and onetime evangelist who had spent years travelling the revival circuit. He had left the ministry and the Lord to traffic in stolen automobiles. During his six-month sentence, he had recommitted himself to Christ with the fervour of a new convert.

Tex was a red-necked, red-headed edition of Popeye, with short bulging biceps and a jutting chin. Standing with him were two other prisoners. One, a tall, handsome black man with a commanding presence, had been active in halfway-house work in Columbus, Georgia. While on probation for a previous narcotics sentence, he was found with a sporting rifle in his possession. Probation was automatically revoked and he was back in prison for nine months. The other, a quiet man with a huge bush of curly hair, was often in the library, reading Scriptures, or working on Bible correspondence courses.

Tex in loud whispers was describing the plight of an inmate named Bob Ferguson who was up for parole hearing the next day. "Bob is in terrible shape. He's crawling on his belly tonight. Oh – Praise the Lord – We gotta help him. Poor devil, wife and five kids and no money. If he doesn't get paroled, they ain't gonna survive. Praise God, we gotta help him. Maybe pray with him. He's going off his head."

I walked over to the little group. "Sorry, but I couldn't help hearing about this fellow Ferguson. I'd like to pray with him, too," I volunteered.

Tex, his eyes sparkling, grabbing me hard by the arm. "Come along, brother. Come along. Praise the Lord." One of the men went to get Ferguson. Paul sent for his close friend Amos, a pharmacist from Atlanta, who was doing six months for filling a prescription on a doctor's orders which exceeded the permissible narcotics content. Within minutes seven of us were assembled. We caucused for a moment at the library door to decide where to go. The guards were always suspicious of small groups of prisoners gathered in dark areas, since this usually meant they were smoking marijuana. We could not pray in the library which was crowded with other inmates, as were the dorms. The auditorium was out-of-bounds. Paul had a key to two small classrooms just off the library, which were locked at night and also out-of-bounds.

The classrooms seemed the best choice. We filed in, locking the door behind us. Memories of my own days in elementary school flooded back. Three rows of simple polished wood tables, chairs neatly pulled up to each one, a teacher's desk in front of a large blackboard covered with chalk scratchings, "See John run – John has a cat – The cat is brown." Basic reading and writing were regularly taught to the 15 per cent or so of the prison population which was totally illiterate. These were largely mountain and rural folk, moonshiners from the tiny Appalachian communities of Alabama, Tennessee, Kentucky, and the Carolinas. By and large God-fearing men, their primitive understandings of right and wrong were no match for the intricacies of the Internal Revenue Code, the complex laws of society, and hordes of federal agents.

Ferguson was just such a rural person – a man in his thirties, half his front teeth missing, eyes reddened, and a confused and worried expression on his face. Ferguson didn't say a word. He didn't have to. His face was pleading for help. Paul, we discovered, was also scheduled for a parole hearing the next day. Tex began by grimly recounting the experiences of those who were given hearings earlier in the day. The prospects were no better for those coming up tomorrow; the Parole Board was showing little mercy, rigidly adhering to its guide-lines.

The Bible student read several Psalms and then passages from the Book of John about Christ's work on our behalf. Tex then suggested we all pray silently or aloud as we wished, and the seven of us were soon on our knees on the cold tile floor. Tex began. In my mind, I could see him on a hot summer night, underneath a tent surrounded by a few dozen wide-eyed country folk, demanding in the name of Jesus that Satan depart, calling on all of the assembled sinners to come forward and confess their sins or be damned eternally to hell.

"Oh, Lord," he cried out, "just spare these men who are coming up for parole tomorrow. We just praise You, Lord. We ask it of You, dear Lord, in the name of Jesus. We are all sinners but we are here on our knees making our claim. We know, dear Lord, You will hear us. We love You, Jesus." In between each rapid-fire petition, Tex would breathe in deeply, sigh, and begin again, his voice trembling with emotion.

Paul followed with a short quiet prayer, as did the others. I was last: "Lord, strip away the calluses on the hearts of these parole judges, hardened by years of dealing so impersonally with criminals," I prayed. "Please give them wisdom, love, and compassion."

As each of us slowly got to his feet, I found myself hugging the big black. Tex was jumping from one foot to the other, praising God for filling him with the Holy Spirit. Ferguson was unashamedly in tears. We filed out quietly and returned in little groups of two or three to our dormitories just in time for the 10:15 count. No guard had intruded upon our little gathering. But what a strange sight it would have been to anyone who might have stumbled across us.

The next afternoon, news spread quickly through the camp: five men paroled, Ferguson among them. Few expected it; he wasn't eligible under the guidelines. The statistics were startling: five out of seven cases heard – a dramatic switch from the day before. It was the best day even the old-timers could remember. Wednesday was almost as good; well over half the cases heard won parole dates, including Paul.

Paul had not prepared for the hearing in the conventional way. No one had accompanied him. He had even volunteered the information that though he was married (that fact adds one point to a prisoner's rating score) he expected to be divorced. When asked about his future, Paul did not try to blow up his situation with an over-optimistic forecast; he simply explained that he had accepted the Lord and believed He would lead him. According to Paul the Parole Board examiners listened with perplexed expressions; nonetheless they scheduled a March hearing for him.

Paul returned to the dormitory that afternoon with a stunned, far away look: "I can't believe it, Chuck, I can't believe it. I'm not eligible under the guidelines for two years. But they told me they would hear my case in the spring. If I keep my nose clean, I'll be released. It's too good to be true. I can't feel anything. I'm numb all over."

It *was* too good to be true, all of it. The parole actions lifted the morale of the whole camp. The mess hall filled with smiling faces. Word of our Monday-night prayer session had also spread. Some of the seven were the butt of wisecracks on Tuesday, but by nightfall all kidding ceased. By Wednesday night even the most cynical non-believers were in awe of what happened in the little classroom on Monday. Many wanted to believe there was something to it, whatever it was.

The Bible began to enjoy a new respect, too. "Be careful now; somebody might steal it," Jimmy, the houseman, warned me with a smile.

24

A Helping Hand

"You guys meet each night to pray?" Standing before me outside the mess hall was Lee Corbin, who had confided to me one night that his sins were too great, that he had gone past the point of redemption. "You know I really believe in what you guys are doing," Corbin said wistfully.

"Come and join us," I urged. That first session in the classroom had been so inspiring that Paul, Amos, and I met again the next night to pray for Tex who was being released that week. There were so many needs we just kept meeting.

I spent much of that night talking with Lee long after lights were out. "I have swindled so many people," he explained. "Even if I had the money to pay them back, I could never find them all." Corbin astonished me with the story of how he became an accomplished con artist. He began as a phony but successful preacher. With his deep resonant voice and command of the Scriptures, he was soon asked to broadcast a weekly sermon over several Alabama radio stations. "I was not preaching Christ but Lee Corbin," he confessed.

Soon he became so involved in business ventures that he dropped his clergy role entirely. There followed a series of get-rich schemes: bank loans to defunct corporations, phony vending-machine concessions, and false credit cards, with each new flim-flam becoming progressively more ingenious than the one before.

"It was wrong, Chuck and I knew it all the time, but I was hooked on my hundred-thousand-dollar house, the new cars, the yacht. It was so easy. I felt sorry for the poor people I was swindling and I hated myself, yet I couldn't stop."

For seven years Lee crisscrossed the South, leaving behind a trail of bewildered, dejected and sometimes-broke victims, and scores of angry police departments. Then it all began to collapse; there was a series of charges and he became a fugitive. When he was arrested, ironically it was while attending a revival session in South Carolina.

"The Lord picked me right out of the crowd. I deserved it," he added.

Corbin faced an awesome array of charges: mail fraud, embezzlement, forgery. "They could have put me away for life and I guess I would have had it coming," he said. Surprisingly, Corbin was tried on only one count of mail fraud, sentenced to one year, and the other charges were dropped.

"But I can never repay all those people whose money I took," he insisted. "Not if I work for the rest of my life. So how can the Lord take me back until I do?"

We talked that night about forgiveness. Corbin had studied the Scriptures, but he seemed more knowledgeable about the Old Testament than the new. The admonition in Leviticus 6:2–5 – that when a man has taken property wrongly from another, he must restore it plus a 20 per cent fine – had burned itself into his consciousness.

I steered Lee to the Gospels and we focused on the fact that Jesus came to save sinners; He wiped the slate clean for each of us when He went to the cross. As we groped our way through the Scriptures that evening, both of us concluded that Jesus would demand from Lee only an open heart, a complete confession, restitution where possible, and a renewed commitment.

We found further illumination in chapter 7 of Romans, where Paul describes the dilemma of Old Testament men who knew the law and wanted to abide by it, but did precisely the opposite because they were unable to conquer their own human imperfections. "For I do not do the good I want, but the evil I do not want is what I do. Now if I do what I do not want, it is no longer I that do it, but sin which dwells within me" (Romans 7: 19, 20 RSV). Paul's point: trying to live by the law only creates in us the very sin we seek to avoid.

But it wasn't enough for Corbin to see the trap into which he had fallen. He needed to be freed from it. The key to this we found in the next chapter of Romans. "For the law of the Spirit of life in Christ Jesus has set me free from the law of sin and death" (Romans 8 : 2 RSV).

This matter of asking the Holy Spirit to take over our lives was something I had been struggling with since the time of my acceptance of Christ. I had felt then the movement of His Spirit in me. Yet I did not fully understand how to get my sinful self out of the way so that this Spirit could take charge. Strange that it was in prison where I was to find this freedom.

Corbin began attending our evening prayer sessions. On our fourth night together Paul asked Lee to lay it all before God, to ask for forgiveness and for the Holy Spirit to come into his life again. Lee prayed as hard as any man I've known, begging the Lord to take him back and to cast Satan out of his life. At one point his prayer seemed to shift gears, the words were unfamiliar, reminding me of the Gregorian chant I'd once heard in a Catholic church. I had not experienced this praying in tongues, nor had I been with anyone before who did, but not for a minute did I doubt that the Spirit was in control of Lee Corbin. When he finished praying, it was just as if every bit of strength left his body and he fell limp.

I watched the change that took place in him in the days that followed. Corbin stopped sleeping his evenings away, reading instead from his Bible, filled with vitality, a renewed sense of purpose in his life. Whether I fully understood it in Scriptural or theological terms, I knew it was real. I would have gladly shared a foxhole with him in battle – Lee had suddenly become that tough, dependable, and loyal.

There were four of us now meeting to pray regularly. Emboldened by the strength of our fellowship, we decided to encourage others to join us. No matter whom we sat with in the mess hall, we agreed always to ask the Lord's blessing before beginning our meal. We would each pass through the cafeteria line with our trays, find an empty seat, and bow our heads for grace.

At first other inmates would stare at us. Yet there were no sneers or ribbing. Soon the blessing became contagious – a man here, another there, following this practice. To my surprise, whenever I would join a table, even if the others were in the midst of their meal they would stop talking and eating,

bowing their heads with me. It was as if a beachhead was
established at Maxwell for the Holy Spirit !

Although we met every night in the classroom, most of
the newcomers chose to come Monday. Within a few weeks
those Monday night meetings became a regular, organised
Bible-study programme. With the warden's permission, Martin Gay, a Christian lay worker from Montgomery, joined us
to lead the instruction.

Did the main group of prisoners consider us "Jesus freaks?"
Some did, perhaps. But it didn't matter. My priorities were
changing. Then one evening during a cleanup period a tough
young prisoner deliberately bumped into me as we were both
running buffing machines across the floor. "Never did this in
the White House, huh?" he said.

I grinned at him. "I did this kind of work before you were
born."

Surprised, he smiled faintly and returned to waxing the
floor. One of the veterans took me aside. "You don't have to
knock yourself out the way you are," he said. "We know why
you're doing it, but you don't have to. We've discussed it.
You're okay."

So it happened. *Okay* was the magic word. I had passed
a test of sorts with the main group of prisoners. Nothing formal, of course, but a silent understanding which signalled
their acceptance of me. It meant an end to the wisecracks,
the curious stares, the suspicions. I would still have to contend
with the loners, the men not part of the system. The threat
on my life most likely came from one of them, a "nut" perhaps. But at least now I would have some allies. The men in
the main-stream would watch out for me, as much as prisoners ever watch out for one another. Ironic that this acceptance
had come when I stopped striving so hard for it.

From my first week at Maxwell, I had wrestled inside over
the warning that I was not to help my fellow inmates with
legal problems. Perhaps there were good reasons for the rule,
but with such a desperate need for legal assistance in prison,
it seemed a misuse of a man's gifts. In the prisoner' eyes it
was just one more example of planned dehumanisation; men
stripped of self-worth and dignity are easier to control. On the

other hand, my role in prison had changed after the revelation that came to me through reading the second chapter of Hebrews. Since then I had become involved.

It was Homer Welsh, the shy, white-haired man in the bunk next to mine, who helped me resolve this dilemma. Homer was such an insecure person he would jump up each time I spoke to him and called me *sir* even when I asked him not to. Piece by piece I pried from him these facts – he had been a construction labourer in the coal mines of eastern Tennessee, was devoted to his wife and grown-up children. He owned his own home. Unfortunately he had chosen whisky-making as his avocation.

Moonshining is considered by these mountain people an honourable, respected profession. The profits are usually small, certainly in relation to the backbreaking work required. Many older moonshiners know no other trade or profession; it is a skill passed down from one generation to the next. Staying ahead of the "revenooers" is simply one challenge of their craft; they recognised its illegality, but do not consider it immoral. Many when caught do not go to jail because of an unwritten "social compact" between local judges and lifelong moonshiners. Those imprisoned do not understand why they are put with men who lie, cheat, and steal – and yet have about the same length of sentence. Moonshiners are usually hardworking, Bible-reading, God-fearing men.

Homer was just such a man. He read at night from a well-worn leather-bound King James Version of the Bible. After I offered him my Phillips translation of the New Testament, he would borrow it, but only after very formally asking my permission each time. It was during one of our exchanges about my Bible that Homer summoned up all his courage to make another request.

"Mr. Colson, if you don't want to do it, I'll understand, but do you suppose you could help me with a letter to my judge? He told me I'd only be here four months. I can't get to see my caseworker and I've been here four months already. I don't think I'm getting a parole like the judge said. I thought I ought to write him and maybe he'll straighten it out. I have a job in November if I can get out, but if I can't, they won't hold it for me. Could you help, sir?"

I explained the constraints upon me and he was instantly apologetic. "Didn't mean to bother you, sir. I understand completely. I hope you didn't mind me asking."

Homer's request lingered in my mind all that night. He was my bunkmate and a decent man. He obviously could not afford a lawyer and even if he could, the mechanics of getting one were probably beyond him. The caseworkers were too harassed to help him. And jobs for men his age were hard to find. And there was also the possibility he would lose his home. The next morning I suggested a solution to Homer. While I could not write the letter for him, if he would do a rough draft, I would look it over and give him my suggestions.

The old man's face brightened. "Yes, sir. I'll write it. I'll go right to work on it today. Thank you, Mr. Colson."

Night after night Homer sat on the edge of his bunk labouring over a white lined pad of paper. *He must be producing a lengthy brief*, I thought to myself.

A week passed before I asked him how he was progressing. "I think I've got it all down," he said, reaching into his nightstand draw and pulling out a single sheet of white paper. The barely legible writing covered only half the page. It was a series of words, not even sentences. "This is the best I can do," he lamely explained. "All the facts are here, anyway."

How blind I had been! Homer could not write. He had been struggling pathetically night after night – simply to get words on paper – and was too embarrassed to tell me. We hurried off to the library together. Within twenty minutes I had written a letter to the judge, using simple language in the hopes it would look as if Homer himself wrote it. Paul typed it, and it was in the next morning's mail.

From that moment my new course was charted: I could not refuse those who needed help. These were my brothers. The Lord had shown the way and now I was following. Most of my evenings thereafter were consumed helping other prisoners write parole applications, furlough requests, and the assorted other appeals men pursue in an effort to secure their freedom or fair treatment. I drew the line in not preparing court documents or writs against the prison officials, which would be a clear violation.

One day while I was regulating the flow of laundry into the washing machines, a new inmate, a young man from Tennessee named Dan, came into the laundry asking for the "louyah, the Watergate man." Nettled by his lack of restraint within the hearing of guards, I told him I wasn't allowed to practise law. His beaming smile disappeared, replaced by such a pathetic sheep-dog look that I relented and told him to return after working hours for a talk. Dan's face lighted up again. "Thank you. Thank you."

That evening Dan was waiting in the doorway with that big broad smile. We found a quiet spot and I asked him to tell me his problem. "Well, suh," he began, "I don't know what mah sentence is and I thought maybe – some of the fellas said you'd help me write to the judge."

"Don't put me on," I cut in impatiently. "Everybody knows what his sentence is. What were you convicted of?"

"I don't know that either, suh, honest I don't," he answered.

I was tired and must have appeared angry because Dan kept saying, "Honest – honest." After weeks of meeting victims of the system, men who had experienced the most bizarre encounters with the law, I should not have been surprised. "Don't you have a lawyer?" I asked.

"The judge gave me one who told me what to do. He said he'd 'copped' something for me with the prosecutor. Then we went back before the judge who looked so mean at me my knees wouldn't stop shakin'. I don't know what he said. Somethin' about four years. That didn't sound so good. Then he said somethin' about probation. That sounded good. My louyah said it was, anyway. But then two men took me away in handcuffs. I never saw the louyah again, and here I is."

I stared at him in total dismay. Dan was, I believed telling me the truth. I knew that such things did happen, that some court-appointed lawyers found such cases a bother and negotiated quick guilty pleas with prosecutors, leaving the unsuspecting defendant to the mercy of the court. What stung me now was that I was face-to-face with a decent, fresh-faced young kid who was in prison and didn't even know why or for how long. When Dan later brought me his papers, I saw that he had been given a four-year sentence for purchasing a stolen car. It was hard to believe that such an offence could warrant that kind of punishment. I agreed to do what I could to help him.

The decision to abandon the Krenshaw advice produced some subtle changes in me. There was a further lessening of resentment towards the forces that put me in prison. I was seeing firsthand that injustice was a part of life. Being so involved, doing something about these sad cases, gave me less time to think about myself, and brought home to me an awareness of a great need in our society. Soon I had almost no time for myself, getting even less sleep as I would sit up after hours in a dimly lit smoke-filled dayroom, preparing papers, advising others.

For many days now I had lived with a threat over my head, sleeping fitfully, watching for those angry, hate-filled eyes which would give me a clue to my would-be assassin. With God's Spirit now so alive in the prison, I had been able to trust Him even about this. When the time was right I would have a face-to-face showdown with this man. Until then I had been given other work.

Another change in me was a new sense of gratitude for family and friends. I knew that there was a vast group of people outside who still hated the "hatchet man." But how much it meant to have the letters flood in from grass-roots Americans who wanted to lift my spirits. One family, the Charles Givlers of Beaver Falls, Pennsylvania, wrote to say that they had adopted me. Each week brought notes from the Givlers children, crayoned drawings, cheery cards, books, small thoughtful gifts, and always expressions of Christian love.

Patty's regular weekend visits were always the week's highlight. For my birthday she gave me a present I had wanted all these months in prison – a wedding band on which she had inscribed: "April 4, 1964 – Forever." This might seem a curious gift for a couple married so long, but this new band was to remind me daily of the bonds we had together, with the word *forever* now having a new meaning for us.

A letter was received from the former President, written on my birthday (see page 331).

October 16, 1974

Dear Chuck,

    During the two months that we have been in
California since the Resignation and during the time
that I have been grounded by the doctors, I just
wanted you to know that my thoughts and prayers have
been with you through this difficult time.

    When I think of the enormous service you
rendered to the Administration, your loyalty to me
personally, and your friendship, my heart really goes
out to you in what I know must be a terribly trying time
for you.

    Fortunately, you are a young man, you're a
strong man, and you are a good man, and in the end
this will pass and we will all live to fight another day.

    God bless you and let's keep in touch.

                             Sincerely,

A birthday visit from two friends and former law partners, Charlie Morin and George Fender, was memorable in a different way. As lawyers they were able to obtain special permission to visit during the week. Since the visiting yard was closed, we were shown into what was called the captain's office, a tastefully furnished room with a large wooden desk in the centre. Although fearing I might be developing my own case of prison paranoia, I could not shake off the suspicion that the captain's office was bugged. The room was used for disciplinary proceedings, which, it seemed logical, prison officers would want recorded.

I knew that all phone calls by prisoners were monitored and probably taped, since one of the inmates had seen the transcribing equipment. (Prisons vary in the telephone freedom they allow. At Maxwell we were permitted to make unlimited personal collect calls on the two public telephones installed, but only at designated hours during the day. With long lines of men always waiting, a ten-minute limit for each call was carefully observed. Making the telephone more available to prisoners has been an important morale factor.)

All outgoing and incoming mail, except from attorneys, was opened and read. This feeling of being watched and listened to all the time was one of the most unsettling aspects of prison life. While George Fender was at his effusive best, telling jokes and funny stories from the office, my mind was searching the room for hidden listening devices. Finally, I passed Charlie Morin a note: "This room is probably bugged."

Charlie read the note and nodded understandingly. George read it over Morin's shoulder and then attempted to lift the desk, only to find it bolted to the floor. He scribbled a note back: "You're right – standard technique – microphone wires run through the bolted desk legs under the floor."

Now I could not suppress my curiosity. I went into the adjacent office, ostensibly to ask the secretary which phone line Morin could use for a call. She appeared flustered, jumped up, and escorted me out of the room, but not before I caught a good look at a large tape recorder on her desk, reel slowly turning, obviously recording something.

Then I remembered that the only other visits I'd had during a weekday had been in this same room. Wally Henley, a local preacher who once served with me in the White House, had visited several times, always in this room. Together we had prayed about a dilemma I'd felt during my first days – if asked by the warden or some other prison official for information about another prisoner, how could I keep from "ratting" on a fellow inmate and still be truthful? Although other prisoners had been pressured to "rat," I never had. Was it because they had listened to our prayers?

Our time together was not the relaxed few hours we had hoped for. Seeing men in prison garb and unable to be myself only increased my friends' distress. Being with two good friends and knowing they could walk out unimpeded suddenly made me yearn for my freedom. The awareness that our conversation was probably being recorded further dampened our spirits. Then an idea was dropped in my mind.

Here might be our God-given opportunity to help Howard. To my friends' surprise, I suddenly became charged with righteous indignation : "This prisoner, Jim Howard, has suffered a nervous breakdown in prison and none of the officials care. It's criminal," I ranted on. "Howard will never get out of here until he dies or commits suicide. It's nothing less than manslaughter – criminal negligence. The warden is so concerned with providing slave labour to the Air Force, he doesn't think about individuals. I can't do anything about it now, but I sure will when I get out of here." Hoping that my words would be heard by the warden, I laid this burden on him as hard as I could. My friends quickly caught on to what I was doing and played straight men to me.

The next morning while in the laundry, I heard Mr. Bleven taking a call to process clothing and linens for a prisoner who was to be transferred immediately. He came out of his office shaking his head and mumbling. "Can't understand what's going on around here. Must be something funny. They never move anybody this way."

That afternoon, escorted by two marshals, Jim Howard was taken to the prison hospital in Atlanta. And that evening Paul, Amos, Lee, and I said heartfelt, thankful prayers together.

Patty was staying in Montgomery that week instead of

commuting back to Washington. For years wives in the area had attended Brother Blow's services on Tuesday night and Methodist services on Thursday night. Inmates and their wives sat together, but wives left immediately after the service. I'd noticed the care with which each couple observed the rules. No visiting, just time to worship together.

Patty arrived Tuesday night shortly before seven in a torrential downpour, escorted by Brother Blow and his wife. Though the auditorium was cold and damp, the service quickly warmed us. The Southern Baptist preacher was in great form, and it was as exciting for Patty as it had been for me the first night. Word must have reached the authorities about Patty's attendance at the service because the next day I was summoned to the office. "Wives of prisoners can't come to church here," the officer on duty told me curtly.

"The men tell me that it has been going on for years," I answered.

"Something is wrong," the officer said. "If wives have been coming to the church services, we'll put a stop to that right now."

My heart sank. Had Patty and I spoiled it for everyone else?

"Men are here to be punished," he snapped, slapping his right hand against the back of his left, a gesture which too often summed up the rehabilitative philosophy at Maxwell. "When prisoners and their wives attend church together during the week, this is visiting," he concluded.

An inmate who served as the base-chaplain's assistant took the case to the warden. "You should come hear Brother Blow yourself, Mr. Grunska. He is very close to God," the man pleaded.

"He'd better be – he's going to need God when I get through with him," Grunska stonily replied.

There were more stormy words. Then came the warden's decision : church services were a privilege not a right. Wives of inmates were an intrusion. I couldn't help but wonder if this overreaction was not related to the Howard matter.

Word quickly spread through the camp that wives had been banned from weekday church services. I was particularly depressed because most knew that it was Patty's attendance which had brought the longstanding practice to an end. The

˙warden's edict struck a sharp blow to morale within the camp. Not that very many men shared worship services with their wives, but the denial of any privilege, no matter how small, was taken seriously. It was a threat to the delicately balanced relationship between the prison population and front office. It was also an omen of worse things to come.

From then on there was increased harassment of our visitors. One weekend Doug Coe and Fred Rhodes flew down from Washington, replacing an exhausted Patty. Fred, who was then the chairman of the U.S. Postal Rate Commission, was stopped by one surly guard who brusquely searched his briefcase, snarling all the while at Fred who kept smiling throughout. The official's rudeness upset us, not the search which uncovered only some allowable food items.

Fred's conclusion was that some of the guards seemed more imprisoned than the inmates themselves. "Let's pray for them, Chuck." And we did so right there in the visitors' yard, probably the first time this particular guard had ever been prayed for, unless it was for his transfer to another prison. Later we continued this prayer in our prison fellowship.

Meanwhile Doug in his irrepressible way spent time with almost all the prisoners in the visiting area, encouraging, exhorting, winning friends. Fred singled out Lee Corbin for a quiet talk. Doug and Fred were then joined by Jim Hiskey, who had a ministry to professional golfers throughout the country. The three of them brought the spirit of love into the prison area despite all manner of obstacles. Later that week Lee Corbin sat up all one night making a string model of a sailing vessel, a beautiful piece of work which he sent to Fred Rhodes. Fred, in turn, mailed Lee a Scofield Bible. The chairman of the Postal Rate Commission and an inmate convicted of mail fraud were thus sharing their faith – through the mail.

That evening I wrote Doug: "I can't tell you how much these visits have meant to me. I often feel like I am on a lonely frontier away from the spiritual home of our fellowship. I know this is the Lord's plan and I accept the mission with joy. But just as I miss my physical home with Patty, I miss my spiritual home with you and the brothers. The Lord is moving here in such a powerful way – and there are few places where His presence is more needed than in this colony of lost souls. There must be such a need in other prisons, too . . ."

Brother Blow had asked me when we first met to talk at one of the Tuesday-night meetings. I declined, explaining that I wanted first to become accepted by the men. Events of the past week convinced me that the time had come to try to explain my conversion to my fellow prisoners. I agreed to speak the following Tuesday.

The warden's action barring the wives from prisoner services during the week had the effect of rallying the prisoners behind Brother Blow. Twice the number of inmates plus a large number of parishioners from his church were on hand the following Tuesday for our service. As the hour approached I became increasingly nervous and apprehensive. In describing my White House experiences I would have a hard time relating to these moonshiners and country folk. What could I say that would be helpful?

Brother Blow opened the service with his usual enthusiasm. After hymns, guitar playing by one of the inmates, and a short sermon by Blow, the pulpit was turned over to me.

I began by praying for the Lord to take charge. Then the words began to flow, haltingly at first, as I explained how I had been separated from God by my own pride and ego and imprisoned by my own sins. Now only eighteen months later and a federal prisoner, I was a free man in my spirit.

"Praise the Lord," shouted Brother Blow and others in the audience. At first I found it awkward to speak through the *Amens* and *Hallelujahs*. Many times I had been heckled and jeered by hostile groups when I was in politics. The memory of an Irish dinner in New York during the 1972 campaign, when I was almost driven off the stage by IRA sympathisers, flashed through my mind. I had tried to outshout the crowd, then had lost my train of thought.

Yet now the more I shouted, the more enthusiastic Blow and his followers became. Then suddenly I found I was no longer being distracted. Instead I was moving right along with the rhythm. The words came out with more feeling and excitement than ever before. Love and joy and power were surging through the room. What began as a quiet testimony almost turned into a revival meeting. Some of the inmates were involved as well. As a windup I said, "Praise the Lord that I am in prison and have this chance to be a witness for Jesus Christ."

Brother Blow bounded out of his chair, rushed to the altar, and nearly smothered me in an embrace. His long arm around me, he prayed, then issued an altar call. "Hallelujah," he shouted out. "Come forward or just raise your hand and you will receive right now the salvation of Jesus Christ and the washing of His blood at Calvary.

The final hymn of the night was sung so loudly that I imagined the warden himself might be able to hear us as he sat in the living room of his home several hundred yards beyond the prison entrance. The repsonse from Brother Blow's parishioners who were present was enthusiastic, but I was not sure how the message had been received by the inmates. Had I spoken over their heads? Had I held myself out to be too important? Did they still look at me as one of them? I walked to the back of the room where most of the inmates were now congregated. Lee, Paul, and Amos were standing together, all flashing the biggest warmest smiles I had ever seen on any faces. Their expressions gave me the answer.

During the week that followed, interest in the prison fellowship grew. God had used the testimony. Men were seeking. The tension and anxiety would continue – I knew that – but for all the oppressiveness of prison life, I had felt that movement of God's Spirit among us. More and more I could see how the Lord was guiding my life. Just knowing this was a foundation of assurance for the rough days ahead.

25

Unexpected Gift

With the first brisk chill of autumn in the air, Mr. Bleven asked me to issue winter clothing to all the prisoners, chiefly surplus dark brown Army field jackets. As we opened box after box, out fell the most threadbare collection of old rags I'd even seen; the jackets had long frayed strings hanging from the cuffs, elbows punched through, large gaping tears in the fabric. Whatever warmth the garments once contained had been so worn or washed out that there would be little protection against the damp, raw Alabama winter.

As we passed them out to the men, I looked again for the hostile eyes that might reveal my would-be assassin. It was useless. Most of the men were angry – but it was at the poor quality of winter clothing they were receiving.

That wasn't all we had to gripe about. In the warehouse we uncovered crates of surplus but little-worn, down-filled officers' flight jackets which an enterprising supply officer had rescued from the Air Force dump. But we could not use them; they were a light green colour and prison regulations demanded that all clothing be deep chocolate-brown. Then we began experimenting by loading them two at a time into the washing machines, trying different dark dyes. Success. They came out limp and shrunken replicas of the originals, but a deep brown shade. Snugness was a small price to pay for keeping warm.

Dye was the next problem. It wasn't on the prison supply list and Bleven's petty-cash account was used up. Obtaining dye was all that stood between 250 fluffy warm jackets and

250 half-frozen prisoners. As word spread of the availability of jackets and my eagerness to dye them, inmates began appearing in the laundry room, usually on Monday mornings, carrying small brown boxes. Bleven was sympathetic, turning the other way as one prisoner after another slipped the contraband into my hand. By mid-October, it was a thriving nonprofit business. I was troubled that the dye had to be smuggled in, but getting around idiotic regulations had always stimulated me and helping the men was now my main purpose in life.

In my enthusiasm, I enlisted the service of Woodie, a well-educated, good-looking young man who had been given an eighteen-month sentence for buying and selling stolen cars. Eager to have a flight jacket, Woodie offered to help bring in the contraband.

On a mid-October weekend Patty reluctantly brought six packets of dye from Washington. During visiting hours Patty and I spent time with Woodie and his attractive young wife in the yard. Glancing around to be sure a guard wasn't watching, Woodie took two packets under the table from Patty, stuffing them into his trouser pockets. I felt no pangs of conscience; the more jackets I could get to the inmates, the better off they would be. Smuggling in personal items was a fairly routine practice, though risky. Prisoners caught at it were sometimes transferred; at the least it meant a couple of nights in the hole.

Patty was worried, but Woodie was completely unconcerned. He had insisted that he bring the dye in, assuring me that he would never be searched. The guards normally spot-check men going in and out of the visitors' area, usually searching only prisoners with narcotics convictions. At the end of the day Woodie and I left the visitors' area together heading straight for our familiar position overlooking the street to wave good-bye to our wives. Woodie was walking a few steps ahead as we passed the Control Room. All at once two guards stepped forward.

"In here," one commanded. The other grabbed Woodie's arm and yanked him through the door.

I dared not stop, but slowed my walk long enough to hear one of the guards shout, "Strip down!"

Was he being shoved into the hole? Had someone seen him take the box from Patty. Had someone "ratted?" With sinking heart I realized that Woodie was due for a parole hearing next month. "What have I done?" I muttered to myself, my stomach churning. If my young friend was in deep trouble, I was responsible. He was almost a kid; I was supposedly the mature one. The idea had been stupid and wrong. No matter how silly the rule seemed to me, it represented authority which I had pledged myself to honour.

I returned to the dormitory and sought out Paul, telling him the whole story. By now the dye had been found for sure and Woodie was in the hole. The next day was a Monday holiday; Woodie's wife would arrive at eight, anxious to be with her husband. I couldn't bear it – the look of pain on her sweet face when she found out. Her husband could very well be hauled off this night to the city jail where he would be held for later transfer. That was often done and families would be out of contact for weeks.

"Okay brother, what do I do?" I asked Paul. "I have to take the responsibility. Should I go to the lieutenant and tell him everything?"

Paul shook his head. "Spilling the story will only get you transferred and that won't help Woodie. The warden sure won't show any favouritism to you. Smuggling is serious with him. Let's see what's happened to Woodie first."

Surely Woodie would come to our dormitory if he had been released. The minutes ticked slowly by. No sign of him. Now I was certain of the worst. We sat waiting right through dinner. Paul volunteered to look in his dorm, just to be certain – and then go to the hole. If a decent guard was on duty, Paul might be allowed to talk with him. I was now resigned to my fate. If Woodie was in the hole, I'd turn myself in. It had to be that way.

Paul, downcast, returned ten minutes later with the dreaded report, "He is in the hole, but he'd like to see you. They're going to ship him out."

Those next few moments were agony. Why had I been so stupid as to destroy everything I had tried to build up at Maxwell? I had refused to heed the reminder in my diary that week – a note to myself to resist succumbing to the little temptations of prison life. "As a Christian I cannot engage in the commonplace things inmates do to make life a little bit more bearable here," I wrote. "I must avoid the little bends and twists in the rules, the little lies."

Looking at those words made me almost physically sick. How could I be so hypocritical as to say one thing to myself and do another? The truth is that to have a chance at a furlough, prisoners lie, enlarge the facts, create emergencies. The prison officials expect it – encourage it, in fact – to build the proper record in the files. Games are played this way in prison as elsewhere, both sides using the same rules.

Sitting there on my bunk, staring bleakly at Paul, a crushing new thought rammed into my consciousness. Did I learn nothing from Watergate? How could I forget that a series of little lies can eventually blur one's capacity to see moral distinctions about big things? Months before at a Monday session at Fellowship House we had concluded that little lies are as corrosive to a man's character as big ones; it is only a question of degree and how long it takes. Now I'd fallen into this trap myself.

I told Paul of my decision and we walked together from the dorm towards the lieutenant's office. All of the worst imaginable thoughts rushed through my mind. Paul was doing his best to console me : "Maybe they'll give you a second chance, Chuck. Maybe you and Woodie will be shipped to the same joint."

Halfway across the courtyard we passed in front of Woodie's dormitory. Paul grabbed my arm, an enigmatic look on his face. "Let's go in here first, Chuck."

"There's no point in postponing things, Paul. Let's get it over with," I said grimly.

But Paul was persistent. Finally a big grin spread over his face. "We'll get Woodie and then the two of you can turn yourselves in together."

I stood staring, aware that all colour had drained from my face. "You're kidding."

"Come on," he laughed. "Woodie is taking a nap."

My friend had made it through the shakedown. The guards were looking for narcotics and paid no attention to the dye he carried. Paul was laughing harder than I'd ever seen him before, pointing at my white face, and doubling over. I was too relieved to be angry, too emotionally drained to speak.

It was a lesson learned. How easy it is to backslide, to succumb unknowingly to temptations of the moment. I was concerned only with helping the other men – or so I thought – but in part it was the old Colson. *Chuck will get it done* was the phrase I so loved to hear in the White House.

Strange are the workings of a prison. When I announced that there would be no more smuggling of dye, Mr. Bleven made arrangements to purchase all the dye we needed. In short order all inmates were outfitted with warm jackets.

The easy way I had slid into my old pattern of behaviour with the dye operation shook me deeply. How had it happened? I was part of a fellowship, praying together with Christians. Ordinarily one of the group should have checked me: "Chuck, about this dye business. Is it really honest – what you are doing? I know it's for a good cause, but does one right and one wrong equal right?" The question would have stopped me cold. It was Watergate all over again. The end justified the means. What a trap that philosophy can be!

There has to be another way to accomplish good besides slipping into grey morality. What does Christ suggest for this special power? In all my intense study of His life over the past fifteen months, He had given me the answer. Yet it was elusive. I went searching through my Bible again. There it was in the first chapter of Acts. Jesus said to his disciples, "But when the Holy Spirit has come upon you, you will receive power..." (Acts 1 : 8 LB).

I had studied the Trinity, learned to understand how the Father, the Son, and the Holy Spirit are different, yet the same. I had asked for the Holy Spirit to guide and strengthen me. But it suddenly occurred to me that I had not asked the Holy Spirit to fill me with power.

And then came one of those marvellous demonstrations of God's timing. That very Monday night Martin Gay announced that the next lesson would be on the power of the Holy Spirit. "It is possible," the soft-spoken teacher explained, "to ask in prayer for God to fill us with the Holy Spirit. It works," he said. "We merely have to turn ourselves over to Him."

During the days before the next lesson I reviewed everything I knew about the Holy Spirit, starting with the Book of Acts. The disciples, I saw, had all been rather ineffective people until the Upper Room experience. Then there was this mighty wind and tongues of fire – and the disciples were filled with the Holy Spirit. Timid men suddenly became bold. Courage replaced fear. They had been given power to establish Christ's church.

Yet in the centuries that followed, the term *Holy Ghost* frightened more people than it helped, while the more acceptable words *Holy Spirit* became just a theological utterance in most churches. Then in recent years the charismatic (Holy Spirit) movement had burst upon our world, rocking churches, changing worship forms, making the term *pentecostal* more respectable. Once again Spirit-filled people were finding a new power and boldness to claim God's audacious promises. I had seen some of the gifts of the Spirit in operation, but I knew little about them. Lee Corbin had prayed in tongues and I had sensed power coming into his life. But there was so much I didn't know about the Spirit.

The following Monday night Martin Gay did not intellectualise about the subject. "Ask for it," he said, "and the Holy Spirit can take total control of your life. He will take charge if you open yourselves and *seek* – like a personal relationship with Christ, but something far deeper than the mere acknowledgement of God."

I bowed my head while Gay was fending off questions being tossed at him by two doubting and inquisitive men at the far end of the long table. "Father," I asked silently, "please fill me with Your Spirit. Fill me so full there's room for nothing else, no hatred, no hurt, no bitterness, no exhaustion. Lift me above it all, Father . . ."

And there sitting on a bench in a bare classroom filled with people who were wrangling over theological terms, the most curious effervescent sensation rushed through my body. It was like the cleansing I had experienced in the Phillipses' driveway. It was persistent and I kept praying. If Gay had called on me to speak, I would have never heard him. Then the bubbling sensation turned into a tingling from head to foot, like fever chills but pleasant, comforting, and energising. Joy and new strength were welling up within me.

I kept my head down until Paul, sitting next to me, nudged me with his elbows. "You asleep?" he whispered.

"If I am, you ought to try it." I looked up to see Paul, his index finger up to his pursed lips. I realised I was speaking too loudly. Gay was peering at us through his thick glasses.

"Brother Gay, this is some lesson tonight," I exclaimed, but said no more. The others around the table were still grappling and I must not frighten them off.

I'd often wondered how a person really knew when he was filled with the Spirit. There is no light which goes on or off like the warning light on a dashboard when seat belts are not fastened. This day I had no more doubts. As I wrote in the diary the next morning, "It was almost like a conversion again – the black cloud passed; it was an incredible experience to have my spirit washed clean."

I've heard of people who have experienced this power and were transformed overnight. An alcoholic completely loses his craving for alcohol; a drug addict is so changed and freed from bondage that he does not even go through a withdrawal period. I believe the power of the Holy Spirit can work dramatically this way in us. More often, I surmise, the Spirit resides in us as a great source of new power, but He serves more as a Helper while we develop our own spiritual disciplines.

From the moment of this infilling, I felt a new sharpness in my awareness of life about me. I felt more understanding for prison officials, more love for fellow inmates.

I did ask the Lord to tell me if I could forget the threat on my life, or to show me who it was. This had hung over me too long now. I still found myself face watching at odd moments. Now I brought Him into it directly – "This one, Lord?" as I saw a glowering face across the table at breakfast. Or – "He, Lord?" as I passed a prisoner in the yard who did not return my greeting.

Once I had awakened suddenly in the night, then bolted upright in my bunk, convinced danger was near. For long moments I sat there, heart pounding. All I saw were sleeping forms, snoring, coughing, muttering in their dreams.

At first I thought he was one of the blacks. As a group they had been deeply hostile to Nixon's policies. In prison the blacks usually kept to themselves. Some were quiet and sullen. But as time passed many became friends.

Several times I questioned Jerry to see if by chance he could have been playing a game with me. Each time he firmly repeated his story and just as firmly refused to reveal the one who threatened to kill me.

A few days after my experience in class, I was walking in the compound on my way to the dormitory. Ahead of me were two men walking side by side. One was a handsome black-haired young man who always wore dark sunglasses; the other was perhaps in his mid-forties, a muscular individual whose head squatted bull-like on his broad shoulders. They had bronzed complexions with dark piercing eyes, probably of Eastern European origin. The two – both ex-policemen I was told – were always together, always unsmiling. As I approached their backs, the inner voice seemed to say – "Now, Chuck."

I quickened my pace until I was alongside, and heard these words come from my lips: "Did you want to talk to me?"

The older, heavyset man wheeled around, his face reddened, squinting eyes smouldering.

"I've been wanting to talk to you," I said.

He stared speechless for a moment, but the scowl deepened. The tall, younger man turned to him and said, "Go ahead and find out now. Ask him."

The older man kept staring at me. Then in a deep, gruff voice he asked, "Do you know what happened to me?"

"Maybe," I replied. "You're a busted cop, right?"

"No, a busted Chicago police lieutenant. And busted because of you politicians in Washington. Framed and hung by your lousy White House, that's what."

"And you blame me?" I asked.

"Does that surprise you? You were the guy who ordered the Chicago investigation. It's true, isn't it?" His voice rose in anger at the bitter memories.

"Look, Lieutenant," I spoke calmly, "I know all about the Mayor Daley investigation. I know who started it. It wasn't the White House; it was the Justice Department. If there were political reasons, they didn't come from me. I had nothing to do with it. That's the truth; you can believe it or not."

As I stared into his tense, angry face, I felt certain at long last that this was the man Jerry had overheard. "And by the way," I added, "I know what it's like to be a political target. Believe me, I know how you feel." The words came out with deep emotion.

"I guess you do. Yeah, I guess you do." His voice was softening, but his eyes still bored into mine.

We swapped tales of the agonies of our prosecutions. His story was of evidence stacked against him, how others had lied and implicated him, how he could have gotten off by laying it on higher-ups, but had refused. I told him about the prosecutors, the angry, bitter questioning, the squeeze put on my staff, how I could have turned on Nixon but did not.

"I think you're levelling with me," he said finally. And his steel grip as we shook hands told me that we were no longer enemies. How serious his threat had been I'll probably never know. But thanks to the work of the Holy Spirit, I had been able to seek out my oppressor and turn hostility into understanding.

26

Spiritual Warfare

The gentle white-haired mountaineer, Homer Welsh fell ill during the third week of October. The flu, we thought. For several days he was excused from work and lay in his bunk hour after hour. Homer had begun attending our evening prayer sessions, and after the fever struck we would adjourn early and pray with him at his bunk just before lights out. Paul brought him food which he rarely ate and cold drinks which he craved for a parched throat.

When Homer did not improve he was taken to the base hospital for tests and then to the tiny, bare two-bedded room just off the infirmary. There Welsh remained while his 103-degree fever stubbornly defied massive doses of antibiotics.

When the lab reports came back, one of the inmates in the infirmary whispered to us the discouraging news – a spot on Welsh's lung, pneumonia at best, and not a good sign for a man who'd spent much of his life in soot-filled mines. There was blood in his urine and his white corpuscle count was high. It was a grim prognosis.

During this same week in rapid succession began a series of setbacks, accidents, and outbursts of violence. It was devastating, bewildering, and brought me face-to-face with the unseen enemy. In my pre-Christian years any talk in my circles of the devil or Satan as an entity had been in a jocular vein. I reasoned that the evil men did was a part of man's nature. Even after my acceptance of Jesus as a Person and later awareness that His Spirit was with us today, I still viewed demonology as something akin to black magic.

My thinking changed in prison. I soon discovered that there

was no clear distinction between good and evil men. Many who had a sense of decency and goodness in them had committed gross sins while in the grip of some kind of evil power. I no longer could accept the idea that some men simply had an evil nature. All men are sinners, Scripture taught me, struggling between the two forces: God and Satan, good and evil. It doesn't matter whether we imagine Satan as a man dressed in a red suit brandishing a pitchfork, or whether we think of him as an invisible force. Whatever you call him (or it), there is an evil power which works in the world touching the lives of men.

Doug Coe once explained that Satan doesn't waste his time on those unbelievers who follow the world's ways; in time they drift into his fold without much persuasion. But those who choose Jesus Christ are Satan's chief enemy and the real threat to his rule. Like any good battlefield commander, the devil saves his best firepower for his foes' best divisions. Thus have history's most stalwart believers been tested, tried, and forced to withstand Satan's fiercest onslaughts.

Obviously Satan had claimed Maxwell as his territory long ago and wasn't about to surrender it easily. He had not worried about a few religious services every now and then, but the changing of men's hearts was something to take seriously. As for inviting the Holy Spirit into Maxwell, and then bringing men together to pray for each other and for the prison officials – well, that called for an all-out counterattack.

A small incident, hardly more than a college-type prank, opened the lid. Two inmates slipped out of their dorms one evening, found a can of yellow paint in one of the worksheds behind the compound, and went to work. Insulting epithets aimed at the warden were scrawled on the walls of buildings and on the side of the rickety prison bus. Early the next morning a tight-lipped warden was on the scene surveying the vandals' work. Barely able to contain his anger, he marched with long determined strides back to his office. Within an hour, over the loudspeaker came the first official reaction: "From now on, all areas behind the dormitories and all grassed areas beyond the roadway are out-of-bounds after dark. This curfew will remain in effect until further notice."

Despite an extensive investigation, the warden never found the inmates responsible. There is seldom any real détente between prisoners and officials. What passes as tranquillity is usually only an uneasy absence of confrontation. The pent-up anger which smoulders inside every prison now began to heat up fast.

That night two prisoners in another dorm started an argument over something trivial. Soon fists were flying, one man throwing the other across several bunks. No one broke it up until the guards arrived. Both men were taken to the hospital where a gash over the younger man's right eye required extensive stitches. Then they were tossed into the hole. The next day prison justice was administered. Who started the fight didn't seem to matter. There were no hearings, no appeals, no second chances. Both men were led out in chains and handed over that afternoon to U.S. Marshals for delivery to other prisons.

Patty had met the young wife of one of these men. She discovered later that he was not allowed to call her, even though she was right there in Montgomery. It would be weeks before the young girl found her husband. Such is the way the PC (Prisoner Coordination) system operates for moving prisoners. The PC system sounds reasonable enough, but in fact is one of the harshest forms of punishment.

When a prisoner is to be moved, local officers notify Washington where, in the headquarters of the U.S. Marshal Service, the information is fed into a computer. Data about the movement of all marshals is similarly recorded in this computer. In machine fashion, prisoners and marshals are brought together. It may be economical and work fine in theory, but in fact prisoners are moved about like pieces of luggage, often "lost" in local jails for weeks at a time waiting to be picked up by a marshal.

These temporary and unnecessary delays in open cement cells jammed full of violent criminals result in some devastating experiences for young or inexperienced prisoners. The Fulton County Jail in Georgia is a favourite dumping ground for men from Maxwell. There in the overcrowded hundred-year-old institution, broiling hot in the summer, icy cold in winter, sixteen men have sometimes been locked in one open twenty-foot-square cell for days. There is only one toilet, one washbasin, no windows, and four tiers of wooden slabs for beds. The inmates may be drunken vagrants, murderers awaiting trial, or federal prisoners in transit. I met men who after a few days in such holes were in severe shock. Some had spent months in transit in the PC system subjected to indescribable horrors. Permanent scars are hard to avoid.

Several nights later, while we were still discussing ways to try and help the wives of the transferred prisoners, the loudspeaker blared: "Return to your dormitories, count time." Then the shrill whistle. Ten minutes went by, usually enough to complete the tally. Sensing something out of the ordinary, we gathered at the door and peered into the compound. In the yard the guards were frantically running back and forth shouting to the Control Room now ablaze with lights. A prisoner had gone over the fence.

We soon discovered that the missing inmate was a gaunt, silent black who had come from fifteen months in maximum-security prisons. Though he had but a few months to serve, something snapped. He could not take another day of confinement. When recaptured days later, years were added to his sentence.

Early that week Doc Krenshaw was scheduled for release. The day before his freedom he discovered that the necessary paperwork had not been completed. Standing before a prison official's desk, Doc flew into a screaming rage. "I almost hit him, Chuck – I was almost out of control," he told me that night. So overwhelming are the pressures during the last days of confinement that even someone as even tempered as Doc nearly snapped.

Tensions continued to mount, fed to a great extent by a prisoner named Knight, who had been given a one-year sentence for passing bad cheques. A bright, scrappy rebel, Knight set up his "office" in the Maxwell library shortly after his arrival. Soon he was producing for himself and a dozen other inmates an array of writs to be filed in court. I watched him each night as he methodically prepared for the assault, counselling with other aggrieved prisoners, carefully studying the tattered legal-form book in the library, pecking away at an old typewriter, amassing logical challenges to the prison's furlough policy, its inadequate medical facilities, the parole process, the whole range of things governing a prisoner's life.

Knight took a perverse delight in antagonising the warden. During that same hectic week he typed out daily announcements describing the writs filed, the reactions of the camp administrators, and their repressive countermeasures. Each night he posted copies on the bulletin boards at the entrance of each dormitory. The guards would then sweep through the camp tearing them off the walls.

One day the warden himself came through each dorm. I watched him angrily fling open the glass door covering the bulletin board, snatch the paper off the wall, crumple it in his hands, slam the door shut, almost breaking the glass, and storm off. An inspection of all typewriters in the camp was ordered to locate the machine used. New regulations were then published – typewriters could no longer be used for other than official business.

Even honest efforts to communicate seemed ill-fated. I was following a tall prisoner through the mess-hall line one day. Warden Grunska was behind the serving counter inspecting a large pan of stew. When the man in front of me was across from the warden, Grunska looked up. Their eyes met. "How's it going fella?" Grunska asked cheerily.

The man was so taken aback – he had probably never had the chance to speak to the warden before – that he stammered for a moment, then told the warden that the TV in his dormitory had been broken for a week. "Any chance of getting it fixed?" he asked timidly.

The warden's smile vanished. "As soon as people around here start behaving themselves," he snapped. With that he turned and marched away leaving the young lad staring in bewilderment.

One prisoner thrown in the hole that week was a middle-aged Texan by the name of Rodriguez. From the day he arrived at Maxwell it was obvious that he was an alcoholic who needed psychiatric and medical help. At night he would sit on his bunk chain-smoking and shaking uncontrollably; then he would pace nervously about the compound. Already he had had two seizures.

Early that demoralising week Rodriguez passed out on the dormitory floor. An ambulance was summoned from the base hospital, and the two corpsmen carried him away on a stretcher. He was placed under heavy sedation and returned the next day to the prison. The next morning Rodriguez became embroiled in an argument in the mess hall with a huge fellow inmate who smashed Rodriguez across the side of his head with his fist, knocking him to the floor. The incident was reported to the Control Room and two guards carted Rodriguez off to the hole. Nothing was done to his assailant who was a favourite of the front office.

Rodriguez spent that day in the hole, most of the time crying in pain, peering out through the small steel mesh-covered opening in the door, calling for a doctor. No one paid any attention to his cries. Late that afternoon, a marshal's van was pulled up outside. Two muscular guards opened the door to Rodriguez's cell and handcuffed him. "Where am I going?" he cried. Prisoners who are being removed for disciplinary reasons are generally not told, but one of the guards answered, "The Montgomery city jail."

"Oh, no," Rodriguez was pleading. "Get me a doctor. Can't you see my ear is bleeding?" A stream of deep red was running from inside his ear, over his earlobe and down his neck, soaking his torn collar.

The two guards looked at Rodriguez's ear, looked at one another, then shrugged. One snapped, "There is no doctor on duty and we have orders to move you right now. The van is here. We can't keep the marshal waiting." I was standing nearby and watched helplessly while the two men dragged the struggling prisoner to the door. Rodriguez turned to me with a frightened expression on his face and shouted, "You see I'm bleeding, don't you, Colson?"

"Yes, I do," I responded firmly. "You need a doctor."

Both guards stopped dead in their tracks, turned and stared at me. For a moment I thought they were going to bring Rodriguez back and take him down the hall to the infirmary. It was only a momentary pause. The two blue-shirted men put their hands under Rodriguez's armpits, lifted his feet off the floor and carried him to the waiting van. There was nothing left now but a few blood stains on the tile floor. I felt nauseous, helpless. Nor was I ever able to learn what happened to this pathetic man.

Late that same tumultuous week Paul found me in the laundry. His eyes were filled with hurt and saying not a word he thrust a small piece of paper into my hands. It was a short terse notice from the regional director of the Parole Board: "There are no circumstances warranting a decision outside the 'guidelines' established for your offence ... continue to expiration. Parole denied." That single sheet of paper went against the ruling given Paul only a few weeks ago and doomed him to another two years in prison.

Remembering how our prayers for Paul and Ferguson had been so miraculously answered, the thought flashed through both our minds: *Could God have now abandoned Paul? Could He revoke His own work?* Hardly. We were being tested.

"Don't worry, Paul. We'll appeal it and beat them," I said. "By now I'm the best jailhouse lawyer around." Paul could not even manage a smile at my forced humour. The challenge to us was clear – with God's help, fight for Paul's freedom.

Next it was Lee Corbin. One night that week while in the library I saw him approach, ashen-faced, lips quivering, "What's the matter, Lee?" I asked.

"Chuck, I've got to see you right away. I need help." We walked into the darkness just outside the library door. "Chuck, it's my wife. She wants to leave me. I don't know what to do."

The big, burly ex-Marine was trembling all over, his shoulders heaving as he fought back the tears. It was painful as he slowly explained it all. When arrested he sold his big home in Atlanta and moved his wife and two small children back to a small town near Asheville, North Carolina, to be close to his relatives. Lee's wife took a job nights in a textile plant, making just enough to feed their children and keep up the payments on the trailer which Lee had purchased with his last dollars before entering prison. At first she wrote faithfully, then less frequently until the letters stopped altogether. She had not been able to visit him in prison because their old car had broken down. She had no phone. Worried, Lee had telephoned his brother-in-law who lived a few miles away. That's when he learned the bad news.

"I guess I deserve it," he sobbed. "It's not her fault. Her brother says she still loves me, and I love her so much. She is on her way to her parents' house now. I've got to get there or I will lose her. She and the little ones are all I have left in the world; they need me. If only I can get home, I can save my marriage."

Surely the prison officials would recognise this situation as a bona fide *emergency*, I thought. In the regulations one of the stated reasons for furloughs is "to maintain family ties."

But when Lee asked the officer on duty for an emergency furlough, it was denied. "If there's been a serious accident or someone is critically ill and the doctor calls, then I can phone the warden," the lieutenant said tersely. "Otherwise, I have no authority."

Lee, sobered by the rebuff, turned to me, "I'm going to leave tonight. I'm going over the fence. You shouldn't know anything about it because I don't want to get you into trouble. But I have to do it."

Corbin was calm, his words measured and cold as steel. He had been in prison since early spring with not one disciplinary mark. Only a few months remained on his sentence. He knew the consequences of trying to escape, but at the moment nothing mattered beyond being with his family. Lee was big and tough; I couldn't hold him if I wanted to.

I said the only thing that might stop him : "Lee, unless you give me your oath to God that you will not do that, I'm going back to the lieutenant and tell him exactly what you said. I'll have him put you in the hole tonight. I'm not going to let you ruin your life."

Lee knew I meant it. "Maybe we'd better do just that," he said, "I can't control myself. I gotta go in the hole."

As Lee calmed down, I explained that if he turned himself in this way, he would lose any chance for furlough and would probably be transferred into a maximum-security prison. Just talking about it brought Corbin to his senses. We prayed together quietly for a few minutes; Lee then left to try to reach his wife on the phone.

Later Lee reported back that he had talked with his wife and asked her to pray with him over the phone. "She told me to cut out all the religious stuff," Lee said, "but I had a feeling that the Lord was really working on her. She says she still loves me and won't do anything foolish until I can come home, if I can come soon." The pressure was eased temporarily, although Lee's painful anxiety was to continue.

That night I was in the office when I saw a young man with pock-marked face and sunken cheeks approach Peyton, the official on duty. "My brother has died. I got to get home for the funeral." The young man's grief-filled eyes were pleading for help.

"What do you expect me to do?" Peyton growled. "Go fill out the forms and bring them to me. I can't do anything without a proper written request. You should know that."

There was no "I'm sorry," not even a sympathetic expression. As the young prisoner walked dejectedly away, Peyton shouted after him, "And do it right the first time. There's nothing that annoys me more than having to do those forms over again." Peyton's lanky frame was draped over the chair, his legs stretched out, his head shaking in disgust that the young man had been so inconsiderate of him.

I bit my tongue and turned away in anger. I couldn't look at Peyton. Christ said to love your oppressor, but I could only feel utter contempt for this guard and his arrogance – for the whole camp, in fact – for the whole ugly week that had just passed.

I wanted to shut it all out of my mind: the disease-ridden body of Welsh as he was taken to the hospital, the bloody, senseless fight which further messed up the lives of two prisoners and their families, the pathetic man who had gone over the fence, the callous treatment of Rodriguez, the hurt in Paul's eyes when parole was denied, the look of pain and anguish on Corbin's face when he feared he had lost his wife. Now the sickening exchange between Peyton and the young prisoner put the cap on this miserable, depressing week.

Thank God for my experience with the Holy Spirit the week before. Beset from all sides, I called upon the power of His Spirit to keep me from doing something foolish – to help me stand firm, to be an encourager to the others. Our foursome continued to meet each night in the classroom. At least they had not closed this off to us. We accepted the fact that prison is friendly terrain for Satan's warriors. As God is Love, so Satan is hate. Hate, hence Satan, abounds in every prison like a mildew-bred fungus, its spores nurtured by suspicion, jealousy, anger, depression. Hate was mushrooming at Maxwell during this terrible week, threatening to engulf all of us. We prayed that the sunshine of our faith would blot out this ugly spongy growth.

Our prayers were answered. It began with Paul. For a while he had been so dejected by the adverse parole ruling that he could do little but wallow in silence and self-pity. Late in the week he broke through the cloud over him. "Chuck, I know this is a testing time for me and I'm not going to allow it to shake my faith."

Something began to sing in me. Too many believe that merely by accepting Christ, they will henceforth be delivered from all hazards and dangers in life, that He will produce all good things from par golf scores to freedom from prison. The disappointments and defeats which inevitably come only make us even more vulnerable than before to Satan's attacks. Paul was learning to tough it out with the Lord. Once more in his quiet way he imparted strength to others, seeking out men in need. The following week he brought to the Lord one young man who was going through a period of great anxiety.

Lee Corbin then began to feel God's love working in him. He decided he could not leave prison with any resentment towards his wife. All he wanted when he was released was for them to be able to share together their love and their faith. Lee's whole demeanor changed. His smile became more radiant. Other inmates began to seek him out for help. During church services the next Tuesday he gave an eloquent spontaneous talk, admitting with a refreshing candour that he had once been a "phoney preacher." He had fallen but was now working his way back. That the prison continued to deny his furlough request did nothing to dim God's Spirit in him.

A standard battlefield tactic I learned in Marine basic training is to cut off your enemy from his main line of supply. Satan had done just that for a while; for days we were so preoccupied with all that was going wrong that we failed to use the power of the Spirit to check the assaults. Once we did, the clouds parted and the sun shone through. The bonds of the fellowship tightened. The power surged back.

Homer Welsh was showing no improvement. He was still lying in one of the infirmary hospital beds, his spirit slowly sinking, his fever uncontrolled. Paul and I took turns sitting with him, bringing him pitchers of cold drinks we'd purchased at the commissary. Homer would force a smile during our visits, but his pathetic fear-filled eyes stabbed us.

The first Saturday of November we knew Homer's condition was grave. Amos, the pharmacist, pointed out that a severe fever over a ten-day period could permanently damage an older man. He was not responding to antibiotics; a red rash had broken out all over his body. The chances of his getting decent medical care were slim. It could be another week before he would be transferred to the base hospital.

"Do each of you guys believe in Christ's power to heal?" I asked my three sombre-faced brothers.

Lee was the first to reply, "I sure do."

Paul thought for a moment and then nodded. Amos was more sceptical. "I'm not sure about this faith-healing business, but I gotta admit that nothing else is working."

I then described an earlier experience with Harold Hughes when, through all-out prayer and a total relinquishment of his ailment to the Lord, he was spared a serious operation. "But," I warned, "each one of us must believe. If any of us has any doubts that Homer can be healed, let's speak them now. We must be as one in our hearts, agreeing totally that Jesus heals today, just as He did two thousand years ago."

While I believed every word I was saying, inside I was just as frightened as my brothers. It is one thing to know the truth in abstract terms; it's something else again to trust, to be bold about it. There is always the fear of failure and embarrassment in the eyes of others. This time I decided I would rather be a fool if need be, than not try anything for the kindly white-haired man lying so helplessly in pools of his own sweat.

We decided to think it over for the next few hours. If there were reservations, the doubters would not participate. Otherwise, we ageed to meet in Welsh's room to pray for his healing at nine o'clock that night. I checked for a late report with one of the prison attendants who seemed to know his business. "There has been no break in his fever and the tests overall were very negative. Don't tell him this, but the doctor at the base is concerned. Possible complications. Maybe a malignancy somewhere. They are talking about clemency – so he can go home to die."

At nine o'clock the four of us gathered in Welsh's room. No dropouts. Homer was happy to see us, but so totally exhausted he would doze off even as we talked to him. We told him that we wanted to put complete faith in Christ's power to heal and that if he would do the same and pray with us, we believed in the depths of our hearts that he would be made well. Homer didn't need to be apprised of the medical reports; he knew that he was a desperately sick man. He looked first into my eyes, then around the bed at each of the brothers. No one spoke. Then he nodded and mumbled a faint "Thank you."

The four of us knelt beside the bed. Homer turned his body towards us and buried his face in his hands. Each of us prayed aloud. Corbin began – in the name of Jesus commanding Satan to come out of Homer's body. Then he asked for the power of the Holy Spirit to fill Homer and continued his prayer in tongues. I felt the Spirit flood into the room, as Corbin's chant gained in intensity and emotion.

"Lord," I prayed, "I thank You in advance for this healing." Then I went on to claim the victory.

Paul, who always prayed in a hushed and subdued voice, boldy proclaimed that night his complete faith in the power of Jesus Christ to heal men's bodies just as He had healed our hearts. Amos thanked God for the miracle of the moment and dropped his head to the floor in total submission.

It would have been an incongruous sight had anyone walked in on us that evening – the former White House hatchet man on his knees beside an old coal miner from the hills of Tennessee; Corbin, a great hulking ex-con man crying out to Jesus and uttering thoroughly unintelligible sounds; Kramer, the young ex-cocaine peddler, in total submission, praising God – all three of us former tough, pragmatic Marines. Finally Amos, in his own quiet way radiating kindness, the humble but scientific-minded pharmacist.

We prayed for more than a half-hour. As we finished, I felt the same surge of joy I first experienced in the Bible study a week before. As if some force was lifting me to my feet, I bounded up and shouted, "Hallelujah !" I had never done that before either, usually being pensive after prayer.

Corbin jumped to his feet grinning. Then he leaned over the bed and grabbed the startled wide-eyed mountaineer in his arms. For a moment I thought he might pull Homer right out of bed. Corbin kept hugging him, indifferent to Homer's soaking-wet body. We all stood there smiling as at a victory celebration. None of us doubted that a healing was under way.

The next morning I was up early to check our patient. Not wanting to wake Homer if he was sleeping, I quietly opened the door to the little room just a crack and peered in. Homer was sitting up in bed wide-awake. He looked towards the door, spotted me and shouted, "Praise the Lord. I love you guys. I love you brothers."

I stood in the door stunned. Even when he was well, Welsh was shy and reserved, usually talking in such a low voice that I had to strain to hear him. Now his voice was strong, firm, ringing through the room. He seemed totally changed, not only physically but in his personality as well. To my relief he no longer called me *sir*. Though still pale and drawn, a giant smile covered his face.

"The fever's gone," he shouted. "It's gone. It left me right after you fellows did last night. I slept like a baby for the first time in a week. I'm ready to get out of bed right now. The Lord has healed me."

I was so excited I ran back to the dormitory, waking the others. They dressed and followed me back to Homer's room. My feet were hardly touching the ground as I found myself praising God for putting me in this prison. "This place needs Your man, Lord, more than it needs a doctor. Thank You for letting me be here. Thank You, thank You. This moment is worth it all."

That evening we visited and prayed again with Homer who was sitting up in bed beaming at us. On Tuesday he was examined at the base hospital. All of the tests – blood, urine, and X-rays – were negative, and the next day he was discharged and returned to the dormitory. "We'll let Squibb and the doctors take all the credit," Lee laughed, "but we know better."

That day I noticed the change in the prison. The angry, oppressive atmosphere was gone. The mood was more relaxed, less tense. Voices had lowered. Even the most melancholy of the men seemed brighter, more alive. The unseen battle between the strongest forces in the world was over – for now.

27

A Time to Be Free

My transfer back to Holabird Prison in Baltimore came unexpectedly in mid-November. Once again I was to be a witness, this time in the Watergate trial of Bob Haldeman, John Ehrlichman, and John Mitchell.

I left Maxwell with strangely mixed feelings, hating the place but loving so many of the people. Saying good-bye to Paul, Lee, Amos, Homer, and the others was a deeply emotional time. Like the four at Fellowship House, these men were now my Christian Brothers; even in a few months close ties had been woven. We had been through a lot together; we cared about each other.

Homer Welsh walked with me to the Control Room. Gone was the obsequious deference he had always shown me. "I'll be praying for you, Chuck," he said smiling.

"I'll need it more than ever the next few months," I said – more a prophet than I realized.

Homer stood by the driveway as I walked towards the marshal's car. I looked back once to wave and saw the old man's eyes glistening in the late autumn sun.

At Holabird there was little change. Some old faces gone, a few new ones. Herb Kalmbach and John Dean greeted me warmly. Jeb Magruder wasn't sure how to take me. The hostility that had once put us in opposing camps had abated somewhat, but there was a healing needed in our relationship.

My testimony at the Watergate trial in Washington was

heatedly assailed – first by the prosecution, then by the defence. Though called as a defence witness, it was Mitchell's counsel who subjected me to the most searing cross-examination. The simple truth as I saw it did not fit either side's strategy for the case.

Mary McGory scorched me in her column, unable to comprehend that I now saw my only loyalty not to the prosecutors in whose chains I was held, not to men I once served, but to the truth. Some wrote that I unexpectedly turned on my former colleagues; others suggested that I helped Ehrlichman. Most were simply confused and baffled as they searched my motives. It mattered little. The prosecutors played miles of Presidential tapes to the endless delight of the jury and spectators. The defendants tried to rebut their own often inaudible words. The outcome was predictable: my onetime cohorts were being marched towards judgement as surely as members of the French aristocracy were made to kneel before the blade two hundred years earlier.

When the verdict of guilty was announced on New Year's Day, Dean bounded into my room, rubbing his hands. "I've been vindicated."

I stared silently at John. There could be no victories now, I felt, for anyone involved in Watergate; reporters might win prizes, a number of us would write books after prison, unknown politicians would be vaulted into the nation's spotlight as others fell in disgrace, but at what price? It was time for lessons to be learned, all right, but how I ached for my country to move on and for wounded men to rebuild their lives.

Though John Dean and I were not allies in the combat of the trial, we became close, spending long evenings talking, planning our futures, discussing the Bible sometimes, exchanging ideas about the books each of us planned. I valued John's keen intellect. Watergate matured him, changed his values, brought to him a stronger core of integrity than I had seen before Watergate broke over us both.

Herb Kalmbach and I had become warm friends. I marvelled at how Herb, at first unsure of himself and sometimes despondent, had steadily gained strength through the long ordeal.

Watergate had toughened Jeb Magruder, too. He had accepted Christ through the help of a covenant group at Washington's National Prestbyterian Church and its indefatigable pastor, Louis Evans, Jr., who had visited him weekly. Sometimes Jeb and I would pray together.

Other wounds were being bound up, too. Senator Lowell Weicker began an independent investigation of CIA abuses. Through the marshals he asked if I would cooperate through a series of interviews. It was only a few months before that we had nearly come to blows. But that was behind us now. Believing that his investigation was needed, I agreed to help. During the hours we spent togther, the old antagonisms dissolved and I saw a different side to the senator: painstaking conscientiousness over his responsibilities and a deep concern for the country.

Al, Graham, Doug, and Harold trekked to Baltimore as often as the marshals would allow the visits. Near the year's end, they came every Saturday morning. After three hours of fellowship and prayer, the four would file through the chain link gate, climb into the same blue Buick which had delivered me to the marshals six months earlier, and drive away. It was harder for them in some ways than for me, having to leave one of their own standing behind the gate, peering through the mesh and waving good-bye.

The prosecutors decided to keep the four fallen Nixon men at Holabird for as long as the trial continued. I was happy about this. I hadn't realized how fatiguing the months at Maxwell had been, never sleeping in the daytime, sitting up late to talk to needy men. I slept twelve hours a night at Holabird until I reminded myself of Bonhoeffer's warning and put myself back on a more disciplined routine.

It was a break for Patty, too, a respite from the rigours of travelling to Alabama. And my mother, now alone, was able to visit. She did so frequently. Despite her age and poor health, she drove alone from Boston and spent long hours with several prisoners, her lively wit cheering us all.

Despite the somewhat easier living conditions at Holabird, however, I missed the brothers in Alabama. I could barely read Paul Kramer's first letter without choking up:

Chuck, everyone asks when you are coming back ...
Our group has grown, in size and in spirit ... Chuck, I
want you to know we pray for you each night at fellowship. We still see you sitting there with us, shorts, T-
shirt, and pipe ... We are close these days also. Our
group has been so personal. Just like you wanted it to be.
We carry each other's burdens ... We love and miss you
more than you realise. God bless you, Chuck and Patty.

Paul et al ...

On Christmas Eve my heart was so heavy for the men at
Maxwell in their lonely outpost that I spent much of the
evening writing Paul and the others. Since we had been denied
permission to attend midnight services at a local church in
Baltimore, the four Watergate prisoners assembled in Dean's
room. Jeb and I read aloud from the Scriptures about the birth
of Christ. We prayed quietly for each other and our families
and in the silence I asked an extra blessing for the men at
Maxwell.

It was while the jury was still out in the Watergate trial
after Christmas that serious rumours began trickling out
about our imminent release. As is standard practice the four
of us had filed motions asking for reduction of sentence; normally they are routinely rejected. But the judges had not yet
acted on them. They were waiting for something, we knew,
perhaps the trial's end. Our hopes grew as the speculation
became epidemic.

Jeb and I became the activists, suggesting that we petition
the Justice Department, flood President Ford with letters, file
new motions with the judges. Dean, too, was mapping his
campaign. Kalmbach was the first of us eligible for parole,
but his application had been ensnarled in red tape. He had the
most legitimate reason to be impatient. Instead he was the
steadiest of the four.

"Look, fellows," Herb said one evening, just after New
Year, "I've done what I can do; my lawyers are doing everything. I'm just going to trust the lawyers" – he paused, staring
at me – "and the Lord."

Herb was right; his words were like dashing cold water on
my face. I had slipped back into trying to do things *my* way.

How easy it is to fall on your face in the Christian walk. Harold had brought me up short on this very point in December. "Look, Chuck, until you surrender this to the Lord, really put your whole trust in Him, you are simply punishing yourself. Just thank Him for everything. Turn it all over to Him, trust Him and you'll be set free."

"Sure," I snapped back. "It's easy enough for you to say that. You'll be home tonight. I go on day after day – the dreary endless sameness, the closed-in, trapped feeling. It is hell." Harold was right. I knew it. But so desperately did I want my freedom that I was fighting again.

On one point the courthouse tipsters, the lawyers, and Herb, John, Jeb, and I were all agreed – the four of us would be released together or none of us would. Dan and Magruder were government witnesses, which had won them favour, but their offences were more severe than mine or Herb's. Our sentences were comparable and Kalmbach was overdue. No, if one went out, all would go out.

On January 8 I was in Washington for more interrogation on other cases at the prosecutor's office. Our meeting was interrupted midmorning by an emergency phone call: Dean's lawyer calling me. He explained that John was at Holabird and could not call me but had asked him to do so. John wanted me to hear it from him first.

"What is it?" I asked impatiently.

"John has been released today by Judge Sirica," the lawyer said. My heart began racing just the way it did when Ford announced that all of us were being considered for pardon. I waited for him to bring me the good news. "John wanted to be sure you heard it from him, not over the radio," he continued.

"Why?" I asked. "It's great news."

"Well – it is for John," he replied, "and for Jeb and Herb, too, but it's kind of tough on you."

For a long moment I couldn't believe the words pounding into my ears. Magruder, Kalmbach and Dean – all sentenced by Judge Sirica – were set free. I was not. Sentenced by a different judge – Gerhard Gesell – my future was still much in doubt.

By the time I arrived back at Holabird, John, Herb, and Jeb

had already left for home. A heavy pall hung over the ramshackle barracks that night. I walked down the hall and stared into Dean's room where each night the four of us had met. There was nothing but the bed, its dirty mattress bare, two chairs, and the small desk. It was quiet – an eerie silence. On my desk I found a hand-scribbled note:

> Dear Chuck –
> It is difficult to know what to say – other than I know you will soon be freed. Rest assured that I will be calling for your freedom when I'm first confronted by the press.
> Also I will be in touch with you soon – to talk about it all.
> My prayers are with you and my actions will do whatever I can to help –
>
> Your friend,
> John

The evening television news highlighted the release of the three men with scenes of the jubilant homecoming in the Magruder's front yard, neighbours gathered for the welcome, interviews with the families. For Patty, watching it was nearly unbearable. Each weekend she had visited with the other families. Patty, Gail Magruder, and Mo Dean were friends, enjoying the dubious camaraderie of being prison widows together.

The next morning I stayed in my room reading the Scriptures, waiting for the phone to ring on the marshal's desk with the news that I felt had to come. Fittingly, the lesson in my devotional literature, *Our Daily Bread*, for this gloomy day – January 9 – was entitled "The Philosophy of Patience." The key Scripture passage: "Rest in the Lord, and wait patiently for him . . ." (Psalms 37 : 7 KJV).

The only call that day was from Shapiro. "No news," he said, "and the scuttle from the courthouse ain't good. Gesell doesn't like to have anyone think he is being forced to follow Sirica's lead. Hang tough, my boy."

The short days and long nights were without beginning or end. Time seemed to stand still. I stared out of my little room at the prickly strands of barbed wire, tried to read and write, but my mind wandered. The marshals were sympathetic, dropping almost all barriers between captor and captive. A lean, rawboned Southerner named Jack, an all-out believer, was the most helpful. "The Lord will handle this," he said confidently.

The visiting hours were precious now – but hard, too, as I watched Patty suffering the agony of the vigil, our hopes fading each day as freedom – and our own homecoming – seemed to be slipping further and further away. Our prayers together, more fervent now, sustained us.

On January 20 the Virginia Supreme Court announced that I was disbarred. It should not have been the shock it was. Most of the lawyers implicated in Watergate were targets of ceaseless cries for reform: "Clean up the bar – Purge the scoundrels." The Ervin Committee had sent to every State Bar Association computer printouts of every allegation – proven or not – affecting each of us.

I had built false hopes. Although unable to attend the hearing before the Supreme Court in Virginia, the members seemed sympathtic, according to Morin and Mason who argued for me. We had asked for a delay until I could appear personally, but now it was denied.

Two days later I was summoned to the prison office. "It's your attorney," the duty marshal told me as he handed me the phone. The trip-hammer went off inside me again. Stupidly I still believed every call would be the one telling me I was free.

"Chuck, are you ready for a tough one?" The voice on the other end was Ken Adams. *How many tough ones are left?* I wondered. "Go ahead, Ken."

"Your son Christian has been arrested for narcotics possession. He's in jail, but we'll have him out on bail in a few hours."

I couldn't reply; my stomach went again, like someone had kicked me in the middle. Chris, now a freshman at the University of South Carolina, had never caused us any trouble, hardly any worry. He had the kind of personality that everybody loved. We'd talked about drugs, Chris and I, and I was certain he never used them. But it was all too true. Chris had taken school board money advanced to him during Christmas vacation and invested a hundred and fifty dollars in fifteen ounces of marijuana. He hoped to sell it for a quick profit and use the proceeds to replace his old car with one in better condition.

I thought I had been through all the tribulations one person could take. My son in prison seemed the worst blow of all. I knew that Chris had been soured by all that had happened to me, but I never dreamed that it might lead him to do this.

"Now you've got both of us," Chris told the arresting officer in a quote that made the front pages of the papers. It was the frustrated outburst of an eighteen-year-old boy, embittered over what had happened to his dad. That I couldn't be at my son's side made the pain intense.

I never once thought, however, that God had forsaken me. More testing, yes, and more teaching from Him. I knew all the Scriptural references which tell us to praise Him no matter what, but alone by my bunk that cold, bleak January night I simply couldn't bring myself to do it. Surely God could not expect me to praise Him for my son's life being ruined!

And how long must the agony continue? My licence to practise law was gone, my son imprisoned, my dad gone, my compatriots freed and over two years of a three-year sentence still staring me in the face. Though I knew I could not give up, those next days were the most difficult of any that I had spent in prison, probably the most difficult of my life.

Word filtered through that during the first week of February I would be returned to Maxwell, that Holabird was to be closed. It would be good to be with my brothers there again, but I was deeply concerned now for Patty who had been through so much the past two years. How would she take many months of commuting to Alabama? Her sweet gentle nature was near the breaking point.

Charlie Morin had nearly abandoned his law practice, visiting me several times a week and organising a campaign to ask President Ford to pardon me. Ken Adams spent full time on motions and procedures for early parole. Both men visited often. The mail poured in, too, from warmhearted people across the country sympathising that the others were freed and I was still imprisoned. Their encouragement helped sustain me.

Along with Charlie and Ken, the brothers at Fellowship House rallied to my aid. On Tuesday, January 28, Al Quie called: "Chuck, I've been thinking about what else we can do to help you. All of us today signed a letter to the President appealing for mercy, but is there anything else?" The voice on the other end didn't sound like Al; the words came slowly and seemed laden with sadness.

"Al, you guys are doing everything possible," I told him, "and I love you for it. I just don't know what else you can do."

"There's got to be something else, Chuck. I have been thinking —" There was a long pause. "There's an old statute someone told me about. I'm going to ask the President if I can serve the rest of your term for you."

Stunned, I could only stammer a protest. Al Quie with twenty years in Congress, was the sixth-ranking Republican in the House, senior minority member of the Education and Labour Committee, and one of the most respected public figures in Washington. He could not be serious.

"I mean it, Chuck," he said. "I haven't come to this decision lightly."

"I won't let you," I said.

"Your family needs you, and I can't sleep while you're in prison; I think I'd be a lot happier being inside myself." The lump in my throat made it impossible to tell Al how much his offer meant, but that I could not accept it.

That very day Doug Coe sent me a handwritten note. All the brothers would volunteer to serve my sentence, he explained, and then added:

These past three weeks you have been on my mind constantly ... Chuck, a band of like-minded men is being formed by God around the world. The thing you always dreamed of doing for our country and for the people — peace and a better life — can still take place — only now God will get the credit. God only needs men totally com-

mitted to Him – and then the mobilisation of His resources for the common good of all people can take place . . .
If I could I would gladly give my life so you could use the wonderful gifts of God, that He has entrusted you with, to the Glory of God.

I love you, friend – all your companions love you – ! !
As always,
Doug

It was almost more than I imagined possible, this love of one man for another. Christ's love. Al Quie would give up his whole career, Doug Coe would lay down his life, Graham and Harold, too. Isn't that what it's really all about? Isn't that the overwhelming gain of knowing Christ Jesus which makes all else as "loss"? And this day I knew Him as never before. I'd felt his presence all right, but now I knew His power and love through the deep caring of four men. All the pain and agony to mind and body was small in comparison.

It was that night in the quiet of my room that I made the total surrender, completing what had begun in Tom Phillips's driveway eighteen long months before: "Lord, if this is what it is all about," I said, "then I thank You. I praise You for leaving me in prison, for letting them take away my licence to practise law, yes – even for my son being arrested. I praise You for giving me your love through these men, for being God, for just letting me walk with Jesus."

With those words came the greatest joy of all – the final release, turning it all over to God as my brother Harold had told me to do. And in the hours that followed I discovered more strength than I'd ever known before. This was the real mountaintop experience. Above and around me the world was filled with joy and love and beauty. For the first time I felt truly free, even as the fortunes of my life seemed at their lowest ebb.

Forty-eight hours later, five o'clock on Friday afternoon, Judge Gerhard Gesell phoned Dave Shapiro: because of family problems – what had happened to Chris – an order was being prepared to release Charles Colson from prison immediately.

Hours later Jack, the marshal who had been so sympathetic, ran over to us as Patty and I were standing at the front gate at Holabird, bidding good-bye to the small band of inmates.

"The Lord really takes care of His own men," Jack said. "I kind of knew He would set you free today."

"Thank you, brother," I said, "but He did it two nights ago."

Since Then . . .

Five days after his release from confinement, Charles Colson returned to Maxwell Prison to visit Paul Kramer and encourage the men he had been so close to while imprisoned there. This was the first of numerous visits to institutions all over the country which have led Chuck Colson into a full-scale prison ministry.

In June 1975 the Bureau of Prisons approved a proposal by Senator Harold Hughes and Colson to furlough men and women from selected federal institutions to attend fourteen-day retreats and training sessions in the Washington area. These furloughed inmates are selected not by prison officials but by members of Fellowship Foundation after careful interviews and investigation. The training, under the auspices of the Fellowship, focuses on leadership development, and Bible study.

The first group – twelve inmates from six federal prisons in the east – gathered together in Washington in early November 1975. The key-note was trust: the furloughed prisoners – ten men and two women (six whites, six blacks) – were driven to Washington in private cars and housed in the Good News Mission. There were no guards, but complete freedom to come and go.

The results more than reassured any sceptics. The training sessions were businesslike, with much give-and-take. The prisoners volunteered to visit and witness to inmates at the nearby Arlington County Jail and at Lorton Reformatory. One of the group composed a song especially for those he met at Lorton. Singing and praise sessions dominated free periods. During one trip through Washington, two of the prisoners separated from the others, found their way back to the Good News Mission on their own – verification of the trust given them.

Following the two-week course, the inmates returned to their prisons trained to be disciples in serving God and their fellow men. Their key mission: to start prison fellowships. Continued friendship and guidance will be given them while they remain inside, while job opportunities await when they are released. Six similar training sessions are planned for the Washington area in 1976

To develop this prison ministry, Charles Colson is donating to it his speaking fees and a portion of the income from this book. His longtime friend Fred Rhodes took an early retirement from the government in 1975 to give his full time to the Lord's work as Colson's special assistant.

Meanwhile, Paul Kramer continues to serve his sentence at Maxwell – and to serve his Lord through his leadership in the prison fellowship there. Homer Welsh and Lee Corbin have been released. Homer is healthy, employed, and joyfully gives his healing testimony at every opportunity. Lee Corbin, his life rebuilt, is once again at work as an evangelist.

The Lord is healing Watergate wounds in the Colson family, too. Chuck's son Christian was released from jail and enrolled in a youth counselling programme. After four months the state of South Carolina dropped all charges and Chris continues in college, his marks improving. The incident – for which Colson could not praise God at first – has brought father and son closer together.

THE EDITOR

With Gratitude . . .

Neither this book nor the story unfolded in its pages is mine alone. Without such a loving, caring wife I would not have had the strength to weather these years or tackle the task of committing the story to paper. Patty and I have shared times of tears, times of joy. We shared this book as well. Patty took dictation, typed reams of manuscript, suffered my many moods and demands for silence around our home – always with good humour.

Following Dad's death, my mother showed real grit, suffering the pains of my experience with me. I have been richly blessed with a wonderfully supportive family – Chris, Wendell, and Emily, each in his or her own way has given me great strength.

Len LeSourd's remarkable editing skill was a source of continual wonderment – and education. Even as Len left big hunks of my prose on the cutting-room floor (writers have good reason to resent editors), we came closer together in true fellowship. Len made all the work seem a joy. His wife, Catherine, and John and Elizabeth (Tibby) Sherrill, the other three of the Chosen Books team, gave constructive criticism and encouragement.

Tibby Sherrill's role is worth special note. She laboured for several weeks polishing the final draft with her gifted deftness. Tibby had been one of those who marched outside the White House in an anti-Vietnam protest back in 1971 while I sat inside, seething with resentment against all demonstrators. In the secular world a Tibby Sherrill could not stomach a Colson manuscript; nor would a Colson let a Tibby Sherrill within a hundred yards of his book. Because we now share a commitment to Christ we could work together with common purpose, our opposite political viewpoints often producing new insights and more clarity in the manuscript.

Along with Patty, there were many who typed – and retyped: Dotty Hellyer from Fellowship House, my secretary these past six months, who laboured tirelessly – days into nights – draft after draft; Holly Holm, with her sparkling personality and strength of character, who served so loyally through it all – the White House, Watergate, and into the beginning chapters of Born Again; Josephine Englat, an old friend who typed several of the early chapters; Patricia Owens, Charlie Morin's secretary and a valued and dear friend for many years; and Connie Otto, Harold Hughes's oldest daughter.

But for the support of "brothers" – Doug Coe, Harold Hughes, Graham Purcell, and Al Quie – there, of course, might be no story to tell. They opened their hearts to me and remained steadfast when others were fleeing Watergate's spreading stain. Together we have come to know the richest bonds in life. Tom Phillips was the steady compass when all else in my life was spinning dizzily out of control. Born Again is a story of how God used men like Tom in mighty ways. For his part in the story and more importantly his part in my life, I shall be grateful always.

Born Again is also the tale of Paul Kramer and the other men I came to know and love in prison. They remain my brothers, an unforgettable chapter in my pilgrimage.

Two of the men in the Fellowship, Paul Temple and Winston Weaver, made available their vacation homes (in Spain and the Virginia mountains respectively) to Patty and me when we needed a place of retreat. Ken Adams, Dave Shapiro, Arthur Mason, Judd Best, Charlie Morin, Sid Dickstein, Myron Mintz, Henry Cashen, and all the lawyers and employees of my old firm not only represented me admirably in my travails – but contributed to and encouraged this manuscript. To Ken Adams is owed a special debt. He not only represented me with devotion, but he took a great interest in this manuscript, helping in his spare time with research reviews, and comments.

Fred Rhodes, with whom I have worked side by side this year, spared me from many distractions while I wrote – and from our prayers together came sustaining strength for this and other work.

Much of the research for this book was made possible because of the indefatigable work of volunteers from Fellowship House who pasted and indexed thousands of clippings. Though the court motions for which the clippings were assembled were denied, their work was not in vain. So my thanks to John and Betsy Curry, Ruth McDaniel, and scores of others who gave of themselves to support a brother in need.

Charles Morin, whose companionship I have treasured for twenty years, reminds me each day of the meaning of true friendship. And so do many others: Mike Balzano, Jesse Calhoon, Frank Fitzsimmons, Brainerd Holmes, Dick Howard, Alexander Lankler, and Bill Maloney, to mention but a few.

Then there are all those – in Washington and across the country – the thousands of warmhearted believers who supported me through encouraging letters and by prayer. How can a man describe his feeling at knowing that hundreds of men and women, most of whom he will never meet on this earth, have been constantly praying on his behalf! Nothing did more to enrich my faith and spur me on.

So to all who have shared this journey with me, my deepest thanks.

CHARLES W. COLSON

Index of Proper Names

379